Guide to HTML, JavaScript and PHP

David R. Brooks

Guide to HTML, JavaScript and PHP

For Scientists and Engineers

 Springer

David R. Brooks
Institute for Earth Science Research and Education
2686 Overhill Drive
Eagleville, PA 19403
USA
brooksdr@drexel.edu

ISBN 978-0-85729-448-7   e-ISBN 978-0-85729-449-4
DOI 10.1007/978-0-85729-449-4
Springer London Dordrecht Heidelberg New York

British Library Cataloguing in Publication Data
A catalogue record for this book is available from the British Library

Library of Congress Control Number: 2011926229

Printed on acid-free paper

Springer is part of Springer Science+Business Media (www.springer.com)

Preface

"The best way to become acquainted with a subject is to write a book about it."

—Benjamin Disraeli

"Each problem that I solved became a rule, which served afterwards to solve other problems."

—René Descartes

i
What Is the Purpose of This Book?

There are many students and professionals in science and engineering, other than those specifically interested in fields such as computer science or computer engineering, who need to know how to solve computational problems on computers. There are basically two approaches to meeting the needs of such people. One is to rely on software applications such as spreadsheets, using built-in functions and perhaps user-defined macros, without requiring any explicit understanding of the principles on which programming languages are based.

A second approach is to learn a programming language, previously Fortran or Pascal, and more recently C, C++, or Java. These languages are important for certain kinds of work, such as computer science or scientific computing, but they may be viewed, possibly with good reason, as irrelevant by many students and professionals.

From a student's point of view, there is no painless solution to this dilemma, but in this book I assume that learning to solve computational problems in an online environment using **HTML**,[1] **JavaScript**, and **PHP** will at least appear to be a more relevant approach. HTML and JavaScript are universally used for developing self-contained online applications. The use of PHP for accessing externally stored data files, a capability that is not available directly through JavaScript, greatly extends the range of science and engineering problems that can be addressed. A working knowledge of these programming languages is a valuable skill for any scientist or engineer. The fact that these are Web-based languages may make such skills more immediately marketable than comparable skills developed with older text-based languages.

---

[1] See Glossary for definitions of terms appearing in bold font.

In some ways, the HTML/JavaScript/PHP environment is more difficult to learn than a traditional text-based programming language such as C. C is a mature (some might prefer "obsolete"), fairly small language with an unambiguous set of syntax rules and a primitive text-based input/output interface. You can view the limitations of C as either a blessing or a curse, depending on your needs. A major advantage of C is that programs written in **ANSI** Standard C should work equally well on any computer that has a C compiler, making the language inherently **platform-independent**.

HTML, JavaScript, and PHP, on the other hand, are immature and unstable programming languages (if we can agree to call HTML a "language") that function within a constantly changing Web environment. There are dialects of HTML and JavaScript that will work only on particular computing platforms and the possibility exists for language "extensions" that may be even more platform-dependent. PHP is more platform-independent, but it is still an evolving language whose standards are set and maintained by a user group – essentially by volunteers. While it is true that there are extensions to languages such as C and other older languages that are platform-dependent, the platform dependence of languages used in the online environment is a major implementation issue rather than an occasional minor inconvenience.

As one indication of the teaching and learning challenges these environments provide, just three popular paperback HTML and JavaScript reference books occupy nearly 6 in. of space (15 cm in deference to a metric audience) on my office bookshelf! A great deal of the material in those books is devoted to explaining the often subtle differences among various versions of HTML and JavaScript.

Fortunately, it is possible to work with some core subsets of HTML and JavaScript which, with PHP, can be used to solve some of the same kinds of computational problems that would be appropriate for a more traditional language such as C or C++. My initial motivation for writing this book was to learn how to use HTML, JavaScript, and PHP to create my own online applications, and I now use this environment for many tasks that I previously would have undertaken in C. Based on this experience, I have concluded that, despite the fact that these languages cannot fairly be defined as "scientific computing" languages, it is nonetheless entirely reasonable to use them to learn basic programming skills, and to create useful and robust science and engineering applications.

Although this book is intended for "scientists and engineers," as suggested by its title, the content is not technically complex. The examples and exercises do not require extensive science, engineering, or mathematics background and only rarely is mathematics beyond basic algebra needed. So, I believe this book could serve as a beginning programming text for undergraduates and even for high school students.

ii
Learning by Example

It is well known that people learn new skills in different ways. Personally, I learn best by having a specific goal and then studying examples that are related to that goal. Once I understand those examples, I can incorporate them into my own work. I have used that learning model in this book, which contains many complete examples that can serve as starting points for your work. (See the second quotation at the beginning of this preface.)

This model works particularly well in an online environment. The amount of online information about HTML, JavaScript, and PHP, including code samples, is so vast that it is only a slight exaggeration to state that nobody writes original code anymore. If you have trouble "learning by example," you will have trouble learning these languages, not just from this book, but in general because that is how most of the available information is presented.

It is an inescapable fact that a great deal of the source code behind Web pages involves nothing more (or less) than creative cutting, pasting, and tweaking of existing code. Aside from the issues of plagiarism and intellectual dishonesty that must be dealt with in an academic environment, there is also the practical matter of an effective learning strategy. You cannot learn to solve your own computational problems just by trying to paste together someone else's work. (Believe me, I've tried!) Until you develop your own independent skills, you will constantly be frustrated because you will never find *exactly* what you need to copy and you will be unable to synthesize what you need from what is available.

So, while you should expect to find yourself constantly recycling your own code based on what you learn from this book, you need to make sure that you really *learn* how to use these languages and don't just *learn to copy*!

If you are reading this book, you almost certainly are not and do not aspire to be a professional programmer. For a casual programmer from a scientific or technical background, it can be very time consuming to cut through the clutter of online information about these languages when the applications are not directly applicable to the needs of scientists and engineers. In my own work, what I need over and over again is some sample code that will jog my memory about how to approach recurring programming problems – how to select items from a pull-down list, how to extract information from a data file, how to pass information from an HTML document to a PHP application, how to display data-based graphics, etc. Throughout the book, I have tried to give examples that serve this need, including an entire chapter devoted to PHP graphics.

iii
The Origin and Uses of This Book

In 2007, Springer published *An Introduction to HTML and JavaScript for Scientists and Engineers*. This was followed in 2008 by *An Introduction to PHP for Scientists and Engineers: Beyond JavaScript*. Those two books followed the sequence in which I learned to use HTML, JavaScript, and PHP in my own work. (See the first quotation at the beginning of this preface.) When the time came to consider a second edition of the *HTML and JavaScript* book, it seemed a better idea to undertake a rewrite that would combine both books into a single volume. This book is the result. I have, hopefully, clarified some of the explanations. There are more examples and exercises and I have added some new material that my students and I have found useful, including a brief introduction to using "pseudo-code" as an approach to organizing solutions to computing problems (see Appendix 4).

I have used both of the original books as texts in an 11-week (one quarter) introductory programming course for biomedical engineering graduate students at Drexel University. I found that a course restricted just to HTML and JavaScript is a little "thin" for this audience. Adding a brief introduction to PHP solves the problem. This book easily provides enough material for a one-semester introductory programming course for science and engineering students because the possibilities for PHP-based applications are limitless. Because of the book's very specific focus on science and engineering applications, I believe the book is also particularly well suited for developing a working knowledge of HTML, JavaScript, and PHP on your own if you are a student or professional in any technical field.

iv
Acknowledgments

I am indebted to several classes of graduate students from Drexel University's School of Biomedical Engineering, Science & Health Systems, who have provided feedback on the material in this book and its predecessors. I am also once again indebted to my wife, Susan Caughlan, for her patient and always helpful proofreading of my manuscripts.

Institute for Earth Science Research and Education   David R. Brooks

Contents

Introducing HTML and JavaScript

1

Abstract Chapter 1 provides a very brief introduction to using HTML and JavaScript for creating simple Web pages. It presents examples of how JavaScript interfaces with an HTML document to display some printed output in a Web browser window. The chapter introduces the concept of an HTML document as an object, with certain methods and properties accessible through JavaScript to act on that object.

Numerous examples show how to modify the appearance of a document by using HTML tags and their attributes, including as part of a text string passed as a calling argument to JavaScript's `write()` method.

1.1
Introducing the Tools

1.1.1
What Is an HTML Document?

HTML is an acronym for **H**yper**T**ext **M**arkup **L**anguage. **HTML documents**, the foundation of all content appearing on the **World Wide Web (WWW)**, consist of two essential parts: information content and a set of instructions that tells your computer how to display that content. The instructions—the "markup," in editorial jargon—comprise the HTML language. It is not a programming language in the traditional sense, but rather a set of instructions about how to display content. The computer application that translates this description is called a **Web browser**. Ideally, online content should look the same regardless of the operating system on which a Web browser resides or the browser used. This goal of complete **platform independence** is achieved only approximately in practice.

A basic HTML document requires a minimum of four sets of **elements**:

```
<html> … </html>
<head> … </head>
<title> … </title>
<body> … </body>
```

D.R. Brooks, *Guide to HTML, JavaScript and PHP: For Scientists and Engineers*,
DOI 10.1007/978-0-85729-449-4_1, © Springer-Verlag London Limited 2011

1

These elements define the essential parts of an HTML document: the document itself, a heading section, a title section, and a body. Each of the elements is defined by two **tags**—a start tag and an end tag. Tags are always enclosed in angle brackets: <...>. End tags start with a slash (/). As will be shown later, some HTML elements have only one tag. Most tags are *supposed* to occur in pairs, although this rule is enforced only loosely in HTML. In order to support a **scripting language** such as JavaScript (much more about that later!), another element must be added to the four basic elements:

```
<script> … </script>
```

As used in this book, a `script` element always contains JavaScript code.

These elements are organized as follows within an HTML document:

```
<html>
  <head>
    <title> … </title>

    …
    <!-- Optional script elements as needed. -->
    <script> … </script>
  </head>
  <body>
    …
  </body>
</html>
```

The `html` tag encloses all other tags and defines the boundaries of the HTML document. We will return to the other tags later. `script` tags often appear inside the <head> tag, but they can appear elsewhere in a document, too. The indenting used to set off pairs of tags is optional, but it makes documents easier to create, read, and edit. This style is part of good programming practice in all languages.

Because JavaScript is so tightly bound to HTML documents, you must learn JavaScript along with at least a subset of HTML. Unfortunately for anyone trying to learn and use HTML and JavaScript, each of the several available browsers is free to implement and support JavaScript in its own way. A browser doesn't even have to support JavaScript at all, although it is hard to imagine why it wouldn't. Browsers can and do incorporate some proprietary HTML and JavaScript features that may not be supported by other browsers. Newer versions of any browser may support features that won't be recognized by earlier versions.

Fortunately, it is possible to work with what is essentially a *de facto* standardized subset of HTML and JavaScript. As a result, some of the descriptions of the details of HTML and JavaScript in this book will be incomplete; this is not necessarily a bad thing!

Although HTML documents are usually considered to be a way of distributing information for remote access on the Web, they are equally useful when used locally on any computer that has a browser. So, in conjunction with JavaScript (and later with PHP), you can create a self-contained problem-solving environment that can be used locally as well as (literally) globally.

Good programming technique often involves separating the **input/output (I/O) interface** from the underlying calculations that do the work of a program. The programming environment provided by HTML/JavaScript provides a conceptually elegant means of implementing this strategy. An HTML document provides the I/O interface and JavaScript (and/or PHP, as will be seen later in this book) handle the calculations. An advantage of HTML is that it provides a wealth of interface possibilities that far surpass those of text-based languages such as C.

1.1.2
What Is JavaScript?

JavaScript is an **interpreted** (rather than **compiled**) **object-oriented programming language** that has been developed for use alongside other Web tools. JavaScript does not operate as a standalone language. It is designed to work together with HTML for creating interactive Web pages. It is not the same as Java, which is a compiled object-oriented language.

JavaScript is used to write **client side applications**, which means that JavaScript code is sent to a user's computer when a Web page is loaded. The code is then executed, basically line by line, by a JavaScript interpreter included as part of the user's (client's) Web browser. This arrangement minimizes security issues that can arise when a client computer interacts with the computer that sent the page. It also makes it easy to package an entire problem, with its own user interface and solution, self-contained within a single document. But the inability to interact dynamically with information stored on a **server** imposes limitations on the kinds of tasks that JavaScript can accomplish.

It is commonplace to refer to any set of written computer instructions as a "program." However, this term is more rigorously applied to a separate entity that can be executed on its own. Because JavaScript is interpreted rather than compiled, a separately executable entity is never created. Instead, JavaScript code statements are interpreted and executed one at a time, essentially "on the fly." Although this may seem inefficient, there is rarely any discernible time lag associated with executing JavaScript commands on modern computers.

JavaScript is one of a class of scripting languages whose purpose is to access and modify components of an existing information interface. (Microsoft's VBScript is another scripting language.) In this case, the interface is an HTML document. As soon as HTML documents on the Web evolved from one-way delivery systems for displaying fixed content, something like JavaScript immediately became necessary. One of its first applications arose from the need to check values entered by users into the fields of HTML forms that can be sent back to the originator. (Forms are discussed in a later chapter.) JavaScript can be used to compare input values against an expected range or set of values and to generate appropriate messages and other actions based on those comparisons.

JavaScript has evolved into a complete programming language with extensive capabilities for manipulating text and handling mathematical operations, useful for a wide range of computing problems. Possible applications include many self-contained scientific and engineering calculations. As noted earlier, JavaScript is restricted to problems that do not need to access external data sources, regardless of whether those sources reside on a local computer or on a remote server.

1

As previously noted, the major challenge in learning HTML/JavaScript is that it is not a completely standardized environment. The various dialects of HTML and JavaScript pose problems even for experienced programmers. These kinds of problems can be minimized by focusing on an appropriate subset of HTML/JavaScript. This is feasible because there is little reason to use browser-specific subsets of HTML/JavaScript in the context of the topics dealt with in this book.

1.1.3
How Do You Create HTML/JavaScript Documents?

Because HTML/JavaScript documents are just text documents, they can be created with any text editor. Even Windows' very basic Notepad application is a workable choice for simple tasks.[1] Once they are created, you can open HTML files in your computer's browser—hopefully without regard to which browser you are using. As long as you give such documents an .htm or .html file name extension, they should automatically open in your browser when you double-click on the file name. Although Windows documents are no longer restricted to three-letter extensions, a convention that dates back to the pre-Windows days of the MS-DOS operating systems, the three-letter .htm extension is often used on Windows systems. The four-letter .html extension is commonly used on UNIX systems.[2]

There is one other consequence of using Windows computers for creating all the code examples in this text: Windows file names are case-insensitive, while in UNIX, all spellings, including file names and commands, are case-sensitive. This shouldn't cause problems, but it is something to keep in mind. In Windows, you can name a document newDocument.htm. Later, you can spell it newdocument.htm, NEWDOCUMENT. HTM, or any other combination of uppercase and lowercase letters and it won't matter. On a UNIX system, that file can be accessed only with the original spelling.

Although you can create text (and, therefore, HTML) documents with a full-featured word processor such as Microsoft Word, this is not recommended. When you save a word processor document it no longer contains just the text you have typed, but also all the layout and formatting information that goes with that document. You can choose to save a document as just text with an .htm extension, but it is easy to forget to do this.

Microsoft Word and other modern word-processing applications can also format any document as an HTML document. However, this is also not recommended. These converted documents may include a huge quantity of extraneous information and HTML

---

[1] When you save a file in Notepad, the default extension is .txt. You may need to enclose the file name plus its .htm extension in quote marks to prevent Notepad from adding the .txt extension.

[2] On Windows computers, you can associate extensions with whatever application you wish. So, for example, if you have more than one browser installed on your computer, you could designate one of them as the default browser and assign it as the application for opening HTML documents.

instructions that make the resulting file much larger and more complex than it needs to be. (To see this for yourself, save a Word document as an HTML document and then look at the result in a text editor such as Notepad!)

RTF ("rich text format") documents are also unacceptable, as they still retain some formatting information that is inappropriate for an HTML document. Any document that contains "smart quotes" rather than "straight quotes" can also cause problems, because smart quotes may not be displayed properly by browsers. (This is much less of a problem on current browsers than it used to be.)

There are commercial Web development tools that allow you to create Web pages without actually knowing anything about HTML or JavaScript. These applications are not suitable for use with this book. The obvious reason is that the primary purpose of the book is to show you how to write your own HTML documents and JavaScript code. Also, these applications may create HTML files that are much larger and more complex than they need to be for basic HTML documents. So, these applications are better suited for Web development projects that involve a lot of graphics and the other "bells and whistles" that make commercial Web pages attractive.

Creating an HTML/JavaScript document that works properly inevitably involves switching back and forth between a text editor and a browser—making changes and observing the effects of those changes. Once you create a basic HTML document, you can open it in your browser and move back and forth between this document and your text editor. Whenever you change the document, you can reload or refresh it in your browser. It is certainly possible, but not particularly convenient, to do this with a simple text editor such as Notepad.

There are many commercial software tools whose purpose is to facilitate writing and editing HTML documents by integrating document creation, editing, and viewing. As noted previously, some of them are intended for large and complicated projects and may be "overkill" for use with this book. For several years, for creating this book and in my own day-to-day work, I have used Visicom Media's AceHTML Freeware V.5 (see www. visicommedia.com). This software provides an HTML/JavaScript editor with some automatic color-based text formatting that makes HTML instructions and JavaScript code easier to read. There is an integrated browser, so it is easy to switch back and forth between creating and editing a document and seeing the results of your work.

AceHTML also has a JavaScript syntax checker. As is typically the case, the checker isn't very good at telling you how to fix a syntax error, but it at least tells you where the error was detected. The freeware version of this editor may or may not be available currently, and it may require you to install other software that you may or may not want on your computer. At the time this book was being published, freeware versions of AceHTML were still available, as were versions available for purchase.[3]

Although, in principle, it *shouldn't* make any difference which browser you use, the outputs displayed in this text come from either AceHTML's internal browser or Mozilla's Firefox, which is the default browser on the author's Windows computers. When you

---

[3]Recent versions of AceHTML assume XHTML as the default language, rather than HTML. If you use such a version with this book, you must override this assumption by saving files with `.htm` or `.html` extensions.

display content in an "alert" box, as will be described later in this book, the appearance of this box is different for different browsers, and hence may be different from what is displayed in this book.

1.1.4
Some Typographic Conventions Used in This Book

HTML tags and JavaScript code are printed in a `monospaced (Courier) font` in document examples and whenever they are referred to in the text. Thus, `document` is interpreted as a reference to an HTML **object**, as opposed to its general use as a term identifying a body of text. Some technical terms used for the first time are printed in **bold font**. Their definitions can be found in the Glossary. Within descriptions of HTML document features and JavaScript code, user-supplied text is denoted by *{italicized text in braces (curly brackets)}*; the curly brackets are *not* necessarily meant to be included in the user-supplied text.

AceHTML and other editors typically apply some combination of color coding, bold fonts, and italicized fonts to various language elements. When HTML code is copied from the editor and inserted into this black-and-white text, bold and italic fonts are retained but of course the color coding is not.

The renderings of HTML documents and other output as displayed in a browser window have been captured and edited on a Windows computer by pressing the PrtScn (or Print Screen) key and copying the resulting screen image into an image editing program. (Pressing Alt-PrtScn copies just the currently active window instead of the entire screen.)

Because of the small format of this book, line breaks in document examples are often necessary and may sometimes be misleading. Although every effort has been made to use line breaks in a way that does not affect the operation of the script, it may sometimes be necessary to remove some line breaks when you reproduce these documents for your own use.

1.1.5
Where Can You Find More Information About HTML and JavaScript?

By now, it should be clear that this book is in no way intended as a reference source for either HTML or JavaScript. Any attempt to provide complete coverage for either language would thoroughly confound the purpose of the book and is far beyond the author's capabilities! Therefore, you must look elsewhere for exhaustive treatments of HTML and JavaScript. Here are three useful language reference sources:

Thomas Powell, *HTML: The Complete Reference, Third Edition*, 2001, Osborne/McGraw-Hill, Berkeley, CA. ISBN 0-07-212951-4.

Thomas Powell and Dan Whitworth, *HTML Programmer's Reference, Second Edition*, 2001, Osborne/McGraw-Hill, Berkeley, CA. ISBN 0-07-213232-9.

Thomas Powell and Fritz Schneider, *JavaScript: The Complete Reference*, 2001, Osborne/McGraw-Hill, Berkeley, CA. ISBN 0-07-219127-9.

If you are at all serious about creating your own online applications ("serious" perhaps being defined as anything past the bare minimum needed to complete a course based on this text), there is no substitute for these or similar references.

The first HTML book the author ever read is out of print, but it is still worth looking for in libraries or remaindered book stores. Even though it addresses an older (and simpler) version of HTML, it is still an excellent resource for the kinds of applications discussed in this book and it is included here for reasons that are only partly nostalgic:

Todd Stauffer, *Using HTML 3.2, Second Edition*, 1996, Que Corporation, Indianapolis, IN. ISBN 0-7897-0985-6.

1.2
Your First HTML/JavaScript Documents

A typical first goal in learning any programming language is to display a simple message. With HTML, this is trivially simple: Just type the message in the body of the document, as shown in Document 1.1. (Appendix 1 contains an index to all documents in the text.) Save the file with the name shown.

Document 1.1 (`HelloWorldHTML.htm`)

```
<html>
<head>
<title>First HTML Document</title>
</head>
<body>
Hello, world!
</body>
</html>
```

Hello, world!

Most document examples presented in this text will include a browser's rendering of the screen output produced by the document. When a border appears around the output, as it does for the output from Document 1.1, the purpose is to distinguish the output from the rest of the text—the document doesn't generate that border. In the text, renderings are always in black and white or grayscale. In some cases, as noted, color renderings are printed on separate color plates. In other cases (such as Document 1.3, below) you will have to try the code yourself to view outputs in color.

Document 1.1 is certainly not very exciting. But the point is that an HTML document simply displays the static content you provide. As you will learn in Chap. 2, HTML provides many facilities for changing the *appearance* of this content, but not the content itself.

You can display content with JavaScript, too. With JavaScript, input and output always pass through an HTML document. Instructions (code) you write in JavaScript are called a **script**. The capability to interpret JavaScript instructions must be built into your browser. Document 1.2 uses JavaScript to generate a simple text message that is displayed in the document. There is no good reason to use JavaScript simply to display fixed content, but this exercise will provide an introduction to JavaScript syntax. Don't worry if the details of this and following examples seem obscure—hopefully, future chapters will clarify all these details!

Document 1.2 (HelloWorld.htm)

```html
<html>
<head>
  <title>Hello, world!</title>
  <script language="javascript" type="text/javascript">
  // These statements display text in a document.
    document.write("Hello, world!");
    document.write("<br />It's a beautiful day!");
  </script>
</head>
<body>
<!-- No content in the body of this document. -->
</body>
</html>
```

```
Hello, world!
It's a beautiful day!
```

A browser must be instructed to interpret certain parts of an HTML document as JavaScript code. To accomplish this, all text appearing inside the script element will be interpreted by a browser as one or more JavaScript statements. This means that HTML elements cannot appear inside the script element, because then the JavaScript interpreter would attempt (inappropriately) to interpret them as JavaScript code. This will generate a JavaScript error. In Document 1.2, the <br /> tag, which generates a line break, is an HTML element, but it is included inside a quoted string of text. This is allowed, but

```
document.write("Hello, world!");
<br /> document.write("It's a beautiful day!");
```

is not.

As noted previously, JavaScript is an object-based language. In programming terminology, an HTML document is an object. Using JavaScript, predefined **methods** can be used to act on a specified object. (Objects will be discussed in more detail starting in Chap. 4.) Document 1.2 accesses ("calls" or "invokes") the write() method of the document object to display text. A method is associated with its object by using "dot notation," as in document.write().

Methods such as write() often, but not always, require one or more inputs, referred to as **calling arguments**. In Document 1.2, the text strings "Hello, world!" and "
It's a beautiful day!"; (enclosed in single or double quotes) are calling arguments for the `write()` method. Calling arguments provide the values on which a method acts.

As you will see, most HTML elements include **attributes** that are used to assign properties to the element. The `script` element *should* include values for the `language` and `type` attributes, as shown:

`<script` `language="javascript"` `type="text/javascript">`

However, HTML does not actual *require* that these attributes be included. Comments within an HTML document are indicated by a specific sequence of symbols:

`<!-- ` *{comments}* ` -->`

In keeping with the style adopted in this book, italicized text enclosed in curly brackets indicates text that is entered by the user. The curly brackets *could* be part of the comment, but are not needed and would normally not be included.

Inside a `script` element, single-line comments begin with two slashes, as in the fifth line of Document 1.2. Comments are a basic part of good programming style, no matter what the language. Some authors prefer not to use many comments in HTML/JavaScript because it increases the size of the file that must be sent to the client computer. However, when you are learning the material presented in this book, there is no excuse for not making liberal use of comments as reminders to yourself of what you are doing.

One use of HTML comments is to hide JavaScript code from browsers that don't have a JavaScript interpreter. This is much less of a problem than it might have been several years ago. It is also irrelevant for now because, of course, your browser must support JavaScript in order to be useful for this book. In any event, JavaScript hiding is done like this:

```
<script language="javascript" type="text/javascript">
  <!-- Start hiding JavaScript code here.
      {Put JavaScript statements here.}
  // Stop hiding code here. -->
</script>
```

Although these HTML comment tags appear to be out of place because HTML elements can't appear inside a `script` element, a browser that does support JavaScript will ignore the HTML comment tags themselves and a browser that doesn't support JavaScript will ignore everything inside the comment tags.

HTML syntax is case-insensitive, which means that `<html>` is equivalent to `<HTML>` or even `<hTmL>`. Some HTML document authors favor uppercase spellings for tags because they stand out from the text content. However, **XHTML** (extended HTML), the apparent successor to HTML, requires tags to be in lowercase letters.[4] Hence, this text will

---

[4]Although this book adopts some XHTML style rules, the documents are written in HTML and are not intended to be fully XHTML-compliant.

always use lowercase letters for tag names. Note that, despite previous warnings that file names and commands are case-sensitive in some systems, browsers should not be case-sensitive in their interpretation of HTML tags, regardless of the underlying operating system.

JavaScript syntax is *always* case-sensitive, regardless of the computer system on which it runs, like the C/C++ languages from which it is derived. So, when you write JavaScript code, you need to be very careful about case. For example, document is an object name recognized by JavaScript, but Document is not. (Try this in Document 1.2 if you need convincing.)

Note that each of the two JavaScript statements (the calls to document.write()) is terminated with a semicolon. JavaScript interprets a semicolon as "end of statement." As a matter of syntax, a line feed at the end of a statement will also be interpreted as marking the end of that statement. However, it is poor programming practice to use this "implied semicolon," and all JavaScript statements appearing in this book *should* terminate with semicolons. (Authors are not perfect!)

You can make Document 1.2 a little fancier by using other HTML elements and their attributes to control the appearance of the text. (Chap. 2 will present much more information about elements and attributes.) In Document 1.3, font (font description), h1 (heading), and hr (horizontal rule) are elements, and color, size, and align are attributes. Of these elements, the hr element requires only a single tag because it does not enclose any HTML content. Single-tag elements should include a forward slash at the end: <hr /> rather than <hr>.

Document 1.3 (HelloWorld2.htm)

```html
<html>
<head>
<title>Hello, world!</title>
</head>
<body>
<h1 align="center">First JavaScript</h1>
<hr />
<script language="javascript" type="text/javascript">
  document.write("<font size='5'
    color='red'><center>Hello, world!</font>");
  document.write("<br /><font size='7' color='blue'>
    It's a beautiful day!</center></font>");
</script>
</body>
</html>
```

First JavaScript

Hello, world!
It's a beautiful day!

(Try this yourself to see the colors displayed.)

As previously noted, there is no good reason to use JavaScript to display this fixed content, but Document 1.3 again makes the point that any HTML tags appearing as part of the calling argument passed to `document.write()` are treated as part of the text string—the characters enclosed in quote marks—and therefore don't violate the rule that HTML elements can't be used inside a `script` element. The HTML tags are essentially "pasted" into the HTML document right along with the text. Within the string

```
"<br /><font size='7' color='blue'>
It's a beautiful day!</center></font>"
```

the attribute values are enclosed in single quotes rather than double quotes. Otherwise, it would not be clear where the quoted string begins and ends. Using double quotes *inside* a statement already enclosed in double quotes will generate a JavaScript error message.

Another difference between Document 1.2 and Document 1.3 is that, in 1.3, the `script` element is inside the `body` element. This is OK, although we will often try to keep the `script` element inside the `head` element, thus ensuring that the JavaScript code is interpreted before the rest of the page is loaded. This detail is of no concern in this example, whose sole purpose is to display some text.

As expected, this attempted modification of the script, containing HTML tags in a context where a browser expects to see only JavaScript code, will produce an error:

```
<script language="javascript" type="text/javascript">
  <font size="5" color="red"><center> // ERROR!!
  document.write("Hello, world");
  </font>
</script>
```

You can include more than one `script` element within an HTML document, as shown in Document 1.4a, in which there are two separate `script` sections, arbitrarily divided into a section above the horizontal rule (see the `<hr />` tag) and another below the rule.

Document 1.4a (`HelloWorld3.htm`)

```
<html>
<head>
<title>Hello, world! (v.3)</title>
</head>
<body bgcolor="lightgreen" text="magenta">
<h1 align="center">First JavaScript</h1>
<script language="javascript" type="text/javascript">
  document.write("<font color='green'>
  This document was last modified on
  "+document.lastModified+"</font>");
</script>
<hr />
```

```
<script language="javascript" type="text/javascript">
  document.write("background = "+document.bgColor);
  document.write("<br />font = " + document.fgColor);
  document.write("<font size='5'
    color='red'><center>Hello,world!</font><br />");
  document.write("<font size='7' color='blue'>
    He said, &quot;It's a beautiful day!&quot;
    </center></font>");
</script>
</body>
</html>
```

First JavaScript

This document was last modified on 02/21/2010 14:47:49

background = #90ee90
font = #ff00ff

Hello,world!

He said, "It's a beautiful day!"

(See Color Example 1 for full-color output.)

Document 1.4a contains an answer to this question: How do you display double quote marks with the document.write() method if you can't use double quotes inside a quoted string? The answer: Use the **escape sequence** ". Escape sequences always start with an ampersand (&) and end with a semicolon (;). There are many escape sequences for displaying characters that are not available directly from the keyboard or would be misinterpreted by HTML if entered directly, and we will discuss them later as needed. A list of commonly used escape sequences appears in Appendix 2.

JavaScript objects have **properties** as well as methods. Like methods, properties are associated with objects through the use of dot notation. One useful property of the document object is lastModified, used in Document 1.4a. As its name suggests, this property accesses the time and date stamp automatically stored along with a document whenever it is modified and saved, based on the calendar and clock on the computer used to create the document. This stamp is automatically attached to the document, without any special action required by the creator of the document. The lastModified property is useful for documents that contain time-sensitive information, or just to give users some idea of whether a page displayed in a browser is current.

Document 1.4a contains these two statements that access two more document properties:

```
document.write("background = "+document.bgColor);
document.write("<br />font = " + document.fgColor);
```

These display a code for the background and font colors.

Attributes such as `size` and `color` have values. These values are *supposed* to be enclosed in quotes, although this is not actually required in HTML. Quotes *are* required in XHTML and they are always used in this book. You can use either double or single quotes. In HTML documents, double quotes are generally accepted as the standard. However, when HTML elements with attributes are included inside quoted strings, as in

```
document.write("<font size='5'
   color='red'><center>Hello,world!</font><br />");
document.write("<font size='7' color='blue'>
   He said, &quot;It's a beautiful day!&quot;
   </center></font>");
```

then single quotes are required for the values in order to avoid conflict with the double quotes around the string.

A more reasonable approach to generating the output shown for Document 1.4a is to use JavaScript only as required to access desired `document` properties (and perhaps display some related text), and use HTML for everything else. Document 1.4b is a modified version of Document 1.4a which does the content formatting with HTML tags inside the document. There is no need to show the output, as it is identical to that for Document 1.4a.

Document 1.4b (`HelloWorld3HTML.htm`)

```
<html>
<head>
<title>Hello, world! (with HTML)</title>
<script language="javascript" type="text/javascript">
   document.write(
    "<font color='green'> This document was last modified on
   "+document.lastModified+"</font>");
</script>
</head>
<body bgcolor="lightgreen" text="magenta">
<h1 align="center">First JavaScript</h1>
<hr />
<script language="javascript" type="text/javascript">
   document.write("background = "+document.bgColor);
   document.write("<br />font = " + document.fgColor);
</script>
<font size="5" color="red"><center>Hello,world!</font><br />
<font size="7" color="blue">
He said, "It's a beautiful day!"</center></font>"
</body>
</html>
```

Table 1.1   Some properties and methods of the document **object**

Property or method	Action
Property document.bgColor	Return or set current value of background (page) color. Returns "#ffffff" for<body bgcolor="white">
Property document.fgColor	Return or set current value of font color. Returns "#0000ff" for <body text="blue">
Property document.lastModified	Return text string containing date the document was last modified.
Method document.write("Hello!")	Print quoted string on document page.
Method document.writeln("Hello!")	Print quoted string on document page, followed by line feed.[a]

[a]Because HTML ignores line feeds, the writeln() method will not normally produce any noticeable difference in output. If the text to be displayed is within a pre element, then the line feed will be present.

In this case, there is actually a justification for putting one of the script sections inside the body of the document: This script is used to display codes for the background and text colors, which are known only after they are set inside the body element.

A summary of some properties and methods of the document object is given in Table 1.1. The bgColor and fgColor properties will tell you what the current colors are. More usefully, they can also be used to *assign* these colors. This means that you can change font and background colors "on the fly" while a JavaScript script is running. Note that bgcolor is an HTML attribute used to set the background color of the body element and is supposed to be (but doesn't have to be in case-insensitive HTML) spelled in lower-case letters. On the other hand, bgColor is a property of the JavaScript document object and must be spelled with a capital C, as shown.

In Document 1.4b, the default background color has been set to light green and the default text color to magenta inside the <body> tag. Inserting these two lines:

```
document.bgColor="red";
document.fgColor="black";
```

as the first two lines inside the <script> tag in Document 1.4b will change the background color from light green to red and the default text color from magenta to black.

1.3
Accessing HTML Documents on the Web

Documents intended for access by others on the World Wide Web are posted on a **Web server**, a computer system connected to the **Internet**. Colleges and universities typically provide Web servers for use by their faculty and students. Individuals not affiliated with an institution may have to purchase space on a commercial Web server or they can set up their own server. In any case, access to Web pages is universal in the sense that any computer with an Internet connection and a browser can request to be connected to a Web site through its Internet address—its Uniform Resource Locator (**URL**).

Not all HTML documents have to be publicly accessible on the Web. They can be protected with logon identifications and passwords, or they can be available only locally through an **intranet** (as opposed to the Internet). The Internet is a global **network** of interconnected computers, whereas an intranet is a local network that may or may not also provide connections to the Internet. For example, a company can provide an intranet with no external access, exclusively for internal use by its own employees.

Note that when you view HTML documents in the browser on your local computer, they are not available on the Internet unless you have specifically set up a server on your computer, assigned it a URL, and placed HTML documents in a folder associated with that server. Usually you have to purchase a URL from a company that specializes in hosting Web sites, but it may also be possible to associate your local network with a free URL obtained from one of these companies.[5]

Internet addresses look something like this:

```
http://www.myUniversity.edu/~myName/index.htm
```

Internet addresses usually start with the `http://` prefix, to indicate that the Hypertext Transfer Protocol (**HTTP**) is being used. There are some variations, such as `https`, which indicates that the address that follows resides on a secure server, as required for financial transactions, for example. The rest of the address identifies a Web server and then a folder or directory on a computer system at `myUniversity` for someone named `myName`. The `.edu` extension identifies this site as belonging to an educational institution, in the same way as `.gov`, `.com`, and `.org` identify government, commercial, and organization sites. The ~ symbol is often used as a "shorthand" identifier for a folder (or directory) set aside for Web pages belonging to a user whose name follows the ~, but there are many ways to specify the location of Web pages. Sometimes names in URLs are case-sensitive, depending on the operating system installed on the computer system containing the Web page. So, if you type `myname` instead of `myName` in the above URL, it may not work. Users of Windows computers should note the use of forward slashes rather than backslashes to separate folders (or directories).

The `index.htm` (or `index.html`) file contains the **home page** for this individual. By default, the `index.htm` file is automatically opened, if it exists, whenever this URL is accessed. That is, the address

```
http://www.myUniversity.edu/~myName/
```

is equivalent to the address that includes the `index.htm` file name.

---

[5]At the time this book was being written, the author was running a server using a free URL provided by www.no-ip.com.

1

As they were being developed, the documents discussed in this book resided neither on the Internet nor on an intranet. Instead, they were simply stored in a folder on a computer and accessed through the file menu in a browser, just as you would access a file with any other software application. For example, the "address" on the author's computer for the first document in this text is

```
file:///C:/Documents%20and%20Settings/David/Desktop/
JavaScript/JavaScriptCode/HelloWorld.htm
```

Spaces are represented by the hexadecimal code %20 and, yes, there are three forward slashes following file:. To view this document stored somewhere on your computer, you don't have to open your browser and type in the complete address. All you *should* have to do is double click on the file and it should automatically open in your browser.

You should create a separate folder on your computer as you work through the examples in this book and write your own documents. You *could* make documents you create yourself accessible on the Internet or an intranet by placing them on a Web server. For example, if you are taking a course based on this book, your instructor may require you to post homework assignments on a Web site.

1.4
Another Example

This example shows how to include an image in an HTML document.

Document 1.5 (house.htm)

```
<html>
<head>
<title>Our New House</title>
<script language="javascript" type="text/javascript">
document.write("<font color='green'>This document was
last   modified on "+document.lastModified+"</font>");
</script>
</head>
<body>
<h1>Our New House</h1>
<p>
Here's the status of our new house. (We know you're
fascinated!)</p>
<!-- Link to your image goes here. -->
<img src="house.jpg" align="left" /><br />
</body>
</html>
```

There are several image formats that are widely used in HTML documents, including image bitmaps (.bmp), Graphics Interchange Format (.gif), and Joint Photographic Experts Group (.jpg).

The original .jpg file has been compressed, and this process can result in jagged edges where edges should be straight. This effect is visible in the house framing and roof lines.

This document was last modified on 05/03/2006 13:12:30

Our New House

Here's the status of our new house. (We know you're fascinated!)

Within the img element, height and width attributes allow you to control the size of the image display (in pixels). However, this is not necessarily a good idea for photos like this because it is not equivalent to actually "resizing" the image, as is possible with image-editing software.[6] Hence, it is important to use images that initially are sized appropriately. The house.jpg image was resized to 300 pixels high by 400 pixels wide, which retained the height-to-width ratio of the original (cropped) photo. If a very large high-resolution image file is displayed as a very small image, using the height and width attributes, the original large file must still be transmitted to the client computer. In view of the fact that high-resolution images can produce very large files (>10 Mb), it is still important to consider appropriate resolution and sizing for images included in HTML documents, even in an age of high-speed broadband Internet connections and large amounts of online storage space. (The size of the compressed grayscale house.jpg image printed here is about 93 Kb.)

Document 1.5 could be made into a default home page simply by changing its name to index.htm.

Here is a final admonition which hopefully does not sound too preachy: Intellectual honesty and fairness in the use of other people's material is important, no matter what the setting. The image displayed by Document 1.5 was taken by this book's author, of his own house under construction. In other words, the author "owns" this image. Whenever you post images (or other material, for that matter) online, please be careful to respect intellectual property rights. Your default approach should be that online materials are copyrighted and cannot be used freely without permission. If you are in doubt about whether you have permission to use an image or other material, don't!

---

[6]IrfanView (www.irfanview.com) has been used for all image processing in this book. This very popular freeware program does an excellent job of resizing images while maintaining detail from the original image. Of course, its future availability cannot be guaranteed to readers of this book.

HTML Document Basics

2

Abstract Chapter 2 describes the characteristics of an HTML document, including some of the basic HTML elements and their attributes. The list of attributes will not necessarily be complete, but includes a subset that will be used in this book. The chapter includes a description of how to set colors in documents and a brief introduction to cascading style sheets (CSS).

2.1
Documents, Elements, Attributes, and Values

2.1.1
Essential Elements

As noted in Chap. 1, JavaScript needs an HTML document to serve as a user interface. (Or, the other way around, HTML documents need a scripting language such as JavaScript to manage interactions with users.) A basic HTML document consists of four sections defined by four sets of elements, arranged as follows:

```
<html>
  <head>
    <title> … </title>
    …
  </head>
  <body>
    …
  </body>
</html>
```

Each of these elements has a start tag and an end tag. Tags are always enclosed in angle brackets <...> and the end tag always includes a forward slash before the element name. The body element supports attributes that can be used to control the overall appearance of an HTML document. Documents, elements, attributes, and values are organized in a specific hierarchy:

HTML document → elements → attributes → values

D.R. Brooks, *Guide to HTML, JavaScript and PHP: For Scientists and Engineers*, DOI 10.1007/978-0-85729-449-4_2, © Springer-Verlag London Limited 2011

Elements exist within a document. Elements can have attributes and attributes (usually) have values. Note that some of the elements are nested inside others. For example, all other elements are nested inside the `html` element, and the `title` element is nested inside the `head` element.

Following is a brief description of the four elements that will be part of every HTML document. Attributes, if any, are listed for each element. Note, however, that not all possible attributes are listed. Thus, a listing of "none" may mean that there are attributes for this element, but that they are not used in this book. Consult an HTML reference manual for a complete list of attributes. Because several elements can share common attributes, attributes and their values are listed separately, following the list of elements.

`<body>` ... `</body>`
   The `body` element contains the HTML document content, along with whatever elements are required to format, access, and manipulate the content.
Attributes: `background`, `bgcolor`, `text`

`<head>` ... `</head>`
   The `head` element contains information about the document. The `head` element must contain a `title` element and under XHTML rules, the `title` must be the first element after `head`. From the perspective of this book, the other important element to be included in `head` is `script`, which will contain JavaScript code.
Attributes: none

`<html>` ... `</html>`
   The `html` element surrounds the entire document. All other HTML elements are nested within this element.
Attributes: none

`<title>` ... `</title>`
   The `title` element contains the text that will be displayed in the browser's title bar. Every HTML document should have a title, included as the first element inside the `head` element.
Attributes: none

2.1.2
Some Other Important Elements

The four basic elements discussed previously constitute no more than a blank template for an HTML document. Other elements are needed to display and control the appearance of content within the document. Here are some important elements that you will use over and over again in your HTML documents. They are listed in alphabetical order. The list of attributes is not necessarily complete, but includes only those which will be used in this book.

`<a> ... </a>`

The a (for "anchor") element provides links to an external resource or to an internal link within a document.

Attributes: `href, name`

`<b> ... </b>`

The b element forces the included text to be displayed in a bold font. This is a "physical element" in the sense that it is associated specifically with displaying text in a bold font, even though the actual appearance may depend on the browser and computer used. In contrast, see the `strong` element below.

Attributes: none

`<br />` or `<br>`

The br element inserts a break (line feed) in the text. Multiple breaks can be used to insert multiple blank lines between sections of text. The break element has no end tag because it encloses no content. Under XHTML rules, a closing slash (after a space) must be included: `<br />`. The slash is rarely seen in older HTML documents, so its use will be encouraged but not required.

Attributes: none

`<center> ... </center>`

The center element causes displayed text to be centered in the browser window.

Attributes: none

`<em> ... </em>`

This is a "logical element" that will typically cause text to be displayed in italics, but it can be redefined to produce different results in different environments. For most purposes, em and i are interchangeable. See the i element below.

Attributes: none

`<font> ... </font>`

The font element controls the appearance of text. The two most commonly used attributes control the size and color of the text.

Attributes: `size, color, face`

`<hr />` or `<hr>`

The horizontal rule element draws a shaded horizontal line across the screen. It does not have an end tag. A closing slash (after a space) is required in XHTML. A `noshade` attribute displays the rule as a solid color, rather than shaded.

Attributes: `align, color, noshade, size, width`

`<h`*n*`> ... </h`*n*`>`

Up to six levels of headings (for *n* ranging from 1 to 6) can be defined, with decreasing font sizes as *n* increases from 1 to 6.

Attributes: `align`

(continued)

2

(continued)

`<i> ... </i>`
　i is a "physical element" that forces the included text to be displayed in italics. The actual appearance may depend on the browser and computer used. Compare with the em element above.
Attributes: none

`<img />`
　The img element provides a link to an image to be displayed within a document. The image is stored in a separate file, perhaps even at another Web address, the location of which is provided by the src attribute.
Attributes: align, border, height, src, vspace, width

`<p> ... </p>`
　The p element marks the beginning and end of a paragraph of text content. Note that HTML does not automatically indent paragraphs. Rather, it separates paragraphs with an empty line, with all the text aligned left. It is common to see only the start tag used in HTML documents, without the corresponding end tag. However, the use of the end tag is enforced by XHTML and this is the style that should be followed.
Attributes: none

`<pre> ... </pre>`
　The default behavior of HTML is to collapse multiple spaces, line feeds, and tabs to a single space. This destroys some of the text formatting that you may wish to preserve in a document, such as tabs at the beginning of paragraphs.
　The pre element forces HTML to recognize multiple spaces, line feeds, and tabs embedded in text. The default action for pre is to use a monospaced font such as Courier. This may not always be appropriate. But, because line feeds and other text placement conventions are recognized, pre is very useful for embedding programming code examples within an HTML document.
Attributes: none

`<strong> ... </strong>`
　strong is a "logical element" that will typically cause text to be displayed in a bold font, but it can be redefined to produce different results in different environments. For most purposes, b and strong are interchangeable. Compare this with the b tag above.
Attributes: none

Note that most of the elements described here require both start and end tags. The general rule is that any element which encloses content requires both a start and end tag. The br and hr elements do not enclose content, so no end tag is needed. However, br and hr should include a closing slash in their tags in order to be XHTML compatible—for example, `<br />` rather than `<br>`, with a space before the slash.

Description of attributes:

These descriptions may not include all possible values. For a complete listing, consult an HTML reference manual.

`align = "..."`
Values: `"left"`, `"right"`, or `"center"`
   Aligns text horizontally.

`background = "..."`
Value: the URL of a gif- or jpeg-format graphics file.
   Setting the background attribute displays the specified image as the background, behind a displayed HTML document page. Depending on the image size (in pixels), background images may automatically be "tiled," resulting in a repeating image that can be visually distracting. It is not necessary to use background images and they should be used with care.

`bgcolor = "..."`
Values: Background colors can be set either by name or by specifying the intensity of red, green, and blue color components. This topic is addressed in section **2.5 Selecting and Using Colors**.

`border="..."`
Value: The width, in pixels, of a border surrounding an image.

`color = "..."`
Values: Text colors can be set either by name or by directly specifying the intensity of red, green, and blue color components. See section **2.5 Selecting and Using Colors.**

`face = "..."`
Values: Font typefaces can be set either generically, with `cursive`, `monospace`, `sans-serif`, or `serif`, or with specific font names supported by the user's computer. The generic names should always produce something that looks reasonable on any computer, but specific font names that are not available on the user's computer may produce unexpected results.

`height = "..."`
Value: The displayed height of an image in pixels (`width="80"`, for example) or, when followed by a `%` sign (`width="80%"`, for example), as a percent of total screen height. The displayed height overrides the actual height of the image file—the number of rows in the image.

`href = "..."`
Value: The URL of an external or internal Web resource, or the name of an internal document reference.

`hspace = "..."`
Value: The horizontal space, in pixels, between an image and the surrounding text.

(continued)

2

(continued)

name = "…"
Value: The name assigned to an internal document reference through an "a" element.

size = "…"
Values: An unsigned integer from 1 to 7 or a signed number from +1 to +6 or −1 to −6.

An unsigned integer is an absolute font size, which may be system dependent. The default value is 3. A signed integer is a font size relative to the current font size, larger for positive values and smaller for negative values.

For the hr element, size is the vertical height of the horizontal rule, in pixels.

src = "…"
Value: As an attribute for an img tag, the URL of a graphics file. For local use, images and their HTML document are usually stored in the same folder.

text = "…"
Values: The text attribute, used with the body element, selects the color of text in a document, which prevails unless overridden by a font attribute.

vspace = "…"
Value: The vertical space, in pixels, between an image and the surrounding text.

width = "…"
Values: The width of an image or horizontal rule, in pixels or as a percent of total screen width, in percent. For example, width="80" is interpreted as a width of 80 pixels, but width="80%" is a width equal to 80 percent of the total screen width. The displayed width overrides the actual pixel width of the image.

Document 2.1 shows how to use some of these elements.

Document 2.1 (tagExamples.htm)

```html
<html>
<head>
<title>Tag Examples</title>
</head>
<body bgcolor="white">
<h1>Here is a Level 1 Heading</h1>
<h2>Here is a Level 2 Heading</h2>
<hr />
<pre>
     Here is some <strong><em>preformatted
text</em></strong> that has
     been created with the pre element. Note that it
retains the
```

```
paragraph tab
included
in the <b><i>original      document</b></i>. Also, it does
not "collapse" line feeds
and
                white    spaces. Often, it is easier to
use preformatted text than it
is to use markup to get the same effect. Note, however, that
the default
rendering of
preformatted text is to use a monospaced Courier font. This
is often a good choice for
displaying code in an HTML document, but perhaps not a good
choice for other kinds of text content.
</pre><p><center>
<img src="checkmark.gif" align="left" />Here, a small
graphic (the check box) has been inserted into
the document using the "img" element. This text is outside
the preformatted
region, so the default font is different. If you look at the
original document, you can also see that
white     spaces and line feeds are now collapsed.
</p><p>
Note too, that the text is now centered. The way the text is
displayed will
depend on how you
have the display window set in your browser. It may change
when you go from full screen to a window, for example.
</center></p><p>
Centering is now turned off. The default text alignment is
to the left of your screen.
You can change the size and color of text <font size="7"
color="blue"> by using the &lt;font&gt;</font>
<font color="purple">element.</font>
</body>
</html>
```

Below is one rendering of Document 2.1. The small checkbox graphic has been created with Windows' Paint program. The actual text displayed in your browser is larger than this, but the output image has been reduced in size (perhaps to the extent of not being readable) to fit on the page. Also, because of the line feeds imposed on the text of this code example by the page width, the output looks a little different from what you might expect. So, you need to try this document on your own browser.

Here is a Level 1 Heading

Here is a Level 2 Heading

```
         Here is some preformatted text that has
         been created with the pre element. Note that it retains the
paragraph tab
included
in the original        document. Also, it does not "collapse" line feeds
and
         white          spaces. Often, it is easier to use preformatted text than it
is to use markup to get the same effect. Note, however, that the default rendering of
preformatted text is to use a monospaced Courier font. This is often a good choice for
displaying code in an HTML document, but perhaps not a good choice for other kinds of text content.
```

 Here, a small graphic (the check box) has been inserted into the document using the "img" element. This text is outside the preformatted region, so the default font is different. If you look at the original document, you can also see that white spaces and line feeds are now collapsed.

Note too, that the text is now centered. The way the text is displayed will depend on how you have the display window set in your browser. It may change when you go from full screen to a window, for example.

Centering is now turned off. The default text alignment is to the left of your screen. You can change the size and color of text by using the ⟨font⟩ element.

Document 2.1 answers an interesting question: How can HTML display characters that already have a special meaning in the HTML language or which do not appear on the keyboard? The angle brackets (< and >) are two such characters because they are part of HTML tags. They can be displayed with the < and > escape sequences (for the "less than" and "greater than" symbols from mathematics). There are many standardized escape sequences for special symbols. A list of some of them is given in Appendix 2.

2.2
HTML Syntax and Style

A general characteristic of programming languages is that they have very strict syntax rules. HTML is different in that regard, as it is not highly standardized. The positive spin on this situation is to call HTML an "open standard," which means that self-described bearers of the standard can treat the language as they see fit, subject only to usefulness and market acceptance. HTML has an established syntax, but it is very forgiving about how that syntax is used. For example, when a browser encounters HTML code that it does not understand, typically it just ignores it rather than crashing, as a "real" program would do.

Fortunately, market forces—the desire to have as many people as possible accept your browser's interpretation of HTML documents—have forced uniformity on a large subset of HTML. This text will adopt some HTML style conventions and syntax that will be as platform independent as possible. Although these "rules" might seem troublesome if you are not used to writing stylistically consistent HTML documents, they should actually help beginners by providing a more stable and predictable working environment. The only things worse than having syntax and style rules are having no rules or rules that nobody follows.

Here are some style rules that will be used in this text. Under the circumstances of HTML, they are more accurately referred to as "guidelines." Some of them will make more sense later on, as you create more complicated documents.

1. Spell the names of HTML elements in lowercase letters.
   Unlike JavaScript and some other languages, the HTML language is not sensitive to case. Thus, `<html>`, `<HTML>`, and `<hTmL>` are equivalent. However, the XHTML standard requires element names to be spelled with lowercase letters. In the earlier days of HTML, many programmers adopted the style of using uppercase letters for element names because they stood out in a document. You will often still see this style in Web documents. Nonetheless, this book will consistently use lowercase letters for element names.
2. Use the `pre` element to enforce text layout whenever it is reasonable to use a mono-spaced font (such as `Courier`).
   HTML always collapses multiple "white space" characters—spaces, tabs, and line breaks—into a single space when text is displayed. The easiest way to retain white space characters is to use the `pre` element. Other approaches may be needed if proportional fonts are required. Also, tabbed text may still not line up, as different browsers have different default settings for tabs.
3. Nest elements properly.
   Improperly nested elements can cause interpretation problems for your browser. Even when browsers do not complain about improperly nested elements, HTML is easier to learn, read, and edit when these restrictions are enforced.
   Recall this markup in Document 2.1:

```
Here is some <strong><em>preformatted
text</em></strong>
```

If you write this as:

```
Here is some
<strong>
      <em>
            ...{text}
      </em>
</strong>
```

it is easy to see that the em element is properly nested inside the `strong` element. If this is changed to

```
<strong><em> ...{text} </strong></em>
```

your browser probably won't complain, but it is not good programming style.

It is more common to use b and i tags instead of strong and em:

```
Here is some
<b>
        <i>
                ...{text}
        </i>
</b>
```

4. Enclose the values of attributes in single or double quotes

In Document 2.1, bgcolor="white" is an attribute of <body>. Browsers generally will accept bgcolor=white, but the XHTML standard enforces the use of quoted attribute values. This text will be consistent about using double quotes unless attribute values appear inside a string that is surrounded with double quotes (for example, an attribute value embedded in a parameter in the document.write() method). Then attribute values will be single-quoted.

2.3
Using the script Element

The script elements (there can be more than one set of script tags in a document) often, but not always, appear inside the head element, after the title element. Here is a description of script along with its essential attributes.

```
<script language="javascript" type="text/javascript">
...
</script>
Attributes: language, type, src
```

The values usually assigned to the language and type attributes are language="javascript" and type="text/javascript". The values shown in the description are default values, so for documents using JavaScript, it is usually not actually required to include these attributes.

The src attribute has a value corresponding to the name of a file containing JavaScript, usually (but not necessarily) with a .js extension. This attribute will be used in a later chapter.

2.4
Creating and Organizing a Web Site

Obviously this is a major topic, a thorough investigation of which would go far beyond the reach of this text. There is an entire industry devoted to hosting and creating Web sites, including helping a user obtain a domain name, providing storage space, developing content, and tracking access. For the purposes of a course based on this text, the goal is extremely simple: create a Web site sufficient to display the results of work done during the course.

The first step toward creating a Web site is establishing its location. In an academic environment, a college, university, or department computer may provide space for Web pages. A URL might look something like this:

```
http://www.myuniversity.edu/~username
```

where the "~" symbol indicates a directory where Web pages are stored. Together with a user name, this URL directs a browser to the home Web directory for that user. As noted in Chap. 1, HTML documents are not automatically Internet accessible, and for the purposes of this book, your Web pages may be accessible only locally on your own computer.

In this home directory there should be at least one file, called `index.htm` (or `index.html`). UNIX systems favor the `.html` extension, but Windows users may prefer the three-character `.htm` extension because it is more consistent with Windows file extension conventions. This is the file that will be opened automatically in response to entering the above URL. That is, the `index.htm` file is the "home page" for the Web site. This home page file could be named something different, but then its name would have to be added to the URL:

```
http://www.myuniversity.edu/~username/HomePage.htm
```

An `index.htm` file can contain both its own content as well as links to other content (hyperlinks), including other pages on the user's Web site and to external URLs. Here are four important kinds of links:

1. Links to other sites on the World Wide Web.
   This is the essential tool for globally linking Web pages.

Syntax: `<a href="`*{URL of Web page}*`">`
   {description of linked Web page}`</a>`

The URL may refer to a completely different Web site or it may be a link to local documents in the current folder or a subfolder within that folder.

2. Links to images.
   The `img` element is used to load images for display or to use as a page background.

Syntax: `<img src="`*{URL plus image name}*`" align="..."`
   `height="..." width="..." />`

The image may exist locally or it may be at a different Web site. The `align`, `height`, and `width` attributes, which can be used to position and size an image, are optional.

2

However, for high-resolution images, it is almost always necessary to specify the height and width as a percentage of the full page or as a number of pixels in order to reduce the image to a manageable size in the context of the rest of the page. Resizing the image, if possible, will solve this problem.

You can also make a "clickable image" to direct the user to another link:

Syntax: `<a href="{URL of Web page}">`
        `<img src="{URL plus image name}" align="..."`
        `height="..." width="..." /></a>`

3. Links to e-mail addresses.
   An e-mail link is an essential feature that allows users to communicate with the author of a Web page.

Syntax: `<a href="mailto:{e-mail address}">`
        `{description of recipient}</a>`

Often, but not necessarily, the *{description of recipient}* is also the e-mail address. The actual sending of an e-mail will be handled by the default mailer on the sender's computer.

4. Internal links within a document.
   Within a large document, it is often convenient to be able to move from place to place within the document, using internal links.

Syntax: `<a href="#{internal link name}">`
        `{description of target position}</a>`
        ...
        `<a name="{internal link name}">{target text}</a>`

The "#" symbol is required when specifying the value of the `href` attribute, to differentiate this internal link from a link to another (external) document.

The careless specification of linked documents can make Web sites very difficult to maintain and modify. As noted previously, every Web site should have a "home" directory containing an `index.htm` file. In order to make a site easy to transport from one computer to another, all other content should be contained either in the home directory or in folders created within that directory. References to folders that are not related in this way should be avoided, as they will typically need to be renamed if the site is moved to a different computer. Although it is allowed as a matter of syntax to give a complete (absolute) URL for a local Web page, this should be avoided in favor of a reference relative to the current folder.

This matter is important enough to warrant a complete example. Document 2.2a–c shows a simple Web site with a home folder on a Windows desktop called home and two subfolders within the home folder named homework and personal. Each subfolder contains a single HTML document, homework.htm in homework and resume.htm in personal.

Document 2.2a (`index.htm`)

```
<html>
<head>
<title>My Page</title>
</head>
<body>
<!-- These absolute links are a bad idea! -->
Here are links to
<a href="C:/Documents and Settings/David/desktop/
JavaScript/Book/homework.htm">homework</a> and
<a href="C:/Documents and Settings/
   David/desktop/JavaScript/Book/resume.htm">
personal documents.</a>
</body>
</html>
```

Document 2.2b (`resume.htm`)

```
<html>
<head>
<title>Resumé</title>
</head>
<body>
Here is my resumé.
</body>
</html>
```

Document 2.2c (`homework.htm`)

```
<html><head>
<title>Homework</title>
</head>
<body>
Here are my homework problems.
</body>
</html>
```

Note that Document 2.2a uses forward slashes to separate the directories and the file names. This is consistent with UNIX syntax, but Windows/DOS systems use backward slashes. Forward slashes are the HTML standard, and they should always be used even though backward slashes may also work. Another point of interest is that UNIX directory paths and filenames are case-sensitive, but Windows paths and filenames are not. This could cause problems if you develop a Web page on a Windows/DOS computer and then move it to a UNIX-based system. As a matter of style, you should be consistent about case in directory and file names even when it appears not to matter.

As a brief diversion, the "é" in resumé in Document 2.2b is produced by entering the escape sequence é.

In Document 2.2a, the absolute references to a folder on a particular Windows computer desktop are a bad idea because this reference will need to be changed if the index. htm file is moved to a different place on the same computer, or to a different computer— for example, to a University department computer with a different directory/folder structure. Document 2.2d shows the preferred solution. Now the paths to homework.htm and resume.htm are given relative to the home folder, wherever the index2.htm file resides. (Remember that this file, no longer named index.htm, will not be recognized as a default home page.) This document assumes that folders homework and personal exist in the home folder. This relative URL should work without modification when the Web site is moved to a different computer. If the Web site is moved, only a single reference, to the index2.htm file, needs to be changed.

Document 2.2d (index2.htm, a new version of index.htm)

```
<html>
<head>
<title>My Page</title>
</head>
<body>
<!-- Use these relative links instead! -->
Here are links to
<a
href="homework/homework.htm">
homework</a> and
<a href="personal/resume.htm">
personal documents.</a>
</body>
</html>
```

Proper attention to using relative URLs from the very beginning when designing a Web site will save a lot of time in the future!

2.5
Selecting and Using Colors

As previously noted, several attributes, such as bgcolor, are used to set colors of text or backgrounds. Colors may be identified by name or by a six-character hexadecimal numeric code that specifies the strength of the signal emitted from the red, green, and blue electron "guns" that excite the corresponding phosphors on a cathode ray tube color monitor screen. This convention has been retained even when other display technologies are used. The **hex code** is in the format #*RRGGBB* where each color value can range from 00 (turned off) to FF (maximum intensity).

Table 2.1   Sixteen standard
HTML color names and hex
codes

Color name	Hexadecimal code
Aqua	#00FFFF
Black	#000000
Blue	#0000FF
Fuchsia	#FF00FF
Gray	#808080
Green	#008000
Lime	#00FF00
Maroon	#800000
Navy	#000080
Olive	#808000
Purple	#800080
Red	#FF0000
Silver	#C0C0C0
Teal	#008080
White	#FFFFFF
Yellow	#FFFF00

There are many color names in use on the Web, but only 16 are completely standardized, representing the 16 colors recognized by the Windows VGA color palette. These colors are listed in Table 2.1. The problem with additional color names is that there is no enforced standard for how browsers should interpret them. Two examples: magenta probably should be, but doesn't have to be, the same as fuchsia; ivory is a nonstandard color that should be rendered as a yellowish off-white. The colors in Table 2.1 are standardized in the sense that all browsers should associate these 16 names with the same hexadecimal code. Of course, variations can still occur because monitors themselves will respond somewhat differently to the same name or hex code; blue on my computer monitor may look somewhat different than blue on your monitor.

Note that the standardized colors use a limited range of hex codes. With the exception of silver (nothing more than a lighter gray), the RGB gun colors are either off (00), on (FF), or halfway on (80).

What should you do about choosing colors? Favor standardized colors, and if you wish to make an exception, try it in as many browser environments as possible. Be careful to choose background and text colors so that text will always be visible against its background. The safest approach for setting colors in the body element is to specify both background and text colors. This will ensure that default colors set in a user's browser will not result in unreadable text.

If you're not sure whether a color name is supported and what it looks like on your monitor, you have nothing to lose by trying it. If you set bgcolor="lightblue", you will either like the result or not. If a color name isn't recognized by your browser, the result will be unpredictable, but not catastrophic. There are (of course) numerous Web sites that will help you work with colors, including getting the desired result with hex codes.

2.6
Using Cascading Style Sheets

As you create more Web pages, you may wish to impose a consistent look for all your pages, or for groups of related pages. It is tedious to insert elements for all the characteristics you may wish to replicate—font size, font color, background color, etc. Style sheets make it much easier to replicate layout information in multiple sheets. A complete discussion of style sheets is far beyond the scope of this book, as there are many different kinds of style sheets, many ways to make use of them, and many browser-specific nuances. This book will use **cascading style sheets** (CSS), which are widely accepted as a default kind of style sheet, but will present only a *small* subset of all the possibilities! By way of introduction, Document 2.3 shows how to use a `style` element to establish the default appearance of the body of an HTML document.

Document 2.3 (`style1.htm`)

```
<html>
<head>
<title>Style Sheets</title>
<style title="David's default" type="text/css">
      body.bright {background: red; font: 16pt serif;
         color: blue; font-style: italic; font-weight: bold}
</style>
</head>
<body class="bright">
Here is the body.
</body>
</html>
```

Here is the body.

The `style` element has an optional `title` attribute and a `type` attribute set equal to `"text/css"`, where the `css` stands for cascading style sheet. Inside the `style` element, dot notation is used to assign a class name, `bright`, to the body element: `body.bright`. Inside curly brackets attributes are assigned values, with each attribute and its value being separated by a semicolon. Then, the `<body>` tag assigns the class name `bright` as the value of the `class` attribute. As a result, the document background color is red, with the font set to a blue, bold, italicized 16-point serif font.

Any HTML tag that encloses content can be assigned a class value defined in a style element. For this simple example, with styles applying only to a single `body` element, the class name is optional. With no class name and no `class` attribute in `<body>`, the style rules will automatically be applied to the entire HTML document.

In general, several different style rules can apply to the same HTML element. For example, several style rules could be established for paragraphs (`<p>` ... `</p>`), each of which would have its own class name.

In summary, style specifications follow a hierarchy:

$$\mathtt{style} \text{ element} \to \text{other HTML elements}\textit{[.class name]} \to$$
$$\text{properties} \to \text{value(s)}$$

where the *[.class name]* is optional.

How did CSSs get that name? Because the properties set for an element cascade down, or are "inherited," by other elements contained within that element unless those elements are assigned their own style properties. So, for example, properties set for the body element are inherited by the p and h1 elements, because these are contained within the body element. Properties set for the head element are inherited by content appearing in the title element.

CSSs can be used to modify the appearance of any HTML element that encloses content. Here are some properties that can be specified in style sheets.

Background properties

`background-color`

When used in a body element, `background-color` sets the background color for an entire document. It can also be used to highlight a paragraph, for example, when used with a p element.

`background-image`

This property is used with a URL to select an image file (gif or jpeg) that will appear as a background. Typically, this is used with a body element, but it can also be used with other elements, such as p. For other background properties that can be used to control the appearance of a background image, consult an HTML reference text.

`background`

This allows you to set all background properties in a single rule.

Color property

The `color` property sets the default color for text, using the descriptions discussed in Sect. 2.5.

Font properties

`font-family`

Font support is not completely standardized. However, browsers that support style sheets should support at least the generic font families given in Table 2.2.

Example: `font-family: Arial, sans-serif;`

Table 2.2 Generic font families

Generic name	Example
Cursive	*Script MT Bold*
Monospace	Courier New
Sans-serif	Arial
Serif	Times New Roman

`font-size`

This property allows you to set the actual or relative size of text. You can use relative values, such as `large`, `small`, `larger`, `smaller` (relative to a default size); a percentage, such as `200%` of the default size; or an actual point size such as `16pt`. Some sources advise against using absolute point sizes because a point size that is perfectly readable on one system might be uncomfortably small on another. For our purposes, specifying the point size is probably the easiest choice.

Example: `font-size: 24pt;`

`font-style`

This property allows you to specify `normal`, `italic`, or `oblique` fonts.

Example: `font-style: italic;`

`font-weight`

This property allows you to select the font weight. You can use values in the range from `100` (extra light) to `900` (extra bold), or words: `extra-light`, `light`, `demi-light`, `medium`, `demi-bold`, `bold`, and `extra-bold`. Some choices may not have a noticeable effect on some fonts in some browsers.

Example: `font-weight: 900;`

`font`

This property allows you to set all font properties with one style rule.

Example: `font: italic 18pt Helvetica, sans-serif;`

How will your browser interpret a generic font name? For the generic name `serif`, it will pick the primary serif font it supports—probably Times or Times Roman. Browsers will probably also recognize specific font names such as Times or Helvetica (a sans-serif font). If you specify a font name not supported by your browser, it will simply ignore your choice and use its default font for text. It is possible to list several fonts, in which case your browser will select the first one it supports. For example, consider this rule:

`font-family: Arial, Helvetica, sans-serif;`

Your browser will use an Arial font if it supports that, Helvetica if it doesn't support Arial but does support Helvetica, or, finally, whatever sans-serif font it does support. By giving your browser choices, with the generic name as the last choice, you can be reasonably sure that text will be displayed with a sans-serif font.

Text properties

Of the many text properties, here are just three that may be useful.

`text-align`

This is used in block elements such as p. It is similar in effect to the HTML `align` attribute. The choices are `left`, `right`, `center`, and `justify`. With large font sizes, `justify` may produce odd-looking results.

Example: `text-align: center;`

`text-indent`

Recall that paragraphs created with the p element do not indent the first word in the paragraph. (HTML inserts a blank line, but left-justifies the text.) This property allows you to set indentation using typesetting notation or actual measurements. An actual English or metric measurement—inches (`in`), millimeters (`mm`), or centimeters (`cm`)—may be easiest and will always give predictable results.

Example: `text-indent: 0.5in;`

`white-space`

The value of this property is that you can prevent spaces from being ignored. (Remember that the default HTML behavior is to collapse multiple spaces and other nonprintable characters into a single blank space.) Some older browsers may not support this property. You can use the HTML `pre` element by itself, instead, but this causes text to be displayed in a monospaced font such as Courier. The example given here retains white space regardless of the typeface being used.

Example: `white-space: pre;`

 Styles aren't restricted just to the body element. For example, paragraphs (`<p>` ... `</p>`) and headings (`<h`*n*`>` ... `</h`*n*`>`) can also have styles associated with them. You can also set styles in selected portions of text, using the `span` element, and in blocks of text using the `div` element.

```
<div> ... </div>
Attributes: align, style

<span> ... </span>
Attributes: align, style
Values for align: "left" (default), "right", "center"
```

You can create style sheets as separate files and then use them whenever you wish to use a particular style on a Web page. This makes it easy to impose a uniform appearance on multiple Web pages. Documents 2.4a and 2.4b show a simple example.

Document 2.4a (`body.css`)

```
body {background:silver; color:white; font:24pt Times}
h1 {color:red; font:18pt Impact;}
h2 {color:blue; font:16pt Courier;}
```

Document 2.4b (`style2.htm`)

```
<html>
<head>
<title>Style Sheet Example</title>
<link href="body.css" rel="stylesheet"
   type="text/css" />
</head>
<body>
   <h1>Heading 1</h1>
   <h2>Heading 2</h2>
   Here is some text.
</body>

</html>
```

(See Color Example 2 for full-color output.)

This example shows how to create a file, `body.css`, containing style elements that can be applied to any document by using the `link` element, as in Document 2.4b. The `.css` extension is standard, but not required. (You could use `.txt`, for example.) Although this example is very simple, the concept is powerful because it makes it easy to create a standard style for all your documents that can be invoked with the `link` element. The `Impact` font chosen for `h1` headings may not be supported by all browsers. If not, a default font will be used in its place.

The attributes of `link` include `href`, which contains the URL of the style sheet file, the `rel="stylesheet"` (relationship) attribute, which describes how to use the file (as a style sheet), and the `type`, which should be `"text/css"`, just as it would be defined if you created a `style` element directly in the `head` element. In this example, `body.css` is in the same folder as `style2.htm`. If you keep all your style sheets in a separate folder, you will of course need to reference that folder.

It is worth emphasizing that this discussion has barely scratched the surface of style sheets. Style sheets can make your Web pages more visually appealing and can greatly simplify your work on large Web projects. Some developers advocate replacing *all* individual formatting elements, such as `font` and its attributes, with style sheet specifications. In newer versions of HTML, the use of individual formatting elements is "deprecated," but there is little likelihood that support for them will disappear from browsers in the foreseeable future. For the kinds of applications discussed in this book, CSSs may sometimes be convenient, but they are not required.

2.7
Another Example

Documents 2.5a, b show how to use a style sheet file to specify different background and text colors for different sections of text.

Document 2.5a (rwb.css)

```
p.red {background:red;color:blue;font:20pt Times}
div.white {background:white;color:red;font:20pt Times}
span.blue {background:blue;color:white;font:20pt Times}
```

Document 2.5b (rwb.htm)

```
<html>
<head>
<title>A Red, White, and Blue Document</title>
<link href="rwb.css" rel="stylesheet" type="text/css" />
</head>
<body>
<img src="stars.jpg" height="150" width="250" />
<p class="red">
This text should be blue on a red background.
</p><p><div class="white" style="font-style: italic;">
This text should be red on a white background.
</div></p>
<p><span class="blue">This text should be white on a blue
background.
</span>
</p>
</body>
</html>
```

This text should be blue on a red background

This text should be red on a white background

This text should be white on a blue background

(See Color Example 3 for full-color output.)

The stars (they are supposed to be red, silver, and blue) have been drawn using Windows' Paint program.

HTML Tables, Forms, Lists, and Frames

3

Abstract Chapter 3 shows how to use HTML tables, forms, lists, and frames. It explains how to organize documents for user input by combining forms and tables, and how to send the contents of a form back to its creator.

3.1
The `table` Element

3.1.1
Basic Table Formatting

HTML **tables** and **forms** are the two most important ways to organize the content of a Web page. Forms are critical because they provide a user interface for JavaScript. Sometimes it is helpful to organize information in a form through the use of one or more tables. With that approach in mind, first consider tables.

Because HTML ignores text formatting, such as white space and line feeds (the Enter key), it can be difficult to control the placement of content on a web page. The addition of images only compounds this problem. An easy way to gain some control is to create a table, using the `table` element. Then the relative locations of text and graphics can be established by entering them into cells of the table. Within the start and end tags, `<table>` ... `</table>`, rows and cells are defined with the `tr` ("table row") and `td` ("table data") elements. These elements are nested as follows:

```
<table>
   <tr>
     <td> ... </td> {as many columns as you need...}
     ...
   </tr>
     {as many rows as you need...}
     ...
</table>
```

D.R. Brooks, *Guide to HTML, JavaScript and PHP: For Scientists and Engineers,*   **41**
DOI 10.1007/978-0-85729-449-4_3, © Springer-Verlag London Limited 2011

The <tr> ... </tr> tags define the rows and the <td> ... </td> tags define cells in columns within those rows. You can define as many rows and columns as you need. With these elements, you can organize information in a familiar spreadsheet-like row-and-column format. Document 3.1 shows how to use a table to organize and display some results from residential radon testing.

Document 3.1 (radonTable.htm)

```
<html>
<head>
<title>Radon Table</title>
</head>
<body>
<h1>Results of radon testing</h1>
<p>
The table below shows some radon levels measured in
residences.<br /> For values greater than or equal to 4
pCi/L, action should be taken<br /> to reduce the
concentration of radon gas. For values greater than or<br />
equal to 3 pCi/L, retesting is recommended.
</p>
<table>
  <tr bgcolor="silver">
    <td>Location</td><td>Value, pCi/L</td>
  <td>Comments</td></tr>
  <tr>
    <td>DB's house, basement</td><td>15.6</td>
    <td bgcolor="pink">Action should be taken!</td></tr>
  <tr>
    <td>ID's house, 2nd floor bedroom</td><td>3.7</td>
    <td bgcolor="yellow">Should be retested.</td></tr>
  <tr>
    <td> FJ's house, 1st floor living room</td><td> 0.9</td>
    <td bgcolor="lightgreen">No action required.</td></tr>
  <tr>
    <td> MB's house, 2nd floor bedroom</td><td>2.9</td>
    <td bgcolor="lightgreen">No action required.</td></tr>
</table>
</body>
</html>
```

Results of radon testing

The table below shows some radon levels measured in residences. For values greater than or equal to 4 pCi/L, action should be taken to reduce the concentration of radon gas. For values greater than or equal to 3 pCi/L, retesting is recommended.

Location	Value, pCi/L	Comments
DB's house, basement	15.6	Action should be taken!
ID's house, 2nd floor bedroom	3.7	Should be retested.
FJ's house, 1st floor living room	0.9	No action required.
MB's house, 2nd floor bedroom	2.9	No action required.

(See Color Example 4 for full-color output.)

The syntax for tables includes several possibilities in addition to `tr` and `td` for customizing the appearance of a table. These include the `caption` element, which associates a caption with the table, and the `th` element, which is used to create a "header" row in a table by automatically displaying text in bold font. (The `th` element can be used anywhere in a table in place of `td`.) The `caption`, `td`, `th`, and `tr` elements are used only inside the start and end tags of a `table` element: `<table>` … `</table>`. With these elements, a more comprehensive table layout looks like this:

```
<table>
  <caption> … </caption>
  <tr>
  <!-- Use of th in place of td is optional. -->
    <th> … </th>
      …
  </tr>
  <tr>
  <td> … </td>
    …
  </tr>
    …
</table>
```

The attributes associated with these tags all have default values, so you don't need to give them values. You can create a table without using any attributes at all and then add attributes as needed. In Document 3.1, the only specified attribute is the background color in some cells. An easy way to familiarize yourself with the effects of specifying table attributes and their values is to experiment with Document 3.1.

3.1.2
Subdividing Tables into Sections

The tbody element allows a table to be divided into two or more groups of rows. Each group of rows enclosed by a `<tbody>` ... `</tbody>` tag can have its own attributes and can have a different predefined `class` attribute value. Document 3.2 shows a simple example in which rows in a table are grouped by background color.

Document 3.2 (tbody.htm)

```html
<html>
<head>
  <title>Using the tbody element</title>
    <style>
      th {background-color:black; color:white;}
      tbody.cold {text-align:center;
      font-weight:bold; background-color:gray;}
    tbody.cool {text-align:center;
      font-weight:bold; background-color:silver;}
    tbody.hot {text-align:center;
      font-weight:bold; background-color:ivory;}
  </style>
</head>
<body>
<table border>
  <tr><th>Month</th><th>Average<br />Temperature
      <br />&deg;F</td></tr>
<tbody class="cold">
  <tr><td >January</td><td>30.4</td></tr>
  <tr><td>February</td><td>33.0</td></tr>
  <tr><td>March</td><td>42.4</td></tr>
</tbody>
<tbody class="cool">
  <tr><td>April</td><td>52.4</td></tr>
  <tr><td>May</td><td>62.9</td></tr>
</tbody>
<tbody class="hot">
  <tr><td>June</td><td>71.8</td></tr>
  <tr><td>July</td><td>76.7</td></tr>
  <tr><td>August</td><td>75.5</td></tr>
</tbody>
<tbody class="cool">
  <tr><td>September</td><td>68.2</td></tr>
  <tr><td>October</td><td>56.4</td></tr>
</tbody>
```

```
<tbody class="cold">
  <tr><td>November</td><td>46.4</td></tr>
  <tr><td>December</td><td>35.8</td></tr>
</body>
</html>
```

January–March and November–December use the "cold" class, April–May and September–October use "cool," and June–August use "hot." Each class has a different background color. (For this grayscale rendering of the output, gray, silver, and ivory have been chosen instead of something more colorful.)

3.1.3
Merging Cells Across Rows and Columns

If you are familiar with creating tables in a word processing application, you know that it is easy to create more complicated table layouts by merging cells across rows and columns. You can also do this with HTML forms, using the colspan and rowspan attributes. Document 3.3 shows a table that displays cloud names, altitudes, and whether they produce precipitation or not.

Document 3.3 (cloudType.htm)

Month	Average Temperature °F
January	30.4
February	33.0
March	42.4
April	52.4
May	62.9
June	71.8
July	76.7
August	75.5
September	68.2
October	56.4
November	46.4
December	35.8

```
<html>
<head>
<title>Cloud Type Chart</title>
</head>
<body>
<table border="2">
<caption>Cloud Type Chart</caption>
<tr>
  <th align="center">Altitude</th>
  <th colspan="2">Cloud Name</th></tr>
<tr><td align="center" rowspan="3">High</td>
   <td colspan="2">Cirrus</td></tr>
   <tr><td colspan="2">Cirrocumulus</td></tr>
   <tr><td colspan="2">Cirrostratus</td></tr></tr>
<tr><td align="center" rowspan="2">Middle</td>
   <td colspan="2">Altocumulus</td></tr>
   <tr><td colspan="2">Altostratus</td></tr></tr>
```

```
<tr><td align="center" rowspan="5">Low</td>
    <td>Cumulus</td>
    <td>nonprecipitating</td></tr>
<tr><td>Altocumulus</td>
    <td>nonprecipitating</td></tr>
<tr><td>Stratocumulus</td>
    <td>nonprecipitating</td></tr>
    <tr><td>Cumulonimbus</td>
    <td align="center"
        bgcolor="silver">precipitating</td></tr>
    <tr><td>Nimbostratus</td> <td align="center"
        bgcolor="silver">precipitating</td></tr></tr>
</table>
</body></html>
```

It is much more tedious to merge cells across rows in columns in an HTML table than it is in a word processor. You need to plan your table in advance, and even then you should be prepared for some trial-and-error editing!

Here is a summary of some table-related elements and their attributes. All the elements except `table` itself should appear only inside a `table` element.

Cloud Type Chart

Altitude	Cloud Name	
High	Cirrus	
	Cirrocumulus	
	Cirrostratus	
Middle	Altocumulus	
	Altostratus	
Low	Cumulus	nonprecipitating
	Altocumulus	nonprecipitating
	Stratocumulus	nonprecipitating
	Cumulonimbus	precipitating
	Nimbostratus	precipitating

```
<caption> ... </caption>
```
Displays the specified text as a caption for a table. Earlier versions of HTML support only "top" (the default value) or "bottom" for the value of the `align` attribute. Some browsers may allow "center" as a value for `align`, which is worth noting because this might often be the alignment of choice for a table caption.
Attributes: `align`

```
<table> ... </table>
```
Contains table-related and other elements.
Attributes: `border`, `bordercolor`, `cellpadding`, `cellspacing`, `width`

```
<tbody> ... </tbody>
```
Groups rows within the body of a table so each group can be given different attributes and styles.
Attributes: `align`, `char`, `charoff`, `valign`

(continued)

(continued)

`<td> ... </td>`
Defines data cells in the rows of a table. Does not contain other table-related elements.
Attributes: `align`, `bgcolor`, `char`, `charoff`, `colspan`, `nowrap`, `rowspan`, `width`

`<th> ... </th>`
The `th` element works just like the `td` element except it automatically displays text in bold font, serving as headings for table columns. Does not contain other elements.
Attributes: `align`, `bgcolor`, `char`, `charoff`, `colspan`, `nowrap`, `rowspan`, `valign`, `width`

`<tr> ... </tr>`
Defines rows in a table. Contains `td` or `th` elements.
Attributes: `align`, `bgcolor`, `valign`

Description of attributes:

`align = "..."`
Values: `"left"`, `"right"`, or `"center"`
Aligns text horizontally. When `align` is specified in a `tr` element, its value will be overridden if it is specified again within a `td` element in that row.

`bgcolor = "..."`
Values: color names or hexadecimal values `"#RRGGBB"`
Sets the background color for a cell or row. When `bgcolor` is specified in a `tr` element, its value will be overridden if it is specified again within a `td` element in that row.

`border = "..."`
Values: an integer number of pixels
Adds a border to the table and its cells. A value is optional. If it is included, a colored (or gray, by default) border is added around the outer boundary of the table.

`bordercolor = "..."`
Values: color names or hexadecimal values `"#RRGGBB"`
Sets the color of a table border.

`cellpadding = "..."`
Values: an integer number of pixels
Defines vertical spacing between cells in a table.

`cellspacing = "..."`
Values: an integer number of pixels
Defines horizontal spacing between cells in a table.

`colspan = "..."`
Values: an integer
Defines how many columns a cell will span.

(continued)

(continued)

nowrap
   Prevents text from being automatically wrapped within a cell. It does not have a value.

rowspan = "..."
Values: an integer
   Defines how many rows a cell will span.

valign = "..."
Values: "top", "middle", or "bottom"
   Aligns text vertically. When valign is specified in a tr element, its value will be overridden if it is specified again within a td element in that row.

width = "..."
Values: a number or a percentage
   Specifies table or cell width in pixels (width="140") or as a percentage of the window or table header width (width="80%").

3.2
The form and input Elements

One of the most important applications of HTML documents is to provide the Web page equivalent of a paper form. In some cases, a form just helps to organize user input to a Web page. Often, an online form includes provisions for sending a completed form back to the author of the Web page. In other cases, the form may act as an I/O interface in which a user provides input and the Web page provides results from calculations or other actions. This use of forms is especially important for the material presented in later chapters of this book.

   HTML forms are defined by the form element, using start and end tags: <form> ... </form> tags. The attributes of the form element are:

action = "..."
Value: a programmer-supplied URL that identifies a processing script, PHP file name, or mailto: followed by an e-mail address. For example,
action="mailto:my_mail@my_univ.edu".

enctype="..."
Value: This book uses only enctype="text/plain". In combination with method="post", this will transmit form data with the name of the form field followed by an "=" sign and the value of the field. This makes it easy to interpret the contents of a form that has been submitted.

method = "..."
Values: "get", "post"
   The method attribute controls how data from a form is sent to the URL, PHP file, or e-mail address identified in the action attribute. In this book, the "post" value is used because it is the easiest way to transmit form data in an easily readable format.

(continued)

(continued)

name = "..."
Value: a programmer-selected name that is used to identify the form.
The name attribute is needed only if a document contains more than one form.

Table 3.1 Values for the input element's type attribute

Field type	Description
type = "button"	Provides a programmer-defined action to be associated with the field through the use of an event handler such as onclick
type = "checkbox"	Allows selection of one or more values from a set of possible values
type = "hidden"	Allows the definition of text fields that can be accessed by a JavaScript script but are not displayed in a document
type = "password"	Allows entry of character data but displays only asterisks
type = "radio"	Allows selection of one and only one value from a set of possible values
type = "reset"	Used to reset all form fields to their default values
type = "submit"	Processes form contents according to method and action
type = "text"	Allows entry of character data

Forms contain one or more input **fields** identified by <input /> tags. Because the input element does not enclose content, it has no end tag, so it requires a closing slash for XHTML compliance. The most important attribute of input is its type. There are several field types that have well-defined default behaviors in HTML. The possible values are listed in Table 3.1.

There is no field type specifically for numerical values. This will be significant when JavaScript is used to process the contents of forms. The use of event handlers, mentioned in the description of the "button" field type, will be discussed in Chaps. 4 and 6.

Here is a list of attributes for the input element.

checked
Value: none
   Applies to type="radio" and type="checkbox" only.

maxlength="..."
Value: Maximum number of characters that can be entered in the field. This value can be greater than the value given for the size attribute.

name="..."
Value: A programmer-supplied name for the field. The name should follow the variable-naming conventions for JavaScript (see Chap. 4) in order to facilitate its use in JavaScript scripts.

(continued)

(continued)

> ```
> readonly
> ```
> *Value*: none
>   Prevents field values in `type="text"` or `text="password"` from being changed.
>
> ```
> size="…"
> ```
> *Value*: width of the displayed field, in characters.
>
> ```
> type="…"
> ```
> *Values*: See Table 3.1.
>
> ```
> value="…"
> ```
> *Value*: a programmer-supplied default value that will be displayed in the field. This value can be overridden by user input unless the `readonly` attribute is also specified.

The `form` element typically contains a combination of document text and input fields. The document text can be used to explain to the user of the form what kind of input is expected. Document 3.4 gives a simple example that uses several input field types:

Document 3.4 (`location.htm`)

```html
<html>
<head>
<title>Data Reporting Site Information</title>
</head>
<body>
<form>
  Please enter your last name:
  <input type="text" name="last_name" size="20"
    maxlength="20" /><br />
  Please enter your latitude:
  <input type="text" name="lat" value="40" size="7"
    maxlength="7" />
    N <input type="radio" name="NS" value="N" checked />
     or S <input type="radio" name="NS" value="S" /><br />
  Please enter your longitude:
  <input type="text" name="lon" value="75" size="8"
    maxlength="8" />
    E <input type="radio" name="EW" value="E" /> or W
  <input type="radio" name="EW" value="W" checked /><br />
  Please enter your elevation:
  <input type="text" name="elevation" size="8" maxlength="8"
      /> meters<br />
```

```
Please indicate the seasons during which your site reports
   data:<br />
Winter: <input type="checkbox" name="seasons"
   value="Winter" />
Spring: <input type="checkbox" name="seasons"
   value="Spring" />
Summer: <input type="checkbox" name="seasons"
   value="Summer" />
Fall: <input type="checkbox" name="seasons"
   value="Fall" />
</form>
</body>
</html>
```

Note that some of the text fields are blank because no default `value` attribute has been specified. These require user input, and there is no way to establish ahead of time what this input might be. However, it may still be worthwhile in some cases to provide a default value if that might help the user to understand what is required. When the allowed input choices can be limited ahead of time by the creator of the document, it is appropriate to use radio buttons and checkboxes. You can create as many different combinations of these kinds of field as your application needs.

Each group of `radio` and `checkbox` buttons has its own unique field name and, within each group, each button should have its own value. In Document 3.4, there are two `radio` button groups, named NS and EW. It is important to specify a value for each button, because the value of the checked button will be captured when the contents of the form are submitted to a recipient's e-mail address. This will be demonstrated in the modified version of this document presented in Sect. 3.5. Default values for the `radio` field can be specified by using the `checked` attribute. When you access the document, the button with the `checked` attribute will be "on." You can change it by clicking on another of the buttons in the group.

The same basic rules apply to `checkbox` fields. You can have more than one group of checkboxes, each with its unique name. The only difference is that you can select as many boxes as you like within each group, rather than just one value with `radio` fields.

3.3
Creating Pull-Down Lists

A common feature on Web pages that use forms is a pull-down list. The `select` and `option` tags provide another way to limit the input choices a user can make on a form. The implementation described here is similar to a group of radio buttons in the sense that only one item can be selected from a list. This can simplify a document interface and eliminate the need for some input checking that might otherwise need to be done if a user is free to type whatever he/she likes in an input field. For example, creating a pull-down list of the months of the year eliminates the need for a user to type (and perhaps to mistype) the name of a month, as shown in Document 3.5

Document 3.5 (`select.htm`)

```
<html>
<head>
<title>Pull-Down List</title>
</head>
<body><form>
Select a month from this menu:
  <select name="testing">
    <option value="1" selected>January</option>
    <option value="2">February</option>
    <option value="3">March</option>
    <option value="4">April</option>
    <option value="5">May</option>
    <option value="6">June</option>
    <option value="7">July</option>
    <option value="8">August</option>
    <option value="9">September</option>
    <option value="10">October</option>
    <option value="11">November</option>
    <option value="12">December</option>
  </select>
</form></body>
</html>
```

In the output shown, the user has chosen the month of April, which is now highlighted. The values of the `value` attribute can be, but do not have to be, the same as the text displayed for each option. In this case, the month values are numbers between 1 and 12, rather than the names of the months. Assigning the `selected` attribute to the first option means that "January" will be highlighted when the pull-down box is first displayed. For longer lists, the default format is for HTML to include a scroll bar alongside the list.

Although it is easy to create pull-down lists as well as groups of radio buttons and checkboxes, as described in Sect. 3.3, it is not yet obvious how a document will make use of the selections a user makes. As will be shown in Chap. 4, JavaScript provides the required capabilities.

Select a month from this menu: January

January
February
March
April
May
June
July
August
September
October
November
December

3.4
Combining Tables and Forms

In terms of organizing an interactive Web page, it is often helpful to create one or more tables in which the cell contents are fields in a form. Document 3.6 gives an example.

Document 3.6 (siteDefinition.htm)

```
<html>
<head>
<title>Observation Site Descriptions</title>
</head>
<body>
<form>
<table border="2" cellpadding="5" cellspacing="2"
  align="center">
  <caption><font size="+2">Observation Site
  Descriptions</font></caption>
  <tr bgcolor="lightblue">
    <th>Site #</th><th>Site Name</th><th>Latitude</th>
    <th>Longitude</td><th>Elevation</th>
  </tr>
  <tr bgcolor="palegreen">
    <td>Site 1</td>
    <td><input type="text" name="Name1" size="10"
      maxlength="10" value="Name1" /></td>
    <td><input type="text" name="Latitude1" size="10"
      maxlength="10"
      value="Latitude1" /></td>
    <td><input type="text" name="Longitude1" size="10"
      maxlength="10" value="Longitude1" /></td>
    <td><input type="text" name="Elevation1" size="10"
      maxlength="10" value="Elevation1" /></td>
  </tr>
  <tr bgcolor="ivory">
    <td>Site 2</td>
```

```
      <td><input type="text" name="Name2" size="10"
        maxlength="10" value="Name2" /></td>
      <td><input type="text" name="Latitude2" size="10"
        maxlength="10" value="Latitude2" /></td>
      <td><input type="text" name="Longitude2" size="10"
        maxlength="10" value="Longitude2" /></td>
      <td><input type="text" name="Elevation2" size="10"
        maxlength="10" value="Elevation2" /></td>
    </tr>
    <tr bgcolor="palegreen">
      <td>Site 3</td>
      <td><input type="text" name="Name3" size="10"
        maxlength="10" value="Name3" /></td>
      <td><input type="text" name="Latitude3" size="10"
        maxlength="10" value="Latitude3" /></td>
      <td><input type="text" name="Longitude3" size="10"
        maxlength="10" value="Longitude3" /></td>
      <td><input type="text" name="Elevation3" size="10"
        maxlength="10" value="Elevation3" /></td>
    </tr>
    <tr bgcolor="ivory">
      <td>Site 4</td>
      <td><input type="text" name="Name4" size="10"
        maxlength="10" value="Name4" /></td>
      <td><input type="text" name="Latitude4" size="10"
        maxlength="10" value="Latitude4" /></td>
      <td><input type="text" name="Longitude4" size="10"
        maxlength="10" value="Longitude4" /></td>
      <td><input type="text" name="Elevation4" size="10"
        maxlength="10" value="Elevation4" /></td>
    </tr>
    <tr bgcolor="palegreen">
      <td>Site 5</td>
      <td><input type="text" name="Name5" size="10"
        maxlength="10" value="Name5" /></td>
      <td><input type="text" name="Latitude5" size="10"
        maxlength="10" value="Latitude5" /></td>
      <td><input type="text" name="Longitude5" size="10"
        maxlength="10" value="Longitude5" /></td>
      <td><input type="text" name="Elevation5" size="10"
        maxlength="10" value="Elevation5" /></td>
    </tr>
  </table>
  </form>
  </body>
  </html>
```

Observation Site Descriptions

Site #	Site Name	Latitude	Longitude	Elevation
Site 1	Name1	Latitude1	Longitude1	Elevation1
Site 2	Name2	Latitude2	Longitude2	Elevation2
Site 3	Name3	Latitude3	Longitude3	Elevation3
Site 4	Name4	Latitude4	Longitude4	Elevation4
Site 5	Name5	Latitude5	Longitude5	Elevation5

The output is shown with the original default field names, before a user starts to add new values.

Although it may seem like a lot of work to create Document 3.6, the task is greatly simplified by copying and pasting information for the rows. When you access this page, the Tab key moves from field to field but skips the first column, which is just fixed text. The user of the page can change the default values of all the input text boxes.

3.5
E-Mailing the Contents of Forms

Document 3.4 would be much more useful if the location information provided by the user could be sent to the creator of the document. In general, if the basic purpose of forms is to provide an interactive interface between the user of a Web page and its creator, there needs to be a way to transmit the user-supplied information on a form back to the creator. Remember that HTML/JavaScript constitutes a purely client-side environment. However, it is possible to use the `form action="mailto…"` and `method` attributes to send the contents of a form indirectly to the originator of the form (or some other specified destination) by using the client computer's e-mail utility.

In principle, this is easy to do, but the method described here is not very reliable. It may be necessary first to resolve conflicts between a user's browser and e-mail utility which have nothing to do with the contents of the Web page itself, or it may simply not be possible to get this method to work across some networks and platforms.

Here is how to direct the contents of a form to a specified e-mail address, at least in principle!

```
<form method="post"
  action="mailto:my_mail@myuniversity.edu"
  enctype="text/plain">
```

Document 3.7 is a modification of Document 3.3 which allows a user to e-mail the contents of the form to a specified address.

Document 3.7 (location2.htm)

```
<html>
<head>
<title>Location information</title>
</head>
<body bgcolor="ivory">
<form method="post"
    action="mailto:my_mail@university.edu"
    enctype="text/plain">
    Please enter your last name:
    <input type="text" name="last_name" size="20"
    maxlength="20" /><br/>
    Please enter your latitude:
    <input type="text" name="lat" size="7"
      maxlength="7" />
    N <input type="radio" name="NS" value="N" />
  or S <input type="radio" name="NS" value="S" /><br/>
    Please enter your longitude:
    <input type="text" name="lon" size="8"
      maxlength="8" />
    E <input type="radio" name="EW" value="E">
  or W <input type="radio" name="EW" value="W" /><br/>
    Please enter your elevation:
    <input type="text" name="elevation" size="8"
      maxlength="8" /> meters<br/>
    <input type="submit"
      value="Click here to send your data." />
</form>
</body>
</html>
```

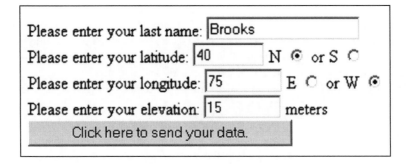

After entering all values, the user clicks on the labeled `submit` button, and the contents of the form *should* be sent to the specified e-mail address. In order to try this document, you must install it on a Web page where it can be accessed online. (It won't work if you try to submit the form locally from an HTML editor, for example.) Sometimes, the `submit` button may not *actually* work. When you click on the `submit` button, it may *appear* that the data have been sent, but the e-mail never actually arrives. When this happens, the problem lies not with the document, but with the relationship between your browser and your e-mail utility. In some cases, it may not be possible to submit forms in this way from your computer.

When the form has been submitted successfully, the field names and values arrive in the body of an e-mail message. The example shown in the screen rendering produces this result:

```
last_name=Brooks
lat=40
NS=N
lon=75
EW=W
elevation=15
```

The names are the field names given in the document and the values are, of course, the values entered by the user.

3.6
The List Elements

As shown earlier in this chapter, the `table` and `form` elements are used as tools for organizing Web pages. **List** elements provide another way to impose formatting on related content. Table 3.2 gives a brief summary of three kinds of lists.

Table 3.2 HTML list elements

Description	HTML tags	Use
Definition (or glossary)	`<dl> ... </dl>`	For a list that includes names and extensive descriptions
Ordered	`<ol> ... </ol>`	When a list of things needs to be numbered
Unordered	`<ul> ... </ul>`	For a list of "bulleted" items
List item	`<li> ... </li>`	Create list entry for `<ul>` or `<ol>`
Glossary head	`<dt> ... </dt>`	Create glossary heading for `<dl>`
Glossary term	`<dd> ... </dd>`	Create glossary term description for `<dl>`

Document 3.8 shows how to use these list tags.

Document 3.8 (lists.htm)

```html
<html>
<head>
  <title>Using HTML Lists</title>
</head>
<body>
This page demonstrates the use of unordered, ordered, and
definition lists.
<ul>
  <li> Use unordered lists for "bulleted" items.</li>
  <li> Use ordered lists for numbered items. </li>
<li> Use definition lists for lists of items to be defined.
</li>
</ul>
Here are three ways to organize content in an HTML document:
<ol>
  <li>Use a table. </li>
  <li>Use a list. </li>
  <li>Use <font face="courier">&lt;pre&gt; ...
&lt;/pre&gt;</font> tags. </li>
</ol>
This is a way to produce a neatly formatted glossary list.
<dl>
  <dt><strong>definition list</strong>
    (<font face="courier">&lt;dl&gt;</font>)</dt>
  <dd>Use this to display a list of glossary items and their
definitions. </dd>
  <dt><strong>ordered list</strong>
    (<font face="courier">&lt;ol&gt;</font>) </dt>
  <dd>Use this to display a numbered list. </dd>
  <dt><strong>unordered list</strong>
    (<font face="courier">&lt;ul&gt;</font>)</dt>
  <dd>Use this to display a list of bulleted items. </dd>
</dl>
</body>
</html>
```

This page demonstrates the use of unordered, ordered, and definition lists.

- Use unordered lists for "bulleted" items.
- Use ordered lists for numbered items.
- Use definition lists for lists of items to be defined.

Here are three ways to organize content in an HTML document:

1. Use a table.
2. Use a list.
3. Use <pre> ... </pre> tags.

This is a way to produce a neatly formatted glossary list.

definition list (<dl>)
    Use this to display a list of glossary items and their definitions.
ordered list (<ol>)
    Use this to display a numbered list.
unordered list (<ul>)
    Use this to display a list of bulleted items.

The use of these tags imposes a preset format for displaying list items. Blank lines are inserted before and after the list, with no <br /> or <p> ... <p> tags required to separate the lists from other text in the document. For ordered and unordered lists, the list items themselves are indented. For the definition list, the items are not indented, but the "definitions" are. The contents of a list item can include text formatting elements. For example, in Document 3.8, the items in the definition list use the strong element to display the item name in a bold font. A list item can be an image, <img src="..." />, or a URL reference, <a href="...">.

Note the use of < and > to display the < and > characters in the document. (Recall that if you simply enter these characters, they will not be displayed on the screen because HTML will try to associate them with tags.)

There are some attributes associated with list elements that provide a little more control over the appearance of lists.

```
start="n"
```
Value: The integer *n* specifies the starting value of an ordered list. The default value is
```
start="1".
```

```
type = "..."
```
Values: For unordered lists: `"disc"` (the default value), `"square"`, `"circle"`
  For ordered lists: `"A"` (uppercase letters), `"a"` (lowercase letters), `"I"` (uppercase
Roman letters), `"i"` (lowercase Roman letters), `"1"` (numbers, the default value)

```
value = "n"
```
Value: The integer *n* specifies a numerical value for an item in an ordered list which
overrides the default value. Subsequent list items will be renumbered starting at this
value.

Finally, it is possible to combine list types to create more complicated list structures.
Document 3.9 shows how list tags can be used to create the table of contents for a
book.

Document 3.9 (`bookContents.htm`)

```html
<html>
<title>Table of Contents for My Book</title>
<body>
<h2>Table of Contents for My Book</h2>
<ol>
<strong><li>Chapter One</strong></li>
   <ol type="I">
     <li>Section 1.1</li>
       <ol type="i">
           <li>First Topic</li>
         <li>Second Topic</li>
           <ul type="circle">
             <li><em> subtopic 1</em></li>
             <li><em> subtopic 2</em></li>
           </ul>
       </ol>
     <li>Section 1.2</li>
     <li>Section 1.3</li>
   </ol>
```

```
<strong><li>Chapter Two</strong></li>
  <ol type="I">
    <li>Section 2.1</li>
  <ol type="i">
    <li>First Topic</li>
    <li>Second Topic</li>
      <ul type="circle">
        <li><em> subtopic 1</em></li>
        <li><em> subtopic 2</em></li>
      </ul>
  </ol>
    <li>Section 2.2</li>
    <li>Section 2.3</li>
  </ol>
<strong><li>Chapter Three</strong></li>
  <ol type="I">
    <li>Section 3.1</li>
      <ol type="i">
        <li>First Topic</li>
        <li>Second Topic</li>
          <ul type="circle">
            <li><em> subtopic 1</em></li>
            <li><em> subtopic 2</em></li>
            <li><em> subtopic 3</em></li>
          </ul>
      </ol>
    <li>Section 3.2</li>
    <li>Section 3.3</li>
      <ol type="i">
        <li>First Topic</li>
        <li>Second Topic</li>
      </ol>
    <li>Section 3.4</li>
  </ol>
</ol>
</body>
</html>
```

Note that if this list were used for an online book, for example, each list item could include a link to a URL or a hypertext link to another location within the same document.

3

┌───┐
│   **Table of Contents for My Book**   │
│   │
│   1. Chapter One   │
│   I. Section 1.1   │
│   i. First Topic   │
│   ii. Second Topic   │
│   ◇ *subtopic 1*   │
│   ◇ *subtopic 2*   │
│   II. Section 1.2   │
│   III. Section 1.3   │
│   2. Chapter Two   │
│   I. Section 2.1   │
│   i. First Topic   │
│   ii. Second Topic   │
│   ◇ *subtopic 1*   │
│   ◇ *subtopic 2*   │
│   II. Section 2.2   │
│   III. Section 2.3   │
│   3. Chapter Three   │
│   I. Section 3.1   │
│   i. First Topic   │
│   ii. Second Topic   │
│   ◇ *subtopic 1*   │
│   ◇ *subtopic 2*   │
│   ◇ *subtopic 3*   │
│   II. Section 3.2   │
│   III. Section 3.3   │
│   i. First Topic   │
│   ii. Second Topic   │
│   IV. Section 3.4   │
└───┘

3.7
Using HTML Frames

Another way of organizing content in HTML documents is through the use of **frames** to divide a window into several separately addressable blocks of content. Frames are built using two elements, `frame` and `frameset`.

```
<frame /> ... </frame>
```
Attributes: `bordercolor`, `frameborder`, `marginheight`, `marginwidth`, `name`, `scrolling` (yes, no, or auto), `src`

Provides a nameable window region, as defined by the `frameset` element, with a link to the content of that region. A value for the `src` attribute must be given, but the

(continued)

(continued)

> other attributes are optional. The default value for the `scrolling` attribute is `auto`,
> which automatically provides a scroll bar if needed to display all of a window's content.
>
> `<frameset> … </frameset>`
> *Attributes*: `border, bordercolor, cols, frameborder, framespacing,`
> `rows`
>   Provides specifications for dividing a web page window into two or more separately
> linkable sub-windows. All attributes are optional except `cols` and `rows`, which must have
> values of n pixels, $n\%$ of the available window, or * to fill the remaining window space.

Consider the following screen display. It is divided into three sections. The upper
left-hand corner contains a clickable image. The lower left-hand corner contains links to
other HTML documents. The right-hand column will be used to display those documents.
When this page is first accessed, a "home page" document should be displayed.

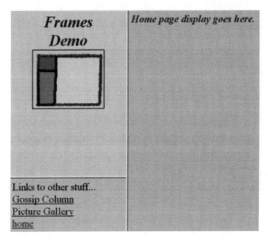

Document 3.10a shows the first step in creating this page.

Document 3.10a (`frameMain.htm`)

```html
<html>
<head>
<title>A simple frameset document</title>
</head>
<frameset cols="30%, 70%" frameborder="1">
      <frameset rows="60%, 40%">
            <frame src="frame1.htm" scrolling="no" />
            <frame src="frame2.htm" />
      </frameset>
      <frame name="homeFrame" src="homeFrame.htm" />
</frameset>
</html>
```

3

The `frameset` element is used to define the frames. In this case, the window is divided into two columns. The left-hand column occupies 30% of the page and the right-hand column occupies the remaining 70%. (In the graphic displayed previously, the proportions look different because the screen display has been cropped to save space.) The line

```
<frameset cols="30%, 70%" frameborder="1">
```

could also be written

```
<frameset cols="30%, *" frameborder="1">
```

where the asterisk is interpreted as "fill the remaining portion of the screen with the right-hand column." If the frame size is given as a number without the % sign, it is interpreted as pixels rather than a percentage of the full window. Setting this frame size to `cols="200,*"` will produce a left-side frame that is always 200 pixels wide, regardless of the screen resolution.

The left-hand column is further divided into two sub-windows. The top window occupies the top 60% and the bottom window occupies the remaining 40%. Each window is associated with a separate HTML document, `frame1.htm` and `frame2.htm`. These windows *could* be given names, but they don't have to have names. The right-hand column is associated with another HTML document, `homeFrame.htm`. This "home frame" will be the destination for content that will be linked from the frame in the lower left-hand corner. This frame needs a name to serve as a "target" for the other documents that will be displayed here. The name can be anything, but `homeFrame` is a self-explanatory and therefore reasonable choice.

Documents 3.10b–d show the HTML code for each of the three frames.

Document 3.10b (`homeFrame.htm`)

```
<html>
<head>
<title>My Home Frame</title>
</head>
<body bgcolor="lightgreen">
<h1><blink><font color="maroon"><b><i>Home page display goes
here.</i></b></font></blink></h1>
</body>
</html>
```

Document 3.10c (`frame1.htm`)

```
<html>
<head>
<title>Title Frame</title>
```

```
</head>
<body bgcolor="pink">
<font size="+6" color="navy"><center><b><i>Frames
<br />Demo<br />
<a href="frameDescription.htm" /><img src="frame.gif"
  border="2"></i></b></center></a>
</font>
</body>
</html>
```

Document 3.10d (frame2.htm)

```
<html>
<head>
<title>Gossip Column</title>
</head>
<body bgcolor="lightblue">
<font size="+3">
Links to other stuff...<br />
<a href="gossip.htm" target="homeFrame" />Gossip Column</a>
<br />
<a href="photoGallery.htm" target="homeFrame" />
  Picture Gallery</a><br />
<a href="homeFrame.htm" target="homeFrame" />home</a><br />
</font>
</body>
</html>
```

Document 3.10e is the HTML document referenced in Document 3.10c.

Document 3.10e (frameDescription.htm)

```
<html>
<head>
<title>How this image was created.</title>
</head>
<body>
This image was created in Windows' Paint program.
<a href="frame1.htm" />Click here to return.</a>
</body>
</html>
```

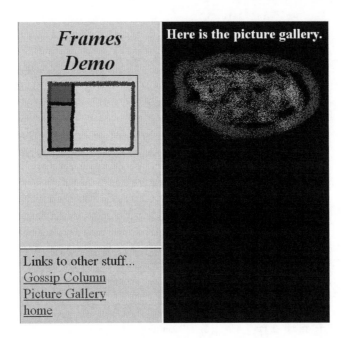

Document 3.10d, for the lower left-hand corner, contains links to several other documents, each of which can be displayed in the right-hand window. This is done by using the `target` attribute, which links to `homeFrame`, the `name` value given in Document 3.10a:

```
<a href="gossip.htm" target="homeFrame">Gossip Column</a>
```

It is up to you to provide the `gossip.htm` and `photoGallery.htm` documents. Document 3.10d also includes a link back to the home page document. The image shown here is the result of clicking on the "Picture Gallery" link to a document on the author's computer; the page image has been cropped to save space.

Document 310b contains the code for the home frame that is displayed when the page is first accessed. (The `blink` element, which causes text to blink on and off, will be ignored by some browsers.) Document 3.10c, for the upper left-hand frame, contains the clickable image, `frame.gif`, with a border drawn around it. Clicking on the image opens a link to descriptive file, `frameDescription.htm` (see Document 3.10e), to be provided by you. This document will be displayed in the "Frames Demo" window (not opened in a new window) and it should contain a link to return to `frame1.htm`:

```
<a href="frame1.htm">Click here to return.</a>
```

HTML frames provide a great deal of flexibility for displaying content, but there is one consequence that may not be immediately obvious. If you try these examples on your own computer, you will see that *only* the main frame document (`frameMain.htm`) is displayed as the URL link, regardless of which document is being displayed in the right-hand column. So, you cannot directly copy or bookmark the URL for a particular document. Accessing the "view source" option on your browser will display the HTML code only for `frameMain.htm`. If you wish to bookmark the "picture gallery" page, for example, you cannot do so directly. You can display the page separately by accessing the document separately:

```
http://... /photoGallery.htm
```

but doing that assumes you already know the name and location of this document.

This situation does not really hide all the code for these documents. You can look at the `frameMain.htm` HTML code and then access separately the `homeFrame.htm`, `frame1.htm`, and `frame2.htm` documents to examine their HTML code.

3.8
More Examples

3.8.1
Selecting Cloud Types from a List of Possibilities

Create a document that allows users to select observed cloud types from a list of possibilities. More than one cloud type can exist simultaneously. The categories are:

High altitude: Cirrus, Cirrocumulus, Cirrostratus
Mid altitude: Altostratus, Altocumulus
Low altitude: Stratus, Stratocumulus, Cumulus
Precipitation-producing: Nimbostratus, Cumulonimbus

A good way to organize this information is to use a table within a form. The form fields should be of type `checkbox` rather than `radio` because multiple selections are possible. Compare this problem with Document 3.3, in which a table was used to display just the cloud types.

Document 3.11 (`cloud1.htm`)

```html
<html>
<head>
<title>Cloud Observations</title>
</head>
<body bgcolor="#aaddff">
<h1>Cloud Observations</h1>
<strong> Cloud Observations </strong>(Select as many cloud
types as observed.)
```

3

```html
<br />
<form>
<table>
  <tr>
   <td><strong>High</strong> </td>
    <td>
     <input type="checkbox" name="high"
       value="Cirrus" /> Cirrus</td>
    <td>
     <input type="checkbox" name="high"
       value="Cirrocumulus" /> Cirrocumulus </td>
    <td>
     <input type="checkbox" name="high"
       value="Cirrostratus" /> Cirrostratus </td></tr>
  <tr>
    <td colspan="4"><hr noshade color="black" />
     </td></tr>
  <tr>
    <td> <strong>Middle</strong> </td>
    <td>
      <input type="checkbox" name="mid"
        value="Altostratus" /> Altostratus </td>
    <td>
      <input type="checkbox" name="mid"
        value="Altocumulus" /> Altocumulus</td></tr>
  <tr>
    <td colspan="4"><hr noshade color="black" />
     </td></tr>
  <tr>
    <td> <strong>Low</strong></td>
    <td>
    <input type="checkbox" name="low" value="Stratus" />
      Stratus</td>
    <td>
    <input type="checkbox" name="low"
      value="Stratocumulus" /> Stratocumulus</td>
    <td>
    <input type="checkbox" name="low" value="Cumulus" />
      Cumulus </td></tr>
  <tr>
    <td colspan="4"><hr noshade color="black" />
     </td></tr>
  <tr>
    <td> <strong>Rain-Producing </strong> </td>
    <td>
```

```
<input type="checkbox" name="rain"
    value="Nimbostratus" /> Nimbostratus</td>
<td>
    <input type="checkbox" name="rain"
        value="Cumulonimbus" /> Cumulonimbus </td></tr>
</table>
</form>
</body>
</html>
```

In Document 3.11, checkboxes for the cloud types are organized into four groups, for high-, mid-, and low-altitude clouds, plus rain-producing clouds. Within each group, each checkbox has a name associated with it. As will be shown in Chap. 5, this arrangement makes it possible for JavaScript to "poll" the checkboxes to see which clouds are observed within each group.

Note that the names given to each checkbox in Document 3.11 are the same as the text entered in the corresponding cell. This is only because these names and text are reasonable descriptions of the cell contents. In general, the text in the cell does not need to be the same as, or even related to, the value of the name attribute of the checkbox.

3.8.2
A Simple "Split Window" Application

Create an application that maintains one or more "header lines" across the top of a Web page window while scrolling through a long text document.

Consider this file:

```
DRB Worcester PA
40.178 -75.3325
4030 5200
Mon day yr   hr min sec EST             PYR-1      PYR-2      T
7   1   2008 0   0   0   1              0.00031    0.00031    20.198
7   1   2008 0   1   0   1.000694444    0.00031    0.00031    20.174
7   1   2008 0   2   0   1.001388889    0.00031    0.00031    20.174
...
```

3

The file contains 1,440 lines of data (24 h times 60 min per hour for July 1, 2008) with the date and time, the day and time converted to a fractional Eastern Standard Time day (EST), data from two instruments, PYR-1 and PYR-2, and air temperature in degree Celsius.

For a file of this size, it might be convenient to be able to display these data under a fixed header that identifies the columns, in the same way that spreadsheets allow creation of a "split window." Documents 3.12a, b show a very simple solution to this problem, using HTML frames.

Document 3.12a (`pyranometerMain.htm`)

```
<html>
<head>
<title>Display pyranometer data</title>
</head>
<frameset rows="10%, *">
        <frame src="header.htm" scrolling="no" />
        <frame src="pyranometer.dat" />
</frameset>
</html>
```

Document 3.12b (`header.htm`)

```
<html>
<head>
  <title></title>
</head>
<body>
<font face="courier" >
This is the header.<br />
mon    day     yr    hr
    min    sec     EST  
        PYR-1  PYR-2  T<br />
</font>
</body>
</html>
```

This is the header.

mon	day	yr	hr	min	sec	EST	PYR-1	PYR-2	T

DRB Worcester PA
40.178 -75.3325
4030 5200 -999

mon	day	yr	hr	min	sec	EST	PYR-1	PYR-2	T
7	1	2008	0	0	0	1	0.00031	0.00031	20.198
7	1	2008	0	1	0	1.000694444	0.00031	0.00031	20.174
7	1	2008	0	2	0	1.001388889	0.00031	0.00031	20.174
7	1	2008	0	3	0	1.002083333	0.00031	0.00031	20.174
7	1	2008	0	4	0	1.002777778	0.00031	0.00031	20.174
7	1	2008	0	5	0	1.003472222	0.00031	0.00031	20.174
7	1	2008	0	6	0	1.004166667	0.00031	0.00031	20.15
7	1	2008	0	7	0	1.004861111	0.00031	0.00031	20.126
7	1	2008	0	8	0	1.005555556	0.00031	0.00031	20.079
7	1	2008	0	9	0	1.00625	0.00031	0.00031	20.055
7	1	2008	0	10	0	1.006944444	0.00031	0.00031	20.031
7	1	2008	0	11	0	1.007638889	0.00031	0.00031	20.031
7	1	2008	0	12	0	1.008333333	0.00031	0.00031	20.007
7	1	2008	0	13	0	1.009027778	0.00031	0.00031	19.984
7	1	2008	0	14	0	1.009722222	0.00031	0.00031	19.984
7	1	2008	0	15	0	1.010416667	0.00031	0.00031	19.984
7	1	2008	0	16	0	1.011111111	0.00031	0.00031	19.984
7	1	2008	0	17	0	1.011805556	0.00031	0.00031	19.96
7	1	2008	0	18	0	1.0125	0.00031	0.00031	19.936
7	1	2008	0	19	0	1.013194444	0.00031	0.00031	19.888
7	1	2008	0	20	0	1.013888889	0.00031	0.00031	19.841
7	1	2008	0	21	0	1.014583333	0.00031	0.00031	19.793
7	1	2008	0	22	0	1.015277778	0.00031	0.00031	19.793
7	1	2008	0	23	0	1.015972222	0.00031	0.00031	19.793
7	1	2008	0	24	0	1.016666667	0.00031	0.00031	19.746
7	1	2008	0	25	0	1.017361111	0.00031	0.00031	19.746
7	1	2008	0	26	0	1.018055556	0.00031	0.00031	19.698
7	1	2008	0	27	0	1.01875	0.00031	0.00031	19.698
7	1	2008	0	28	0	1.019444444	0.00031	0.00031	19.651
7	1	2008	0	29	0	1.020138889	0.00031	0.00031	19.627
7	1	2008	0	30	0	1.020833333	0.00031	0.00031	19.603

The `frameset rows` attribute allocates the top 10% of the page to the header and the output file, `pyranometer.dat`, is displayed in the remainder of the page. For a display that is too long to fit in one window, HTML automatically creates a scroll bar down the right-hand side of the window. A border has been retained under the top frame, just to make clear how the page is divided, but it is optional; to remove the border, set the `frameset` attribute `border="0"`.

A simple modification of the `frameset` code in Document 3.12a would allow listing a number of different files in a left-hand column, each of which could be displayed in the home page frame simply by clicking on the file name. To do this, the direct link to `pyranometer.dat` in Document 3.12a would be replaced with another name specified as the value of a `target` attribute in the reference to each document to be displayed:

```
<a href="..." target="..." ... />
```

Note that the `pyranometer.dat` file is just a tab-delimited text file, not an HTML document.

Fundamentals of the JavaScript Language

4

Abstract Chapter 4 presents the core programming capabilities of JavaScript. The topics include basic programming terminology and concepts, code structure, data and objects, variables, operators, mathematical and string-manipulation functions, decision-making structures, and constructs for repetitive calculations.

4.1
Capabilities of JavaScript

Previous chapters have presented the features of HTML that provide the potential for interacting with a scripting language such as JavaScript. In order to work in this environment, you must understand some of the fundamental concepts underlying programming languages as well as the details of how JavaScript implements these concepts. Although an HTML document interface is still required to manage input and output in the HTML/ JavaScript environment, the material in this chapter attempts to minimize the details of interactions between JavaScript and HTML in favor of presenting programming concepts and their JavaScript implementation as directly as possible.

JavaScript shares capabilities with other languages such as C/C++. In general, what are the capabilities of these kinds of languages? What kinds of tasks can programmers expect them to perform? Here is a list.

1. *Manage input and output.*
   To be useful, any language must provide an input/output (I/O) interface with a user. When a computer program is executed or a script is interpreted (in the case of JavaScript, as a result of loading a Web page into a user's browser), the user provides input. The language instructs the user's computer to perform tasks based on that input. The language then instructs the computer to display the results. A simple interface (for a text-based language such as C, for example) will accept keyboard input and display text output on a computer monitor. As noted several times in previous chapters, HTML and JavaScript work together to provide an elegant and universal I/O interface.

2. *Permit values to be manipulated in a symbolic way, independent of the way a particular computer stores that information internally.*
   The essential thrust of programming languages is to provide a name-based symbolic interface between a computer and a programmer. When quantities can be given names instead of memory addresses, they can then be accessed and manipulated through those names rather than requiring a programmer to keep track of where values are stored in a computer's memory.

3. *Perform arithmetic operations on numbers.*
   A general-purpose programming language must include a range of arithmetic operations on numbers. Although JavaScript is not intended as a "number-crunching" language for serious scientific computing, it does support many arithmetic operations and functions including, for example, trigonometric, logarithmic, and exponential functions. So, it is useful for a wide range of numerical calculations of interest in science and engineering.

4. *Perform operations on characters and strings of characters.*
   A great deal of the work JavaScript is asked to do involves manipulating characters and strings of characters rather than numbers. For example, JavaScript may be asked to compare a name provided as input against a predefined set of names. An HTML document is inherently character-based, so JavaScript must support the manipulation of characters and strings of characters, including interpreting strings of characters as numbers and vice versa. This is necessary because computers store numerical values in ways that differ fundamentally from the way characters are stored.

5. *Make decisions based on comparing values.*
   Computers cannot make decisions by "thinking" about multiple possibilities in a human-like way. However, they can compare values and act on the results of those comparisons. Typically, a program will compare values and then execute instructions based on the results of those comparisons. In particular, such decisions are often embedded in **branching structures** that execute one set of instructions to the exclusion of others, based on a comparison of values.

6. *Perform repetitive calculations.*
   Loop structures are used to allow computers to perform repetitive calculations. These calculations may be terminated after they have been executed a specified number of times, or they may be executed only until or while some set of conditions is satisfied.

4.2
Some Essential Terminology

The terminology of programming languages can be confusing. Nonetheless, it is essential to agree upon the meaning and use of terms in order to discuss programming concepts, especially because the programming-specific meaning of some terms must be

Table 4.1 Definitions of some essential programming language terms

Term	Definitions and Examples

expression	A group of tokens that can be evaluated as part of a statement to yield a result.
	 `y + z`
	 `"This is a string."`

identifier	The name associated with a variable, object, or function. Any allowed name, *e.g.*, x, `getArea`, `my_name`, without embedded spaces.
keyword	A word that is part of a language and has a specific meaning. Keywords cannot be used as identifiers. `function`, `var`, `for`

literal	A value (as opposed to an identifier) embedded in a script.
	 `3.14159`
	 `"Here's a string."`

operator	A symbol that represents a mathematical or other operation. `=, +, -, *, /, %`
program	Loosely, a series of statements or a compiled equivalent. In JavaScript, a "program" is better referred to as a script. Scripts are interpreted one line at a time, not compiled.
reserved word	A word that might become part of a language. Reserved words should not be used as identifiers. `class`, `const`
script	A series of statements written in JavaScript or some other scripting language.

statement	A command that changes the status of a program as it executes, by defining variables, changing the value of a variable, or modifying the order in which other statements are executed.
	 `x = y + z;`
	 `area=Math.PI*radius*radius;`

token	An indivisible lexical unit defined within a programming language. All variables, keywords, operators, and literals.
variable	A place in memory that holds data and is represented by a unique identifier. (see "identifier")

distinguished from their everyday conversational use. Table 4.1 gives some essential terms and their definitions.

These terms define the building blocks of a JavaScript script, starting with **tokens**:

tokens (identifiers, keywords, literals, operators) → expressions → statements → script

Individual tokens form expressions. Expressions form statements. A script consists of a collection of statements.

4

4.3
Structure of JavaScript Code

4.3.1
JavaScript Statements

Instructions in JavaScript are conveyed through a series of **statements**. As indicated in the previous section, statements are built from expressions consisting of tokens. To begin a statement, simply start typing something that follows the syntax rules of JavaScript. When it is time to terminate a programming language statement, there are two choices. One choice is to press the Enter or Return key on your computer. This will terminate both the physical line and the statement. This means that each physical line can contain no more than one statement. (It could be a blank line with no statement at all.) The second choice is to use a unique **terminating character** to mark the end of a statement.

As a matter of syntax, JavaScript allows both these choices. An "end of line" mark (created by pushing the Enter or Return key) will mark the end of a statement. Because of JavaScript's roots in C/C++, the preferred syntax is to terminate each statement with a semicolon. In this book, JavaScript statements will *always* be terminated with a semicolon. As a bonus, this style choice allows multiple statements to appear on the same line.

A set of JavaScript statements is called a script. Presumably, the goal of a script is to do something useful. So, the implication of calling something a "script" is that it contains all the instructions required to complete a specific task. As noted in Chap. 1, even the simplest text editor can be used to create a script, which is nothing more than a text document. But, as was the case for creating HTML documents, it will be easier to create JavaScript scripts with an editor intended for this purpose.

JavaScript is a **free-format language**. This means that statements can appear anywhere on a line. As long as you terminate each statement with a semicolon, you can even put multiple statements on a single line. This flexibility is *supposed* to encourage the writing of code that is logically organized and easy to read. Good programmers always adopt a consistent approach to the layout of their code. Hopefully, the examples in this book will point the way to producing easily readable code. See Appendix 4 for a "pseudocode" approach to designing accurate and readable code.

4.3.2
Statement Blocks

Often, several code statements are grouped together in a **statement block**. These blocks begin and end with curly brackets:

```
{
    {statements go here}
}
```

Later in this chapter, there will be several examples of how to use statement blocks.

4.3.3
Comments

Comments are an essential part of good programming style, no matter what the language. Comments are inserted into code by using certain combinations of characters that will always be interpreted unambiguously as marking the beginning or end of a comment. JavaScript supports two kinds of comments: single- and multiple-line comments. You can use either or both of these comment formats within the same script. However, they cannot be mixed in the same comment. Also, you cannot have "nested" multiple-line comments:

```
// This is a single-line comment.
/* This
     is a
          multiple-line
               comment.
*/
/* This code
/* will generate a syntax error! */
*/
```

Because a JavaScript interpreter ignores comments when it executes statements, comments can occur on separate lines or on the same line as a statement. Comments started with a double slash cannot be placed at the beginning of a statement because JavaScript has no way of knowing where the comment ends and the code begins. This code will work because there is an (invisible) "return" character at the end of the line that is interpreted as the end of the comment:

```
// The gravitational constant is
var g=9.8; // m/s^2
```

This will not work

```
// The gravitational constant is var g=9.8; // m/s^2
```

but this will:

```
/* The gravitational constant is */ var g=9.8; //m/s^2
```

It is easy to overlook the importance of including comments in your code. Intelligently commented code is easier to understand, both for you when you return to it at a later date and for others who need to examine your code. If you don't develop the habit of including comments in all your code, eventually you will be sorry!

4

4.4
Data and Objects

In general, programming languages can work with different kinds of information. Each kind of information is associated with a **data type**. Each data type is stored differently within the programming environment, and each is associated with a specific set of operations. For example, it is obvious that you can add two numbers ($3.3 + 12.9$), but it is less obvious what (if anything) it means to associate an addition operation with character literals (`'A' + 'c'`). In the latter case, A and c are not being used as symbolic names, but as the "literal values" of the characters `'A'` and `'c'`.

A concept central to all high-level programming languages is that discrete units of information called **variables** can be associated with specific locations in computer memory. Variables serve as "containers" for data. A data container is established by giving it a symbolic name, called an **identifier**. This process is called **data declaration**. Once identifiers have been established with meaningful names, you can write code to manipulate information symbolically by using the identifier names, thereby freeing you from having to think directly about where information is actually stored in your computer's memory. (As a practical matter, you can't figure out exactly where this information is stored even if you think you need to know.) This symbolic approach makes it possible to write scripts that will work without modification on any computer with a Web browser that supports JavaScript.

4.4.1
Data Declarations and Variables

A basic programming rule, no matter what the language, is that variables must be declared before they are used elsewhere in a program. Data declaration assigns an identifier (a variable name) to a data container and associates the identifier with a particular location in your computer's memory. The allocation of memory is handled by the programming environment (in this case, your browser and its JavaScript interpreter) and is of no concern to you as a programmer.

The data declaration process, whether explicit or implicit, is required to enable a programming environment to manage its memory resources and perform appropriate operations. In JavaScript, the keyword `var` is used to declare variables and their identifiers. Consider this code:

```
var g;
g=9.8;
g="gravitational acceleration";
```

Unlike some other languages such as C and C++, a single keyword serves to declare *all* variables, regardless of their data type. In the above example, the `var` statement asks the JavaScript interpreter to set aside space for a variable named g. At the time of the declaration, it is not yet clear what kind of information the identifier g is going to represent.

JavaScript is a **weakly typed language**, which means that the programmer has a great deal of latitude in associating an identifier with data of a particular type. Consider the second and third lines in the above code fragment. The second line associates g with the numerical value 9.8. The third associates g with the string "`gravitational acceleration`" and replaces the previous value with the new one. These statements imply that the "container" associated with the identifier g can hold anything you want it to hold and that you can change your mind about the nature as well as the value of the information held in the container. The data declaration statement in JavaScript reserves the *name* of an identifier associated with a data container, but not the nature of its *contents*. To put it another way, JavaScript *infers* data type from the current contents of a variable container. If the nature of the contents of the container (not just the value) is changed, then the data type associated with that container will change, too. If you use spreadsheets such as Excel, you will be familiar with this kind of data typing. When you enter content in a spreadsheet cell, the spreadsheet imposes its own default typing for the content—as a number or text, for example. If you enter something different in the same cell, the spreadsheet reinterprets the contents accordingly.

Because of weak typing, it is almost always possible to omit the `var` keyword when using a variable name for the first time. The statement

```
pi=3.14159;
```

without a previous `var pi;` is an implicit data declaration for the variable identifier `pi`. Although this is generally allowed in JavaScript, there are a few situations where an explicit data declaration is actually required. Even when they are allowed, implied declarations are poor programming practice in any language and should be avoided in your code. So, to avoid potential problems, it is best to be diligent about explicitly declaring *all* variables, using the `var` keyword, before you use them.

4.4.2
Data Types

JavaScript supports three basic data types (**primitives**): numbers, strings, and Boolean values. JavaScript does not distinguish between integers and real numbers. That is, it does not provide separate data types for integers and real numbers. Instead, JavaScript stores *all* numbers in a **floating point** format, which provides what is, in general, an approximation of the actual value. In contrast, integers, in languages that support a separate data type, are stored as exact values, in a binary format. This distinction can have significant consequences in some kinds of numerical calculations.

Some languages, such as C/C++, have a separate data type for representing individual characters, from which string representations are built. JavaScript works essentially the other way around, with a single character being represented as a string variable of length one.

Boolean data have one of two values, `true` or `false`. Boolean variables can be assigned one of these two values:

```
var x=true,y=false;
```

Note that the words `true` and `false` are values, not "names" (or string literals, as defined in the next section), so they are not enclosed in quote marks.

4.4.3
Literals

Literals are actual numbers, character strings, or Boolean values embedded in code. In the statement `var pi=3.14159;`, `3.14159` is a number literal. In the statement `var name="David";`, `"David"` is a string literal. The advantage of using literals is that their value is self-evident.

In general, it is good programming style to limit the use of the same literal value in many places in your code. For example, rather than using the literal `3.14159` whenever you need the value of π, you should assign a value to the quantity π by using a data declaration statement `var pi=3.14159;`. Now you can insert the value of π anywhere in your program just by referring to its identifier. Suppose you declare `var B = 5.195;` and use this variable name in several places in your code. If, later on, you decide you need to change the value of B to `5.196`, you can make this change just once, in the data declaration statement, and the change will automatically apply everywhere the B identifier is used.

4.4.4
Case Sensitivity

JavaScript is case sensitive. This means that all reserved words and identifiers must be spelled exactly as they have been defined. For example, `Var` is *not* the same as `var`; the statement `Var pi=3.14159;` will generate a syntax error. If you define a variable named `radius`, you cannot later change that spelling to `Radius` or `RADIUS`. Because of case sensitivity, you *could* define three separate identifiers as `radius`, `Radius`, and `RADIUS`. However, this is potentially confusing and should be avoided.

There are two reasons why it is especially important to be very careful when you spell names in JavaScript. First, recall that JavaScript doesn't require an explicit data declaration statement for variable identifiers. So, you could write the declaration statement `var taxes,income,rate;` and then, later in your script, type `texas=income*rate;`. This misspelling of `taxes` as `texas` would be an obvious mistake on your part, but JavaScript will not see anything wrong with what you have done.

Second, remember that HTML is *not* case sensitive. Since you will be using HTML and JavaScript together in the same document, it is easy to forget this distinction between the two languages. Be careful!

4.4.5
Objects and Methods for Input and Output

In plain language usage, an object is a thing—any kind of thing. An object has properties. Perhaps it is a ball—round, 6 cm in diameter, shiny, and red. Objects can do things. A ball can roll and bounce. In the world of programming, objects also have properties and they can do things. For example, there is a `Math` object in JavaScript that knows about mathematical constants (properties) and how to do certain kinds of mathematical calculations. (See Sect. 4.6 below.) In programming terminology, implementations of actions associated with an object are called methods. For example, you might define a method to describe how high a ball will bounce when you drop it onto a hard surface.

The reason objects are introduced now is that in order to see how JavaScript works, you need to display the results of calculations done in response to user input. For now, the `document.write()` method of the `document` object, first introduced in Chap. 1, or `window.alert()`, a method of the `window` object will be used to display output. It is not necessary to include the `window` object name, so it is OK simply to write `alert()`. The purpose of using these methods is to avoid, for now, worrying about the interface between JavaScript and `input` fields in HTML forms. In later chapters, these methods will be used much less frequently.

For the same reason, to avoid interactions with an HTML document, the `window.prompt()`, or `prompt()` method will be used for input. Both `prompt()` and `alert()` will be used much less frequently after JavaScript and HTML forms are integrated, although they will remain useful for monitoring the performance of scripts.

Suppose you wish to ask the user of a script to provide the radius of a circle. The statement

```
var radius=prompt("Give the radius of a circle: ");
```

results in a message box being opened on the user's monitor. The "undefined" message that may appear in the input box means that the variable named `radius` does not currently have a value assigned to it. When a value is typed in the input box, that value will be assigned to the variable `radius`.

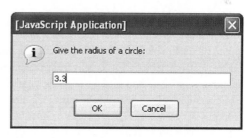

Then, additional lines of code can be written to use that value. Subsequent sections of this chapter make frequent use of the `prompt()` method to get user input for a script. Document 4.1 shows how to use the `prompt()` and `alert()` methods.

Document 4.1 (`circle.htm`)

```
<html>
<head>
<title>Calculate area of a circle.</title>
<script>
```

```
var radius=prompt("Give the radius of a circle: ");
radius=parseFloat(radius);
var area=Math.PI*radius*radius;
alert("The area of the circle with radius="+radius+" is
"+area+".");
</script>
</head>
<body>
</body>
</html>
```

Suppose you type 3.3 in the input box. The following alert message box will then appear on your screen.

The formats of the `prompt()` and `alert()` windows are browser-dependent and can't be changed from within your script.[1]

Note the shaded line in Document 4.1:

```
radius=parseFloat(radius);
```

The purpose of `parseFloat()`, which is a "global" method not associated with a particular object, is to convert appropriate strings of characters into a numerical representation. (Global methods will be discussed again in Chap. 6.) In document 4.1, the variable `radius` is replaced by the output from the `parseFloat()` function. Why? Because anything entered in the `prompt()` input window is considered to be a string of characters, regardless of whether those characters "look" like a number. Often, code will work properly without the `parseFloat()` method, because JavaScript will automatically apply an appropriate **type conversion** (typically from a string of characters to a number). But there are some potential problems with relying on implicit type conversions, as will be discussed in later examples. For now, suffice it to say that you should always apply `parseFloat()` to numerical data entered through a `prompt()` regardless of whether it appears to be necessary.[2]

---

[1] Author's note: Some of my students complain that the alert box looks too much like a "warning," rather than an information window. For the examples in this chapter, you can use `document.write()` instead of `alert()` if that is your preference.

[2] In some cases, the `parseInt()` method, discussed in Chap. 6, might be the preferred choice if the number is to be treated as an integer.

4.4.6
String Methods

Because of the importance of manipulating strings in interactions with HTML documents, JavaScript treats strings as objects and supports a long list of string-related methods. Table 4.2 lists some useful methods.

Table 4.2 Some useful methods for the `String` object

Method Name	Description and Examples
`charAt(n)`	Returns a string containing n^{th} character. n = 0 returns leftmost character. `"HTML".charAt(3);` returns a value of `L`.
`charCodeAt(n)`	Returns the base-10 ASCII code for the nth character. n = 0 returns code for leftmost character. `var s="acid",t;` `t=s.charCodeAt(0);` T has value 97.

`concat({two or more string arguments})`	Concatenates (adds) the string arguments. (Equivalent to using + operator with strings.)
	`var`
	`s="I".concat(" love"," HTML.");`
	`s` has value `I love HTML`.

`fromCharCode (n₁[,n₂,,nₙ])`	Builds string from base-10 ASCII values. `var s= String.fromCharCode(65,66,67);` `s` has value `ABC`.
`indexOf(s[,n])`	Returns index of first appearance of string `s`, at or after the optional starting index *n*. If *n* is not specified, search starts at index 0. Returns −1 if `s` is not found. `"excel".indexOf("x");` returns 1. `"excel".indexOf("xce",2);` returns −1.

`lastIndexOf (s[,n])`	Returns index of last appearance of string `s`, searching from *right* to *left*, at or before the optional starting index *n*. If *n* is not specified, search starts at the end of the string. Returns −1 if `s` is not found.
	`"excel".lastIndexOf("e");`
	returns 3.
	`"excel".lastIndexOf("l",3);`
	returns −1.

`substr(m[,len])`	Returns a new string containing a substring of the target string of length `len`, starting at index m. If `len` is not specified, the substring contains all characters from m to end of target string. `"excel".substr(0,5);` returns `excel`. `"excel".substr(2);` returns `cel`.

(continued)

Table 4.2 (continued)

Method Name	Description and Examples
substring (m[, *end*])	Returns a new string containing a substring of the target string from index m up to but not including index end. If end is not specified, substring contains all characters from m to end of target string. `"excel".substring(1,3);` returns xc.

toLowerCase()	Returns new string that converts all characters in target string to lower case.
	`var h="HTML";`
	`h=h.toLowerCase();`
	replaces h with the new value html.

toUpperCase()	Returns a new string that converts all characters in the target string to upper case.
	`var a="ascii",A;`
	`A=a.toUpperCase();`
	assigns a value of ASCII to A.

The methods of the String object in JavaScript can be applied directly to string primitives—variables or literals. Therefore, the reference to the String object name is rarely needed. This is in contrast to other objects, such as Math, which will be discussed later in this chapter.

Characters in strings are always numbered from left to right, starting with 0. So, "HTML".charAt(3); returns "L" and not "M". There is only one string property: length. The value is set automatically whenever the contents of a string are changed; the value of length cannot otherwise be set. For example, "ThisIsJavaScript". length; returns a value of 16.

It is important to understand that string methods do not change the contents of a string simply as a result of invoking that method. Rather, the method returns a value that must be assigned appropriately. Hence, in the example

```
var h="HTML";
h=h.toLowerCase();
```

the string variable h is replaced by a new value, html, through the assignment statement. In the example

```
var a="ascii",A;
-
A=a.toUpperCase();
```

the value of string variable a is unchanged, while the result of invoking the toUpper-Case() method is assigned to the string variable A, which now has a value of ASCII.

4.5
Tokens, Operators, Expressions, and Statements

4.5.1
Tokens

As noted previously, tokens are the smallest lexical units of a language. One way to think about tokens is to consider how a script might be stored in compressed form. Each unique piece of information will be represented by a token. For example, variable name identifiers will be stored as tokens. The concept of tokens explains why `myname` or `my_name` are allowed variable names, but `my  name` is not—`my  name` will be interpreted as two separate names (two tokens).

4.5.2
Arithmetic Operators

Operators are also tokens. JavaScript operators, shown in Table 4.3, include arithmetic operators for addition, subtraction, multiplication, division, and the modulus operator for returning the remainder from division. These are all binary operators, which means that they require two operands, one to the left of the operator and one to the right. The addition and subtraction operators can also function as unary operators, with a single operand to the right of the operator; for example, `-x`.

With the exception of the modulus, or remainder, operator, these should all be familiar. The modulus operator works with either integer or real number operands. (Remember that JavaScript does not support a separate integer data type.) The result of dividing 17 by 3 is 5 with a remainder of 2. The result of dividing 16.6 by 2.7 is 6 (6 times $2.7 = 16.2$) with a remainder of $16.6 - 16.2 = 0.4$.

The addition operator also works as a concatenation operator for strings. The expression `var author = "David" + " " + "Brooks";` makes perfect sense to JavaScript and will give variable `author` the expected value of `"David Brooks"`. Note that the expression `"David" + "Brooks"` will produce the result `"DavidBrooks."`

When JavaScript interprets an expression, it scans the expression from left to right one or more times. Operations implied by the presence of operators are evaluated according to **precedence rules**. Fortunately, these rules are the same ones that apply in algebraic expressions. Suppose $a=3$, $b=4$, and $c=5$. What is the value of x in the algebraic expression $x = a + bc$? Based on precedence rules, multiplication and division operations are carried out before addition and subtraction. So, $x = 3 + 4 \cdot 5 = 3 + 20 = 23$. That is, a multiplication operation has precedence over an addition operation, so the addition operation is delayed until after the multiplication is performed, even though the addition operator is to the left of the multiplication operator. Parentheses are required to alter the precedence rules: $x = (3 + 4) \cdot 5 = 35$.

Table 4.3 JavaScript's arithmetic operators

Operator	Symbol	Examples	Precedence
Addition	+	`3 + 4`	2
Subtraction	–	`z - 10`	2
Multiplication	*	`A*b`	1
Division	/	`z/3.333`	1
Modulus (remainder)	%	`17%3 (=2)`, `16.6%2.7 (=0.4)`	1

The same rules apply in JavaScript. As indicated in Table 4.3, multiplication and division (including the modulus operation) take precedence over addition and subtraction. So, in this code:

```
var a=3,b=4,c=5;
var x,y;
x=a+b*c;
y=(a+b)*c;
```

the variable x has a value of 23. In the fourth statement, parentheses are used to override the natural order in which operations are evaluated, so y has a value of 35. The expression is evaluated from the innermost set of parentheses outward, so the a+b operation is performed before the multiplication by c.

4.5.3
The Assignment Operator

The JavaScript assignment operator is the symbol =. Thus, the JavaScript statement x=a+b; looks very much like the algebraic equation $x = a + b$. However, they are not at all the same thing! In programming, the assignment operator has a completely different meaning from the symbolic equality implied by the algebraic use of the = sign. In algebra, the equation $x = a + b$ defines a symbolic relationship among a, b, and x; whatever the values of x, a, and b, x must be equal to the sum of a and b. Given values for a and b, you can determine the value of x. Given the values of x and a, you can solve for the value of b: $b = x - a$. Note also that $a + b = x$ is algebraically equivalent to $x = a + b$.

But, in programming,

> **The meaning of the assignment operator is: "Evaluate the expression on the right side of the assignment operator and assign the result to the identifier on the left side of the assignment operator."**

For the statement x=a+b;, the specific meaning is "If a and b have been given numerical values, calculate their sum and assign the result to the identifier x. If a and/or b are strings, concatenate b to a."

With this definition of the assignment operator, it is clear that the JavaScript statement a+b=x; makes no sense, and will generate a syntax error. Why? Because:

Only an identifier can appear on the left side of the assignment operator.

Finally, note that the algebraic expression $x = x + 1$ makes no sense at all because it is not possible for x to be equal itself plus 1. However, the JavaScript statement x=x+1; makes perfect sense. It means "Add 1 to the current value of x and then replace the value of x with this new value." So, as a result of executing these statements:

```
var x=5.5;
x=x+1;
```

x will have a value of 6.5.

It is sometimes difficult for beginning programmers to remember that an assignment statement is not the same thing as an algebraic equation. Although JavaScript (and other programming languages) allow you to perform mathematical operations with variable identifiers, these languages do not understand the concepts of algebra. When it sees an assignment operator, all it knows how to do is evaluate the expression on the right side of the operator and assign that result to the identifier on the left side of the expression. In doing the expression evaluation, it assumes that every identifier has already been assigned an actual, and not just a symbolic, value.

As a result of how the assignment operator works, a general rule about assignment statements is:

An identifier should never appear on the right side of an assignment operator unless it has previously been assigned an appropriate value.

Identifiers that do not follow this rule are called **uninitialized variables**. They are often assigned a value of 0 by default, but you should never violate the rule based on this assumption.

4.5.4
Shorthand Arithmetic/Assignment Operators

Table 4.4 shows some shorthand operators for combining arithmetic operations and assignments. They are popular among programmers because they are easy to write quickly, but their use is never actually required.

The increment operator (++) adds 1 to the value of the variable to which it is applied, and the decrement operator (--) subtracts 1. These operators are commonly used in looping structures, as discussed later in this chapter.

As shown in Table 4.4, you can apply the increment or decrement operators either before the variable name (pre-increment or pre-decrement) or after (post-increment or post-decrement). This choice can lead to some unexpected results. Consider Document 4.2.

Table 4.4 Shorthand arithmetic/assignment operators

Operator	Implementation	Interpretation
+=	x+=y;	x=x+y;
-=	x-=y;	x=x-y;
*=	x*=y;	x=x*y;
/=	x/=y;	x=x/y;
%=	x%=y;	x=x%y;
++	x++; or ++x;	x=x+1;
--	y--; or --y;	x=x-1;

Document 4.2 (`incrementDecrement.htm`)

```
<html>
<head>
<title>Increment/decrement operators</title>
<script>
      var x=3,y;
      y=(x++)+3;
      document.write("post-increment: y="+y+"<br />");
      document.write("x="+x+"<br />");
      x=3;
      y=(++x)+3;
      document.write("pre-increment: y="+y+"<br />");
      document.write("x="+x+"<br />");
</script>
</head>
<body>
</body>
</html>
```

```
post-increment: y=6
x=4
pre-increment: y=7
x=4
```

In the post-increment case, the value of x is incremented *after* the expression is evaluated to provide a value for y. In the pre-increment case, the value of x is incremented *before* the value of y is calculated. A similar result would occur for the decrement operator. For the most part, you should avoid combining the increment/decrement operators with other operations in a single expression. Also, do not apply both pre- and post-operators at the same time (that is, do not write ++x++; or --x--;) and do not apply these operators to the same variable more than once in an expression.

4.6
The JavaScript Math Object

In order for a programming language to be useful for scientific and engineering calculations, it needs not only basic arithmetic operators, but also the ability to carry out other mathematical operations, such as you would find on a scientific calculator. In JavaScript, these operations are packaged as methods in the Math object. The Math object also has properties that provide some useful mathematical values, such as π. The methods implement mathematical functions, such as trigonometric functions. The methods (with a single exception as noted below) have one or two real-number arguments and always return a real-number result, even when that result is a whole number that looks like an integer. Some methods and properties of the Math object are summarized in Table 4.5.

Table 4.5   Some properties and methods of the JavaScript Math object

Property	Description
Math.E	Base of the natural logarithm, e, 2.71828
Math.LN2	Natural logarithm of 2, 0.693147
Math.LN10	Natural logarithm of 10, 2.302585
Math.LOG2E	Log to the base 2 of e, 1.442695
Math.LOG10E	Log to the base 10 of e, 0.434294
Math.PI	π, 3.1415927
Math.SQRT1_2	Square root of ½, 0.7071067
Math.SQRT2	Square root of 2, 1.4142136
Method	**Returns**
Math.abs(x)	Absolute value of x
Math.acos(x)	Arc cosine of x, $\pm\pi$, for $-1 \le x \le 1$
Math.asin(x)	Arc sine of x, $\pm\pi/2$, for $-1 \le x \le 1$
Math.atan(x)	Arc tangent of x, $\pm\pi/2$, for $-\infty < x < \infty$ (compare with Math.atan2(y,x))
Math.atan2(y,x)	Arc tangent of angle between x-axis and the point (x,y), measured counterclockwise (compare with Math.atan(x))
Math.ceil(x)	Smallest integer greater than or equal to x
Math.cos(x)	Cosine of x, ± 1
Math.exp(x)	e to the x power (e^x)
Math.floor(x)	Greatest integer less than or equal to x
Math.log(x)	Natural (base e) logarithm of x, $x > 0$
Math.max(x,y)	Greater of x or y
Math.min(x,y)	Lesser of x or y
Math.pow(x,y)	x to the y power (x^y)
Math.random()	Random real number in the range [0,1]
Math.round(x)	x rounded to the nearest integer
Math.sin(x)	Sine of x
Math.sqrt(x)	Square root of x
Math.tan(x)	Tangent of x, $\pm\infty$

These methods must be used appropriately in order to produce meaningful results. For example, it makes no sense (at least in real-number mathematics) to ask `Math.sqrt()` to calculate the square root of a negative number. Fortunately or unfortunately, depending on your point of view, JavaScript is very forgiving about such abuses. It will return a "value" of NaN if you ask it to do an inappropriate calculation, but it won't tell you what the problem is.

Trigonometric and inverse trigonometric functions always work in *radians*, not degrees. So `Math.sin(30);` will calculate the sine of 30 rad, not 30°. This is an easy error to make. It will not produce an error message because the requested calculation does not represent a problem from JavaScript's point of view. To convert from degrees to radians, multiply degrees by $\pi/180$.

When functions are called with very large or very small arguments, or when they should produce answers that are algebraically equal to 0 (as in the sin of 0 or π radians) or approaching infinity (as in the tangent of $\pi/2$ radians), problems can arise due to the imprecision inherent in real-number calculations. For example, `Math.sin(Math.PI);` will produce a value `1.2246e-16` rather than 0. (Try it and see.)

Despite the fact that "log" is often used to denote base 10 logarithms, with "ln" used for base e logarithms, the `Math.log()` object supports only natural (base e) logarithms and uses `log` rather than `ln`. Logarithms to some other base n can be calculated as

$$\log_n(x) = \log_e(x) / \log_e(n)$$

Base 10 logarithms are often used in engineering calculations. So, a JavaScript expression to calculate the base 10 logarithm of a variable x is

```
Math.log(x)/Math.log(10);
```

or, using the `Math.LN10` property,

```
Math.log(x)/Math.LN10;
```

The `Math` object methods mostly work just as you would expect. However, `random()` (the parentheses are required even though there is no calling argument) deserves a closer look. As is true for random number generators in all programming languages, JavaScript's `random()` method is really only a "pseudorandom" number generator. It relies on an algorithm which follows a predetermined path whenever the method is used. The randomness results from "seeding" the algorithm with a starting value based on a value read from your computer system's internal clock. This "seed" value is not predictable, for all practical purposes, and therefore should produce a sequence of numbers that *appears* to be random.

A call to an algorithm-driven random number generator such as `Math.random()` should generate a real number x randomly located within the interval $0 \leq x < 1$. (That is, it is possible that x might be exactly 0, but not exactly 1.) This range can be expressed mathematically as [0,1). Repeated calls to `Math.random()*n` should produce real numbers uniformly distributed over the interval [0,n). However, practical applications of random numbers are more likely to require uniformly distributed integers over a specified range.

Caution is required when converting uniformly distributed real numbers to uniformly distributed integers. Some sources suggest

```
Math.round(n*Math.random() + 1) //Not a good idea!
```

This will produce integers in the range [1,n], but those integers will *not* be uniformly distributed![3] The correct code is

```
Math.floor(n*(Math.random()%1) + 1);
```

One of the Chap. 4 exercises explores this problem in more detail. See Document 4.3, below, for an appropriate approach to generating uniformly distributed integers.

Whenever a script contains many references to the `Math` object's properties and methods, it is convenient to use the `with` keyword. Within a `with` statement block, references to an object's properties and methods do not have to be prefixed with the object name and dot operator.

```
with (Math) {
   {statements that refer to properties and/or methods of the Math
      object, such as...}
   var x=sin(.197);
}
```

Finally, it is interesting to note that you can create your own extensions to the `Math` object—for example, a method that correctly returns the value of an angle expressed in degrees rather than radians. These extensions exist only for the document in which they are defined, but you can save your own library of extensions that can be pasted into any script. For more information, see the exercises for Chap. 6.

Document 4.3 shows how to use some `Math` object methods. The `for` statement block will be discussed later in the chapter. For now, its purpose should be clear from the output:

Document 4.3 (`mathFunctions2.htm`)

```
<html>
<head>
   <title>Demonstration of the Math object.</title>
<script language="javascript" type="text/javascript">
   for (var i=1; i<=10; i++)
    with (Math) {
     var x=floor(100*(random()%1))+1;
     document.write(x+"  "+sqrt(x)+"  "+pow(x,3)+"<br />");
    }
```

---

[3] Even *JavaScript: The Complete Reference*, the book referenced in Chap. 1, makes this mistake.

```
</script>
</head>
<body>
</body>
</html>
```

```
93 9.643650760992955 804357
73 8.54400374531753 389017
63 7.937253933193772 250047
69 8.306623862918074 328509
20 4.47213595499958 8000
95 9.746794344808963 857375
43 6.557438524302 79507
31 5.5677643628300215 29791
49 7 117649
10 3.1622776601683795 1000
```

This code will generate integer values of *x* in the range [1,100]. Why write `Math.random()%1` rather than just `Math.random()`? If the random number generator happens to produce a value of exactly 1, the modulus operation replaces it with 0, because `1%1` equals 0. Any other number in the range [0,1) is unchanged by the modulus operation.[4]

The output from Document 4.3 illustrates an interesting point: Even though JavaScript does not have a data type for integers, it nonetheless knows how to display whole numbers not as real numbers with 0's to the right of a decimal point, but as integers. On the other hand, real numbers that are not whole numbers are typically displayed with 15 digits to the right of the decimal point! This is a consequence of how JavaScript stores numbers internally, but it is hardly ever desirable or meaningful to display this many digits.

Languages such as C/C++ have formatting options to gain more control over the appearance of output. JavaScript provides only limited options. One solution makes use of the `Math.round()` method. If this statement from Document 4.3:

```
document.write(x+" "+sqrt(x)+" "+pow(x,3)+"<br />");
```

is replaced with:

```
document.write(x+" "+round(sqrt(x)*100)/100+" "+
    pow(x,3)+"<br />");
```

```
4 2 64
44 6.63 85184
75 8.66 421875
15 3.87 3375
38 6.16 54872
39 6.24 59319
18 4.24 5832
77 8.77 456533
57 7.55 185193
63 7.94 250047
```

the output will be changed as shown, with no more than two digits to the right of the decimal point. Other values can be substituted for 100, as appropriate. The output is not simply truncated to the selected number of digits, but rounded appropriately, just as you would round numbers by hand. That is, if you wish to display the value of pi with four digits to the right of the decimal point, both you and JavaScript would display 3.1415927 as 3.1416.

A better solution makes use of the fact that JavaScript numbers are objects, with properties and methods. Here is some code that makes use of the `toFixed()` method for number objects:

[4]Author's note: I have seen some online references claiming that some implementations of `Math.random()` might, in fact, occasionally produce a value exactly equal to 1.

```
var x=2,n=3.3,z=3.777777;
document.write(x.toFixed(3)+"<br />");
document.write(n.toFixed(3)+"<br />");
document.write(z.toFixed(5)+"<br />");
/*
  This statement generates a syntax error.
  document.write(7.toFixed(2)+"<br />");
  but these work:
*/
document.write((7).toFixed(2)+"<br />");
document.write(13.3.toFixed(2)+"<br />");
```

The displayed results are:

```
2.000
3.300
3.77778
7.00
13.30
```

Note that you can use `toFixed()` to retain 0's to the right of the decimal point even for whole numbers, which you cannot do when you use `Math.round()`. So, `toFixed()` is probably the best way to exert some control over the appearance of JavaScript output.

4.7
Comparison Operators and Decision-Making Structures

4.7.1
Relational and Logical Operators

As noted at the beginning of this chapter, a programming language should be able to make decisions based on comparing values. JavaScript provides a set of operators for comparing values and a syntax for taking actions based on the results of comparisons. Table 4.6 summarizes JavaScript's **relational** and **logical operators**.

Some of these operators are familiar from mathematics. When two characters are required, it is because some mathematical symbols are not standard keyboard characters.

4.7.2
The if Construct (Branching Structures)

Branching structures are based on a translation into programming syntax of spoken-language statements such as: "If x is greater than y, then let $z=10$, otherwise let $z=0$" or "If

Table 4.6 Relational and logical operators

Operator	Interpretation	Math Symbol	Precedence	Example	Value
Relational					
<	Less than	<	2	-3.3<0	true
>	Greater than	>	2	17.7>17.5	true
>=	Greater than or equal to	≥	2	7.7>=7.7	true
<=	Less than or equal to	≤	2	7.6<=7.7	true
==	Equal to, allowing for type conversion	=	3	9=="9"	true
===	Equal to, no type conversion	=	3	9==="9" "a"==="a"	false true
!=	Not equal to, allowing for type conversion	≠	3	9!="8" 9!="9"	true false
!==	Not equal to, no type conversion	≠	3	9!=="9"	true
Logical					
&&	AND		4	(x==3)&&(y<0)	
||	OR		5	(x==3)||(z==4)	
!	NOT		1[a]	!(x==3)	

[a]Higher precedence than arithmetic operators

today is Tuesday, I should be in class." Translating such statements into relational and logical tests makes it possible to build decision-making capabilities into a programming language.

JavaScript syntax is close to the spoken language, but of course it follows strict syntax rules. Here is a generic outline:

```
if  ({an expression. If true, statements are executed})
{
        {statements here}
}
// optionally
else if  ({an expression. If true, statements are executed})
{
        {statements here}
}
// optionally, more else if statements
// optionally
else
{
        {statements here}
}
```

The syntax requires only the if statement. The "then" word that you might use in conversation is implied—there is no then keyword in JavaScript. The expressions to be evaluated must be enclosed in parentheses. The else if's and else's are optional. The curly brackets are required to form a statement block whenever there is more than one statement for each branch.

If you consider an if structure as defining branches in a road that eventually rejoin at a main road, the minimum choice is a road with no branches, with the option to continue along the road toward your destination or to bypass the road completely.

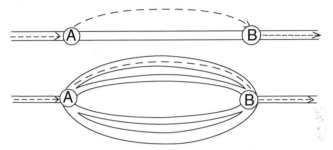

With multiple possible branches, it is important to understand that

> **Only the *first* branch of an if statement for which the expression evaluates as true will be taken.**

To use the road analogy, once you select a branch in the road, you take only that branch and no other.

This principle is illustrated in Document 4.4, which assigns a letter grade based on a 90/80/70/60 grading system. Suppose the numerical grade is 83. This is less than 90, so the first branch is not executed. However, 83 is greater than or equal to 80, so a letter grade of B is assigned. But, 83 is also greater than or equal to 70. Does this mean that the letter grade is now reassigned to a C, etc.? No, because only the first true branch (assign a B) is executed; the subsequent branches are ignored.

Document 4.4 (grades.htm)

```
<html>
<head>
<title>Get letter grade</title>
<script language="javascript" type="text/javascript">
    var grade=
        parseFloat(prompt("What is your numerical grade?"));
    document.write("For a numerical grade of "+grade+
                   ", your letter grade is ");
    if (grade >= 90) document.write("A");
    else if (grade >= 80) document.write("B");
    else if (grade >= 70) document.write("C");
```

4

```
else if (grade >= 60) document.write("D");
else document.write("F");
document.write(".");
```
```
</script>
</head>
<body>
</body>
</html>
```

[JavaScript Application]   ⊠
ⓘ What is your numerical grade?
88
OK   Cancel

For a numerical grade of 88, your letter grade is B.

Note how identifier grade is given its value, with prompt() and parseFloat() combined in a single statement; for comparison, look again at Document 4.1. This script will actually work without applying parseFloat(), because comparisons such as (grade >= 90) will initiate an appropriate type conversion. However, neglecting to apply the parseFloat() requires JavaScript to compare "apples and oranges," and should be avoided both as a matter of good programming style and to prevent possible unforeseen problems in other circumstances.

Document 4.5 is another example of a calculation that uses an if structure. It calculates income tax when there are two tax rates, one of which applies to all income up to $50,000, and the other which applies to just that portion of income that is in excess of $50,000.

Document 4.5 (taxes.htm)

```
<html>
<head>
<title>Calculate income tax</title>
<script language="javascript" type="text/javascript">
var income=
prompt("Enter your income (no commas!): $");
income=parseFloat(income);
var tax,loRate=.17,hiRate=.37;
if (income<=50000.)
       tax=income*loRate;
else
       tax=50000.*loRate+(income-50000.)*hiRate;
document.write("For an income of $"+income+", your tax
is $"+tax.toFixed(2)+".");
</script>
</head>
</body>
</html>
```

[JavaScript Application]   ⊠
ⓘ Enter your income (no commas!): $
73000
OK   Cancel

For an income of $73000, your tax is $17010.00.

For the example shown, the tax is ($50,000)(0.17) + ($23,000)(0.37) = $17,010.00. The `toFixed(2)` method displays the result with two 0's to the right of the decimal point.

When comparisons get more complicated, you must be careful about how you form logical/relational expressions. Suppose you want your code to respond to the statement: "If today is Tuesday or Thursday, I should be in class." The proper implementation is:

```
if ((today == "Tuesday") || (today == "Thursday"))
```

If this expression is rewritten as

```
(today == "Tuesday" || "Thursday") // don't do it!
```

it has a value of `true` if `today` is `"Tuesday"` but a value of `"Thursday"` (rather than `false`) if `today` is `"Monday"`. This is not at all what you intended!

An alternate version of the original expression, without the two inner sets of parentheses, is:

```
// poor style!
(today == "Tuesday" || today == "Thursday")
```

This will be interpreted correctly, but it depends on the fact that the equality operator has precedence over the OR operator. In cases like this, the use of "extra" parentheses, as in

```
((today == "Tuesday") || (today == "Thursday"))
```

is better programming style. It makes clear the order in which you wish the operations to be performed and also makes it unnecessary to memorize the precedence rules for relational and logical operators.

Finally, the expression

```
// don't do it!
(today = "Tuesday") || (today = "Thursday")
```

may *look* OK but, again, it is not at all what you intended because the equality operator has been replaced with an assignmen t operator. The expression has a value of `"Thursday"` rather than `true`.

> Using an assignment operator (=) when you intend to use an equality operator (==) is a common programming mistake that is very hard to pinpoint because it does not generate a JavaScript error. Be careful!

4.7.3
The switch Construct

There is one more type of branching construct that is useful for certain kinds of comparisons. Suppose you would like to write code that will tell a user how many days are in a particular month.

Document 4.6 (daysInMonth.htm)

```html
<html>
<head>
<title>Days in Month</title>
<script language="javascript" type="text/javascript">
var month=prompt("Give month (1-12): ");
switch (month) {
  case "1":
  case "3":
  case "5":
  case "7":
  case "8":
  case "10":
  case "12":
    alert("There are 31 days in this month."); break;
  case "4":
  case "6":
  case "9":
  case "11":
    alert("There are 30 days in this month."); break;
  case "2":
    alert("There are either 28 or 29 days in this
           month."); break;
default:
    alert("I do not understand your month entry.");
}
</script>
</head>
<body>
</body>
</html>
```

Although this code could be implemented with if syntax, the switch construct is perhaps a little more clear. The syntax should be clear from Document 4.6. The switch keyword is followed by an expression enclosed in parentheses. The possible values of the expression are enumerated in the case labels that follow. The "numbers" of the months are given as text because the value from `prompt()` is text. It will *not* work to replace the case statements with, for example, `case 5:` instead of `case "5":` because, unlike comparisons made with the `==` and other relational operators, no automatic type conversion will be performed. (See also the `===` and `!==` operators previously defined in Table 4.6.) If the line `month=parseFloat(month);` is inserted after the prompt, then the case values must all be numbers, and not text.

Each `case` and its value is followed by a colon. The values do not have to be in any particular order. The `default` keyword provides an opportunity to respond to unexpected or other values. The statements following the first `case` label whose value matches the expression are executed. Note that these statements are not enclosed in curly brackets. They are executed in order and, unlike the "single branch" behavior of `if...` statements, will continue to execute subsequent statements that apply to other `case` values unless the `break` keyword appears as the last statement in a group of statements to be executed.

4.8
Loop Structures

The ability to perform repetitive calculations is important in computer algorithms. This is enabled through the use of loop structures. Loops can be written to execute the same code statements a prescribed number of times, or they can be written so that loop execution (or termination) is based on conditions that change while statements in the loop are being executed. The former situation uses **count-controlled loops** and the latter uses **conditional loops**.

4.8.1
Count-Controlled Loops

Count-controlled loops are managed with the `for` keyword. The general syntax of a count-controlled loop is:

```
for (counter= {expression giving on initial value of counter};
    {expression giving high (or low) value of counter};
    {expression controlling incrementing (or decrementing) of counter})
```

The `for` keyword is followed by three statements inside a pair of parentheses. The first statement sets the initial value of a counter. You can give the identifier name—`counter` in the above example—any name you like. The second expression sets conditions under which the loop should continue to execute; the loop continues to execute as long as the value of the second expression is `true`. The third expression controls how the counter is incremented or decremented. It is up to you to make sure that these three related expressions are consistent and will actually cause the loop to terminate. For example, the loop

```
for (i=1; i=12; i+=2)
```

will never terminate because i will never equal 12. Perhaps you meant to write the second expression as i<=12;. If so, then the loop will execute for i=1, 3, 5, 7, 9, and 11.

Now, consider Document 4.7, which displays the integers 0–10, in order. The counter k is initialized to 1. It is incremented in steps of 1, and the loop executes as long as k is less than 10. Use of the shortcut incrementing or decrementing operators, as in k++, is very common in for loops.

Document 4.7 (counter2.htm)

```
<html>
<head>
<title>Counter</title>
<script>
var k;
document.write("Here's a simple counter: "+"<br />");
for (k=0; k<=10; k++) { //curly brackets optional
        document.write(k+"<br />");}
</script>
</head>
<body>
</body>
</html>
```

Here's a simple counter:
0
1
2
3
4
5
6
7
8
9
10

For this example, a statement block enclosed in curly brackets following the for... loop is not required because only one statement is executed in the loop. Document 4.8 shows a version of Document 4.6 which counts backward from 10.

Document 4.8 (countdown2.htm)

```
<html>
<head>
  <title>Countdown</title>
<script>
var k;
document.write("Start launch sequence!"
  +"<br />");
```

```
for (k=10; k>=0; k--) { //curly brackets optional
   document.write(k+"<br />");
}
document.write("FIRE!!");
</script>
</head>
<body>
</body>
</html>
```

| Start launch sequence! |
| 10 |
| 9 |
| 8 |
| 7 |
| 6 |
| 5 |
| 4 |
| 3 |
| 2 |
| 1 |
| 0 |
| FIRE!! |

Recall that a for... loop was used previously in Document 4.3. Now would be a good time to look back at that code and make sure you understand how that loop worked.

4.8.2
Conditional Loops

It is often the case that conditions under which repetitive calculations will or will not be executed cannot be determined in advance. Instead, conditions that control the execution or termination of a loop structure must be determined by values calculated inside the loop, while the script is running. Such circumstances require conditional loops.

There are two kinds of conditional loops: **pre-test** and **post-test loops**. The statements in pre-test loops may or may not be executed at all, depending on the original values of loop-related variables. Post-test loops are always executed at least once, and the values of loop-related variables are tested at the end of the loop. The syntax is slightly different:

pre-test loop:

```
while  ({logical expression})  {
   {statements that result in changing the value of the pre-test logical
    expression}
}
```

post-test loop:

```
do {
   {statements that result in changing the value of the post-test logical
    expression}
} while ({logical expression}) ;
```

Conditional loops can always be written either as post- or pre-test loops. The choice is based on how a problem is stated. Consider this problem:

4

A small elevator has a maximum capacity of 500 lb. People waiting in line to enter the elevator are weighed. If they can get on the elevator without exceeding the load limit, they are allowed to enter. If not, the elevator leaves without trying to find someone who weighs less than the person currently first in line. If the elevator is overloaded, it crashes. It is possible that there might be a large gorilla in line, weighing more than 500 lb. This gorilla shouldn't be allowed on the elevator under any circumstances. Write a document that will supply random weights for people (or gorillas) waiting in line, control access to the elevator, and stop allowing people (or gorillas) to enter if the weight limit would be exceeded.

One solution to this problem is shown in Document 4.9.

Document 4.9 (gorilla1.htm)

```html
<html>
<head>
<title>The elevator problem (with gorillas).</title>
<script language="javascript" type="text/javascript">
  var totalWeight=0.,limitWeight=500.,maxWeight=550.;
  var newWeight;
do {
  newWeight=Math.floor(maxWeight*(Math.random()%1))+1;
  if ((totalWeight + newWeight) <= limitWeight) {
    totalWeight += newWeight;
    document.write(
      "New weight = " + newWeight + " total weight = "
      +totalWeight + "<br />");
    newWeight=0.;
  }
  else document.write("You weigh " + newWeight +
      " lb. I'm sorry, but you can't get on.");
} while ((totalWeight + newWeight)
      <= limitWeight);
</script>
</head>
<body>
</body>
</html>
```

New weight = 191 total weight = 191
New weight = 154 total weight = 345
New weight = 151 total weight = 496
You weigh 108 lb. I'm sorry, but you can't get on.

This solution to the problem uses the Math.random() method to generate random weights between 0 and 500 lb. The calculations are done inside a post-test loop. The code is arranged so that the effect of adding a new person to the elevator is tested before the person is allowed on the elevator. It is left as an exercise to rewrite this loop as a pre-test loop.

In principle, count-controlled loops can also be written as conditional loops. However, it is better programming style to reserve conditional loop structures for problems that actually need them. Clearly, Document 4.9 is such a problem because there is no way for the script to determine ahead of time what weights the Math.random() method will generate. Another example of a problem that demands a conditional loop calculation is Newton's algorithm for finding the square root of a number.

Given a number n:

1. Make a guess (g) for the square root of n. $n/2$ is a reasonable guess.
2. Replace g with $(g + n/g)/2$.
3. Repeat step 2 until the absolute difference between g^2 and n is smaller than some specified value.

This algorithm is easy to write as a conditional loop. Consider Document 4.10.

Document 4.10 (newtonSqrt2.htm)

```
<html>
<head>
<title>Newton's square root algorithm</title>
<script language="javascript" type="text/javascript">
var n=prompt("Enter a positive number:");
n=parseFloat(n);
var g=n/2;
do {
   g = (g + n/g)/2.;
} while (Math.abs(g*g-n) > 1e-5);
alert(g+" is the square root of "+n+".");
</script>
</head>
<body>
</body>
</html>
```

[JavaScript Application]

⚠ 3.0000000000393214 is the square root of 9.

OK

This algorithm is implemented as a post-test loop because a reasonable assumption is that the calculation inside the loop will always need to be done at least once. In fact, considering that the initial guess for the square root of n is $n/2$, this assumption is true for all values of n except 4. The statement g=(g+n/g)/2; is an excellent example of how an assignment operator differs from the same symbol (=) when it is used in an algebraic context. This kind of "replacement assignment" is often seen in conditional loops.

The terminating condition while (Math.abs(g*g-n)>1e-5); is important. It is not obvious whether g^2 will be larger or smaller than n. So, you must test the absolute value of $g^2 - n$ to ensure that the value being compared to 10^{-5} is always positive (because any negative number is less than $+10^{-5}$).

This algorithm will work for any positive number. Note that the algorithm does not give *exactly* 3 as the square root of 9. On the other hand, if you calculate the square root of 4, it will give exactly 2. These kinds of discrepancies are a result of how numbers are stored and how numerical calculations are done. Newton's square root algorithm is a numerical approximation, so in general, it will *approach* the actual answer (within the specified accuracy), but won't necessarily give the exact answer for a perfect square. Except for annoying strings of zeros and digits—to the right of the 3 in the output shown here—these discrepancies are usually of no practical concern. If desired, the extraneous digits can be removed with the `Math.round()` or `toFixed()` method.

4.9
Using JavaScript to Change Values in Form Fields

In an interactive environment, you would like to be able to calculate new values based on user input. HTML form fields can serve both purposes: users can enter values and the document can use JavaScript to calculate new values for other fields. Consider this problem:

Atmospheric pressure decreases with elevation. When barometric pressure is given in weather reports, it is always referenced to sea level. (Otherwise it wouldn't be possible to draw weather maps that show the movement of air masses.) Scientists often need to know the actual barometric pressure at a site. This is called station pressure. An approximate conversion from sea level pressure to station pressure is:

$$P_{station} = P_{sea\ level} - h/9.2$$

where pressure P is expressed in millibars and elevation h is expressed in meters. U.S. users will need to convert from inches of mercury to millibars: $P_{millibars} = 33.864 \cdot P_{inches\ of\ Hg}$. Write an application that calculates station pressure from sea level pressure and elevation.

Document 4.11 demonstrates several new HTML and JavaScript features.

Document 4.11 (`stationPressure.htm`)

```
<html>
<head>
<title>Convert sea level pressure to station
pressure.</title>
<font size="+1">
<b>Convert sea level pressure to station pressure (true
pressure)</b></font><br /><br />
```

```
</head>
<body bgcolor="lightblue">
This application converts sea level pressure to
station pressure.<br />
Station pressure is the actual pressure at an
observer's observing site.<br />
It is always less than or equal to sea level pressure
(unless you are below<br />
sea level).
<br />
<form>
Fill in elevation and sea-level pressure:
<input type="text" name="elevation" value="0" size="8"
maxlength="7" /> (m)
<input type="text" name="sea_level_pressure" value="1013.25"
size="8" maxlength="7" /> (mbar) <br />
<input type="button" name="Calculate"
  value="Click here to get station pressure:"
  onclick="result.value=
    parseFloat(sea_level_pressure.value)-
parseFloat(elevation.value)/9.2;" />
input type="text" name="result" size="8"
  maxlength="7" /> (mbar)<br />
<input type="reset" value="Reset all fields." />
</form>
</body>
</html>
```

Convert sea level pressure to station pressure (true pressure)

This application converts sea level pressure to station pressure.
Station pressure is the actual pressure at an observer's observing site.
It is always less than or equal to sea level pressure (unless you are below
sea level).

Fill in elevation and sea-level pressure: 0   (m) 1013.25   (mbar)
    Click here to get station pressure: 1013.25   (mbar)
    Reset all fields.

    The HTML code in Document 4.11 provides default values for the input fields. The
output reproduced here is for these default values.

    Earlier discussions noted that JavaScript script was often, but not always, contained
within a script element in the head of a document. But, Document 4.11 shows that
JavaScript statements can appear in a document without a script element. It is not

obvious that this should be so—you could easily imagine a scenario in which JavaScript statements were allowed to exist *only* inside a `script` element.

The `"button"` field allows a user to initiate an action by clicking anywhere on the button. In this case, a click initiates the calculation of station pressure based on the values currently in the `elevation` and `sea_level_pressure` fields—either the default values or new values entered by the user. In order to respond to a moving a mouse cursor over the button field and clicking, HTML uses an **event handler**, an important means of providing interaction between a document and its user. Event handlers are attributes (of `input`) whose "values" consist of a set of JavaScript instructions enclosed in quotes. There are several event handlers, but in this chapter only `onclick` will be used. (We will return to the topic of event handlers in Chap. 6.) In Document 4.11, the event to be "handled" is a click of a mouse when its cursor is somewhere in the screen space defined by the "Click here to get station pressure" button.

How is information transmitted from a form field to JavaScript? It will not work to use, for example, just the `elevation` name from the form field. Why not? Because `elevation` is just the *name* of the field, not its *value*. Form fields have attributes, such as `name`, and those attributes have values, such as `elevation`. The attributes have values, too, accessed through the "dot notation"

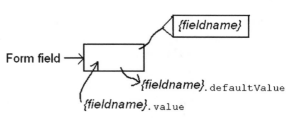

shown. One of the values of a field name is its `defaultValue`, which is the value originally assigned to the form field in the HTML document; this value can be left blank.

Of interest here is `value`, either the same as `defaultValue` or a new value entered by the user. It is the `value` attribute that provides the input for a calculation and will also receive calculated results in other form fields. Applying the `parseFloat (elevation.value)` method translates the text in `value` into a numerical value. Using just `elevation` as the argument for `parseFloat()` makes no sense at all from JavaScript's point of view. It may seem cumbersome to use this notation, but remember that the name assigned to an HTML form field is simply not the same thing as an identifier in JavaScript.

Once a mouse is clicked over the button field in Document 4.11, the JavaScript statement is executed. The application of `parseFloat()` to the values in the `elevation` and `sea_level_pressure` fields is required for the same reasons previously discussed for numerical values entered through `prompt()`. The distinction between text and numerical values is easy to forget because JavaScript often applies type conversions to text values, on its own. In Document 4.11, the calculation for the `result` field *could* also be written as

```
result.value = sea_level_pressure.value -
               elevation.value/9.2; // Bad idea!
```

However, if you replace the "−" sign with a "+" sign, the numerical calculation will **_not_** be done! (Try it and see.) What is the difference? The "+" operator has a specific meaning when applied to strings (it is interpreted as a concatenation operator), but the "−" operator does not.

When it encounters a subtraction operator, JavaScript is "smart enough" to understand that the text values must be converted to numbers in order to carry out the specified action but, from JavaScript's point of view, this is not necessary for the "addition" operator.

Type conversion issues also apply when results of a numerical operation are assigned to a form field name. Although `result.value=`... looks like an assignment of one numerical value to another, the numerical result must actually be converted back to text before it can be assigned to `result.value`. You might think that some kind of "convert this number to text" method is required, and in some sense it is, but you don't have to specify this conversion in your script because JavaScript automatically does it for you.

Finally, clicking anywhere on the "Reset all fields" button sets all inputs back to their original values. JavaScript does this by accessing the `defaultValue` assigned to each field.

4.10
More Examples

4.10.1
Solving the Quadratic Equation

Here is a simple algebraic calculation that is easy to implement.

For the quadratic equation $ax^2 + bx + c = 0$,find the real roots:

$$r_1 = \left[-b + \left(b^2 - 4ac\right)^{1/2}\right]\Big/2a \quad r_2 = \left[-b - \left(b^2 - 4ac\right)^{1/2}\right]\Big/2a$$

The "a" coefficient must not be 0. If the discriminant $b^2 - 4ac = 0$, there is only one root. If $b^2 - 4ac$ is less than 0, there are no real roots.

Document 4.12 (`quadratic.htm`)

```
<html>
<head>
<title>Solving the Quadratic Equation</title>
</head><body><form>
Enter coefficients for ax<sup>2</sup> + bx + c = 0:
<br />
a = <input type="text" value="1" name="a" />
    (must not be 0)<br />
b = <input type="text" value="2" name="b" /><br />
c = <input type="text" value="-8" name="c" /><br />
click for r1 = <input type="text" value="0" name="r1"
onclick="var A=parseFloat(a.value),B=parseFloat(b.value),
C=parseFloat(c.value);
```

```
r1.value=(-B+Math.sqrt(B*B-4.*A*C))/2./A;" /><br />
click for r2 = <input type="text"
value="0" name="r2" onclick="var
A=parseFloat(a.value),B=parseFloat(b.value),
C=parseFloat(c.value);
r2.value=(-B-Math.sqrt(B*B-4.*A*C))/2./A;" /><br />
</form></body></html>
```

This is a workable solution to the problem, but it is certainly not elegant or thorough. (It's the kind of application you might write for your own use, but you might not want to distribute it globally on the Web!) For example, no check is performed on the discriminant to see if it's non-negative

Enter coefficients for $ax^2 + bx + c = 0$:

$a =$ | 1 | (must not be 0)

$b =$ | 2 |

$c =$ | -8 |

click for $r_1 =$ | 2 |

click for $r_2 =$ | -4 |

before the Math.sqrt() method is applied. However, if the discriminant is negative, then JavaScript will simply assign a value of NaN to the result, which can be interpreted as a message that there are no real roots.

Note the use in Document 4.12 of the ^{...} tag to display exponents and other superscripts in HTML. The _{...} tag will display subscripts.

4.10.2
Rectangular Rule Numerical Integration

Programming languages such as JavaScript do not "know" about symbolic mathematics, including calculus, so they can't be used to perform analytic integration of functions. However, there are several ways to integrate functions numerically. This is especially useful for functions that do not have analytic integrals, such as the normal probability density function (see Exercise 6.6). Rectangular Rule integration is the simplest of these methods.

Assume $f(x)=x^2$. To calculate an approximation to the integral of $f(x)$, specify the lower and upper boundaries for the integration, x_0 and x_1. Divide the interval (x_1-x_0) into n equal intervals, $dx=(x_1-x_0)/n$. Then,

INITIALIZE integral$=0$ (Initialize the value to 0.)
LOOP for i$=0$ to n-1,
    $x = x_0 + i \cdot dx + dx/2$
    $y=x \cdot x$ (This could be any function of x.)
    integral$=$integral$+y$
END LOOP
ASSIGN integral$=$integral $\cdot dx$

The graph illustrates the Rectangular Rule integration of $f(x)=x^2$ over the interval 1–4, with $n=3$. The sum of the areas of the gray rectangles is the approximation to the integral. For implementation in code, n should be much larger than 3!

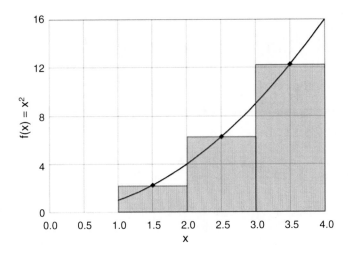

Document 4.13 (`RectangularRule.htm`)

```
<html>
<head>
<title></title>
</head>
<body>
<h2>Rectangular Rule integration</h2>
for f(x)=x<sup>2</sup>
<form>
  x<sub>0</sub>: <input type="text" name="x0" value="1" />
  <br />
  x<sub>1</sub>: <input type="text" name="x1" value="3" />
  <br />
  <input type="button" value="Click here to integrate."
    onclick="var x,X0,X1,i,n=20,integral=0,y;  //y=x*x
      X1=parseFloat(x1.value);
      X0=parseFloat(x0.value);
      dx=(X1-X0)/n;
      for(i=0; i<n; i++) {
        x=X0 + i*dx + dx/2;
        y=x*x;
        integral+=y;
      }
```

```
        result.value=integral*dx;  "/>
   <input type="text" name="result" value="result" /></br />
</form>
</body>
</html>
```

Rectangular Rule integration

for f(x)=x^2

xo: 1

x1: 4

Click here to integrate.   result

The analytic integral of $f(x)=x^2$ is $x^3/3$. The value of the integral over the interval 1–4 is $4^3/3-1^3/3=(64-1)/3=21$. Document 4.13 gives a value that is close but not exact. Increasing n will improve the approximation. In general, numerical integration algorithms work well for "well behaved" functions but they will not give exact values.

It is possible to write code that allows a user to enter a function in an <input> field, expressed in proper JavaScript syntax, rather than having to "hard code" the function as in this example. (See Exercise 6.6.)

Using Arrays in HTML/JavaScript

5

Abstract Chapter 5 presents an introduction to arrays. It explains how to define arrays in JavaScript, how to use them, and how to use arrays to interact with an HTML form.

5.1
Basic Array Properties

The concept of **arrays** is extremely important in programming, as it provides a way to organize, access, and manipulate related quantities. It is important to form a mental model of how arrays are implemented, as shown in the sketch. It may be helpful to think of a post office analogy. The post office has a name, equivalent to the name of an array. Inside the post office are numbered mail boxes. The numbers on the boxes correspond to array "addresses," called **indices**. The contents of the boxes correspond to array **elements**. In many programming languages, including JavaScript, the numbering of array elements always begins at 0 rather than 1.

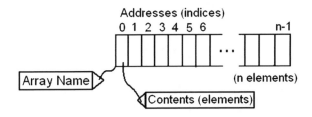

JavaScript supports an `Array` object for creating, using, and manipulating related values. The most important `Array` method is the **constructor** `new Array()`, which allows you to create arrays. Syntax possibilities for doing this include:

```
var Array1 = new Array();
var Array2 = new Array(value_1,value_2,…,value_n);
var Array3 = new Array(10);
```

The first statement creates an empty array named `Array1`. The second statement creates an array of n elements with initial values as provided by the arguments. The third statement creates an array with ten elements whose values are unspecified. Because, as will be shown later, the declared size of an array is easily overridden, it makes little sense to declare an array using the syntax of the third statement.

It is not actually necessary to invoke the `Array()` constructor in order to create a JavaScript array. Each of these statements will create an array:

```
var Array1 = [];
var Array2 = [value_1,value_2,…,value_n];
var Array3 = [,,,,,,,,,];
```

Note the use of **square bracket notation** rather than parentheses in this syntax. The third statement, with nine commas, implies an empty array of ten elements. This syntax might be useful for declaring sparse (mostly empty) arrays:

```
var SparseArray = [1.1,,3.3,,,,];
```

Array elements can also be assigned by using variable names that already have appropriate values. The statements

```
var a = 3.3, b= 5.5, c = 7.7;
var A = [a,b,c];
```

create array A with three elements equal to 3.3, 5.5, and 7.7.

Square bracket notation is also used to access the elements of an array. Individual array elements can appear to either the right or the left of an assignment operator, with the usual provision that array elements appearing on the right side of an assignment operator should already have been given an appropriate value. That is, you can use assignment statements to assign values to undefined array elements or to change previously assigned values:

```
var a = 3.3, b = 5.5, c = 7.7;
var A = [a,b,c];
var x,y = 17.9, z= 13.3;
x = A[0] + A[1] + A[2];
A[2] = y + z;
```

Array indices can be numbers, as in the above example, or identifiers, such as `x[i]`, or even expressions, such as `x[2*j+3]`, assuming the identifier or expression represents an integer value. If, for example, $j=2.5$, the index is $(2)(2.5)+3=8$, and this is an allowed index, assuming there are at least nine elements in x. However, if $j=2.3$, `x[2*j+3]` is undefined because $(2)(2.3)+3$ is not a whole number. For the same reason, `x[1]` is defined, but `x[4/3]` is not.

Unlike some other languages, JavaScript allows an array declaration to be overridden later in the script. Continuing with the above example, it is easy to add one or more additional elements:

```
A[3] = A[0] + A[1];
A[4] = 15.6;
```

Bearing in mind that arrays are objects, the current length of an array is contained in the length property. For the above example, A.length has a value of 5. The value of length is equal to the number of declared locations in the array. To look at it another way, length gives the value of the next available array index. This is true regardless of whether any or all of the array elements have been assigned values. For example, the statements

```
var A = new Array(5);
alert(A.length);
```

display a value of 5 despite the fact that the array A is empty.

A useful feature of JavaScript arrays is that not all elements must contain the same kind of data. Document 5.1 gives a simple example in which array elements are a mixture of numbers and text strings.

Document 5.1 (siteData.htm)

```
<html>
<head>
<title>Site Names</title>
<script>
  var siteID = ["Drexel",3,"home",101];
  var i;
  for (i=0; i<siteID.length; i++)
    document.write(i+", "+siteID[i]+"<br />");
</script>
</head>
<body>
</body>
</html>
```

```
0, Drexel
1, 3
2, home
3, 101
```

Document 5.1 shows how the length property of an array is used to determine the terminating condition in a for... loop to access all the elements of the array. Remember that the index value of the last element in an array is always one less than the total number of elements in the array. This is why the terminating condition is i<siteID.length and not i<=siteID.length. The latter choice won't produce an error message, but it is an inappropriate choice for termination because the element A[A.length] does not exist.

Because the number of elements in a JavaScript array can be expanded while a script is running, the code in Document 5.1 demonstrates the most reliable way to control a for loop when accessing arrays. Using the length property is usually preferable to using a numeric literal as the terminating condition for accessing an entire array.

Note that it is also possible to use a for... loop to access just parts of an array. For example,

```
for (i=1; i<A.length; i+=2) {
  ...
}
```

accesses just the even elements of A—the second, fourth, etc. (Starting the loop at an index of 1 first accesses the second element of A.)

This code:

```
for (i=A.length-1; i>=0; i--) {
  ...
}
```

accesses the elements of A backwards. A for... loop does not have to start at the first element of an array—it can start anywhere—and it can terminate anywhere up to and including the last element in an array. Attempts to access array elements that do not exist will produce unpredictable results. This code:

```
var a=Array(1,2,3,4,5,6,7);
for (var i=0; i<=7;i++) document.write(a[i]+' ');
```

produces this output:

1 2 3 4 5 6 7 undefined

because the upper limit of the loop counter is 7 (i<=7) instead of 6 (i<7) and the seventh element of array a does not exist.

Another interesting feature of JavaScript is that the assignment operator can be used to assign one array name to another. But, you need to be careful about interpreting this action. Consider this modification to Document 5.1:

```
var siteID = ["Drexel",3,"home",101];
var newSite = [];
var i;
newSite = siteID;
for (i=0; i<newSite.length; i++)
  alert(newSite[i]);
```

You could also have written var newSite = siteID;, which eliminates the need for the separate newSite = siteID; statement. A reasonable interpretation of such statements is that newSite is an independent copy of siteID, stored in different memory locations from siteID. *However, this is **not** true!* This code does not actually create an independent copy of siteID. Instead, both siteID and newSite are now identified with the *same* data in memory. This is because an array name doesn't literally represent the contents of the array. Rather, the name simply identifies a location in memory where the first element of the array is stored. If you assign one array name to another array name, all that happens is that the "box" in memory holding the array elements now has two "name tags" instead of just one. As a result, changes made to elements in either array name will affect elements in the other array, too.

The interpretation of an array name as a "pointer" to a location in memory helps to explain why the first element of an array is identified by an index of 0 rather than 1. The index is an offset—the "distance" from the memory location "pointed to" by the array name. For the very first element in an array, this offset is 0.

5.2
Some Operations on Arrays

There are some `Array` methods that are useful for the kinds of problems addressed in this book.

5.2.1
Manipulating Stacks and Queues

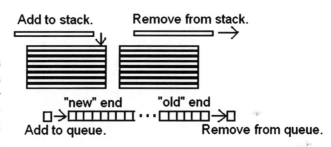

Stacks and **queues** are abstract data types familiar to computer science students. They are used to store and retrieve data in a particular way. A stack uses a last-in first-out (LIFO) data storage model. You can think of it as a stack of dinner plates. You put new dinner plates on the top of the stack, and when you retrieve a dinner plate, it always comes from the top of the stack. So, the last value added on a stack is the first value retrieved.

A queue uses a first-in first-out (FIFO) data storage model. It operates like a queue (a line, in American English) of people waiting. A new person joins the line at the end, and people leave the line according to who has been in line the longest. So, a value removed from the queue is always the "oldest" value.

JavaScript arrays provide a very friendly environment for implementing stacks and queues because arrays can be resized dynamically, while a script is running. However, the methods shown here for operating on stacks and queues may not work in all browsers. For example, they don't work in the internal browser supplied with the AceHTML freeware used for developing the code in this book.[1] You will just have to try the code to see if it works with your browser.

---

[1]You can specify an external browser to use from within AceHTML, to replace its internal browser.

The push() and pop() methods are used for managing stacks and queues. push() adds ("pushes") the specified arguments to the end of the target array (the "top" of the stack), in order, as you would for either a stack or a queue. The length property is automatically updated. The pop() method (no calling arguments) removes ("pops") the last (most recent) element from the array, returns the value of that element, and decreases length by 1, as you would for a stack.

The shift() and unshift() methods are similar to push() and pop(), except that they operate from the front (index 0) of an array. shift() (no arguments) removes the first element from the array (as you would for a queue), returns the value of that element, shifts the remaining elements down one position, and decreases length by 1. The unshift() method shifts current array elements up one position for each argument, inserts its arguments in order at the beginning of the array, and increases length by 1 for each argument. This action wouldn't be used with either a stack or queue—it amounts to allowing "line crashers." The use of these methods might seem backwards because unshift() adds elements and shift() removes them.

To summarize:

For a queue: use push() to add a new value at the end of the queue and shift() to remove the "oldest" value (the value at index 0).

For a stack: use push() to add a new value to the top of the stack and pop() to remove a value from the top of the stack.

Documents 5.2 illustrates how to use these methods to treat an array first as a stack and then as a queue.

Document 5.2 (stacksAndQueues.htm)

```html
<html>
<head>
<title>Stacks and Queues</title>
<script language="javascript" type="text/javascript">
  var a=[1,3,5,7], i;
// Treat the array like a stack.
  document.write("STACK:" + a + " length of a = " +
a.length+"<br />");
  a.push(11,12,13);
  document.write(a + " length of a = " + a.length
+"<br />");
  for (i=1; i<=3; i++) {
    a.pop();
    document.write(a + " length of a = " +
    a.length+"<br />");
  }
// Treat the array like a queue.
document.write("QUEUE:" + a + " length of a = " +
a.length+"<br />");
```

```
a.push(11,12,13);
document.write(a + " length of a = " + a.length
+"<br />");
for (i=1; i<=3; i++) {
a.shift();
document.write(a + " length of a = " + a.length
+"<br />");
}
</script>
</head>
<body></body>
</html>
```

Note the use of an entire array name in the document.write() parameter list. This automatically displays all the elements of the array, separated by commas.

STACK:1,3,5,7 length of a = 4
1,3,5,7,11,12,13 length of a = 7
1,3,5,7,11,12 length of a = 6
1,3,5,7,11 length of a = 5
1,3,5,7 length of a = 4
QUEUE:1,3,5,7 length of a = 4
1,3,5,7,11,12,13 length of a = 7
3,5,7,11,12,13 length of a = 6
5,7,11,12,13 length of a = 5
7,11,12,13 length of a = 4

5.2.2
Sorting

Sorting array elements in ascending or descending order is a fundamental computing task. However, it can be challenging to write efficient sorting algorithms. (Understanding and developing sorting algorithms is a standard topic in basic computer science courses.) Fortunately, JavaScript has an Array method, sort(), that will operate on arrays without much work on your part. Document 5.3 shows how to use this method to sort an array in ascending order. Unfortunately, as you will see, this code does not produce the expected result!

Document 5.3 (sort.htm)

```
<html>
<head>
<title>Sorting Arrays</title>
<script language="javascript" type="text/javascript">
var a=[7,5,13,3];
document.write(a + " length of a = " + a.length+"<br />");
a.sort();
document.write(a + " length of a = " + a.length+"<br />");
</script>
</head>
<body>
  </body>
</html>
```

7,5,13,3 length of a = 4
13,3,5,7 length of a = 4

The contents of the array are displayed before and after application of the sort()
method. The array is clearly not sorted, as 13 is not less than 3! It is apparent that the
sort() method has performed a "lexical" sort based on the order of characters in the
ASCII character sequence even when the characters represent numbers; the character "1"
comes before the character "3" in this sequence in the same sense that "a" comes before
"c" in the dictionary, and therefore, "ac" comes before "c." This result would be easier to
understand if the values from the array came from a prompt() or from the input fields
of a form because it has already been demonstrated that "numbers" are treated like strings
of characters. However, for sorting arrays of user-defined numbers, this behavior is less
obvious and is clearly a potential disaster.

The sort() method can cause problems even with text. If, for example, you replace
the array declaration with

```
var a=["zena","David","apple","pie"];
```

the result is still probably not what you
intended. Uppercase letters come
before lowercase letters in the standard ASCII character sequence, so
"David" is still "less than" "apple."

zena,David,apple,pie length of a = 4
David,apple,pie,zena length of a = 4

The behavior of the sort() method constitutes a serious implementation problem. If
you are sorting just text, you could consider using the toUpperCase() or toLower-
Case() methods to convert all of the letters to either uppercase or lowercase letters prior
to applying the sort() method, but this isn't a very satisfying solution in general.
A more comprehensive solution is to supply the sort() method with your own code for
deciding whether one item is larger than, smaller than, or equal to another item in an array.
This solution will be addressed in Chap. 6.

5.3
More about Array Methods

Several array methods and the length property have been described in previous sections
in the context of stacks and queues. Table 5.1 summarizes these and some other array
methods.

The reverse() method could be used to change the order in a sorted array from
ascending to descending, for example. The join() method, which converts array elements into a string with user-selected separator characters, is paired with the string object's
split() method, which converts a delimited string of values into an array of elements.
The toString() method converts array elements into a string, too, but the separator
character is always a comma. slice() can be used to create a new array from a subset
of contiguous elements in the original array.

Table 5.1 Array methods

Method Description	Usage
`concat()`	`C=A.concat(B);`
Array C contains the concatenation of arrays A and B.	
`join()`	`B=A.join(".")`
B is a string created from the elements of A, separated by periods. If the separator character is omitted, a comma is used as the default separator. See also the string method `split(ch,n)`, which splits the first n values in a string of values separated by the `ch` character into an array. If `ch` is omitted, the entire string is returned as a one-element array. If `ch` is empty (`""`) the string is split between each character. If n is omitted, the entire string will be split.	
`pop()`	`A[0]=17;A[1]=-3; A[2]=4; B=A.pop();`
Removes the last element from an array. B is a scalar (not an array) and its value is 4. A now has a length of 2 instead of 3. The output from `A.pop()` does not have to be assigned to a variable.	
`push()`	`A[0]=17;A[1]=-3; A[2]=4; B=A.push(14,13);`
Adds elements to the end of an array. B is a scalar equal to the new length of A (5). The elements of A are now 17, -3, 4, 14, and 13. The output of `A.push()` does not have to be assigned to a variable.	
`reverse()`	`A.reverse;`
Reverses the order of the elements in A.	
`shift()`	`A[0]=17;A[1]=-3; A[2]=4; B=A.shift();`
Removes the first element from A. B has a value of 17. The output from `A.shirt()` does not have to be assigned to a variable.	
`slice()`	`A[0]=17;A[1]=-3;A[2]=4;A[3]=14;A[4]=13;`
	`var B=Array(); B=A.slice(2,4);`
`slice(a,b)` returns elements of its array starting at position a and stopping before the element at position b. The elements of B are 4 and 14.	
`sort()`	`A.sort(compare);`
Sorts elements of an array, with caveats as discussed in Sect. 5.2.2 and later in Chap. 6.	
`toString()`	`B=A.toString();`
B is a comma-separated string constructed from the elements of A, similar to `join()` but without optional separators.	
`unshift()`	`A[0]=17;A[1]=-3;A[2]=4; B=A.unshift(14,13);`
Adds elements to the beginning of an array. B is a scalar equal to the new length of A (5). The elements of A are now 14, 13, 17, -3, 4. (Note the order of the inserted elements.) The output of `A.unshift()` does not have to be assigned to a variable.	

5.4
Creating Two-Dimensional Arrays

Document 5.1 showed how to store information about an observing site in a one-dimensional array. It would be more useful to have an array structure that allows storing information about multiple sites—perhaps each site's ID, longitude, latitude, and elevation. Table 5.2 gives some sample data.

5

Table 5.2 Site information to be stored in an array

Site ID	Latitude	Longitude	Elevation (m)
Drexel	39.955	−75.188	10
Home	40.178	−75.333	140
North Carolina	35.452	−81.022	246
Argentina	−34.617	−58.367	30
Netherlands	52.382	4.933	−1

A logical way to store these data is in some array equivalent of this row-and-column table. This array structure would need two indices—one to refer to the row and another to refer to the column. Document 5.4 shows one way to do this.

Document 5.4 (TwoDArray.htm)

```
<html>
<head>
<title>Two-D arrays</title>
<script language="javascript" type="text/javascript">
var siteID = new Array();
siteID[0]=new Array("Drexel",39.955,-75.188,10.);
siteID[1]=new Array("home",40.178,-75.333,140.);
siteID[2]=new Array("NC",35.452,-81.022,246);
siteID[3]=new Array("Argentina",-34.617,-58.37,30.);
siteID[4]=new Array("Netherlands",52.382,4.933,-1);
var r,c,n_rows=siteID.length,n_cols=siteID[0].length;
for (r=0; r<n_rows; r++) {
  document.write(siteID[r][0]);
  for (c=1; c<n_cols; c++) {
    document.write(", "+siteID[r][c]);
  }
  document.write("<br />");
}
</script>
</head>
<body>
</body>
</html>
```

```
Drexel, 39.955, -75.188, 10
home, 40.178, -75.333, 140
NC, 35.452, -81.022, 246
Argentina, -34.617, -58.37, 30
Netherlands, 52.382, 4.933, -1
```

The siteID array consists of an array of arrays. That is, each element of siteID is an array. The nested for... loops are constructed so that the elements of the array are printed row-by-row, with the elements in each row separated by a comma and a line break at the end of each row. Note the use of double square bracket notation `[r][c]` to access the individual "cells" in the two-dimensional table.

In some cases it might be helpful to have the columns identified by name rather than by an index and Document 5.5 shows how this can be done. This code will make more sense after reading Chap. 6, which deals with the topic of JavaScript functions. Basically, each element of the array `siteID` is created as an object with properties, using the `new` keyword to reference a user-defined array constructor, `function IDArray()`. This function creates properties for the elements of `siteID`, with names that are appropriate for the values passed as arguments.

Document 5.5 (TwoDArray_2.htm)

```
<html>
<head>
<html>
<head>
<title>"Multidimensional" arrays</title>
<script language="javascript" type="text/javascript">
var siteID = new Array();
function IDArray(ID,lat,lon,elev) {
   this.ID=ID;
   this.lat=lat;
   this.lon=lon;
   this.elev=elev;
}
siteID[0]=new IDArray("Drexel",39.955,-75.188,10.);
siteID[1]=new IDArray("home",40.178,-75.333,140.);
siteID[2]=new IDArray("NC",35.452,-81.022,246);
siteID[3]=new IDArray("Argentina",-34.617,-58.37,30.);
siteID[4]=new IDArray("Netherlands",52.382,4.933,-1);

var i;
for (i=0; i<siteID.length; i++) {
      document.write(siteID[i].ID+
      ", "+siteID[i].lat+", "+siteID[i].lon+",
      "+siteID[i].elev+"<br />");
}
</script>
</head>
<body>
</body>
</html>
```

The output is the same as for Document 5.4. The "`this`" in `this.ID=ID;` is interpreted as defining a property of "this" array object. The output from this code is the same

5

as for Document 5.4. It is convenient to use the same names both as "placeholders" for the arguments and for the property names themselves. However, this is *just* a convenience. Rewriting function IDArray() as

```
function IDArray(a,b,c,d) {
  this.ID=a; this.lat=b; this.lon=c; this.elev=d;
  ...
}
```

does not change the results.

5.5
Using Arrays to Access the Contents of Forms

5.5.1
Accessing Values of type="text" Fields

Consider this generic problem: A form stores several values in <input> fields in a table. You want the last row of the table to hold the sum of all the previous values. Based on previous material, you can give each form field a name: v1, v2, v3, etc. Then, you can sum the values:

```
sum.value =
  parseFloat(v1.value)+parseFloat(v2.value)+ ...
```

This is not a very satisfying solution, if for no other reason than the fact that large tables will require a *lot* of typing.

Fortunately, there is a more elegant alternative. When you create an HTML form, all the elements are automatically stored in an array called elements. You can access the contents of this array just as you would the contents of any other array. Consider the following very simple document.

Document 5.6 (formArray.htm)

```
<html>
<head>
<title>Using the elements[] array to access values in forms.
</title>
</head>
<body>
<form name="myform">
  A[0]<input type="text" value="3" /><br />
  A[1]<input type="text" value="2" /><br />
</form>
```

```
<script language="javascript" type="text/javascript">
for(var i=0; i<document.myform.elements.length; i++) {
   document.write("A["+i+"] =
"+document.myform.elements[i].value+"<br />");
}
</script>
</body>
</html>
```

```
A[0] 3
A[1] 2

A[0] = 3
A[1] = 2
```

First of all, note that these form fields haven't been given names in the <input /> tags. They *could* have names, but the point here is to avoid having to assign many different field names to something that can be treated as a unit, under a single name. Not surprisingly, the elements of the elements array are assigned, starting with index 0, in the order in which they appear in the form.

Previously, forms themselves haven't been given names. However, it is entirely possible that you might wish to have more than one group of form fields in a document, each of which would have its own elements array and could be accessed through its own name. Hence, the use of the name attribute in the form tag in Document 5.6. In this example, the use of "document" in, for example,

```
document.myform.elements[i].value;
```

is optional.

Document 5.7 shows a solution to the generic problem given at the beginning of this section.

Document 5.7 (sumForm.htm)

```
<html>
<head>
<title>Sum a column of values</title>
</head>
<body>
<form name="sumform">
   <input type="text" value="3.3" /><br />
   <input type="text" value="3.9" /><br />
   <input type="text" value="7.1" /><br />
Here is the sum of all the values.<br />
   <input type="text" name="sum" value="0"
      /><br />
</form>
<script language="javascript" type="text/javascript">
        var sum=0;
        for (var i=0;
```

```
i<(sumform.elements.length-1);
i++)
sum+=parseFloat(sumform.
elements[i].value);
sumform.elements[sumform.
elements.length-1].value=sum;
</script>
</body>
</html>
```

3.3
3.9
7.1

Here is the sum of all the values.

14.299999999999999

The terminating condition on the for... loop is

```
i<(sumform.elements.length-1)
```

rather than

```
i<sumform.elements.length
```

because the last element in the elements array does not contain one of the values to be summed.

With multiple columns in a table, you will need to implement the for... loop appropriately. For example, in a form that should be treated as two columns, the index values 0, 2, 4, ... will access the left column and 1, 3, 5, ... will access the right column. Document 5.8 gives an example.

Document 5.8 (sumForm2.htm)

```
<html>
<head>
<title>Sum a column of values</title>
</head>
<body>
<form name="sumform">
<table border>
  <tr><td><input type="text" value="Value 1" /></td>
  <td><input type="text" value="3.3" /></td></tr>
  <tr><td><input type="text" value="Value 2" /></td>
  <td><input type="text" value="3.9" /></td></tr>
  <tr><td><input type="text" value="Value 3" /></td>
  <td><input type="text" value="7.1" /></td></tr>
</table>
Here is the sum of all the values.<br />
  <input type="text" name="sum" value="0"
    /><br />
</form>
```

```
<script language="javascript" type="text/javascript">
  var sum=0;
  for (var i=1; i<(sumform.elements.length-1); i+=2)
    sum+=parseFloat(sumform.elements[i].value);
  sumform.elements[sumform.elements.length-1].value=sum;
</script>
</body>
</html>
```

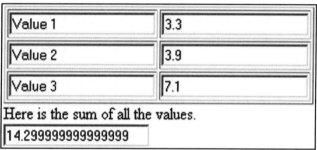

Document 5.8 sums the right hand column of values. Although the output from Document 5.8 looks like a table that could be represented by a two-dimensional array, that is not the case here. The input fields are still numbered consecutively, left to right and top to bottom, in the order in which they appear. Also, remember that if the input fields containing the values you wish to process don't appear first inside the <form>...</form> tag, then the starting position will need to be offset appropriately.

5.5.2
Accessing type="radio" and type="checkbox" Fields

Consider this fragment from an HTML document.

```
Employee is punctual:
  Y <input type="radio" name="punctual" value="Y"
    checked />     
  N <input type="radio" name="punctual" value="N"
    /><br />
```

This code defines a type="radio" field with two possible values. If you look at the elements array associated with the form containing this fragment, each field will be stored as a separate element in the elements array. However, what you really want to know is which button in the "punctual" group has been pressed. Similarly, with a group of type="checkbox" fields, you want to know which choices are selected. Conveniently, each group of radio buttons or checkboxes is associated with its own array, assigned the name you have provided for that group. Document 5.9 provides some examples of how to use arrays to access the contents of radio buttons and checkboxes.

Document 5.9 (buttonAccess.htm)

```html
<html>
<head>
<title>Accessing Radio Buttons and Checkboxes</title>
</head>
<body>
Access contents of form fields...<br />
<form>
Give name: <input type="text" name="Ename" size="15"
value="Mr. Bland" /><br />
Employee is punctual:
Y <input type="radio" name="punctual" value="Y"
    checked />     
N <input type="radio" name="punctual" value="N" /><br />
Employee likes these animals:
Dogs <input type="checkbox" name="animals" value="dogs" />
Cats <input type="checkbox" name="animals" value="cats"
    checked />
Boa constrictors <input type="checkbox" name="animals"
    value="boas" checked /><br />
<input type="button"
    value="Check here to examine form contents."
  onclick="howMany.value=elements.length;
    contents.value=elements[parseFloat(n.value)].value;
      var i;
      if (punctual[0].checked)
          alert(Ename.value+' is always on time.');
      else
          alert(Ename.value+' is always late.');
      for (i=0; i<animals.length; i++) {
        if (animals[i].checked) alert(Ename.value+
          ' likes '+animals[i].value);
      }; " /><br />
# elements: <input type="text" name="howMany"
    value="0" /><br />
Which one (0 to # elements - 1)? <input type="text" name="n"
    value="1" />
Contents: <input type="text" name="contents"
    value="--" /><br />
</form>
</body>
</html>
```

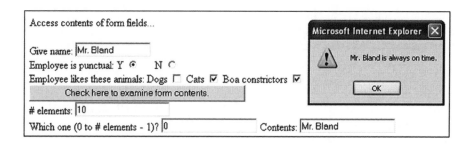

The output shows the screen after the button box has been clicked and the first `alert()` box is displayed.

5.5.3
Accessing Multiple Options Chosen in `<select>` Tags

Previously, the `select` tag used to create pull-down lists has allowed selecting only one value from the list. However, it is also possible to select multiple values from a list of options. Document 5.10 shows how to extract the value or values selected from a pull-down list, using the `options` array that is automatically generated for these lists.

Document 5.10 (`chooseSelect.htm`)

```
<html>
<head>
<title>Using values from a select list</title>
<script language="JavaScript" type="text/javascript" >
  function whichSelected(list) {
    var n=list.length;
      var i;
      var s="";
      for (i=0; i<n; i++) {
        if (list.options[i].selected)
            s = s+" "+list.options[i].value;
    }
      return s;
  }
</script>
</head>
<body >
<h2>Shows how to access values from a <font
face="courier">&lt;select&gt;</font> tag.</h2>
```

5

```
<h3>Only one item can be chosen...</h3>
  <select name="unique" size="3">
    <option value="unique1" selected>unique 1</option>
    <option value="unique2" >unique 2</option>
    <option value="unique3" >unique 3</option>
</select><br />
Click in this field to see what you have chosen: <input
type="text" name="selectedUnique"
onfocus="selectedUnique.value =
  unique.options[unique.selectedIndex].value ;" /><br />
<h3>Multiple items can be chosen...</h3>
Hold down <font face="Arial"><b>Shift</b></font> or
<font face="Arial"><b>Ctrl</b></font>
key to make multiple selections.<br />
<select name="multiple" size="3" multiple>
  <option value="multiple1" selected>multiple 1</option>
  <option value="multiple2">multiple 2</option>
  <option value="multiple3" >multiple 3</option>
</select><br />
      Click on this field to see what you have chosen:
<input size="40" type="text" name="selectedMultiple"
  onfocus="selectedMultiple.value=whichSelected(multiple);"
/><br />
</body>
</html>
```

Accessing selected values from a `<select>` tag.

Only one item can be chosen...

> unique 1
> unique 2
> unique 3

Click in this field to see what you have chosen: `unique1`

Multiple items can be chosen...

Hold down **Shift** or **Ctrl** key to make multiple selections.

> multiple 1
> multiple 2
> multiple 3

Click on this field to see what you have chosen: `multiple1, multiple2, multiple3`

In the first case illustrated in Document 5.10, where only one item can be selected, the selected item in the unique list is obtained from the options array created by JavaScript, using the selectedIndex property of the select element:

```
unique.options[unique.selectedIndex].value
```

The shaded line in Document 5.10 shows how to define a multiple-choice pull-down list—by including the `multiple` attribute. These choices can be identified, again by using the `options` array. In this case, a function has been written to accomplish this task, using code like this to search through all the elements of `options` to find `selected` elements:

```
if (list.options[i].selected)…
```

JavaScript functions will be discussed in detail in Chap. 6.

5.6
Hiding the Contents of a JavaScript Script

Basic security might seem to be the most obvious reason to hide part or all of a script. However, a better reason in the JavaScript context is to make it easy to modify or update part of a script without disturbing the HTML document of which it is a part; this is especially useful if the same script is used in several different HTML documents.

To do this, it is possible to save JavaScript code in a separate file that is referenced in an HTML document. Note that this does not overcome the limitation that a script is always loaded into a client computer when the HTML document containing the script is accessed. All that actually happens is that the "hidden" file is sent to the client computer and inserted into the script when the script is executed. Although this file isn't visible when the HTML document source is viewed from a browser, it is certainly a mistake to assume that this provides any serious security protection for the hidden file.

Based on the discussion of arrays in the previous section, another obvious use for a hidden file is to hold data that will be used to build an array within a script. If these data are stored in a separate file, you can then keep the data up-to-date by editing just the data file rather than an entire HTML document. Document 5.11 is a version of Document 5.4 in which the ID data are stored in a separate file.

Arrays are used to store values in memory and manipulate them while a program is running. With traditional programming languages, data can be stored in a file that is "loaded" into memory to be read from and written to when needed. In the same way, a program can create new data to be stored permanently in a file that exists externally from the program itself.

However, this model does not work with HTML/JavaScript. Why not? Remember that a JavaScript script is loaded into a client computer when a Web page is accessed. The client computer has access only to the contents of this script. Hence, it is not possible to access data from a file that remains behind on the server computer. This limits the usefulness of JavaScript arrays for accessing large amounts of data stored in a central location. This restriction applies even when JavaScript is used locally on your own computer, because JavaScript simply does not provide the tools for accessing or creating external data files even when they reside physically on the same computer as the script that is running.

5

The alternative is to send along all the required data as part of the script. This is a workable solution for small amounts of data that do not need to be protected in a secure environment. This solution works for both online and local applications of JavaScript. In a local environment, it is even reasonable to store large amounts of data, although there are some formatting issues for storing data. Unlike other languages, JavaScript cannot simply read data stored in a specified text format. Instead, as shown in Document 5.11, the data should be stored as part of an array definition.

Document 5.11 (siteData4.htm)

```
<html>
<head>
<title>"Multidimensional" arrays</title>
<script language="javascript" src="siteData.dat">
// This file defines the site characteristics.
</script>
<script language="javascript" type="text/javascript">
var i;
for (i=0; i<siteID.length; i++) {
      document.write(siteID[i].ID+
      ", "+siteID[i].lat+", "+siteID[i].lon+",
      "+siteID[i].elev+
      "<br />");
}
</script>
</head>
<body>
</body>
</html>
```

Data file siteData.dat for siteData4.htm:

```
var siteID = new Array();
function IDArray(ID,lat,lon,elev) {
  this.ID=ID;
  this.lat=lat;
  this.lon=lon;
  this.elev=elev;
}
siteID[0]=new IDArray("Drexel",39.955,-75.188,10);
siteID[1]=new IDArray("home",40.178,-75.333,140);
siteID[2]=new IDArray("NC",35.452,-81.022,246);
siteID[3]=new IDArray("Argentina",-34.617,-58.367,30);
siteID[4]=new IDArray("Netherlands",52.382,4.933,-1);
```

The file `site_data.dat` is referenced within its own `script` element:

```
<script language="javascript" src="site_data.dat">
</script>
```

It is more typical to give such a "hidden" file a `.js` (for JavaScript) extension, but it is not required. In this case, the `.dat` extension seemed to more accurately reflect the purpose of the file.

The `siteData.dat` file doesn't hold just the raw site ID information. Rather, it holds the values plus all the code required to define an array holding this information. This is convenient approach that minimizes the number of separate `<script>` ... `</script>` elements required. Because JavaScript arrays are expandable while a script is running, there is no restriction on how many new sites can be added to the file or, for that matter, on how many sites can be removed.

5.7
More Examples

5.7.1
Checking IDs and Passwords

Here is a typical problem that involves comparing the contents of a form field against a set of predetermined values.

> Provide a form that asks a user for a password. Check their entry against a list of passwords and provide an appropriate message depending on whether the password is valid or not. (It's not necessary to take any action other than printing an appropriate message.)

Document 5.12 provides a "solution" to this problem, but without addressing the problem of password security at all. In fact, this example just serves as a reminder that *there is no security associated with anything sent as part of a JavaScript script!* So, this is just a demonstration of how to search through a list of items to see if a user-specified item is present, rather than an application you would want to use to safeguard information.

Document 5.12 (`password1.htm`)

```
<html>
<head>
<title>Check a password</title>
<script language="javascript" type="text/javascript">
var PWArray=new Array();
PWArray[0]="mypass";
PWArray[1]="yourpass";
```

```
</script>
</head>
<body>
<form>
Enter your password: <input type="password" name="PW"
value=""
onchange="var found=false; result.value='not OK';
  for (var i=0; i<PWArray.length; i++)
    if (PW.value == PWArray[i]) {
      found=true;
      result.value='OK';
    } " /><br />
(Tab to or click on this box to check your password.)<br />
<input type="text" name="result"
value="Click to check password." />
</form>
</body>
</html>
```

Enter your password: ●●●●●●
(Tab to or click on this box to check your password.)
OK

In general, it would make more sense to store the IDs and passwords in a separate .js file, as described in Sect. 5.6.

5.7.2
Magic Squares

Define a 3×3 two-dimensional array of integers, with values 1–9, and display the contents row-by-row. The integer values should be arranged so they form a "magic square," defined as an $n \times n$ square matrix of integers, with values 1 through n^2, each of which appears once and only once, arranged so that each row and column, and each main diagonal, all add to the same value. It can be shown that for a matrix of size $n \times n$, this value is $n(n^2+1)/2$. For a 3×3 matrix, the value is 15.

Here is some JavaScript code for constructing such a matrix, which can be addressed by row and column indices:

Document 5.13 (magicSquare.htm)

```
<html>
<head>
<title>magic Square</title>
<script language="javascript" type="text/javascript">
```

```
var a=[[8,1,6],[3,5,7],[4,9,2]];
var r,c; //alert(a[0].length);
for (r=0; r<a.length; r++) {
      for (c=0; c<a[0].length; c++)
            document.write(a[r][c]+" ");
      document.write("<br />");
   }
</script>
</head>
<body>
</body>
</html>
```

```
8 1 6
3 5 7
4 9 2
```

The shaded line of code in Document 5.13 demonstrates an alternate way of defining an array of arrays—compare this with Document 5.4, for example. The number of rows can be different from the number of columns. As is true for all JavaScript arrays, there is no restriction on the nature of the contents of the individual "cells" in this table. The square bracket notation is not limited just to an array of arrays, but an "array of arrays of arrays" is already conceptually unwieldy.

It is left as an exercise to write appropriate code for adding up the rows, columns, and diagonals of a square matrix to determine whether the matrix forms a magic square.

JavaScript Functions

6

Abstract Chapter 6 introduces the important concept of functions in programming and shows how to integrate documents, forms, JavaScript, and functions to create a complete HTML/JavaScript problem-solving environment.

6.1
The Purpose of Functions in Programming

Functions are self-contained code modules which accept input, perform operations on that input, and return one or more results. The built-in JavaScript methods previously discussed in Chap. 4 are examples of functions. For example, the `Math.sin()` method accepts a single value as input—an angle expressed in radians—and returns the sine of that value. User-defined functions also accept input, often more than one value, and return a value. They are an important concept in any programming language. Here are three reasons to use functions:

1. *Organizing solutions to computational problems*
   A problem to be solved on a computer often consists of several related parts, in which output from one part is used as input to the next part. Functions provide a mechanism for creating a code structure that reflects the nature of this kind of problem. By organizing code into a series of self-contained modules, and by controlling the flow of information among these modules, the problem can be solved in a logical fashion, one part at a time. Basically, this is a matter of separating large problems into smaller and more manageable parts.

2. *Creating reusable code*
   Often, identical calculations must be done several times within a program, but with different values. Functions allow you to write code to perform the calculations just once, using variable names as "placeholders" that will represent actual values when the function is used. Once a function has been written and tested, it can be used in other programs, too, allowing you to create a library of useful calculations. JavaScript's `Math` method is an example of a function library that has already been written for you.

3. *Sharing authorship of large programming projects*
   Large programming projects often involve more than one person. When a project is broken down into several smaller tasks, individual programmers can work independently

D.R. Brooks, *Guide to HTML, JavaScript and PHP: For Scientists and Engineers*,   **135**
DOI 10.1007/978-0-85729-449-4_6, © Springer-Verlag London Limited 2011

and then collaborate to assemble the finished product. Without the separation of tasks made possible by functions, this kind of collaborative approach would not be practical.

The sketch shows schematically how this task-based approach works. Output from each task serves as input to the next task until the solution is reached. Some problems might not have such a "linear" solution structure, but in any case a function-based approach makes it easier to organize a solution to a large problem.

In general, functions are "called" (or "invoked," in the same sense as previously described for object methods) by passing values from a calling program (or another function) to the function. The function executes some operations and then returns a result.

In addition to providing a mechanism for modularizing the solution to a problem, functions play an important role in program design. The syntax of function implementation forces a programmer (or, for large projects, groups of programmers) to think carefully about a problem and its solution: "What information is required to complete this task? What information is provided when the task is completed? What steps are required to solve the problem? What information must be provided by the user of a program? Can the problem be divided into smaller related parts? How does each part relate to the others? Are the specified inputs and outputs for each part consistent with the relationships among the parts?" Once these questions are answered, the structure of a program should be clear. Often, working out an appropriate function structure is the hardest part of solving a large computational problem.

6.2
Defining JavaScript Functions

Functions are essential for JavaScript programming. In fact, a large portion of all JavaScript code is written as functions called from HTML documents. One of JavaScript's first applications was to use functions to check values entered in forms. Inappropriate values are flagged and a warning message is displayed. Forms can be used in conjunction with functions for many kinds of calculations, as will be done throughout this chapter.

It is important to understand how information is provided to and extracted from a function. The basic "mental model" shown in the sketch is applicable to JavaScript and many other languages. A function resides in an isolated subset of computer memory. Communications with the contents of this space are strictly controlled and limited to specific pathways. The box represents the computer memory set aside for the function. This space and the operations carried out within it are not visible to the rest of a script, including to other functions within that

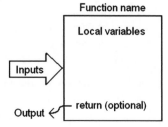

script. Access to the function's memory space is available along only two paths. The large arrow represents the input pathway to the function, through its **parameter list**. The small arrow represents a single output from the function, generated as a result of a `return` statement.

Here is the syntax for a generic function.

```
function doSomething(input1,input2,input3,...) {
    var local1,local2,local3,... outputName;
    local1 = {an expression using one or more inputs...};
    local2 =
        {an expression using one or more inputs and (optionally) local1...};
    local3 =
        {an expression using one or more inputs and (optionally) local1
         and local2...};
    {Do some calculations here with some combination of parameters
        and local variables...};
    return outputName; // or some other value
}
```

The `function` keyword is required at the beginning of every function. Every function must have a user-provided name, `doSomething` in this generic example. Spaces between parts of a function name are not allowed, but underlines are. So, for example, you could name the function `do_something`, but not `do something` (because `do something` is interpreted as two tokens rather than one). JavaScript function names are case-sensitive. As in all aspects of programming, it will be helpful in your own work to settle upon a function-naming convention and use it consistently.

The parameter list contains the names of one or more input parameters, separated by commas and enclosed in parentheses. These names are placeholders for input values passed to the function when it is called. Occasionally, a function will have no values in its parameter list. However, parentheses are still required.

All the code in a function constitutes a statement block, enclosed in right and left curly brackets. The opening bracket can appear either at the end of the `function()` line or on the next line. Your code will be more easily readable if you adopt a consistent style of indenting the body of the code, as shown in the example.

Within the function, one or more **local variables** can be defined in statements that begin with the `var` keyword. Local variables may not be required for some calculations, but code may be clearer if the results of intermediate calculations are stored in separate variables. In any event, the required calculations are done using appropriate combinations of the input parameters and local variables. The general programming rule that a variable should never be used until it has first been assigned a value applies equally to local variables in functions. To put it another way, a local variable should never appear on the right-hand side of an assignment operator until it has first appeared on the left.

It is important to understand that the local variables defined within a function are invisible to the rest of your script, including to other functions. This means that you can select local variable names, assign values, and change those values without regard to what

6

happens in other functions and elsewhere in a script, even when the same variable name is used elsewhere.

The result of calculations performed in a function is returned to the place from which the function was called by using the `return` keyword in a statement. Only one `return` statement can be executed in a function. A function can have more than one `return` statement, perhaps in various possible branches of an `if...` construct, but only one of these can actually be executed. The value to be returned can be declared as a local variable, too, as shown in the shaded items in the code above, but it is also possible to return the result of a calculation without first assigning that result to a variable name.

There are two critical points about functions:

> **The parameter list is a one way path for input only. Information can be passed *in* to the function along this path, but no information passes *out* along this path.**

> **The `return` statement is a one way path for a single value flowing *out* of the function.**

Successful programming requires accurate mental pictures of how programming paradigms work. The function model shown here, including the restricted input/output paths and the protected nature of locally declared variables, is one of the most important paradigms in all of programming. It makes it possible to separate large and complex computational problems into a series of smaller (and hopefully simpler) problems, linked through a series of function interfaces. This modularization makes even small scripts easier to write, and it also makes it practical for large programming projects to be written, tested, and maintained by more than one person.

6.3
Using JavaScript Functions with HTML Forms

In a sense, all the previous material in this book has been directed toward this section. Why? Because the basic problem-solving model for the HTML/JavaScript environment is to use JavaScript functions together with forms in HTML documents.

The function model described in the preceding section would be very simple except for the fact that, in JavaScript, a value passed to a function through a parameter list can be one of three distinctly different things: a value (a character string or number), a form field, or an entire form. These are not interchangeable, and each must be treated differently. In order to explain these differences, consider the simple problem of calculating the area of a circle. Given a radius r:

$$\text{Area} = \pi r^2$$

Recall that `prompt()` and `alert()` and `document.write()` methods provided an I/O interface for these kinds of calculations in Chap. 4. Later in Chap. 4, some JavaScript calculations were initiated as a result of using the `onclick` event handler in a `button` field. These approaches were acceptable at the time, but they are too limited to be good solutions for more complex problems. The following detailed analysis of several approaches to implementing this simple calculation in a function may seem tedious and unnecessary because the problem itself is so simple, but a thorough understanding of the analysis is absolutely essential to successful JavaScript programming.

6.3.1
Passing Numerical Values to a Function

A JavaScript function to solve the problem of calculating the area of a circle is:

```
function getArea(r) {
        return Math.PI*r*r;
}
```

The parameter `r` is assumed to be a number representing the radius of a circle. The calculation is straightforward, using the `PI` property of the `Math` object (`Math.PI`). There is no exponential operator in JavaScript (r^2 can't be represented as `r^2` as it could in a spreadsheet, for example), so `r` is just multiplied by itself.

It seems clear that you should be able to pass a value of the radius from a form field to `getArea()`. However, previous examples in Chap. 4 have provided ample evidence that caution is required! Consider this `input` element appearing within a form:

```
<form>
<input type="text" name="radius" maxlength ="6"
size="6" value="-99" />
...
```

What "value" can be passed from this form to the function? Recall that the *name* of the field, `radius` in this case, is not the same as the *value* associated with this field. In this context, it is important to make sure that a function receiving information through its input parameter list understands how to interpret that input. Consider Document 6.1, which shows one way pass information. Passing `radius` to `getArea` will *not* produce the desired result, nor will `radius.value`. Why not? Because `radius` is only the "value" of the `name` attribute, and `radius.value` is still only a character representation of the required numerical input.

You should not be surprised to learn that the calling argument to `function getArea()` should be `parseFloat(radius.value)`, as shown in Document 6.1.

6

Document 6.1 (`circle1.htm`)

```html
<html>
<head>
<title>Circle Area (1)</title>
<script language="javascript" type ="text/javascript">
        function getArea(r) {
          return Math.PI*r*r;
        }
</script>
</head>
<body>
<h1>Circle Area (1)</h1>
<p>
<form>
  Enter radius, then press tab key or click on "area"
box.<br />
  radius (cm):
  <input type="text" name="radius" size="6" maxlength="7"
  value="-99",
  onblur = "area.value=getArea(parseFloat(radius.value));">
  area (cm<sup>2</sup>):
  <input type="text" name="area" size="6" maxlength="7"
value="-99">
</form>
</body>
</html>
```

Circle Area (1)

Enter radius, then press tab key or click on "area" box.

radius (cm): 3   area (cm^2): 28.274333

In Document 6.1, function `getArea(r)` expects a numerical value equal to the radius of the circle. The name of the function is appropriate to its purpose and is a name unlikely to be associated with a variable name. The shaded line of code uses the `onblur` event handler to "call" the function when the user clicks elsewhere on the document or presses the Tab key. The value passed to function `getArea(r)` is `parseFloat(radius.value)`, which converts the value of the radius field from a string to a number. Note that, in this case, the `parseFloat()` is not actually required because JavaScript will perform an appropriate type conversion, but it is much better style to perform an explicit type conversion whenever string values need to be interpreted as numbers.

The approach taken in Document 6.1 is called "pass by value." Another option is to "pass by name." The field name is provided as input to the function, which then must do the job of converting the value attribute to a number, as shown in Document 6.2.

Document 6.2 (circle2.htm)

```html
<html>
<head>
<title>Circle Area (2)</title>
<script language="javascript" type ="text/javascript">
   function getArea(r) {
     var radius=parseFloat(r.value);
     return Math.PI*radius*radius;
   }
</script>
</head>
<body>
<h1>Circle Area (1)</h1>
<p>
<form>
  Enter radius, then press tab key or click on "area"
box.<br />
   radius (cm):
   <input type="text" name="radius" size="6" maxlength="7"
   value="-99", onblur = "area.value=getArea(radius);">
   area (cm<sup>2</sup>):
   <input type="text" name="area" size="6" maxlength="7"
value="-99">
</form>
</body></html>
```

There is no difference in the results produced by these two approaches, and either is acceptable as long as you are careful not to confuse a field *name* with its *value*. If you pass something inappropriate to a function, such as a string value that isn't converted to a numerical value, then the function will generate a syntax error or return a result of NaN, for "not a number."

There is another subtlety worth noting about using functions with forms. Consider this modification of Document 6.1:

```html
<script language="javascript" type="text/javascript">
   // UNACCEPTABLE CHOICE FOR FUNCTION NAME!
   function area(r) {
     return Math.PI*r*r;
   }
</script>
...
<form>
```

```
Enter radius, then press tab key or click on "area"
    box.<br />
  radius (cm):
  <input type="text" name="radius" size="6"
    maxlength="7" value="-99",
    onblur =
"area.value=area(parseFloat(radius.value));" />
  area (cm<sup>2</sup>):
  <input type="text" name="area" size="6"
    maxlength="7" value="-99" />
...
```

In this code, the function name, area, is the same as a field name in the form. Although one could envision a programming environment in which this conflict could be resolved based on the context, this code will simply not work in JavaScript. So,

> **The names of functions should never be the same as the names of form** input **fields.**

6.3.2
Using Entire Forms as Input

There is yet another way to write a function that calculates the area of a circle. Consider Document 6.3.

Document 6.3 (circle3.htm)

```
<html>
<head>
<title>Circle Area (4)</title>
<script language="javascript" type ="text/javascript">
    function getArea(f) {
      var r=parseFloat(f.radius.value);
      f.area.value = Math.PI*r*r;
    }
</script>
</head>
<body>
<h1>Circle Area (3)</h1>
<form>
  Enter radius, then press tab key or click on "area"
box.<br />
  radius (cm):
```

```
<input type="text" name="radius" size="6"
   maxlength="7" value="-99",
   onblur = "getArea(form);" />
area (cm<sup>2</sup>):
<input type="text" name="area" size="6"
   maxlength="7" value="-99" />
</form>
</body>
</html>
```

In this version of `function getArea()`, the entire form (actually, just information about where the form is located in computer memory) is passed to the function, through the parameter name `f`. There is no `return` statement. How, then, is the result of the calculation made available to the `area` form field? The answer lies in these two statements:

```
var r=parseFloat(f.radius.value);
f.area.value = Math.PI*r*r;
```

The first statement extracts the numerical value of the radius. The second statement modifies not the `form` parameter itself, but the `value` property of one of its fields. (It automatically converts the number back to text, too.) Note that this approach requires the function to "know" the names of the fields in the form passed as input to the function. This is a major conceptual difference compared to the previous approaches. The fact that the form and the JavaScript function are linked in this way is not a problem for self-contained documents such as this. The only disadvantage is that it could limit the use of the function in other scripts that use different field names for the same physical quantities.

In the previous discussion of JavaScript's function model, it was clear that the parameter list acted as a one-way path for input to be passed to a function, but it could not be used to deliver output. Document 6.3 appears to violate this rule because the output has, in fact, been delivered back to the form "through" the parameter `f`. However, this result does not, in fact, compromise the model. When you pass a "value" to a function, you are actually passing memory addresses telling the function where particular parameters are stored. The function is allowed to make use of information stored at these addresses, but not to change the addresses themselves. Specifically, when the location of a form is passed as a parameter, what the function *can* do is modify the contents of fields stored in the form. This is what the

```
f.area.value = Math.PI*r*r;
```

statement does.

It is important to understand that the name f appearing in the function `getArea(form)` has *nothing* to do with names used in the HTML document. This is a consequence of the "protected" environment created by a function definition, in which names defined within the function are invisible to the rest of a document and script. In fact, it would be acceptable from JavaScript's point of view to use `form` as a parameter name, although this might not be a good choice as a matter of style.

The ability of a function to modify fields within a form is important because it is one way to circumvent the restriction that a `return` statement can return only a single value as output. Suppose you wanted to calculate both the area and circumference of a circle. Does this require two separate functions? No. Consider Document 6.4.

Document 6.4 (`circleStuff.htm`)

```
<html>
<head>
<title>Circle Stuff</title>
<script language="javascript" type ="text/javascript">
      function circleStuff(f) {
          var r=parseFloat(f.radius.value);
          f.area.value=Math.PI*r*r;
          f.circumference.value=2*Math.PI*r;
      }
</script>
</head>
<body bgcolor="#99ccff">
<h1>Circle Stuff</h1>
<form>
   Enter radius, then press tab key or click on "area"
box.<br />
   radius (cm):
   <input type="text" name="radius" size="6"
     maxlength="7" value="-99",
     onblur = "circleStuff(form);" />
   area (cm<sup>2</sup>):
   <input type="text" name="area" size="6"
     maxlength="7" value="-99" />
   circumference(cm):
   <input type="text" name="circumference" size="6"
     maxlength="7" value="-99" />
</form>
</body>
</html>
```

Circle Stuff

Enter radius, then press tab key or click on "area" box.
radius (cm): 3   area (cm^2): 28.274333 circumference(cm): 18.849555

Document 6.4 includes an additional form field for the circumference, calculated in the

```
f.circumference.value=2*Math.PI*radius;
```

statement in `circleStuff()`. Both the area and the circumference are calculated within the function, but no `return` statement is used.

It is not quite true that a function accepting a form name as a parameter must know the values of all the `<input... />` tag name attributes. Recall from Chap. 5 that all form fields are available in an array called `elements[]` which is automatically created along with a form. The following modification of the function in Document 6.4 will also work. It uses the `elements[]` array to access the form fields.

```
function circleStuff(f) {
      var r=parseFloat(f.elements[0].value);
      f.elements[1].value=Math.PI*r*r;
      f.elements[2].value=2*Math.PI*r;
}
```

In this case, the function must still be aware of the physical meaning of each form field as well as its position among the other fields.

It is important to understand that the significance of Document 6.5 rests on its demonstration of how to use a single function to generate more than one output value, to circumvent the requirement that a function can `return` only a single value.

6.3.3
Using Arrays to Return Output Values

Yet another way to return multiple values from a function is to have the function return an array, the elements of which contain the output values of interest. Document 6.5 shows how to do this by presenting another version of the "circle stuff" code given in Document 6.4.

Document 6.5 (`circleStuff2.htm`)

```
<html>
<head>
<title>Circle Stuff with Arrays</title>
<script language="javascript" type ="text/javascript">
   function circleStuff(r) {
     var A = Array();
     A[0] = Math.PI*r*r;
     A[1] = 2*Math.PI*r;
     return A;
   }
</script>
</head>
```

6

```
<body bgcolor="#99ccff">
<h1>Circle Stuff</h1>
<form>
  Enter radius, then press tab key or click on "area" or
"circumference" field.<br />
  radius (cm):
  <input type="text" name="radius" size="6"
    maxlength="7" value="-99",
    onblur = "var A = Array();
    A = circleStuff(parseFloat(radius.value));
    area.value = A[0]; circumference.value = A[1]; " />
  area (cm<sup>2</sup>):
  <input type="text" name="area" size="6"
    maxlength="7" value="-99" />
  circumference(cm):
  <input type="text" name="circumference" size="6"
    maxlength="7" value="-99" />
</form>
</body>
</html>
```

Of course, with this approach it is necessary for the programmer to keep track of which output value is stored in which array element.

6.4
Some Global Methods and Event Handlers

6.4.1
Global Methods

This book has already made extensive use of the parseFloat() method. Table 6.1 lists several methods of the Global object, including parseFloat().

The last three methods are particularly important because they provide mechanisms for converting the text values of form fields into numerical values. The parseFloat() method tries to analyze its text argument as a number, starting at the left. The characters +, −, ., e (in proper context as part of scientific notation), and the digits 1–9 are allowed. If parseFloat() encounters some other character it stops. So, parseFloat(7.17x) returns 7.17 but parseFloat(x7.17) returns NaN.

The parseInt() method, which converts a text string into an integer, requires additional discussion. Consider Document 6.6.

Table 6.1   Some Global methods for evaluating and converting strings

Global method	Descriptions and Examples
eval("s")	Evaluates string "s" as though it were JavaScript code.
	Eval("3+4/5") returns a value of 3.8.
isNaN("s")	Returns "true" if the argument **cannot** be interpreted as a number, "false" otherwise.
	isNaN("a17") returns a value of true.
Number(x)	Converts an object to a number.
	Number(7.17); returns 7.17
	Number(7.17x); returns NaN
	Number(x7.17); returns NaN
	var x=new Boolean(true);Number(x); returns 1
	var x=new Date(); Number(x); returns milliseconds since January 1, 1970 UT
parseFloat("s")	Converts a string to a real (floating point) number.
	parseFloat(7.17); returns 7.17
	parseFloat(7.17x); returns 7.17
	parseFloat(x7.17); returns NaN
	parseFloat("17.7") returns a value of 17.7.
parseInt("s",b)	Converts a string to an integer number using base "b" arithmetic.
	parseInt("17.7",10)
	returns a value of 17.

Document 6.6 (parseIntBug.htm)

```html
<html>
<head>
<title>parseInt() "bug"</title>
</head>
<body>
<form>
integer value: <input name="x" value="09" /><br />
Click for parseInt("string") result: <input name="x_int"
  onclick="x_int.value=parseInt(x.value); " /><br />
Click for parseInt("string",10) result: <input
name="x_int10"
  onclick="x_int10.value=parseInt(x.value,10); " /><br />
Click for parseFloat("string") result:
  <input name= "x_float"
  onclick="x_float.value=parseFloat(x.value); " />
</form>
</body>
</html>
```

integer value: |09

Click for parseInt("string") result: |0

Click for parseInt("string",10) result: |9

Click for parseFloat("string") result: |9

The `parseFloat()` method produces the expected value, but `parseInt()` with a single string argument does not. Why not? The problem lies in how `parseInt()` interprets numbers. This method can accept two arguments. The first is the text that is to be converted to an integer. The second argument, described as "optional" in JavaScript documentation, is the "radix," or the number base used for the conversion of the string given as the first argument. When the second argument is absent, `parseInt()` tries to determine the appropriate base from the string itself. Strings of digits beginning with a zero are assumed to be base-8 (octal) numbers, not base 10! In Document 6.6, an entry of "07" will not cause a problem because 7 is an allowed digit in a base-8 system. However, 8 and 9 are not allowed digits in the base-8 system, so `parseInt("09")` returns 0 rather than 9! This is a perfect example of behavior that some might consider a "feature," but which others might consider a very annoying bug.[1]

The behavior of `parseInt()` is cause for concern because it is always tempting to ignore "optional" arguments. Consider that a two-digit format is standard for entering months, days, hours, minutes, degrees, etc., and there may be good reasons for treating whole numbers as integers rather than floating point numbers.[2] For example, it is reasonable to expect users to enter November 8, 2006, as 11/08/2006 rather than 11/8/2006. In this case, a day entered as 08 and converted to an integer using `parseInt()` would have a value of 0 rather than 8—a serious error! Hence, `parseInt()` should *always* be called with both arguments. Without exception for the topics addressed in this book, the second argument should be 10, to force conversion to a base-10 integer even with one or more leading zeros.

The `Number()` method provides a third way to convert text strings to a number. Unlike `parseFloat()`, `Number()` will not ignore trailing characters that are not part of a number. That is, `Number(7.17x)` or `Number("123 456")` returns NaN instead of 7.17 or 123. As shown in Table 6.1, `Number()` will convert other objects to numbers, too. `Number(true)` returns a value of 1 and `Number(false)` returns 0. `Number(new Date())` will return the number of milliseconds since midnight, January 1, 1970, Universal Time.

For the purposes of this book, and for applications you will write for your own use as opposed to distributing them globally on the Web, it is probably not worth the effort to check the validity of all entries in fields that are supposed to be numbers. The `isNaN()` method provides a way to do this, but it has some limitations. Referring to Document 6.6, `isNaN(parseInt(x.value))` would return a value of "false" for the default entry of 09 in the `"x"` field (meaning that it is a valid number) even though Document 6.6 makes clear that the value returned from `parseInt()` without the second base argument is in error. The fact that `isNaN(parseInt(x.value))` would return a value of "true" for an entry of .09 is perhaps not so surprising, because .09 is not an integer, but it might be a misleading result.

The `eval()` method listed in Table 6.1 is very powerful because it allows user entry of JavaScript expressions. Document 6.7 shows how to use the `eval()` method to implement

---

[1]Author's note: I admit to learning about this "feature" only when someone pointed out that one of my own applications sometimes gave erroneous results.

[2]In some programming environments, integers are stored internally in a different format than floating point numbers, which has implications for mathematical operations carried out on integers.

a very simple calculator that recognizes the four basic arithmetic operators (+, −, *, and /) and knows how to interpret parentheses. The same approach can be used to evaluate much more complicated expressions, too—basically anything that can be interpreted as one or more JavaScript statements.

Document 6.7 (`calculator.htm`)

```
<html>
<head>
<title>Simple Calculator</title>
</head>
<body bgcolor="silver">
<form>
  Type expression to be evaluated, using numbers
    and +, -, *, /:<br />
  <input type="text" name="expression" size="30"
    maxlength="30"
    onchange="result.value=eval(expression.value);"
  />
  <input type="text" name="result" size="8"
    maxlength="8" />
</form>
</body>
</html>
```

Type expression to be evaluated, using numbers and +, -, *, /:

| 3*(5-13.5)/17 | -1.5 |

6.4.2
Using Event Handlers with Forms and Functions

JavaScript is an event driven language, meaning that scripts are activated as a result of events that happen in an HTML form. The `onblur` event handler was first used in Document 6.1 and `onclick` in Chap. 4. Whenever a user tabs to a form field or clicks on that field with a mouse, that field is said to be **in focus**. The `onblur` event handler initiates JavaScript activity whenever a document user presses the Tab key to leave a particular form field or clicks elsewhere on a document. Several event handlers that can be used in this way are summarized in Table 6.2. Note the spelling of the names using only lowercase letters. These are the "official" names, and the convention should be followed even though spellings using some uppercase letters (`onBlur` is common, for example) will be accepted by case-insensitive HTML.

The primary use for these event handlers is to execute code that will perform operations with field values, including changing those values.

Table 6.2 Summary of some event handlers used in forms

Event handler	Action
onblur	Initiates action when a user tabs from a form field or clicks elsewhere in a document.
onchange	Initiates action when a user changes the contents of a form field.
onclick	Initiates action when a user clicks on form input field.
onfocus	Initiates action when a user tabs to or clicks on a form field.
onload	Inside a <body> tag, initiates action when a document is loaded into the user's browser.

6.5
Recursive Functions

There is an important class of calculations that can be implemented with **recursive algorithms**. A standard example is the factorial function n!, which is defined for non-negative integer values of n and which is equal to $n \cdot (n-1) \cdot (n-2) \ldots (1)$. For example, $5! = 5 \cdot 4 \cdot 3 \cdot 2 \cdot 1 = 120$. This function can be defined as:

$n! = 1$ for $n = 1$ or $n = 0$
$n! = n \cdot (n-1)!$ for $n > 1$

This is a recursive definition, in which $n!$ is defined in terms of $(n-1)!$.

Like other modern programming languages, JavaScript supports **recursive functions**—functions that call themselves. Document 6.8 demonstrates a recursive function that calculates $n!$.

Document 6.8 (factorial2.htm)

```
<html>
<title>Calculate n!</title>
<body>
<script language="JavaScript" type="text/javascript">
function nFactorial(n) {
            if (n<=1) return 1;
            else return n*nFactorial(n-1);
      }
</script>
</head>
<h1>Calculate n factorial (n!)</h1>
<p>
<form>
```

```
Enter n (a non-negative integer):
<input type="text" name="n" size="2" maxlength="3"
value="0"
   onblur="factorial.value=
     nFactorial(parseInt(n.value,10));" />
   (Press Tab to get n!.)<br>
   <input type="text" name="factorial" size="10"
     maxlength="11" value="1" /> <br />
</form>
</body>
</html>
```

Calculate n factorial (n!)

Enter n (a non-negative integer): 8   (Press Tab to get n!.)

40320

The shaded line contains the critical code, in which the function calls itself. For certain mathematical functions, such as $n!$, the structure of the recursive function is easy to see from the mathematical definition of the function. Recursive algorithms always require at least two branches. One branch generates a recursive call and the other terminates the function. In Document 6.8, the relationship between the recursive definition for $n!$ and the code required to evaluate $n!$ should be obvious. Note that the code does not check to make sure that only non-negative integer values of n have been entered as input.

The success of recursive functions depends on the function model discussed at the beginning of this chapter, in which information flows into a function through the parameter list. When the function is called with the current value of $n - 1$, this value is associated with the parameter n in the new call. Because of the way the algorithm is written, the local value of $n - 1$ will eventually equal 1 (for any value of n originally greater than 1) and the recursive calls will be terminated. The intermediate values of the factorial function are stored within the programming environment. Table 6.3 shows the sequence of events for calculating 4!.

You can think of each function call as adding a "plate" to a stack of plates. The initial call plus the three recursive calls add a total of four plates to the stack. At the third recursive call, $n = 1$ and a value of 1 is returned. Executing a `return` statement is equivalent to removing one of the plates. Subsequently, the three remaining plates are removed as the

Table 6.3 Calculating 4! using a recursive algorithm

Local value of n	Action	Value returned
$n = 4$	Initial call	Deferred
$n = 3$	First recursive call	Deferred
$n = 2$	Second recursive call	Deferred
$n = 1$	Third recursive call	1
$n = 2$	Complete multiplication 2·1	2
$n = 3$	Complete multiplication 3·2	6
$n = 4$	Complete multiplication 4·6	24

deferred multiplications are carried out and a value is returned. When the function returns control of the script back to the point from which it was initially called, all the "plates" have been removed from the stack.

For more complicated recursive algorithms, it can be difficult to actually follow the course of the calculations. Fortunately, it isn't necessary to do this. As long as the algorithm is properly designed, with a condition that will eventually terminate the recursive calls, the programming environment takes care of keeping track of all the intermediate values generated during the execution of the algorithm.

Here's another example of a well-known function that is defined recursively. The Fibonacci numbers F_n that form the sequence 1, 1, 2, 3, 5, 8, 13, 21, ... are defined for positive integer values of n as

$F_n = 1$ if $n = 1$ or $n = 2$
$F_n = F_{n-1} + F_{n-2}$ if $n > 2$

Document 6.9 shows how simple it is to evaluate this function using a recursive algorithm.

Document 6.9 (fibonacci.htm)

```html
<html>
<title>Calculate Fibonacci numbers</title>
<body>
<script language="JavaScript" type="text/javascript">
  function Fib(n) {
    if (n<=2) return 1;
    else return Fib(n-1)+Fib(n-2);
  }
</script>
</head>
<h1>Calculate the n<sup>th</sup> Fibonacci number</h1>
<p>
<form>
  Enter n (a positive integer):
  <input type="text" name="n" size="2" maxlength="3"
value="1"
  onblur="FibN.value=Fib(parseInt(n.value));" />
(Press Tab to get n<sup>th</sup>
  Fibonacci number.)<br>
  <input type="text" name="FibN" size="8"
    maxlength="8" value="1" />
</form>
</body>
</html>
```

Calculate the nth Fibonacci number

Enter n (a positive integer): |8   (Press Tab to get nth Fibonacci number.)
|21

Because this function requires multiple recursive calls, it is not easy to follow the sequence of events. However, you don't have to worry about these details as long as the algorithm is written properly!

Recursive algorithms can also be formulated using count-controlled or conditional loop structures. However, a recursive formulation is often much shorter and more direct to implement in code. The famous "Towers of Hanoi" problem is an excellent example of a problem that is difficult to solve "directly" but is trivial to solve recursively.

Consider three poles, on one of which are stacked 64 golden rings. The bottom ring is the largest and the others decrease in size. The object is to move the 64 rings from one pole to another, using the remaining pole as a temporary storage place for rings. There are two rules for moving rings:

1. Only one ring can be moved at a time.
2. A ring can never be placed on top of a smaller ring.

Describe how to move the entire stack of rings from one pole to another.

It can be shown that it will take $2^n - 1$ moves to move n rings. For $n = 64$, if you could move one ring per second without ever making a mistake, it would take roughly 100 times the estimated age of the universe! However, you can develop an algorithm that will work, in principle, for any number of rings and apply it to a value of n that is small enough to be practical. For $n = 4$, it will take 15 moves.

In a conceptual sense, the solution is easy (but perhaps not obvious). Suppose the poles are labeled A, B, and C. Initially, all the rings are on A and the goal is to move them all to C. The steps are:

1. Move $n - 1$ rings from A to B.
2. Move the nth ring from A to C.
3. Move $n - 1$ rings from B to C.

This solution is "conceptual" in the sense that it has not yet been specified how to do steps 1 and 3; only step 2 defines a specific action that can be taken. However, the power of recursive functions allows this problem to be solved without giving additional specific steps! Consider Document 6.10.

6

Document 6.10 (`towers.htm`)

```
<html>
<head>
<title></title>
<script language="javascript" type="text/javascript">
  function move(n,start,end,intermediate) {
    if (n > "0") {
    move(n-1,start,intermediate,end);
    document.write("move ring "+n+
      " from "+start+" to "+end+".<br />");
    move(n-1,intermediate,end,start);
    }
  }
  var n=prompt("Give n:");
  move(n,"A","C","B");
</script>
</head>
<body>
</body>
</html>
```

```
move ring 1 from A to B.
move ring 2 from A to C.
move ring 1 from B to C.
move ring 3 from A to B.
move ring 1 from C to A.
move ring 2 from C to B.
move ring 1 from A to B.
move ring 4 from A to C.
move ring 1 from B to C.
move ring 2 from B to A.
move ring 1 from C to A.
move ring 3 from B to C.
move ring 1 from A to B.
move ring 2 from A to C.
move ring 1 from B to C.
```

Amazingly, this simple "conceptual" code is all that is required to solve this problem in the sense that all the steps are explicitly written out. Do not try this code with large values of *n*!

The success of this algorithm depends, once again, on how parameter lists work—passing information along a "one-way street" into a function. In principle, you can manually follow the individual values of the parameters during the recursive calls, but it is hardly worth the effort. All that is actually required is that the algorithm be stated appropriately.

6.6
Passing Values from One Document to Another

Just as it is useful to be able to pass values to functions within an HTML document, it might be useful to be able to pass values from one document to another document. Here's a typical problem:

> Create a "sign on" page that asks a user for an ID and password. Check the values provided and if they are OK, provide access to a second page. Otherwise, access to the second page will be denied. The second page will be able to make use of information about the user that can be accessed through the user's ID.

JavaScript is not actually a suitable language for solving this problem because of the lack of two-way interaction between the client and the server. This means, essentially, that a list of approved IDs and passwords must be sent to the client computer—not a great idea! (You can "hide" this information in a separate file, as described in Chap. 5, but this is still not a real solution.) Nonetheless, it is still interesting to see how to pass information from one document to another. Document 6.11 provides a simple example.

Document 6.11a (`passID.htm`)

```html
<html>
<head>
<title>Get ID and password.</title>
<script language="javascript" type="text/javascript">
   function checkIDPW() {
     var PWinput=login_form.PW.value;
     var IDinput=login_form.ID.value;
     var flag=prompt("ID = "+IDinput+
       ", PW = "+PWinput+". OK (y or n)?");
     if (flag == "y") return true; else return false;
   }
</script>
</head>
<body>
  <form method="link" action="catchID.htm"
    name="login_form" onsubmit="checkIDPW();">
  ID: <input type="text" name="ID">
  PW: <input type="text" name="PW">
  <input type="submit" value="Access protected page.">
</form>
</body>
</html>
```

Document 6.11b (`catchID.htm`)

```html
<html>
<head>
<title>Receive ID and password from another
  document.</title>
</head>
<body>
<form name="catchForm">
<input type="hidden" name="info">
</form>
<script language="javascript" type="text/javascript">
catchForm.info.value=window.location;
```

```
// alert(window.location);
function getID(str)
{
  theleft=str.indexOf("=")+1;
  theright=str.lastIndexOf("&");
  return str.substring(theleft,theright);
}
function getPW(str) {
  theleft=str.lastIndexOf("=")+1;
  return str.substring(theleft);
}
document.write("ID is "+getID(catchForm.info.value)+
  ", PW is "+getPW(catchForm.info.value));
</script>
</body>
</html>
```

Document 6.11a is the "sign on" page. It asks the user for an ID and password. The form uses method="link" to submit data to another document—catchID.htm. Because no additional location information is given in this example, the second document must reside in the same directory (or folder) as the first document. When the link is made to the second form, the first form provides a text string that can be accessed as window. location. This consists of the URL of the first form plus values of all the form fields defined in the first document. If you know the format of this string, it is possible to extract the form field values—an ID and password, in this case.

In Document 6.11b, methods of the String object are used to extract substrings of window.location. By removing the comment characters from the // alert(window. location); statement and "commenting out" the document.write() statement near the end of the code, you can see the entire string and how it is formatted:

This window shows the result of passing "xxx" and "ssss" for the ID and password.

This code requires that there be no "surprises" in the ID and password values. Their contents should be restricted to letters and digits. Other characters may be translated into their hex code representations, which will complicate their extraction from window. location. Although it might be possible, in principle, to extract several passed values, using more values will complicate the code.

Although it hasn't been done in Document 6.11b, the implication of the code is that you can save the ID and password by assigning them to the value of a form field in the new document. Then you can use these values just as you would any value created directly within this document.

6.7
Revisiting the JavaScript sort () Method

Recall Document 5.3 in Chap. 5, which introduced JavaScript's sort () method. That example demonstrated that the results are browser-dependent and therefore unreliable. In at least some browsers, sort () treats array elements that "look" like numbers as though they were characters. Thus, 13 is less than 3 in the same sense that "ac" is less than "c." To fix that problem, you need to create a separate function that is passed as a parameter to the sort () method. This function should accept as input two values x and y (elements in the array being sorted) and should return a value less than 0, 0, or greater than 0, depending on whether x is less than, equal to, or greater than y.

In this way, you can provide your own code for comparing values. In this case, you wish to force a type conversion from text to number so that 13 will be greater than 3. Consider this modification of Document 5.3:

Document 6.12 (sort2.htm)

```
<html>
<head>
<title>Sorting Arrays</title>
<script language="javascript" type="text/javascript">
  function compare(x,y) {
    var X=parseFloat(x); Y=parseFloat(y);
      if (X<Y) return -1;
      else if (X==Y) return 0;
      else return 1;
  }
  var a=[7,5,13,3];
  var i;
  document.write(a + " length of a = " + a.length+"<br />");
  a.sort(compare);
  document.write(a + " length of a = " + a.length+"<br />");
</script>
</head>
<body>
</body>
</html>
```

```
7,5,13,3 length of a = 4
3,5,7,13 length of a = 4
```

The two calls to document.write() in Document 6.12 show the array before and after sorting; it is clear that this code works as expected. Your "compare" function can have any name you choose, as long as you use it consistently. The general idea is that, in order to force JavaScript to sort an array correctly, you need to do appropriate data type conversions in the "compare" function along with type-appropriate comparisons.

6

In Document 6.12, the code

```
if (X<Y) return -1;
else if (X==Y) return 0;
else return 1;
```

could be replaced with

```
return parseFloat(X) - parseFloat(Y);
```

Because the only operation is subtraction, even `return X - Y` would work, even if that is not very good JavaScript programming style.

6.8
More Examples

A thorough understanding of how functions and methods work is essential to using HTML/JavaScript as a reliable problem-solving environment. As described earlier in Sect. 6.3, there are several different approaches to getting information to and from a function. By design, the problem to be solved in these earlier examples—calculating the area and/or circumference of a circle—was conceptually trivial. The purpose of the solutions presented was to provide templates that you can adapt for use in your own code. When JavaScript code doesn't work, the reason is often that a function interface has been implemented incorrectly. Hopefully, the examples presented in this section will provide some points of reference for your own code.

6.8.1
Dewpoint Temperature

The dewpoint temperature is the temperature at which water vapor condenses from the atmosphere. It is related to air temperature and relative humidity through the following equations:

$$a = 17.27$$

$$b = 237.7$$

$$\alpha = aT_a / (b + T_a) + \ln(\text{RH})$$

$$T_{dp} = (b + \alpha)/(a - \alpha)$$

where relative humidity RH is expressed as a decimal fraction (between 0 and 1) and air and dewpoint temperatures T_a and T_{dp} are in degree Celsius.

Document 6.13 (dewpoint.htm)

```
<html>
<head>
<title>Dewpoint Calculator</title>
<body>
<script language="JavaScript" type="text/javascript">
  function getDewpoint(T,RH) {
    var a=17.27,b=237.7,alpha;
    var temp=parseFloat(T.value);
    var rh=parseFloat(RH.value)/100;
    alpha=a*temp/(b+temp)+Math.log(rh);
    return ((b*alpha)/(a-alpha)).toFixed(2);
  }
</script>
</head>
<h1>Dewpoint Temperature Calculator</h1>
<p>
<form>
<input type="reset" value="Reset" /><br />
Temperature:
<input type="text" name="T" size="5" maxlength="6"
  value="-99" /> °C <br />
Relative Humidity:
<input type="text" name="RH" size="6" maxlength="6"
  value="-99" /> % <br />
<br />
<input type="button"
  value= "Click here to get dewpoint temperature (deg
C)."
  onclick="DP.value=getDewpoint(T,RH)" />
<br /><br />
Dewpoint Temperature: <input type="text" name="DP" size="5"
maxlength="6" value="-99" /> °C<br />
</p>
</form>
</body>
</html>
```

6

Dewpoint Temperature Calculator

Reset

Temperature: 25   °C

Relative Humidity: 63   %

Click here to get dewpoint temperature (deg C).

Dewpoint Temperature: 17.46   °C

It is not absolutely necessary to define the local variables a, b, and alpha in function getDewpoint(), but it makes the conversion of the equations into JavaScript easier to understand. Note the use of the toFixed() method to control the display of the result.

6.8.2
Loan Repayment Schedule

Given the principal amount P of a loan, an annual interest rate R in percent, and a repayment period of n months, the monthly payment M is given by:

$$r = R / (100 \cdot R) \quad M = (P \cdot r) / [1 - 1 / (1 + r)^n]$$

Create an HTML document that asks the user to enter P, R, and n and then calculates and displays the monthly payment.

Document 6.14 (loan.htm)

```
<html>
<head>
<title>Loan Calculator</title>
<body bgcolor="#99ccff">
<script language="JavaScript" type="text/javascript">
    function getPayment(P,r,n) {
      r=r/100/12;
      var M=P*r/(1-1/Math.pow(1+r,n));
      return M.toFixed(2)
    }
```

```
</script>
</head>
<h1>Loan Calculator</h1>
<p>
<form>
Principal Amount: $:
<input type="text" name="amount" size="9"
  maxlength="9" value="0" /><br />
Annual rate: %
<input type="text" name="rate" size="6"
  maxlength="6" value="0" />
<br />
Number of Months:
<input type="text" name="n" size="3"
maxlength="3" value="0" /><br />
<input type="button"
  value="Click here to get monthly payment."
  onclick=
    "monthly.value=getPayment(parseFloat(amount.value),
    parseFloat(rate.value),parseInt(n.value,10));" />
<br />
Monthly Payment: $
<input type="text" name="monthly" size="9"
  maxlength="9" />
</form>
</body>
</html>
```

6.8.3
Legendre Polynomials

A set of functions called Legendre polynomials are sometimes required in science and engineering applications. Here is a table of the first eight Legendre polynomials.

n	$P_n(x)$
0	1
1	x
2	$(3x^2 - 1)/2$
3	$(5x^3 - 3x)/2$
4	$(35x^4 - 30x^2 + 3)/8$
5	$(63x^5 - 70x^3 + 15x)/8$
6	$(231x^6 - 315x^4 + 105x^2 - 5)16$
7	$(429x^7 - 693x^5 + 315x^3 - 35x)/16$

By making use of the fact that $P_0(x) = 1$ and $P_1(x) = x$, Legendre polynomials of order $n \geq 2$ can be generated through a recursion relation:

$$P_n(x) = [(2n-1)/n]xP_{n-1}(x) - [(n-1)/n]P_{n-2}(x)$$

Write an application that will generate the value of the nth Legendre polynomial for any value of x and $n \geq 0$.

Document 6.15 (`legendre.htm`)

```html
<html>
<head>
  <title>Legendre Polynomials</title>
  <script language="JavaScript" type="text/javascript">
  function Legendre(n,x) {
    if (n == 0) return 1;
    else if (n == 1) return x;
    else
    return (2*n-1)/n*Legendre(n-1,x)-(n-1)/n*Legendre(n-2,x);
  }
  </script>
</head>
<body>
<h3>Calculate the n<sup>th</sup> Legendre polynomial,
P<sub>n</sub>(x), for any x and n &ge; 0</h3>
```

```
<form>
  n (&ge; 0):
<input type="text" name="n" value="3" /><br />
  x:
<input type="text" name="x" value="1.5" /><br />
<input type="button"
  value="Click here to calculate Legendre polynomial"
onclick="L.value=
  Legendre(parseInt(n.value,10),parseFloat(x.value));" />
<br />
  Legendre polynomial: <input type="text" name="L" />
</form>
</body>
</html>
```

Calculate the nth Legendre polynomial, P$_n$(x), for any x and n $\geq$ 0

n ($\geq$ 0): 3

x: 1.5

Click here to calculate Legendre polynomial

Legendre polynomial: 1.916666666666667

As previously noted, the power of recursive algorithms allows this calculation to be done very easily simply by "translating" the recursive definition into code.

6.8.4
Array-Derived Pull-Down Menus

In the previous introduction to creating pull-down menus with the select tag (see Document 3.4, for example), the options in the list were "hard coded" into the HTML document using the option tag. It is also possible to let JavaScript create the menu entries using an array of items and the new Option() constructor. Document 6.16 shows how to do this.

Document 6.16 (buildMenu.htm)

```
<html>
<head>
<title>Build a variable-length pull-down menu</title>
<script language="javascript" type="text/javascript">
  var listItems = new Array();
  listItems[0]="thing1";
```

```
listItems[1]="thing2";
listItems[2]="thing3";
listItems[3]="things4";
listItems[4]="newthing";
function buildSelect(list,things) {
  var i; //alert(things);
  for (i=0; i<things.length; i++)
    list.options[i]=new Option(things[i],things[i]);
}
function getSelected(list) {
  var i;
  for (i=0; i<list.length; i++)
    if (list.options[i].selected)
      return list.options[i].value;
}
</script>
</head>
<body onload="buildSelect(menuForm.stuff,listItems);" >
<form name="menuForm" >
Here's the menu:<br />
Click on an item to select it.<br />
<select name="stuff" size="10"
  onchange="listChoice.value=getSelected(stuff); ">
</select><br />
This is the item selected:
<input type="text" name="listChoice" value=""/>
</form>
</body>
</html>
```

By placing the onload event handler in the body tag, the call to buildSelect() creates the stuff options list when the application is loaded into the user's browser. buildSelect() gets its values from a user-created array of options and uses the new Option() constructor to copy those values into the options array associated with the pull-down list. The options array is a property of the select tag (do not try to change its name) whose ele-

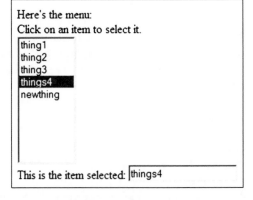

ments contain all the option tags defined within the select tag. The syntax for using the new Option() constructor is:

new option identifier = new Option (*text to appear in options list,*
                                      text assigned to value attribute);

The selected item in the options list is displayed whenever a choice is made in the pull-down menu, by using the onchange event handler inside the <select> tag.

The text to be displayed in the pull-down menu can be the same as the text assigned to the value attribute for the option tag, as it is in Document 6.16, but it doesn't have to be the same. If the two input parameters for new Option() constructor are different, instead of new Option(things[i],things[i]), as in this case, then you would need two arrays to generate these values, or perhaps a two-dimensional array, as discussed in Chap. 5.

As Document 6.16 demonstrates, you don't have to "hard code" any of the option tags within the select tag. You could also just define the options array elements directly instead of assigning them indirectly through an additional array of items. The point of using this additional array is that you could maintain an array of menu options in another file which can be pasted into your script as needed. In fact, this array could be a simulated two-dimensional "data array" that contains many additional values for each entry into the pull-down menu. After the user selects an item in the menu, then additional form fields can be populated with information contained in the selected element of the data array.

This approach might be worth using for a long list of menu items even if it was a "static" list that didn't have to be changed, to make the body of the HTML shorter and easier to read. Document 6.16 includes a function showing how to determine which item in the list has been selected. It uses a for... loop rather than a conditional loop because it is also possible in principle to specify multiple selections in a pull-down list. (See Document 5.10).

6.8.5
Creating a "Password-Protected" HTML Document

Document 5.12 in Chap. 5 suggested how to use arrays to store user IDs and passwords and to check user input against entries in that array. However, that application didn't show how to use a password to access a "protected" site.

Document 6.17 provides a very simple solution to this problem: assume that the password is the name of the protected file. Unless users know the name of that file, they cannot access it. This "solution" is not really secure, though, because anyone who has access to the directory in which the "protected" file exists could possibly figure out what to enter for the "password."

Document 6.17a (passwordProtect.htm)

```
<html>
<script language="JavaScript"><!--
function check() {
/* This code uses the name of an htm file as a "password."
Prompt the user for the password.
*/
```

6

```
  var pwd = prompt('Enter password before continuing...');
/* Access the file, assuming it's in the same directory.
If it's not, then include a string pointing to the location.
*/
  location.href=pwd + ".htm";
}
// -->
</script>
<head>
<title></title>
</head>
<body>
<p>You will need a password to visit my site.</p>
  <form>
    <input type="button" onClick="check()"
    value="Click here to enter site." />
  </form>
</body>
</html>
```

You will need a password to visit my site.

Click here to enter site.

Document 6.17b (&_crazy.htm)

```
<html>
<head>
  <title></title>
</head>
<body>
<p>You have entered &_crazy.htm.</p>
</body>
</html>
```

The protected file name can be any combination of keyboard characters that can be part of a file name. In this case, access is provided only if the user enters &_crazy at the prompt. A somewhat better implementation would ask the user to enter the password in an <input type="password" ... /> field, so that the typed characters will not appear on the screen. This value would be passed to function check(), with the addition of an input parameter in the function definition.

This code makes use of JavaScript's location object, which is a property of the window object. It acts essentially as the JavaScript equivalent of the HTML <a href="...">...</a> tag. Document 6.17b is very simple but, of course, this document can be as complicated as needed.

Creating a Server-Side Environment with PHP

7

Abstract Chapter 7 compares the concepts of a server-side language, PHP, with the client-side environment provided by HTML and JavaScript. It shows how to create an environment in which information from an HTML document can be acted upon by a PHP document located on a server.

7.1
Getting Started with PHP

JavaScript's primary limitation relative to languages such as C/C++ is that it is a client-side language embedded in Web browsers. When an HTML/JavaScript document is accessed online or locally with a browser, only the contents of that document are available. JavaScript code cannot access data stored elsewhere on a server. This restriction is inherent in the language syntax and operating environment and applies regardless of whether the server is actually at a different location—a remote server—or whether external data exist on a **local server** residing elsewhere on the same computer where the HTML/JavaScript document resides.

As a result, the only way to access information from a JavaScript application is to have all that information embedded within the application itself. Data can be formatted as a JavaScript array and contained in a file (often with a .js extension) that can be "included" when the HTML document is opened. This at least allows the data part of an application to be maintained separately from the processing part, but it does not overcome the inherent limitations of client-side processing.

Because the ability to read and write data files is so important for science and engineering applications, it is necessary to use some other language in place of or in addition to JavaScript. One solution is to use PHP, a full-featured programming language similar in syntax to JavaScript and other languages derived from a C/C++ heritage. PHP is a **server-side language**, which means that PHP documents reside on a remote or local server rather than being downloaded onto a browser on a **client-side** computer. Not only does PHP provide capabilities for accessing files stored on a remote or local server, it also allows an application to receive information from an HTML document and act on that information. For PHP to be used in this way, even on a local computer, PHP must be installed in an appropriately configured server environment, and not just installed as an application.

D.R. Brooks, *Guide to HTML, JavaScript and PHP: For Scientists and Engineers*,   **167**
DOI 10.1007/978-0-85729-449-4_7, © Springer-Verlag London Limited 2011

Newcomers to PHP may hope that PHP will work just like a JavaScript function. They will send a PHP document some information. That document would process the information and "return" some results that could then be used within the HTML/JavaScript document.

But PHP doesn't work this way! Passing information from an HTML document is a one-way street, from client to server. The PHP document can display output on your browser screen, by creating an HTML-formatted web page as output, but it doesn't return information that can be used within an HTML document or by a JavaScript script. For example, you cannot send information to a PHP application from the form fields in an HTML/JavaScript document, ask the PHP application to do some calculations, and then write the results back into form fields in the calling document for additional modifications through JavaScript. However, you *can* create and save data in files on the server, as will be shown later in this chapter.

As an example of how PHP works together with an HTML document, consider this problem:

> A user enters information about measurements taken with a sun viewing instrument (called a sun photometer) that is used to measure total column water vapor in the atmosphere. The information provided by the user consists of the instrument's serial number, the location and time of the measurements, and voltage outputs from the instrument. The application must use this information to find the location of the sun at the time and place of the measurement and then calculate total column water vapor based on calibration constants stored for the instrument that was used to collect the data.

The purpose of most of the calculations in this application will be first to determine the elevation (or zenith) angle of the sun based on the location and time of the measurements, to obtain what is called the relative air mass. Next, the calibration constants for the specified instrument must be retrieved. Finally, the precipitable water (PW) can be calculated. Apart from the actual calculations of solar position and PW, which are organizationally trivial, if computationally a little involved, this is a conceptually simple and typical data entry and processing problem that will provide a framework within which to learn about PHP.

Assume that the calibration constants (A, B, C, β, and τ) for several water vapor instruments are entered in a space-separated text file, `WVdata.dat`, and stored on a server:

```
SN  A  B  C  beta  tau
WV2-113   0.762   0.468   0.20   0.65   0.10
WV2-114   0.814   0.468   0.20   0.65   0.10
. . .
WV2-157   0.911   0.468   0.20   0.65   0.10
. . .
```

A typical approach to programming problems is to separate a large problem into smaller problems. For this problem, the first step will be to write an HTML document that will pass

an instrument serial number to a PHP application on a server. The second step is to write a
server-side application that will receive this serial number and will then search through
WVdata.dat and display the calibration constants for that instrument. These two documents must be linked through an interface that passes information from the first document
to the second.

Document 7.1 is an HTML document that will pass an instrument serial number to a
server application.

Document 71. (getCalib.htm)

```
<html>
<head>
<title>Get calibration constant</title>
<script language="javascript">
  document.write("This document last modified on "
    + document.lastModified+". ")
</script>
</head>
<body>
<h2>Get calibration constants for water vapor instrument</h2>
<p>
<form method="post" action="getCalib.php">
Enter serial number here: <input type="text" name="SN"
value="WV2-157" /><br />
<input type="submit"
  value="Click here to get calibration constants..." />
</body>
</html>
```

This document last modified on Thursday, February 01, 2007 11:05:02.

Get calibration constants for water vapor instrument

Enter serial number here: WV2-157

Click here to get calibration constants...

In this document, an instrument serial number is entered in typical fashion, as a value
in a type="text" input field in a form. A type="submit" form field button is
used to send this value to a server-side application named getCalib.php. There is no
reason why the PHP application needs to have the same name as the client-side HTML/
JavaScript document, but using identical names (with different extensions) makes clear
which HTML files are associated with which PHP files.

Note that JavaScript is used only incidentally in this document, to display the most recent document modification date and time. The transfer to a PHP document is done simply through the mechanism of an HTML form and does not require any other action such as a JavaScript script.

Information is sent to a PHP application simply by setting the method and action attributes in the form tag:

```
<form method="post" action="getCalib.php">
```

The value of the action attribute gives the location of the PHP document. The fact that, in this example, the value is simply the PHP file name rather than a longer URL reference implies that both the calling HTML document and the receiving PHP document reside in the same folder on a local computer—in this case, the folder designated as the local host on which PHP applications run. As will be shown below, this action automatically transmits the name and value of every form field defined in the calling document. In this case, there is only one value, the instrument serial number.

Now write the PHP application to receive and process this information. This requires code that will be completely unfamiliar to JavaScript programmers.

Document 7.2. (getCalib.php)

```php
<?php
// Extract instrument ID from POST data...
  $SN=$_POST["SN"];
  $len=strlen($SN);
// Open WV instrument calibration constant file...
  $inFile = "WVdata.dat";
  $in = fopen($inFile, "r") or die("Can't open file");
// Read one header line...
  $line=fgets($in);

// Search rest of file for SN match...
  $found=0;
  while ((!feof($in)) && ($found == 0)) {
// Could do it like this...
//      $line=fgets($in);
//      $values=sscanf($line,"%s %f %f %f %f %f");
// or like this...
//      fscanf($in,"%s %f %f %f %f %f",
//              $SN_dat,$A,$B,$C,$beta,$tau);
list($SN_dat,$A,$B,$C,$beta,$tau)=fscanf($in,
                      "%s %f %f %f %f %f");
      if (strncasecmp($SN_dat,$SN,$len)==0)
$found=1;
  }
fclose($in);
```

```php
if ($found == 0) echo
      "Couldn't find this instrument.";
else {
// Build table of outputs...
  echo "<p><table
border='2'><tr><th>Quantity</th><th>Value</th></tr>"."
</td></tr>";
  echo "<tr><td>Instrument ID</td><td>$SN</td></tr>";
  echo "<tr bgcolor='silver'><td colspan='2'>
    Calibration Constants</td></tr>";
  echo "<tr><td>A</td><td>$A</td></tr>";
  echo "<tr><td>B</td><td>$B</td></tr>";
  echo "<tr><td>C</td><td>$C</td></tr>";
  echo "<tr><td>&tau;</td><td>$tau</td></tr>";
  echo "<tr><td>&beta;</td><td>$beta</td></tr>";
  echo "</table>";
  }
?>
```

What is required to create and use such a document? The following steps proceed "from scratch," based on the assumption that you already understand how to use HTML and JavaScript but have never used a server-side programming language.

Quantity	Value
Instrument ID	WV2-157
Calibration Constants	
A	0.911
B	0.468
C	0.2
τ	0.1
β	0.65

Step 1. Setting up a PHP environment.

There is a very significant difference between HTML/JavaScript documents and PHP applications. JavaScript is, essentially, universally and automatically available through any modern browser, so you shouldn't have to do anything special to process JavaScript code (unless, for some reason, your browser's JavaScript interpreter has been disabled). In contrast, the ability to use an HTML document as a source of input for a PHP application requires access to a server on which a **PHP interpreter** has been installed. (PHP is an interpreted, as opposed to a compiled, language in the sense that stand-alone executable binary files are not generated.) The server must be configured specifically to allow PHP scripts to be processed and all PHP applications must be saved on the server in an appropriate location.

Because of the potential for carelessly written or malicious code to wreak havoc on any computer that allows remote access to its contents (in this case, through an HTML document that passes information to a PHP application), appropriate safeguards must be established to limit the ability to read and write data from or to specific locations on the server. Because of these potential problems, some institutions do not support the use of server-side applications on *any* of their computers.

7

Even if the client browser and server reside on the same physical computer, a server and PHP interpreter must still be installed and configured, and precautions should still be taken to protect the computer's contents. Server software may already exist on Windows and Macintosh computers, but it may need to be activated. Options include the popular Apache server, which is available through free downloads in versions for Windows (WAMP), Macintosh (MAMP), and Linux (LAMP) computers. On the author's Windows computers, a default installation of the WAMP local server has automatically provided all the required capability to run PHP applications, including graphics-based applications.

The steps involved in setting up a **PHP environment** for developing PHP applications on a local computer include:

1. Install a server (or activate an existing server) on a local computer. Although it is possible in principle to use PHP on a remote server, it will be much easier to learn how to use this language if it is available on your own computer. This is the default situation assumed for all the PHP code examples in the rest of this book.
2. Download and install a PHP interpreter. PHP may already be part of your server—it is for a WAMP server, for example. If not, installation packages for PHP are available as free downloads from http://www.php.net/downloads.php. For this book, a WAMP installation on a Windows computer running XP Pro has been used, although this fact *should* be irrelevant for using any of the PHP applications discussed in the book. That is, the interpretation of PHP code *should* be platform-independent.
3. On your computer, configure the server to recognize PHP documents and to locate the PHP interpreter. It is entirely possible that this will be done automatically when you install a server and you may not need to change any configuration settings.

Fortunately, there are many online sources of help with installing PHP on your own computer. For using PHP on a remote server, you don't have to carry out the above steps yourself, but you still need to know how to access the server. The details vary from system to system, and you may need to get help from your system administrator.

Step 2. Creating, editing, and executing PHP documents

Just like HTML documents, **PHP documents** are text files that can be created with any text editor. AceHTML, the editor used to produce all the code in this book, provides convenient editing and color-coded syntax formatting capabilities for creating PHP documents just as it does for creating HTML/JavaScript documents.

At first, it may not be obvious that you cannot execute PHP scripts directly from an editor's browser window, as you can JavaScript scripts in HTML documents. However, this is clearly the case. You can create and edit PHP scripts with an editor, but you must then execute them on a server, even if that server resides on your own computer. For example, on a Windows XP computer with a WAMP installation, PHP documents are saved in the `C:/wamp/www` folder and executed by entering

```
localhost/{PHP document name}
```

as the URL in a browser window. These required folders are automatically created when the WAMP package is installed. For convenience, you can also store the corresponding HTML/JavaScript documents in the same folder (recall Document 7.1).

So, to execute a PHP document, create it in a code or text editor, save it in www (for a WAMP installation) then switch to a browser to execute it at localhost on a local Windows server. Whenever you make changes, save them and refresh the PHP document in your browser window.

When you create applications, whether in JavaScript, PHP, or some other language, it is important to develop a consistent approach that minimizes the time spent correcting the errors you will inevitably make. It is rarely a good idea to create an entire application all at once. A much better plan (in any language) is to proceed step-by-step, adding small sections of code and testing each addition to make sure the results are what you expect. When you pass information from an HTML document to a PHP application, it is *always* a good idea to display the values passed to the PHP application *before* writing more PHP code.

The error messages you will receive when you make mistakes in your code will almost never be very helpful, although experience and practice will improve your ability to interpret these messages. They may tell you where an error has been encountered but not what the error actually is. You might like to see a message like "You forgot to put a semicolon at the end of line 17." But that will *not* happen! PHP interpreters seem to be a little more helpful than JavaScript interpreters when it comes to describing errors, but neither of them will tell you what you really need to know—exactly what you did wrong and how to fix it. And of course, no syntax checker will protect you against the worst error of all—code that works perfectly well but is logically flawed and gives the wrong answers!

To test your PHP/server environment, start with this minimal PHP document. Name it helloWorld.php and save it in www (or the equivalent location on your system).

Document 7.3. (helloWorld.php)

```php
<?php
  echo "Hello, world!";
?>
```

Open a browser and type localhost/helloWorld.php (or whatever is the appropriate URL for your system). You should see the text, "Hello, world!" displayed in your browser window.

Another difference between HTML files and PHP files is that your computer is probably configured to automatically associate an .htm or .html extension with your browser. So, if you double-click on a file with such an extension, it will open in your browser. But, if you double-click on a file with a .php extension, the result is uncertain. On a Windows computer, such files may open as text files in the Notepad utility unless you have specifically associated the .php extension with some other application, such as a code editor. In any case, you cannot "execute" this file by double-clicking on it. Instead, you must enter its URL in a browser, as noted above.

You can also save and execute this file:

7

Document 7.4. (`PHPInfo.php`)

```php
<?php
  echo phpinfo();
?>
```

This file will display a great deal of information about how PHP is configured on your server. (If you view the source code for this document, you can also learn a lot about formatting output from PHP.)

The `echo` **language construct** in Document 7.3 displays the specified string literal and in Document 7.4 displays the (very long) string output returned by `phpinfo()`, a PHP function that displays information about your PHP installation.

Even more simply, you can just type `http://localhost/` (for a WAMP server). There *should* be an index.php file that will display some information about your server and PHP configuration.

The first thing to notice about these Documents 7.3 and 7.4 is that PHP files do not need to be embedded within an HTML document template, with its basic tags; they serve as stand-alone applications. Although you will often see PHP documents that place PHP scripts inside the `body` tag of an HTML document, these two examples demonstrate that PHP can work on its own without any HTML "shell," basically with the assumption that any HTML syntax appearing in formatted output will be interpreted appropriately when that output is echoed to your browser.

PHP code—a **PHP script**—is enclosed inside a **PHP tag**:

```php
<?php
  . . .
?>
```

There are other ways of implementing PHP scripts, including

```
<script language="PHP">
  ...
</script>
```

but the `<?php … ?>` tag found in the examples in this book is widely used for stand-alone PHP applications.

If you get error messages, or if nothing happens when you try to execute the documents in this chapter, then something is wrong with your server/PHP installation. It is hopeless to try to offer system-specific advice for resolving this kind of problem, but the most likely sources of trouble at this level, assuming that you have installed both a server and PHP, is that some server configuration options have been overlooked or have been given inappropriate settings, that you haven't stored your PHP document in an appropriate folder on a local computer, or that you do not understand the procedure for running PHP applications on a remote server. You may need to consult with your system administrator (if you have one!) to resolve these problems.

Step 3. Passing information from an HTML/JavaScript document to a PHP application.

The next thing you need to know to use PHP for anything other than displaying text output in a browser window is how to pass information to a PHP document. By design (since this is the essential reason for the existence of PHP), this is *very* easy to do, using the `action` and `method` attributes of the `form` element.

```
<form action="{URL of PHP document}" method="post">
...
<input type="submit" value="{Put submit button text here.}" />
</form>
```

The example from Document 7.1,

```
<form method="post" action="getCalib.php">
```

passes information to `getCalib.php`.

This code in this book will always use `method="post"`, although it is also possible to use `method="get"` in some circumstances. A PHP document is identified through its URL and not just by a directory/folder reference on the server. For the examples in this book, the assumption is that the HTML document and the PHP document reside in the same folder/directory on the same local server. For local use on a Windows computer using a WAMP installation, this location could be `C:/wamp/www` with an automatically assigned URL of `localhost`. This co-location of files is done just for convenience in a local server environment. When you use PHP on a remote server, you will store the HTML interface document on your local computer or download it from a server, and the URL for the PHP document will be different, of course.

What makes the process of calling a PHP document from an HTML document so painless is the fact that the contents of *all* form `input` fields in the calling document are *automatically* available to the target PHP document, without any additional programming effort on your part! There are some nuances and useful modifications to this very simple procedure, including ways to ensure that the "submit" action is carried out only once per visit to the calling document, but that discussion isn't essential for now.

On the **server side**, `getCalib.php` receives the information from `getCalib.htm` in a system-generated array named `$_POST` whose elements are accessed by using the names associated with the form fields in the calling document. In Document 7.2, the statements

```
$SN=$_POST["SN"];
$len=strlen($SN);
```

assign the value of the ID form field—it is named `SN` and its default value is `WV2-157`—to the PHP variable `$SN` and save the length of `$SN` in variable `$len`. In PHP scripts, all variable identifiers, whether user- or PHP-defined, begin with a `$` character.

7

Step 4. Reading and interpreting information stored in server-side text files.

The next step in solving the problem addressed in Document 7.2 is to compare the value of $SN against the instrument serial numbers stored in WVdata.dat. Open the file and assign a name—a **file handle** in programming terminology:

```
$inFile = "WVdata.dat";
$in = fopen($inFile, "r") or exit("Can't open file.");
```

The file handle $in (it can be any name you like) provides a link between the physical file stored on the server and the "logical" name by which that file will be known in a PHP script. If the file exists, it is opened and the value of the file handle variable is the location in memory of the first byte of the physical file. If the file doesn't exist, the exit() function prints a message and terminates the application. (Note the syntax of this line of code, which is a "short-hand" PHP version of an if... else... statement using the or operator instead of the || operator.)

The parameters for the fopen() function are the file name and a string that specifies the operations that are allowed to be performed on the file. It is not necessary to assign a separate variable name to the physical file. The single statement

```
$in = fopen("WVdata.dat", "r") or
  exit("Can't open file.");
```

will work the same as the previous two statements, but the single "hard-coded" file name doesn't allow you to pass the name of the physical file from an HTML document to a variable in the PHP document. Of course, for some applications, you might *want* to use a hard-coded file name that can't be changed by a user calling the PHP document.

A value of "r" (or 'r') identifies the file as a **read-only text file**. This means that the PHP document can extract information from WVdata.dat but cannot change its contents in any way. Text files are subject to an important restriction: they are **sequential access** file whose contents can only be read sequentially, starting at the beginning. Even if a program does not need all the information in a text file, it must still be read and then, perhaps, ignored.

With this restriction in mind, there are several ways to read text files and extract information from them. The basic requirement is that the programmer must know *exactly* how data in the file are stored. The first line in WVdata.dat is a **header line**:

```
SN A B C beta tau
```

The header line is followed by calibration values for instruments. From the PHP script's point of view, the number of instrument calibrations stored in this file is unknown—additions to or deletions from the file can be made offline at any time. So, the script must first read past the header line (which is assumed always to be present in this application) and then search through an unknown number of instrument calibration data lines to find the specified instrument:

```
// Read one header line...
$line=fgets($in);
// Search rest of file for SN match...
$found=0;
while ((!feof($in)) && ($found == 0)) {
// Could do it like this...
// $line=fgets($in);
// $values=sscanf($line,"%s %f %f %f %f %f");
   $values=fscanf($in, "%s %f %f %f %f %f");
   list($SN_dat,$A,$B,$C,$beta,$tau)=$values;
   if (strncasecmp($SN_dat,$SN,$len)==0) $found=1;
   }
fclose($in);
```

The syntax is similar to JavaScript syntax for conditional loops, even if the file-handling functions are unfamiliar because they have no equivalent in JavaScript. The variable $found is assigned an initial value of 0 before starting the loop. You could also assume that $found is a boolean value and initialize it with a value of false, to be changed later to true rather than 1, along with changing ($found == 0) to (!$found) in the while (...) statement.

Inside the loop, the file is read one line at a time. The feof() function terminates the conditional loop when an end-of-file mark is encountered, and the test on $found terminates the loop when the specified instrument serial number is found. Since every line is formatted the same way, the fscanf() function is a simple choice for extracting data from the file. The shaded line in the above code stores six values in the user-named array $values. The elements of this array are then assigned to separate variable names using the list() language construct.

An alternative approach shown in the comment lines is to use the fgets() function again to read a line of text into a user-specified string variable called $line. The sscanf() function is used to extract the values. For this application there is no reason to replace one statement for extracting values with two statements that accomplish the same goal.

A third alternative is to use the fscanf() function to assign values directly to variables:

```
fscanf($in,"%s %f %f %f %f %f",
        $SN_dat,$A,$B,$C,$beta,$tau);
```

This is actually the easiest way to read these values.

The **format specification string** in the fscanf() function tells PHP to look for a text string followed by five real numbers. This string contains one or more **format specifiers**— characters that tell how a value in the file is to be interpreted. In the example being discussed here, "s" describes a character string and the "f" describes a floating point number. Each value in the text file must be separated by one or more spaces. This code will not work as written if other printable characters, such as commas, are present. However, extra spaces and even tabs are OK—tabs are treated as "white space" separating the values and are ignored by the format specification.

Except for white space, the contents of the data file must *exactly* match what the format specifier string tells your code to expect. If the data records in the WVdata.dat file were separated by commas instead of white space:

```
SN A B C beta tau
WV2-113, 0.762, 0.468, 0.20, 0.65, 0.10
...
```

Then the format specification string would have to be:

```
$values=fscanf($in, "%s, %f, %f, %f, %f, %f");
```

There is more discussion of format specifications in Sect. 10.4.1.

The list() construct (which looks like a function because of the parentheses, but in programming terms is a language construct) associates the elements of $values with the values read from one line of data in the calibration file. The names of these values can be whatever you like. In this case, the choice that makes the most sense is to use the descriptive names that appear in the header line of the data file.

The strncasecmp() function performs a case-*in*sensitive comparison of the instrument serial number passed from getCalib.htm against serial numbers in the WVdata.dat file. (That is, a value of either WV2-157 or wv2-157 passed from getCalib.htm will be treated as a match with the WV2-157 value in WVdata.dat.) If a serial number match is found, strncasecmp() returns a value of 0 and the $found value is changed to 1. The feof() function looks for an "end-of-file" mark in the file and terminates the loop if it gets to the end of the file without finding a match with the user-specified serial number. When the loop terminates, the fclose() function closes the data file.

If a calibration for the specified instrument doesn't exist, then the script should print an appropriate message. Otherwise, it should display the calibration values for that instrument. Use an if... else... statement, with syntax similar to JavaScript:

```php
if ($found == 0)
echo "Couldn't find this instrument.";
  else {
// Build table of outputs…
  echo "<p><table
border='2'><tr><th>Quantity</th><th>Value</th></tr>";
  echo "</td></tr>";
  echo "<tr><td>Instrument ID</td><td>$SN</td></tr>";
  echo "<tr bgcolor='silver'>
    <td colspan='2'>Calibration Constants</td></tr>";
  echo "<tr><td>A</td><td>$A</td></tr>";
  echo "<tr><td>B</td><td>$B</td></tr>";
  echo "<tr><td>C</td><td>$C</td></tr>";
```

```
   echo "<tr><td>&tau;</td><td>$tau</td></tr>";
   echo "<tr><td>&beta;</td><td>$beta</td></tr>";
   echo "</table>";
}
```

This code shows how to use echo to build output strings that include HTML tags. Tags are used here to build a table, just as you would do in an HTML document. The multiple echo statements in this example could be reduced by using PHP's string concatenation operator, a period. The statements building the output table could also be written like this:

```
echo "<p><table border='2'>
 . <tr><th>Quantity</th><th>Value</th></tr>"
 . "</td></tr>"
 . "<tr><td>Instrument ID</td><td>$SN</td></tr>"
 . "<tr bgcolor='silver'><td colspan='2'>"
 . "Calibration Constants</td></tr>"
 . "<tr><td>A</td><td>$A</td></tr>"
 . "<tr><td>B</td><td>$B</td></tr>"
 . "<tr><td>C</td><td>$C</td></tr>"
 . "<tr><td>&tau;</td><td>$tau</td></tr>"
 . "<tr><td>&beta;</td><td>$beta</td></tr>"
 . "</table>";
```

This completes the task of finding calibration constants for an instrument serial number passed from an HTML document and displaying the results of that search.

Step 5. Saving PHP output in a server-side file.

Now suppose you wish to process data submitted by a user and save it in a server-side file. Document 7.5 is an expansion of Document 7.2 which demonstrates how to save the data shown in the output image for Document 7.2 in a file. The few additional lines that are required are shaded.

Document 7.5. (writeCalib.php)

```
<html>
<head>
<title>Get calibrations for water vapor instrument</title>
</head>
<body>
<?php
// Extract instrument ID from POST data…
   $SN=$_POST["SN"];
   $len=strlen($SN);
```

```php
// Open WV instrument calibration constant file…
  $inFile = "WVdata.dat";
  $outFile="WVreport.csv";
  $in = fopen($inFile, "r") or
                   exit("Can't open file.");
  $out=fopen($outFile,"a");
// Read one header line…
// Read one header line…
      $line=fgets($in);
// Search rest of file for SN match…
      $found=1;
      while ((!feof($in)) && ($found == 1)) {
        $line=fgets($in);
        $values=sscanf($line,"%s %f %f %f %f %f");
        list($SN_dat,$A,$B,$C,$beta,$tau)=$values;
        if (strncasecmp($SN_dat,$SN,$len)==0)
          $found=0;
      }
      fclose($in);
      if ($found == 1)
        echo "Couldn't find this instrument.";
      else {
// Build table of outputs…
echo "<p><table border='2'>
      <tr><th>Quantity</th><th>Value</th></tr>";
echo "</td></tr>";
echo "<tr><td>Instrument ID</td><td>$SN</td></tr>";
echo "<tr bgcolor='silver'>
      <td colspan='2'>Calibration Constants</td></tr>";
echo "<tr><td>A</td><td>$A</td></tr>";
echo "<tr><td>B</td><td>$B</td></tr>";
echo "<tr><td>C</td><td>$C</td></tr>";
echo "<tr><td>&tau;</td><td>$tau</td></tr>";
echo "<tr><td>&beta;</td><td>$beta</td></tr>";
echo "</table>";
}
fprintf($out,"Data have been reported for:
%s,%f,%f,%f,%f,%f\n",$SN,$A,$B,$C,$tau,$beta);
fclose($out);
?>
</body>
</html>
```

The first two highlighted lines create an output file with a .csv extension.

```
$outFile="WVreport.csv";
$out=fopen($outFile,"a");
```

You can use any **file name extension** you like—PHP doesn't care—but `.csv` is the standard extension for "comma-delimited" files that can be opened in Excel and other spreadsheet applications. PHP *does* care where you try to store this file. Files can be written only to locations on a server with appropriate write permissions. On a Windows XP computer, running an Apache server with default configurations, you should be able to write files in the `/wamp/www` folder. With some other server, such as the Windows IIS server, it might be necessary to write data into a directory that is shared by all users (as opposed to just the administrator, for example). One possibility might be to create a folder in a directory *just* for writing PHP output files:

```
C:/Documents and Settings/All Users/Documents/phpout/.
```

The second of the highlighted lines assigns a file handle, `$out`, and opens a file with `"a"` (**append**) permission. This means that if the file already exists, new data will be appended to the end of the file. If the file doesn't already exist, it will be created.

The other common permission is `"w"` (**write-only**) permission. If the file doesn't already exist, it will be created. If it already exists, all the existing contents of the file will be destroyed and only the results from executing this PHP script will be written in the file. Basically, "write" permission wipes the slate clean each time an output file is created. This may or may not be what you intend, so be careful! In this case, the desired result is to append new data to the end of existing data, not to start over again with an empty file, every time the PHP application executes.

The second group of highlighted lines

```
fprintf($out,"Data have been reported for:
%s,%f,%f,%f,%f,%f\n",$SN,$A,$B,$C,$tau,$beta);
fclose($out);
```

uses a format specifier string to write some text and the values of variables to the output file. The output format specifiers mirror the specifiers used to read these values from the input data file and should match the data type of the information that is going to be written. The commas in the specifier string are there by choice, not by necessity, because we wish to create a comma-delimited text file (a ".csv" file). After one call to `writeCalib.php` the file will look like this:

```
Data have been reported for:
WV2-157,0.911,0.468,0.2,0.1,0.65
```

It is important to understand that the output created by this PHP application is not in any sense a special "PHP file." It is simply a text file that can be used by other software and applications, including spreadsheets and even other PHP scripts, as needed. If the data in an output file are comma-delimited, for example, the file can be opened directly into a spreadsheet.

Finally, the "sequential access" restrictions on text files apply to files opened with append or write-only permission. Just as text files can be read from only sequentially, they can be written to only sequentially. Writing starts at the beginning of a write-only file (regardless of its current contents), and at the current end of an append file. It is not possible to "jump around" in this kind of file to write new information in random locations, anymore than it is possible to read information from random locations.

As noted previously, the kinds of file access tasks described in this chapter are impossible with JavaScript alone. Of course, there are many PHP language details to be explored, but these are just details compared to the conceptual framework. The examples given here show that by passing values to a PHP document, you can use those values to initiate processing that takes place on a remote server, including accessing existing data and creating new data that can be stored permanently on that server. Many Web programmers use PHP primarily to access databases or validate the contents of submitted online forms. From a science and engineering applications perspective, this will not be the primary use. With PHP's capabilities, and without knowing anything about formal database structure, you can send information from a client-side application—input values for a calculation, for example—to a PHP application and permanently store that information in whatever text-based format you desire, along with results of operations performed on those data, including operations that require access to other information stored on the server. These capabilities vastly expand the range of online applications beyond those that can be carried out with JavaScript alone.

7.2
More Examples

7.2.1
Solving the Quadratic Equation

For the quadratic equation $ax^2 + bx + c = 0$, find the real roots:

$$r_1 = \frac{\left[-b + \left(b^2 - 4ac\right)^{1/2}\right]}{2a} \qquad r_2 = \frac{\left[-b - \left(b^2 - 4ac\right)^{1/2}\right]}{2a}$$

The "a" is the coefficient must not be 0. If the discriminant $b^2 - 4ac = 0$, there is only one root. If the discriminant is less than 0, there are no real roots.

This problem can be solved easily just with JavaScript, but it provides another example of passing HTML from field values to a PHP application.

Document 7.6a (quadrat.htm)

```
<head>
<title>Solving the Quadratic Equation</title>
</head>
<body>
<form method="post" action="quadrat.php">
Enter coefficients for ax<sup>2</sup> + bx + c = 0:
<br />
a = <input type="text" value="1" name="a" />
   (must not be 0)<br />
b = <input type="text" value="2" name="b" /><br />
c = <input type="text" value="-8" name="c" /><br /><br />
<input type="submit" value="click to get roots..." />
</form>
</body>
</html>
```

Enter coefficients for $ax^2 + bx + c = 0$:

a = [1]   (must not be 0)

b = [2]

c = [-8]

[click to get roots...]

Document 7.6b (quadrat.php)

```
<?php
$a = $_POST["a"];
$b = $_POST["b"];
$c = $_POST["c"];
$d = $b*$b - 4*$a*$c;
if ($d == 0) {
   $r1 = $b/(2*$a);
   $r2 = "undefined";
}
else if ($d < 0) {
   $r1 = "undefined";
   $r2 = "undefined";
}
```

```
else {
    $r1 = (-$b + sqrt($b*$b - 4*$a*$c))/2/$a;;
    $r2 = (-$b - sqrt($b*$b - 4*$a*$c))/2/$a;;
}
echo "r1 = " . $r1 . ", r2 = " . $r2;
?>
```

$$r1 = 2, r2 = -4$$

If the coefficient c is changed from -8 to 8, the equation has no real roots:

$$r1 = \text{undefined}, r2 = \text{undefined}$$

Note that in this example, the PHP variable names are the same as the form field names in the corresponding HTML document. These are reasonable names for coefficients of a quadratic equation, but they could be given any other names, such as p, q, and r, if there were some reason to do that. The PHP document needs to know only the field names by which these values were identified in the calling HTML document, because those names must be available to extract values from $\_POST[]$. For the kinds of problems presented in this book, in which an HTML/JavaScript document is typically paired with a PHP document, it is a reasonable style choice to use the same names for variables in the PHP code as were used in the HTML document.

7.2.2
Preventing Multiple Submissions from a Form

> Create an HTML document that allows a user to enter some meteorological observations. Pass these observations to a PHP document and append them to a file of observations. Take some steps to prevent a user from submitting the same set of observations more than once.

A typical problem when using a form to send data to a remote server is that it is too easy to submit the same data multiple times by clicking repeatedly on the "submit" button. If you are using a PHP application to store data in a file, the result of multiple submissions will be a data file with many duplicate data records.

The amount of effort that should be expended to write code that minimizes duplicate submissions depends on the application and how hard you wish to make it to change data and resubmit them as a new entry. Document 7.7 takes a somewhat relaxed approach based on the assumption that a user may legitimately wish to submit several sets of data on the same "visit" to the form, but should be prevented from sending the same data more than once. Hence, the user is forced to reset the form before the "submit" button will work again.

Note that this is a JavaScript solution, having nothing to do with PHP in the sense that the PHP application doesn't check to see if data that are submitted already exist in the "append" file. It is certainly possible within the PHP application to prevent duplicate data from being appended to the file, but it requires less effort to eliminate duplicate submissions in the first place.

Document 7.7a (`WeatherReport.htm`)

```html
<html>
<head>
<title>Weather Report</title>
<script language="javascript" type="text/javascript" >
  var alreadySubmitted = false;
  function submitForm ( )
  {
    if (alreadySubmitted)
    {
      alert("Data already submitted. Click on 'Reset Button'
and start over." );
      return false;
    }
    else
    {
      alreadySubmitted = true;
      return true;
    }
}
</script>
</head>
<body>
<h2>Report weather observations</h2>
<form method="post" action="WeatherReport.php"
    onSubmit="return submitForm(this.form);" >
Date (mm/dd/yyyy) : <input type="text" name="date"
    value="09/23/2007" /><br />
Time (UT hh:mm:ss): <input type="text" name="time"
    value="17:00:00" /><br />
Air temperature (deg C):<input type="text" name="T"
    value="23" /><br />
Barometric pressure (millibar): <input type="text"
    name="BP" value="1010" /><br />
Cloud cover (octas 0-8): <input type="text" name="octas"
    value="7" /><br />
Precipitation today (total mm): <input type="text"
    name="precip" value="2.3" /><br />
<input type="submit" name="PushButton"
    value="Click to submit..." /><br />
```

```
<input type="reset" value="Reset Button"
    onClick="alreadySubmitted=false;"/>
</body>
</html>
```

The comma-delimited text file that will contain the reported data should be created ahead of time, starting with just a header line:

```
Date,Time,T,BP,Octas,Precipitation
```

Document 7.7b (`WeatherReport.php`)

```php
<?php
$date=$_POST["date"];
$time=$_POST["time"];
$T=$_POST["T"];
$BP=$_POST["BP"];
$octas=$_POST["octas"];
$precip=$_POST["precip"];
echo "You have reported:<br />" .
    "date:" . $date . "<br />" .
    "time: " . $time . "<br />" .
    "BP : " . $BP . "<br />" .
    "octas: " . $octas . "<br />" .
    "precip: " . $precip . "<br />";
$out=fopen("WeatherReport.csv","a");
fprintf($out,"%s, %s, %.1f, %.2f, %u, %.2f\r\n",
            $date,$time,$T,$BP,$octas,$precip);
fclose($out);
?>
```

You may have to change the location of the output file to suit your situation. After two submissions, the `WeatherReport.csv` file might look like this:

```
Date,Time,T,BP,Octas,Precipitation
09/23/2007, 17:00:00, 23.0, 1010.00, 7, 2.30
09/24/2007, 17:10:00, 25.0, 1012.00, 1, 0.00
```

Note that the `fprintf()` format string includes $\backslash$r$\backslash$n as a line terminator, so the line breaks will be visible if the file is opened in a Windows text editor such as Notepad, rather than in Excel. Additional format specifiers limit the number of digits associated with the floating-point numbers. See Sect. 10.4.1 for more details about how to use these specifiers.

Working with PHP

8

Abstract Chapter 8 describes the syntax of PHP and shows how to perform calculations and work with text-based files. The chapter returns to the problem defined in Chap. 7 and provides a complete PHP-based solution. Further information about reading and writing files is also provided.

8.1
Structure of PHP Scripts

For this chapter, it is assumed that you are familiar with how basic programming concepts such as variables, operators, assignment statements, functions, and loops are implemented in JavaScript. These same concepts apply to PHP; thus little attention will be given to general explanations. Although the file-handling syntax will be unfamiliar to JavaScript programmers, because JavaScript does not have these capabilities, it is not difficult to learn how to write PHP scripts if you are comfortable with JavaScript. A summary of selected PHP language elements is provided in Chap. 10.

PHP scripts do not appear very different from JavaScript scripts, but there are some important distinctions. For example, PHP scripts *require* a semicolon to terminate each line, but JavaScript scripts do not. Every PHP variable name must be preceded by a "$" symbol. (There is no compelling explanation for why this is the case.) Variables are not declared ahead of time and there is no equivalent of the JavaScript `var` keyword for declaring variables without assigning a value. If you use a variable name (for example, $taxes) and misspell it later in your script, for example, $texas, PHP will not flag this as an error, but your program obviously will no longer give correct results.

PHP scripts can be embedded in HTML documents or created as standalone documents using the `<?php … ?>` tag, and this is the style used in this book. (PHP scripts can also be embedded in HTML documents within `<script> … </script>` elements.) `/* … */` is used for block (multiline) comments. Single-line or in-line comments can begin with either `//` or `#`.

PHP supports functions, similar to syntax in JavaScript functions. However, argument passing is simpler because there is no need to distinguish among forms, form fields, and the values of form fields passed as inputs. There is no need in PHP for an equivalent of the

D.R. Brooks, *Guide to HTML, JavaScript and PHP: For Scientists and Engineers*, **187**
DOI 10.1007/978-0-85729-449-4_8, © Springer-Verlag London Limited 2011

8

JavaScript `.value` property, or for the `parseFloat()` or `parseInt()` functions needed to transform form field strings into their corresponding numerical values in calculations or when strings are passed as function arguments.

Recall that when JavaScript functions need to return multiple values, one possibility is to pass a form as input and assign values to fields in that form. Another possibility is to return an array of values. The second option, but not the first, is available for PHP.

Values returned from a JavaScript function can be used elsewhere in a JavaScript script and then "returned" directly into form fields. PHP values, including output from functions, can also be used anywhere within a PHP script, but values cannot be returned to form fields in the calling HTML document. Output is returned to a client computer in the form of HTML-formatted output that can be displayed in a browser window.

JavaScript processing is interactive in the sense that you can change inputs and recalculate outputs, sometimes automatically, simply by changing a value in a form field, and sometimes by clicking on a button, all from within the same document. In this sense, PHP works more like old-fashioned command-line "batch processing." If you need another set of outputs, you need to return to the calling document, change the input values in one or more form fields, and send the new values for reprocessing by the PHP script.

From a user's point of view, the biggest difference between JavaScript and PHP is the fact that PHP scripts can read data from and write data to a file on a server. This presents potential system security issues, and as a result, institutions that provide web space for authorized users may prohibit the use of *any* server-side languages such as PHP. However, there are no such restrictions with setting up a server on your own computer for your own personal use, although it is certainly possible to overwrite a file that you really couldn't afford to lose!

8.2
Calculations with PHP

As a focus for learning how to do calculations with PHP, return to the problem of calculating column water vapor (total precipitable vapor) based on measurements from a sun photometer, as outlined in Chap. 7. As a first step toward solving this problem, Chap. 7 showed how to pass an instrument serial number to a PHP application so that its calibration constants could be retrieved from a server-side data file.

The next step in this application requires some extensive calculations of the sun's position at a specified location and time on Earth's surface. Although the details of the algorithms involved are incidental to learning about PHP, the fact that the code is fairly lengthy, involving exponential, logarithmic, and trigonometric functions, will provide many examples of how to do math with PHP.

There are two approaches to doing the calculations required for this problem. The (very short) water vapor calculation requires as input the output voltages and calibration constants for a specified instrument, and a value for the relative air mass (a dimensionless quantity that has a value of 1 when the sun is overhead, with a solar zenith angle z of $0°$, and which increases as the zenith angle increases, approximately as $1/\cos(z)$).

The relative air mass calculation for a particular time and place requires some lengthy astronomical equations, but they are self-contained and can be done within JavaScript. Hence, one option is to calculate the relative air mass in the HTML/JavaScript document and send its value to a PHP application. The other option is to send just the input values—instrument serial number, measurement location, time, and instrument output voltages—to a PHP application, which will then do *all* the required calculations.

There is no compelling reason why one option is better than the other for this problem (and other similar problems), unless it is considered important to prevent the user from seeing the actual code required to perform the solar position and relative air mass calculations, as would be possible within JavaScript. The justification for choosing the second option here is to take advantage of the opportunity to learn a great deal about the details of using the PHP language.

As a starting point, Document 8.1 below is a complete HTML/JavaScript application that calculates precipitable water vapor based on the assumption that the user already knows the calibration constants for the instrument used to collect the data. All the equations for calculating solar position are incorporated into this document, so all that will be required later is to translate them into PHP. This document is a good place to review your understanding of how to do math calculations with JavaScript!

Document 8.1 (PWcalc2.htm)

```html
<html>
<head>
<title>WV calculations for calibrated instrument</title>
<script language="javascript">
      document.write("This document last modified on
      "+document.lastModified+".");
</script>
<script language="javascript">
function getSunpos(m,d,y,hour,minute,second,Lat,Lon) {
with (Math) {
// Explicit type conversions to make sure inputs are
treated like numbers,
// not strings.
  m=parseInt(m,10); d=parseInt(d,10);
  y=parseInt(y,10);
  hour=parseFloat(hour); minute=parseFloat(minute);
  second=parseFloat(second); Lat=parseFloat(Lat);
  Lon=parseFloat(Lon);
// Julian date
  var temp=ceil((m-14)/12);
```

8

```
//This number is always <=0.
  var JD = d - 32075 + floor(1461*(y+4800+temp)/4)
    +floor(367*(m-2-temp*12)/12)
// m-2-temp*12 is always > 0
    -floor(3*(floor((y+4900+temp)/100))/4);
  JD =JD-0.5+hour/24+minute/1440+second/86400;
// Solar position, ecliptic coordinates
  var dr=PI/180;
  var T=(JD-2451545)/36525;
  var L0=280.46645+36000.76983*T+0.0003032*T*T;
  var M=357.52910+35999.05030*T-0.0001559*T*T-0.00000048*T*T*T;
  var M_rad=M*dr;
  var e=0.016708617-0.000042037*T-0.0000001236*T*T;
  var C=(1.914600-0.004817*T-0.000014*T*T)*sin(M_rad)
    +(0.019993-0.000101*T)*sin(2*M_rad)+0.000290*sin(3*M_rad);
  var L_save=(L0+C)/360;
  if (L_save < 0) var L_true=(L0+C)-ceil(L_save)*360;
  else var L_true=(L0+C)-floor(L_save)*360;

  if (L_true < 0) L_true+=360;
  var f=M_rad+C*dr;
  var R =1.000001018*(1-e*e)/(1+e*cos(f));
// Sidereal time
  var Sidereal_time=280.46061837+360.98564736629*
(JD-2451545)+0.0003879*T*T-T*T*T/38710000;
  S_save=Sidereal_time/360;
  if (S_save < 0) Sidereal_time=Sidereal_time-ceil(S_save)*360;
  else Sidereal_time=Sidereal_time-floor(S_save)*360;
  if (Sidereal_time < 0) Sidereal_time+=360;
// Obliquity
  var obliquity=23+26/60+21.448/3600-46.8150/3600*
T-0.00059/3600*T*T +0.001813/3600*T*T*T;
// Ecliptic to equatorial
  var right_Ascension =
    atan2(sin(L_true*dr)*cos(obliquity*dr),
    cos(L_true*dr));
  var declination =
    asin(sin(obliquity*dr)*sin(L_true*dr));
  var Hour_Angle = Sidereal_time + Lon -
    right_Ascension/dr; // Don't know why!!
  var Elev=asin(sin(Lat*dr)*sin(declination)+
    cos(Lat*dr)*cos(declination)*cos(Hour_Angle*dr));
```

```
/* relative air mass from Andrew T. Young, Air mass and
   refraction (Eq. 5), Appl. Opt., 33, 6, 1108-1110 (1994) */
   var cosz=cos(PI/2-Elev);
   } // End with (Math) &
   var airm=(1.002432*cosz*cosz+0.148386*cosz+
     0.0096467)/(cosz*cosz*cosz+0.149864*cosz*cosz+
     0.0102963*cosz+0.000303978);
   return airm;
}
function get_PW(IR1,IR2,A,B,C,beta,tau,airm,p) {
/* NOTE:
     1. Station pressure may be included in these
calculations in the future.
     2. No addition operations in these calculations, so
explicit string conversions to numbers are not required.
*/
   var x = C*airm*tau - (Math.log(IR2/IR1)-A)/B;
   var PW = Math.pow(x,1/beta)/airm;
   return Math.round(PW*1000)/1000;
}
</script>
</head>
<body bgcolor="white">
<h2>Calculations for Total Precipitable Water Vapor (PW)</h2>
<p>
<form>
<table border="2">
   <tr bgcolor="silver"><td colspan="4">
     <b>Location:</b></td></tr>
     <td>longitude (decimal degrees): </td>
     <td> <input type="text" name="lon" value="-75.188"
size="8"> </td>
     <td>latitude (decimal degrees): </td><td>
<input type="text" name="lat"
     value="39.955" size="8"></td>
   </tr>
   <tr bgcolor="silver"><td colspan="4">
<b>Calibration constants:</b></td>
   </tr>
   <tr><td><b>A (you <u><i>must</i></u> provide a
value)</b>, B, and C:</td>
   <td><input type="text" name="A" value=""
```

8

```
size="8"></td>
  <td><input type="text" name="B" value="0.468"
size="8"></td>
  <td><input type="text" name="C" value="0.2"
size="8"></td>
  <tr><td colspan="2">&beta; and &tau;:</td>
  <td><input type="text" name="beta" value="0.65"
size="4"></td>
  <td><input type="text" name="tau" value="0.10"
size="4"></td>
</tr>
<tr bgcolor="silver"><td colspan="4"><b>Date:</b></td>
</tr>
<tr><td>mm/dd/yyyy</td>
  <td><input type="text" name="mon" value="4" size="3"></td>
  <td><input type="text" name="day" value="5" size="3"></td>
  <td><input  type="text" name="yr" value="2007" size="5"></td>
</tr>
<tr bgcolor="silver"><td colspan="4"><b>Time:</b></td></tr>
<tr><td>hh:mm:ss (<b><i><u>must</u></i> be Universal Time
</b>)</td>
  <td><input type="text" name="hr" value="14" size="3"></td>
  <td><input type="text" name="min" value="33" size="3"></td>
  <td><input type="text" name="sec" value="15" size="3"></td>
</tr>
<tr><td colspan="2" bgcolor="silver">
  <b>Station pressure (mbar, not currently used in
calculation):</b></td>
  <td colspan="2"><input type="text" name="p"
value="1013"size="7"></td>
</tr>
<tr bgcolor="silver"><td colspan="4"><b>Instrument
voltages:</b></td></tr>
<tr>
    <td>IR1</td>
    <td><input type="text" name="IR1" value="0.742"
size="5"> </td>
    <td>IR1<sub>dark</sub></td>
    <td><input type="text" name="IR1_dark"
value="0.003" size="5"></td>
  </tr>
```

```
<tr>
  <td>IR2</td>
  <td><input type="text" name="IR2" value="0.963"
size="5"></td>
<td>IR2<sub>dark</sub></td>
<td><input type="text" name="IR2_dark"
value="0.004" size="5"></td>
  </tr>
</table>
<input type="button" value="Click here to calculate
relative air mass and PW"
onclick="
// Get relative air mass &
airm.value=getSunpos(this.form.mon.value,
  this.form.day.value,this.form.yr.value,
  this.form.hr.value,this.form.min.value,
  this.form.sec.value,
  this.form.lat.value,this.form.lon.value);
// then PW &
PW.value=get_PW(this.form.IR1.value-
this.form.IR1_dark.value,
  this.form.IR2.value-this.form.IR2_dark.value,
  this.form.A.value,this.form.B.value,
  this.form.C.value,this.form.beta.value,
  this.form.tau.value,
  this.form.airm.value,this.form.p.value);
airm.value=Math.round(airm.value*10000)/10000;">
<br />
Relative air mass: <input type="text" name="airm"
value="0" size="7">
<br />
Overhead precipitable water vapor (cm H<sub>2</sub>O):
<input type="text" name="PW" value="0" size="7">
</form>
</body>
</html>
```

8

Location:			
longitude (decimal degrees):	-75.188	latitude (decimal degrees):	39.955
Calibration constants:			
A (you *must* provide a value), B, and C:	1.123	0.468	0.2
β and τ:		0.65	0.10
Date:			
mm/dd/yyyy	4	5	2007
Time:			
hh:mm:ss (*must* be Universal Time)	14	33	15
Station pressure (mbar, not currently used in calculation):	1013		
Instrument voltages:			
IR1	0.742	IR1$_{dark}$	0.003
IR2	0.963	IR2$_{dark}$	0.004
Click here to calculate relative air mass and PW			

Relative air mass: 1.4852

Overhead precipitable water vapor (cm H_2O): 1.767

To start the transition from JavaScript to PHP, Document 8.2a below is an HTML document that will pass instrument and measurement data to a PHP application. See Appendix 4 for a "pseudocode" approach to organize an HTML/PHP solution to this problem.

Document 8.2a (PWcalc3.htm)

```
<html>
<head>
<title>WV calculations for calibrated instrument</title>
<script language="javascript">
 document.write("This document last modified on "
    +document.lastModified+".");
</script>
</head>
<body bgcolor="white">
<h2>Calculations for Total Precipitable Water Vapor
(PW)</h2>
<p>
<form method="post" action="PWcalc3.php">
<table border="2">
  <tr bgcolor="silver"><td
     colspan="4"><b>Location:</b></td></tr>
  <td>longitude (decimal degrees): </td>
  <td> <input type="text" name="lon" value="-75.188"
    size="8"> </td>
```

```
<td>latitude (decimal degrees): </td>
<td><input type="text" name="lat" value="39.955"
   size="8"></td></tr>
<tr bgcolor="silver"><td colspan="4">
   <b>Instrument Serial Number:</b></td></tr>
<tr><td colspan="4"><input type="text" name="SN"
   value="WV2-117" /></td></tr>
<tr bgcolor="silver">
   <td colspan="4"><b>Date:</b></td></tr>
<tr><td>mm/dd/yyyy</td>
<td><input type="text" name="mon" value="4"
   size="3"></td>
<td><input type="text" name="day" value="5"
   size="3"></td>
<td><input type="text" name="yr" value="2005"
   size="5"></td></tr>
<tr bgcolor="silver"><td
colspan="4"><b>Time:</b></td>
<tr><td>hh:mm:ss (<b><i><u>must</u></i> be Universal
   Time</b>)</td>
<td><input type="text" name="hr" value="14"
   size="3"></td>
<td><input type="text" name="min" value="33"
   size="3"></td>
<td><input type="text" name="sec" value="15"
size="3"></td></tr>
<tr><td colspan="2" bgcolor="silver"><b>Station
   pressure (mbar, not currently used in
   calculation):</b></td>
<td colspan="2"><input type="text" name="p"
   value="1013" size="7"></td></tr>
<tr bgcolor="silver"><td colspan="4">
   <b>Instrument voltages:</b></td></tr>
<tr>
<td>IR1</td>
<td><input type="text" name="IR1" value="0.742"
   size="5"> </td>
<td>IR1<sub>dark</sub></td>
<td><input type="text" name="IR1_dark" value="0.003"
   size="5"></td>
</tr>
<tr>
<td>IR2</td>
<td><input type="text" name="IR2" value="0.963"
  size="5"></td>
<td>IR2<sub>dark</sub></td>
```

```
<td><input type="text" name="IR2_dark" value="0.004"
  size="5"></td>
</tr>
</table>
<input type="submit"
  value="Click here to calculate PW..." />
</form>
</body>
</html>
```

This document last modified on 01/16/2008 10:39:39.

Calculations for Total Precipitable Water Vapor (PW)

Location:				
longitude (decimal degrees):	-75.188		latitude (decimal degrees):	39.955
Instrument Serial Number:				
WV2-117				
Date:				
mm/dd/yyyy	4	5		2005
Time:				
hh:mm:ss (*must* be Universal Time)	14	33		15
Station pressure (mbar, not currently used in calculation):	1013			
Instrument voltages:				
IR1	0.742	IR1$_{dark}$		0.003
IR2	0.963	IR2$_{dark}$		0.004

Click here to calculate PW...

The output looks similar to the output for Document 8.1, except that the PW calculations are replaced with a "submit" button that will pass values to a PHP document. The companion Document 8.2b, below, is a PHP application that will accept input values from Document 8.2, look up calibration constants in a file stored on a server, and then calculate PW. It incorporates the previous code for these calculations from Document 8.1, translated into PHP.

Document 8.2b (PWcalc3.php)

```
<html>
<title>WV calculations for calibrated instrument
</title>
<?php
```

```php
function getJD($m,$d,$y,$hour,$minute,$second) {
// Julian date
  $temp=ceil(($m-14)/12);//This number is always <= 0.
  $JD = $d - 32075 + floor(1461*($y+4800+$temp)/4)
    +floor(367*($m-2-$temp*12)/12) // m-2-temp*12 is always > 0.
    -floor(3*(floor(($y+4900+$temp)/100))/4);
  $JD =$JD-0.5+$hour/24+$minute/1440+$second/86400;
  return $JD;
}
function getSunpos($m,$d,$y,$hour,$minute,$second,$Lat,$Lon) {
// Retrieve Julian date
  $JD=getJD($m,$d,$y,$hour,$minute,$second);
// Solar position, ecliptic coordinates
  $dr=pi()/180;
  $T=($JD-2451545)/36525;
  $L0=280.46645+36000.76983*$T+0.0003032*$T*$T;
  $M=357.52910+35999.05030*$T-0.0001559*$T*$T-0.00000048*$T*$T*$T;
  $M_rad=$M*$dr;
  $e=0.016708617-0.000042037*$T-0.0000001236*$T*$T;
  $C=(1.914600-0.004817*$T-0.000014*$T*$T)*sin($M_rad)
    +(0.019993-0.000101*$T)*sin(2.*$M_rad)+0.000290*sin(3.*
  $M_rad);
// Replacement code for L_true=fmod(L0+c,360)
  $L_save=($L0+$C)/360;
  if ($L_save < 0) $L_true=($L0+$C)-ceil($L_save)*360;
  else $L_true=($L0+$C)-floor($L_save)*360;
  if ($L_true < 0) $L_true+=360;
  $f=$M_rad+$C*$dr;
  $R =1.000001018*(1-$e*$e)/(1+$e*cos($f));
// Sidereal time
$Sidereal_time=280.46061837+360.98564736629*($JD-
  2451545)+0.0003879*$T*$T-$T*$T*$T/38710000;
// Replacement code for Sidereal=fmod(Sidereal,360)
  $S_save=$Sidereal_time/360;
  if ($S_save < 0) $Sidereal_time=$Sidereal_time-
ceil($S_save)*360;
  else $Sidereal_time=$Sidereal_time-
floor($S_save)*360;
  if ($Sidereal_time < 0) $Sidereal_time+=360;
// Obliquity
  $obliquity=23+26/60+21448/3600-46.8150/3600*
$T-0.00059/3600*$T*$T +0.001813/3600*$T*$T*$T;
// Ecliptic to equatorial
```

```php
   $right_Ascension = atan2(sin($L_true*$dr)*cos($obliquity*
$dr),cos($L_true*$dr));
   $declination = asin(sin($obliquity*$dr)*sin($L_true*$dr));
   $Hour_Angle = $Sidereal_time + $Lon - $right_Ascension/$dr;
$elev=asin(sin($Lat*$dr)*sin($declination)+cos($Lat*
$dr)*cos($declination)*cos($Hour_Angle*$dr));
/* relative air mass from Andrew T. Young, Air mass and
refraction (Eq. 5),
   Appl. Opt., 33, 6, 1108-1110 (1994) */
   $cosz=cos(pi()/2-$elev);
// echo $cosz;
$airm=(1.002432*$cosz*$cosz+0.148386*$cosz+0.0096467)/
($cosz*$cosz*$cosz+
0.149864*$cosz*$cosz+0.0102963*$cosz+0.000303978);
   return $airm;
}
?>
</head>
<body bgcolor="white">
<?php
echo "<h2>Calculations for Total Precipitable Water
Vapor (PW)</h2>";
$m=getSunpos($_POST["mon"],$_POST["day"],$_POST["yr"],
$_POST["hr"],$_POST["min"],$_POST["sec"],
$_POST["lat"],$_POST["lon"]);
$IR1=$_POST["IR1"]-$_POST["IR1_dark"];
$IR2=$_POST["IR2"]-$_POST["IR2_dark"];
        $A=$_POST["A"];
        $B=$_POST["B"];
        $C=$_POST["C"];
        $beta=$_POST["beta"];
        $tau=$_POST["tau"];
        $SN=$_POST["SN"];
        $len=strlen($SN);
// Open WV instrument calibration constant file &
        $inFile = "WVdata.dat";
        $in = fopen($inFile,'r') or die("Can't open file");
// Read one header line &
        $line=fgets($in);
// Search rest of file for SN match &
        $found=1;
        while ((!feof($in)) && ($found == 1)) {
```

```php
      $line=fgets($in);
      $values=sscanf($line,"%s %f %f %f %f %f\n");
      list($SN_dat,$A,$B,$C,$beta,$tau)=$values;
      if (strncasecmp($SN_dat,$SN,$len)==0) {
        $found=0;
      }
    }
  fclose($in);
// Build table of outputs &

echo "<p><table
border='2'><tr><th>Input</th><th>Value</th></tr>";
echo "</td></tr>";
echo "<tr><td>Instrument SN</td><td>$SN</td></tr>";
echo "<tr bgcolor='silver'><td colspan='2'>Calibration
Constants</td></tr>";
echo "<tr><td>A</td><td>$A</td></tr>";
echo "<tr><td>B</td><td>$B</td></tr>";
echo "<tr><td>C</td><td>$C</td></tr>";
echo "<tr><td>&tau;</td><td>$tau</td></tr>";
echo "<tr><td>&beta;</td><td>$beta</td></tr>";
echo "<tr bgcolor='silver'>
  <td colspan='2'>Measurements</td></tr>";
echo "<tr><td>IR1 (sunlight - dark)</td><td>$IR1</td></tr>";
echo "<tr><td>IR2 (sunlight - dark)</td><td>$IR2</td></tr>";
echo "</table></p>";
$x = $C*$m*$tau - (log($IR2/$IR1)-$A)/$B;
$PW = pow($x,1/$beta)/$m;
echo "<p><table border='2'><tr><th>Output</th>
  <th>Value</th></tr>";
echo "<tr><td>relative air mass</td><td>";
echo round($m,4);
echo "</td></tr>";
echo "<tr><td>PW, cm H<sub>2</sub>O</td><td>";
echo round($PW,4);
echo "</table></p>";
?>
</body>
</html>
```

8

Calculations for Total Precipitable Water Vapor (PW)

Input	Value
Instrument SN	WV2-117
Calibration Constants	
A	0.9793
B	0.4687
C	0.2
τ	0.1
β	0.65
Measurements	
IR1 (sunlight - dark)	0.739
IR2 (sunlight - dark)	0.959

Output	Value
relative air mass	1.4806
PW, cm H_2O	1.3427

Needless to say, Document 8.2 deserves close attention and line-by-line comparison with Document 8.1, because it contains a great deal of information about using PHP in your own applications. Here are some general observations about similarities and differences between JavaScript and PHP.

1. The syntax of writing expressions and statements is essentially the same.
2. The syntax for user-defined functions is essentially the same.
3. In PHP, mathematical calculations are carried out with built-in functions, such as `sin(x)`, rather than the "methods" such as `Math.sin(x)` used in JavaScript. distinctions between a "function" and a "method" at the conceptual and language design level don't matter in these applications.
4. Values passed to a PHP application do not need to be converted explicitly from strings to numbers. In other words, there is no PHP equivalent to JavaScript's `parseFloat()` method. Recall that, in JavaScript, the result of adding two "numbers" passed from a form field would be a string that contained the concatenation of the two "numbers," interpreted as though they were strings of characters. In PHP, the concatenation operator is a period, not a "+" sign, so there is no chance for confusion. It is safe to conclude that the operator determines how its operands will be treated; the statement `$C = $A + $B;` interprets `$A` and `$B` as two numbers because this is the only interpretation that makes sense for the addition operator.

Considering that PHP and JavaScript are two different languages, the translation from JavaScript to PHP is remarkably easy. The explicit conversions of form field value from strings to numbers that are required in JavaScript is replaced by PHP code that assigns variables based on the values passed to the $_POST[] array in Document 8.3:

```php
$m=getSunpos($_POST["mon"],$_POST["day"],$_POST["yr"],
$_POST["hr"],
$_POST["min"],$_POST["sec"],$_POST["lat"],
$_POST["lon"]);
//$m=$_POST["airm"];
$IR1=$_POST["IR1"]-$_POST["IR1_dark"];
$IR2=$_POST["IR2"]-$_POST["IR2_dark"];
$A=$_POST["A"];
$B=$_POST["B"];
$C=$_POST["C"];
$beta=$_POST["beta"];
$tau=$_POST["tau"];
$SN=$_POST["SN"];
$len=strlen($SN);
```

$_POST is the PHP-generated array containing all the form field values passed to the application. For the most part, the new variable names created in Document 8.3 are the same as the names in the form fields from the calling HTML/JavaScript application. However, this doesn't have to be true. The statements

```php
$IR1=$_POST["IR1"]-$_POST["IR1_dark"];
$IR2=$_POST["IR2"]-$_POST["IR2_dark"];
```

take advantage of the fact that the voltage from each channel required for the precipitable water vapor calculation

```php
$x = $C*$m*$tau - (log($IR2/$IR1)-$A)/$B;
$PW = pow($x,1./$beta)/$m;
```

is the voltage reported when the instrument is pointed at the sun, minus the "dark" voltage produced by the instrument's electronics. So, $IR1 and $IR2 are defined as the difference between the sunlight and dark voltages for each channel, as posted from the calling document.

When converting JavaScript to PHP it is critical to remember to add a $ character to the beginning of all variable names. If you forget this character, PHP may not produce an error message, but your program will certainly not work!

The PHP syntax for creating user-defined functions that return a single value is just like JavaScript:

```
function
getSunpos($m,$d,$y,$hour,$minute,$second,$Lat,$Lon) {
...

$airm=(1.002432*$cosz*$cosz+0.148386*$cosz+0.0096467)/
($cosz*$cosz*$cosz+
    0.149864*$cosz*$cosz+0.0102963*$cosz+0.000303978);
  return $airm;
}
```

A PHP function for rounding numbers to a specified number of digits to the right of the decimal point can be used to limit the number of digits that would otherwise be displayed in an output string. For calculations based on the physical world, many of the digits displayed by default are meaningless. This statement rounds off the relative air mass to four digits:

```
echo round($m,4);
```

The `round()` function will not retain significant digits when they are 0. In other words, `round(5.444,4)` displays 5.444 rather than 5.4440. (You can gain more control over output using other output functions such as `printf()`.)

With PHP functions, it is the programmer's responsibility to ensure that input arguments are used appropriately because no syntax distinction is made between, for example, arguments intended to be used as character strings and those intended to be used as numbers. On the other hand, it is not necessary to worry about arguments that "look" like numbers being treated as strings, as could be the case in JavaScript.

The statement below from `function getSunpos()` in Document 8.3 demonstrates that a user-defined PHP function can be called from inside another PHP function, as expected:

```
$JD=getJD($m,$d,$y,$hour,$minute,$second);
```

One important topic not addressed by Document 8.3 is how to return multiple values from a PHP function. As previously noted, PHP functions can also return multiple values. Use the `array()` constructor to create an array of the values you wish to return from a function and then `return` that array. (PHP arrays will be discussed in detail in Chap. 9.) The `list()` construct can then be used to extract the values from that array. Document 8.3 shows how to do this. (It might be worthwhile to compare this example with Document 6.5.)

Document 8.3 (`circleStuff.php`)

```php
<?php
/* function CIRCLESTUFF($r) {...}
   will also work because PHP function names are case-
   insensitive!
*/
```

```
    function CircleStuff($r) {
        $area=M_PI*$r*$r;
        $circumference=2.*M_PI*$r;
    return array($area,$circumference);
}
        list($area,$circumference) = CircleStuff(3.);
        echo $area . ", " . $circumference;
?>
```

The echo statement displays the following:

```
28.274333882308, 18.849555921539
```

(This result begs for application of the round() function!)

It is a peculiarity of PHP that function names are case-*in*sensitive. Thus, function CircleStuff() and function CIRCLESTUFF() will both work in this example. Because variable names are case-sensitive, and because great care is generally required in matching cases in all other aspects of programming, it makes little sense to take advantage of this PHP "feature."

8.3
More About PHP File Input/Output

Consider the following problem:

A text file contains wind speed data:

```
1  1991  31
 3.2,  0.4,  3.8,  4.5,  3.3,  1.9,  1.6,  3.7,  0.8,  2.3,
2.8,  2.4,  2.5,  3.2,  4.1,  3.9,  5.0,  4.4,  4.4,  5.5,  3.0,
3.7,  2.2,  2.0
 2.6,  2.8,  2.3,  2.3,  1.2,  2.4,  3.1,  4.0,  3.6,  2.9,
6.0,  4.4,  0.8,  3.8,  3.5,  4.5,  2.7,  3.4,  6.6,  5.2,  1.6,
1.2,  2.3,  2.4
...
2  1991  28
 4.6,  5.9,  3.1,  3.2,  4.5,  4.4,  3.9,  4.4,  7.5,
8.4,10.2,  9.2,  8.1,  6.3,  3.1,  3.5,  2.2,  1.4,  0.4,  4.2,
5.4,  4.0,  2.9,  1.7
 2.5,  2.3,  2.1,  1.5,  2.3,  4.1,  5.3,  6.0,  6.0,
9.7,11.3,12.7,13.0,13.0,11.6,  9.9,  9.6,  8.7,  5.4,  5.1,
5.3,  5.6,  4.4,  4.2
...
```

(continued)

8

(continued)

> The three numbers in the first line of the file are the month, year, and number of days in the month. Then, for each day in the month, 24 hourly wind speeds are given (in units of miles per hour), separated by commas. Each set of 24 hourly values is on the same line of text in the file, even though each of those lines occupies three lines as displayed here. This pattern is repeated for all 12 months. Missing data are represented by a value of –1.
>
> Write a PHP script that will read this file and count the number of missing values for each month. The script should display as output the number of each month (1–12) of the year, and the number of missing values for that month. Write the results into a file and save it.

The calculations required for this problem are simple, but reading the data file correctly is more complicated and requires some care. Document 8.4 shows the code for solving this problem.

Document 8.4 (`windspd.php`)

```php
<?php
$inFile="windspd.dat";
$outFile="windspd.out";
$in = fopen($inFile, "r") or die("Can't open file.");
$out=fopen($outFile, "w");
while (!feof($in)) {
// Read one month, year, # of days.
  fscanf($in, "%u %u %u",$m,$y,$nDays);
  if (feof($in)) exit;
  echo $m . ', ' . $y . ', ' . $nDays . '<br />';
  $nMissing=0;
  for ($i=1; $i<=$nDays; $i++) {
    $hrly = fscanf($in, "%f,%f,%f,%f,%f,%f,%f,%f,%f, %f,%f,
%f,%f,%f,%f,%f,%f,%f,%f,%f,%f,%f,%f,%f");
    for ($hr=0; $hr<24; $hr++) {
        // echo $hrly[$hr] . ', ';
        if ($hrly[$hr] == -1) $nMissing++;
    }
    // echo $hrly[23] . '<br />';
  }
  echo 'Number of missing hours this month is ' . $nMissing
        .'.<br />';
      fprintf($out, "%u, %u, %u\r\n",$m,$y,$nMissing);
}
echo "All done.<br />"
// fclose($in);
// fclose($out);
?>
```

> 1, 1991, 31
> Number of missing hours this month is 22.
> 2, 1991, 28
> Number of missing hours this month is 0.
> All done.

The input file required by Document 8.4, `windspd.dat`, is stored in the PHP document folder, and the output file is written to the same directory. (You might want to create a separate directory just for output files created by PHP scripts, or for a particular project.) The output shown here is for a short version of this file, with data for only 2 months.

It is often the case that the code to read data from a data file should not assume ahead of time how many values are in the file. Thus, a conditional loop is most often the appropriate approach. The `feof()` function is used to test for an end-of-file mark that, when found, uses `exit` to close all the open files and terminate the program. If additional processing is required after reaching the end of the file, the alternative is to use `break` rather than `exit`:

```php
while (!feof($in)) {
// Read one month, year, # of days.
        fscanf($in, "%u %u %u", $m, $y, $nDays);
        if (feof($in)) break;
...
}
echo "All done.<br />";
fclose($in);
fclose($out);
// possibly more code here...
```

Executing a `break` exits the loop and code execution continues starting with the first statement after the loop.

The hourly data are read with `fscanf()`. You might be tempted to try reading the 24 hourly wind speed values like this[1]:

```php
// PHP code that won't work!
for ($hr = 0; $hr<23; $hr++)
        fscanf($in, "%f,", $hrly[i]);
fscanf($in,"%f",$hrly[23]);
```

This code assumes that `fscanf()` can be used to read values from the file one at a time. However, this won't work in PHP. The `fscanf()` function reads an entire line of text, just as `fgets()` does, regardless of what appears in the format string. The difference is that, without providing specific variable names to be read from the file, `fscanf()` puts values in an array, whereas `fgets()` puts everything in a string that must then be parsed

---

[1]Actually, you might be tempted only if you have programmed in C/C++.

with `sscanf()`. So, you can read the entire 24 h worth of wind speeds with a single call to `fscanf()`, but you need to write out 24 format specifiers, as shown.

Note these two `echo` statements inside the `while`... loop in Document 8.4:

```
// echo $hrly[$hr] . ', ';
...
// echo $hrly[23] . '<br />';
```

If the `//`'s are removed, all the wind speed values will be displayed. Whenever you are reading a file, it is important to ensure that you are reading the file correctly. The best way to do this is to echo back values from the file. If they all have the expected values, by comparison with the original data file, then you can proceed.

Part of the output for this problem is an output file that summarizes the missing data:

```
(windspd.out)
```

```
1, 1991, 22
2, 1991, 0
```

The file is opened in write-only mode and the data are written with `fprintf()` in the shaded line in Document 8.4. `fprintf()` is the basic function for creating formatted text files as output. In this case, the format specifier string `"%u, %u, %u\r\n"` writes three comma-separated integer values for the output file.

Because this code was written on a Windows computer and the output file will be used on a Windows computer, each line is terminated not just with `\n`, but with `\r\n`. This is because Windows text files have both a "linefeed" and a "return" character at the end of each line. Recall Document 7.5, in which only the `\n` character was used as a line termination. Although it is not obvious, the fact that this file was created as a `.csv` file and opened directly into Excel means that only the line feed `\n` character was needed. If you open the same file in Windows' Notepad, for example, there will be no line breaks.

8.4
More Examples

8.4.1
Calculating Volumes of Solid Objects

> Write an HTML document that allows a user to select a solid object shape and enter its dimensions and the material from which it is made. The choices could be a cube, a rectangular block, a cylinder, or a sphere. You could choose a number of possible materials—air, gold, water, etc. Then call a PHP application that will find the mass of the object by calculating its volume based on the specified shape and the density of the material as retrieved from a data file.

Document 8.5a shows an HTML interface for this problem. The possible shapes and materials are placed in `<select>` lists.

Document 8.5a (`getMass.htm`)

```html
<html>
<head>
<title>Calculate mass</title>
</head>
<body>
<form name="form1" method="post" action="getMass.php">
Enter length: <input type="text" name="L" value="3" /><br
/>
Enter width: <input type="text" name="W" value="2" /><br />
Enter height: <input type="text" name="H" value="10" /><br />
Enter radius: <input type="text" name="R" value="3" /><br />
<select name="shapes" size="10">
  <option value="cube">cube</option>
  <option value="cylinder">cylinder</option>
  <option value="block">rectangular block</option>
  <option value="sphere">sphere</option>
</select>
<select name="material" size="10">
  <option value="air">air</option>
  <option value="aluminum">aluminum</option>
  <option value="gold">gold</option>
  <option value="oxygen">oxygen</option>
  <option value="silver">silver</option>
  <option value="water">water</option>
</select>
<input type="submit" value="Click to get volume."
<!--
<input type="button" value="click"
onclick="alert(shapes.selectedIndex);
alert(material.options[material.selectedIndex].value); " />
  -->
    />
</form></body></html>
```

Note that the value attribute of the `<option>` tag can be, but does not have to be, the same as the text for the option. For the "rectangular block" shape, `value` is assigned as a single word (`block`), which will look like a single string literal value when it is used later in the PHP application.

In the original version of Document 8.5a, the first line of the input tag line,

8

```
<input type="submit" value="Click to get volume."
```

was replaced with the shaded lines that are now commented out of the <input> tag near the
end of Document 8.5a. This code will show which item has been chosen for each <select>
list. It remains to be seen how this information will be handled by the PHP application.

It is almost never a good idea to try to write an entire JavaScript or PHP application all
at once. A much better approach is to proceed step by step, testing your results one step at
a time. Once you understand Document 8.5a, it is then worth writing a single-line PHP
application that will simply look at what is posted to the application using the print_r()
function to display the contents of the $_POST array:

```
<?php
  print_r($_POST);
?>
```

This code will display something like this:

Array ([L] => 1 [W] => 1 [H] => 1 [R] => 3 [shapes] => cube [material] => oxygen)

Although it may not be obvious at first glance, this is an amazingly helpful result! In
JavaScript, it is necessary to invoke the selectedIndex properties of the two select
objects, shapes and material, in order to determine which option has been selected.
But, the output shown here demonstrates that this is not necessary in the PHP application.
PHP already "knows" which option has been selected without any effort on your part.
These values have been stored in the system-generated PHP array $_POST, whose ele-
ments are identified by name rather than with an integer index starting at 0. The details of
this output will make more sense when PHP arrays are discussed in Chap. 9.

Once you are convinced that the inputs are successfully passed to PHP, the calculations
can be done. The first step is to create a data file containing materials and their densities:

```
(density.dat)

material density (kg/m^3)
water 1000
aluminum 2700
gold 19300
silver 10500
oxygen 1.429
air 1.2
```

The header line is optional, but it is always a good idea to describe the contents of a data
file, including, in this case, the physical units in which the densities should be supplied.

The next step is less obvious. Although it is certainly possible to "hard code" volume
calculations for each allowed shape, a more interesting solution is to create a second data
file that contains PHP code for calculating the volume of each shape:

```
(volume.dat)

shape volume
cube $L*$L*$L
sphere 4./3.*M_PI*$R*$R*$R
cylinder M_PI*$R*$R*$L
block $L*$W*$H
```

The code string for each allowed shape assumes specific variable names for the dimensions—$L, $W, $H, and $R—as already defined in Document 8.5a.

Start building the PHP application like this:

```php
<?php
print_r($_POST);
$material=$_POST[material];
$shape=$_POST[shapes];
$L=$_POST[L];
$W=$_POST[W];
$H=$_POST[H];
$R=$_POST[R];
echo "<br />" . $material . ", " . $shape . "<br />";
?>
```

This code will display:

> Array ([L] => 1 [W] => 1 [H] => 1 [R] => 3 [shapes] => cube [material] => oxygen)
> oxygen, cube

Now it is clear that the PHP application is properly receiving the inputs passed from Document 8.5a and has stored them in local variables. (You could also echo the values of $L, $W, $H, and $R if you like.) In Document 8.5a, the fields were given the names L, W, H, and R, but this would not need to be the case. All that is important for the PHP application is to give the variables the same names used in the volume.dat file.

Document 8.5b gives the entire solution to this problem. This code should be written in three sections: first, the definition of the variables as shown above, then the code to search for the material in its data file, and finally the code to do the mass calculation.

Document 8.5b (getMass.php)

```php
<?php
print_r($_POST);
$material=$_POST[material];
$shape=$_POST[shapes];
$L=$_POST[L];
$W=$_POST[W];
```

```php
$H=$_POST[H];
$R=$_POST[R];
echo "<br />" . $material . ", " . $shape . "<br />";
$materialFile=fopen("density.dat","r");
$shapeFile=fopen("volume.dat","r");
// Read materials file.
$found=false;
$line=fgets($materialFile);
while ((!feof($materialFile)) && (!$found)) {
  $values=fscanf($materialFile,"%s %f",$m,$d);
  if (strcasecmp($material,$m) == 0) {
    echo $material . ", " . $m . ", " . $d . "<br />";
      $found=true;
  }
}
// Read volume file.
$found=false;
$line=fgets($shapeFile);
while ((!feof($shapeFile)) && (!$found)) {
  $values=fscanf($shapeFile,"%s %s",$s,$v);
  if (strcasecmp($shape,$s) == 0) {
    echo $shape . ", " . $v . "<br />";
      $found=true;
  }
}
// Close both data files.
fclose($materialFile);
fclose($shapeFile);
// Calculate mass.
$vv=$v . "*$d";
echo "Result: ".eval("return round($vv,3);")." kg<br />";
?>
```

In the interests of demonstrating just the essential code needed to solve this problem, Document 8.5b does not include code to determine whether the supplied material is included in the file of materials or whether there is a match with the shape supplied, but this would not be difficult to do.

The not-so-obvious and rather clever part of this application is included in the two shaded lines of the code in Document 8.5b:

```php
$vv=$v . "*$d";
echo "Result: " . eval("return round($vv,3);") . "<br />";
```

The first of these lines appends $"*\$d"$ to the volume calculation string—mass equals volume times density. This string now looks like "legal" PHP code, for example:

```
M_PI*$R*$R*$L*$d
```

(You could echo the value of $vv if you want to see what it contains.) The next line of the code "executes" this statement, using the eval() construct (it looks like a function, but is not), which is similar to the JavaScript eval() global method. The return keyword is required to get back the numerical result, and the round() function is applied to the calculation to remove extraneous digits from the output.

The obvious advantage of this approach is that you can add new materials and shapes without altering the PHP code, assuming that, at most, four variables—length, width, height, and radius—will be sufficient to describe all dimensions needed for the volume calculations. For more complicated shapes, it might be necessary to add new variables or apply different interpretations to existing variables.

8.4.2
Processing .bmp Image Files

Image files come in a variety of formats—jpg, gif, bmp, etc. Of these, bitmapped files are conceptually the simplest. A bitmap file (indicated with a .bmp extension) consists of two sections—an information section that contains information about the structure of the file and the image section itself. For 24-bit color images, the image is represented as a series of three bytes per pixel, with each byte containing values for the blue, green, and red color "guns" (in that order) that are used to produce that pixel. This arrangement allows for $256 \times 256 \times 256 = 16,777,216$ possible colors. There are other kinds of .bmp files that have fewer colors, but these will not be considered here—they actually require more code to process.

Because each pixel in a 24-bit color image requires three color bytes to define, bitmap images can be very large. In principle, .bmp files can be compressed, but this is generally not done. It is possible to apply "lossless compression" algorithms, such as the widely used ZIP compression algorithm, to .bmp files. The results depend greatly on the nature of the image itself. For example, an image with large blocks of single colors could be compressed significantly. However, this process has nothing to do with the image format itself because a compressed file needs to be uncompressed back to its original state before it can be used as an image file. Consequently, bitmap file compression is irrelevant to this discussion.

The simple structure of .bmp files makes them very easy to analyze with PHP (and other programming languages that can access external files). Although an image file is obviously not a "text" file, .bmp files can nonetheless be *treated* as text files that can be read and written one byte at a time, interpreting each byte as a "character." Here are the necessary details about the contents of each section in a .bmp file:

8

Header record

The header consists of 14 8-bit bytes.

Image information record

The image information record consists of 40 bytes.

Image data

The image pixels are stored "upside down." In other words, the first pixel in the image section represents the lower left-hand corner of the image as it is viewed. The pixels proceed from left to right, and row-by-row to the top of the image. If required, each row in the image is padded on the right end with extra bytes so that each row contains a multiple of 4 bytes. The value of these bytes is not specified, but they are not necessarily filled with zeros.

As an example of extracting from these records the values needed to work with a .bmp image, consider this image of a male wild turkey. This image, printed here in grayscale, is a 24-bit color .bmp file. Document 8.6 reads the header and image information records and interprets the values according to Tables 8.1 and 8.2. If you want to try this code, you will of course need to find your own .bmp image. Any photo processing utility should let you save an image in .bmp format, or you can create your own bitmap image with a drawing utility such as Windows' Paint program.

Document 8.6 (bmp_info.php)

```php
<?php
$inFile="turkey.bmp";
// Get the size of this file.
echo "File size: " . filesize($inFile)."<br />";
$in=fopen($inFile, 'r');
// Read header.
```

Table 8.1 Contents of header record

Byte Position (offset index + 1)	Contents
1–2	Image type field (BM)
3–6	File size, bytes
7–8	Not needed
9–10	Not needed
11–14	Offset to image data, bytes

Table 8.2 Contents of file information record

Byte Position (offset index + 1)	Contents
1–4	Header size, in bytes
5–8	Width of image, bytes
9–12	Height of image, bytes
13–14	Number of color planes
15–16	Bits per pixel
17–20	Compression type (0 for uncompressed 24-bit color images)
21–24	Image size, bytes
25–28	X-resolution
29–32	Y-resolution
33–36	Number of colors
37–40	Important colors

```php
$c=array();
for ($i=0; $i<14; $i++) {
    $c[$i]=ord(fgetc($in));
    echo $c[$i]." ";
}
echo "<br />";
// Calculate file size.
$size=$c[5]*16777216+$c[4]*65536+$c[3]*256+$c[2];
echo "File size = ".$size." bytes.<br />";
// Find offset to start of image.
$offset=$c[10];
echo "Offset to start of image = ".$offset."<br />";
// Read image information record.
for ($i=0; $i<40; $i++) {
$c[$i]=ord(fgetc($in));
echo $c[$i]." ";
}
echo "<br />";
// Get # of rows and columns.
$cols=$c[7]*16777216+$c[6]*65536+$c[5]*256+$c[4];
$rows=$c[11]*16777216+$c[10]*65536+$c[9]*256+$c[8];
echo "This image has ".$rows." rows and ".$cols."
columns.<br />";
// Get some other information.
$nPlanes=$c[13]*256+$c[12];
echo "# of color planes = ".$nPlanes."<br />";
$bitsPerPixel=$c[15]*256+$c[14];
echo "Bits per pixel = ".$bitsPerPixel."<br />";
$compressionType=$c[19]*16777216+$c[18]*65536+$c[17]*256+$c[16];
```

```php
echo "Compression type = ".$compressionType."<br />";
$imageSize=$c[23]*16777216+$c[22]*65536+$c[21]*256+$c[20];
echo "Image size = ".$imageSize."<br />";
$Xresolution=$c[27]*16777216+$c[26]*65536+$c[25]*256+$c[24];
echo "X-resolution = ".$Xresolution."<br />";
$Yresolution=$c[31]*16777216+$c[30]*65536+$c[29]*256+$c[28];
echo "Y-resolution = ".$Yresolution."<br />";
$nColors=$c[35]*16777216+$c[34]*65536+$c[33]*256+$c[32];
echo "number of colors = ".$nColors."<br />";
$importantColors=$c[39]*16777216+$c[38]*65536+$c[37]*256+$c[36];
echo "important colors = ".$importantColors."<br />";
// Close the file.
fclose($in);
?>
```

The shaded line of code in Document 8.6 shows how to use `fgetc()` to read a single character and then to use `ord()` to convert that character into its base-10 integer value.

As indicated in Table 8.1, the first two bytes , $c[0] and $c[1], contain ASCII values 66 and 77, corresponding to the upper-case letters B and M, which identify this as a bitmap file. Bytes $c[2] through $c[5] contain the file size, represented as a 32-bit integer. This integer is stored in four bytes, in low-to-high (reversed) order, and the base-10 integer is extracted like this:

file size =
`$c[2]+256*$c[3]+65536*$c[4]+16777216*$c[5]`
           $= 18 + 144 \cdot 256 = 36882$

This value is the same as the value obtained from `filesize($inFile)`.

> File size: 36882
> 66 77 18 144 0 0 0 0 0 0 54 0 0 0
> File size = 36882 bytes.
> Offset to start of image = 54
> 40 0 0 0 131 0 0 0 93 0 0 0 1 0 24 0
> 0 0 0 0 220 143 0 0 19 11 0 0 19 11 0 0
> 0 0 0 0 0 0 0 0
> This image has 93 rows and 131 columns.
> # of color planes = 1
> Bits per pixel = 24
> Compression type = 0
> Image size = 36828
> X-resolution = 2835
> Y-resolution = 2835
> number of colors = 0
> important colors = 0

The next four bytes can be ignored. The last four bytes give the offset to the start of the image data, also stored in four reverse-order bytes even though for 24-bit images only the first (lowest order) byte will have a value other than 0:

Offset to image =
`$c[10]+256*$c[11]+65536*$c[12]+16777216*$c[13]` $= 54$

This value is as expected because 14+40, the number of bytes in the header and image information records, equals 54.

The image information record shows that this image is 91 pixels high and 131 pixels wide. There are 24 bits per color. The only compression type of interest in this discussion is 0, for an uncompressed image. The image size is 32,828 bytes, equal to the file size minus 54 bytes for the header and image information records. The *X*- and *Y*-resolution are given in the somewhat puzzling units of pixels per meter, which might be useful for deciding how to display this image on a computer monitor. For 24-bit color images, the number of colors is not specified here, and all colors are "important," so the number of important colors can be ignored.

With this information, it is now possible to read and interpret the image section of a .bmp file. As a test of whether images are being interpreted properly, a reasonable goal is to read the image, convert the pixels to their grayscale equivalent, and create a new .bmp file containing this grayscale image. An easy way to convert a color image to grayscale is to average the blue, green, and red values for each pixel and replace each of those values with that average value. With this approach, the format of the grayscale image file will be exactly the same as the 24-bit color image.

Document 8.7 shows how to read a .bmp file.

Document 8.7 (bmp_read.php)

```php
<?php
$inFile="turkey.bmp";
echo filesize($inFile)."<br />";
$in=fopen($inFile,'r');
// Read header.
$ch=array();
for ($i=0; $i<14; $i++) {
      $ch[$i]=ord(fgetc($in));
      echo $ch[$i]." ";
}
echo "<br />";
//$offset=$ch[10];
for ($i=0; $i<40; $i++) {
  $ch[$i]=ord(fgetc($in));
  echo $ch[$i]." ";
}
echo "<br />";
$cols=$ch[5]*256+$ch[4];
$bytes=3*$cols;
// Each row is padded to contain a multiple of 4 bytes.
$nPad=4-$bytes%4;
echo "# of pad bytes = ".$nPad."<br />";
$rows=$ch[9]*256+$ch[8];
echo "rows and columns: ".$rows." ".$cols."<br />";
```

8

```
// Read image.
for ($r=1; $r<=$rows; $r++) {
  for ($c=1; $c<=$cols; $c++) {
    for ($i=0; $i<=2; $i++) {
        $ch[$i]=fgetc($in);
        echo ord($ch[$i]);
      }
      echo " ";
}
// Read pad bytes at end of line.
for ($p=1; $p<=$nPad; $p++) {
    $pad=fgetc($in);
    echo "pad";
}
echo "<br />";
}
fclose($in);
?>
```

```
3688266 77 18 144 0 0 0 0 0 0 54 0 0 0
40 0 0 0 131 0 0 0 93 0 0 0 1 0 24 0 0 0 0 0 220 143 0 0 19 11 0 0 19 11 0 0 0 0 0 0 0 0
0 0
# of pad bytes = 3
rows and columns: 93 131
488478 488478 488478 659993 75109103 639791 85119113 599387 609488 78110105
92124119 80112107 83113108 649489 88118113 83113108 86116111 97129124
669893 75103103 679393 729597 668789 8199106 607885 8096103 95111117 769298
99118121 80100101 82104102 749896 436864 729793 729793 729995 709591
98125121 92117113 618884 739894 649187 85110106 77104100 689389 588680
659086 7510397 84109105 81109103 508172 599382 6710190 7611099 77111100
629685 619584 80116104 6810492 478573 569482 84122110 81119107 6610694
6110189 6710593 6710593 6710593 6610191 85119109 77108101 7610399 114138138
138159161 126145150 115133140 110125134 146161170 124139148 137154163
101120128 112134140 130152158 80108109 92128122 73113102 115155144
74114103 79119108 76116105 6010089 101141130 78118107 122162151 121160152
90130119 88127119 97137126 101140132 101140132 80122111 74118105 107152136
122167151 88131116 100141126 115156141 86124112 101139127 106143133
111148138 81121110 539584 82123115 84127118 84129120 106146141 142171176
126149157 92118124 87116120 104135136 87122118 6710397 74114103 569684
87127115 7011196 347560 529176 79118103 padpadpad
...
```

(continued)

(continued)

```
1392685 1392685 1392685 1392685 1392685 1392685 1392685 1392685 1392685
1392685 1392685 1392685 1392685 1392685 1392685 1392685 1392685 1392685
1392685 1392685 1392685 1392685 1392685 1392685 1392685 1392685 1392685
1392685 1392685 1392685 1392685 1392685 1392685 1392685 1392685 1392685
1392685 1392685 1392685 1392685 1392685 1392685 1392685 1392685 1392685
1392685 1392685 1392685 1392685 1392685 1392685 1392685 1392685 1392685
1392685 1392685 1392685 1392685 1392685 1392685 1392685 1392685 1392685
1392685 1392685 1392685 1392685 1392685 1392685 1392685 1392685 1392685
1392685 1392685 1392685 1392685 1392685 1392685 1392685 1392685 1392685
1392685 1392685 1392685 1392685 1392685 1392685 1392685 1392685 1392685
1392685 1392685 1392685 1392685 1392685 1392685 1392685 1392685 1392685
1392685 1392685 1392685 1392685 1392685 1392685 1392685 1392685 1392685
1392685 1392685 1392685 1392685 1392685 1392685 1392685 1392685 1392685
1392685 1392685 1392685 1392685 1392685 1392685 1392685 1392685 1392685
1392685 1392685 1392685 1392685 1392685 padpadpad
```

Document 8.8 is a version of Document 8.7 that reads the original file and modifies the color values to create a grayscale version of the image.

Document 8.8 (bmp_grayscale.php)

```php
<?php
$inFile="turkey.bmp";
$outFile="turkey_grayscale.bmp";
echo filesize($inFile)."<br />";
$in=fopen($inFile,'r');
$out=fopen($outFile,'w');
// Read header.
$ch=array();
for ($i=0; $i<14; $i++) {
  //$ch[$i]=ord(fgetc($in));
  //echo $ch[$i]." ";
  //fwrite($out,chr($ch[$i]),1);
  fwrite($out, fgetc($in));
}
echo "<br />";
//$offset=$ch[10];
for ($i=0; $i<40; $i++) {
  $ch[$i]=ord(fgetc($in));
  echo $ch[$i]." ";
  fwrite($out,chr($ch[$i]),1);
}
echo "<br />";
$cols=$ch[5]*256+$ch[4];
```

```php
$bytes=3*$cols;
$nPad=4-$bytes%4; // Each row padded to contain a multiple
of 4 bytes.
echo "# of pad bytes = ".$nPad."<br />";
$rows=$ch[9]*256+$ch[8];
echo "rows and columns: ".$rows." ".$cols."<br />";
// Read image.
for ($r=1; $r<=$rows; $r++) {
  for ($c=1; $c<=$cols; $c++) {
    for ($i=0; $i<=2; $i++) {
        $ch[$i]=fgetc($in);
    }
        $avg=(ord($ch[0])+ord($ch[1])+ord($ch[2]))/3;
        fwrite($out,chr($avg),1); fwrite($out,chr($avg),1);
        fwrite($out,chr($avg),1);
  }
  // Read pad bytes at end of line.
  for ($p=1; $p<=$nPad; $p++) {
      $pad=fgetc($in);
      fwrite($out,$pad);
  }
}
fclose($in);
fclose($out);
echo "A grayscale file has been created.<br />";
?>
```

All that is required to create a new .bmp file is to write every character that is read from the original file into the new file. If no changes are made in these characters, then the new file is a copy of the original file. In this case, the color values will be changed. The resulting grayscale image created by Document 8.8 is not shown here because it looks just like the original image of the turkey shown above, which was converted to grayscale for printing.[2]

The first block of highlighted text shows that it is not necessary to convert the character to its decimal value, using the ord() function, unless these values are actually needed for something. In this case, the character is read from the original file and written to the new file in a single statement, using the fwrite() function.

The second block of highlighted text shows the code used to replace the color settings with their average grayscale settings before writing them to the new file. In this case, it is necessary to convert the characters to base-10 values in order to compute their average.

---

[2]As is the case for other images in this book that were originally in color, the grayscale conversion was done with the excellent freeware image editing program IrfanView.

This simple example of how to manipulate the contents of a .bmp file opens the door to many possibilities for processing images. The contrast in images can be stretched or compressed, linearly or nonlinearly. Starting with a grayscale image, it is easy to generate false-color images based on the grayscale values. All these possibilities are applicable to medical and other kinds of X-ray imaging, for example.

A less obvious application is to use .bmp files to transmit text messages. In fact, although it seems like a silly use of the .bmp file format, there is no reason why a .bmp file can't contain *just* text in the bytes that assign RGB color settings, rather than "real" color values. "Image processing" then becomes simply a matter of appropriately interpreting the file contents as text.

Because of the structure of .bmp files, it is easy to embed "hidden" text within an image. Even in a relatively small bitmap image, there are places to hide text where it will be virtually undetectable in the image itself. Individual color values can be replaced with ASCII character codes that still look like legitimate color settings. Even better, the padding bytes that may be added to the end of each row of an image (depending on its width, to make each row a multiple of four bytes) are completely invisible within the image. They are not needed for anything and they can be used to store text.

Within the 14-byte image header record, there are four unused bytes that can be used to hold the location—perhaps the row and column—of the start of the text message. This information could also be included in the padding bytes for the first (bottom) row of the image, for example. While not actually encrypted, a small text message embedded within a large .bmp file will be very hard to find unless you know what you are looking for and where to look for it.

Document 8.9 writes the message "Please don't eat me!" into the padding bytes, starting at row 9—this value is written into the unused seventh byte of the header record.

Document 8.9 (bmp_hidetext.php)

```php
<?php
$inFile="turkey.bmp";
$outFile="turkey_text.bmp";
echo filesize($inFile)."<br />";
$in=fopen($inFile,'r');
$out=fopen($outFile,'w');
$hiddenText="Please don't eat me!";
$startRow=9;
// Read header.
$ch=array();
for ($i=0; $i<14; $i++) {
  $ch[$i]=ord(fgetc($in));
  echo $ch[$i]." ";
  // Write starting row for text here, in unused byte.
  if ($i==6) fwrite($out,chr($startRow),1);
  else fwrite($out,chr($ch[$i]),1);
}
```

8

```php
echo "<br />";
//$offset=$ch[10];
for ($i=0; $i<40; $i++) {
  $ch[$i]=ord(fgetc($in));
  echo $ch[$i]." ";
  fwrite($out,chr($ch[$i]),1);
}
echo "<br />";
$cols=$ch[7]*16777216+$ch[6]*65536+$ch[5]*256+$ch[4];
$bytes=3*$cols;
$nPad=4-$bytes%4; // Each row padded to contain a multiple
of 4 bytes.
echo "# of pad bytes = ".$nPad."<br />";
$rows=$ch[11]*16777216+$ch[10]*65536+$ch[9]*256+$ch[8];
echo "rows and columns: ".$rows." ".$cols."<br />";
// Read image.
$K=strlen($hiddenText);
$knt=0;
for ($r=1; $r<=$rows; $r++) {
  for ($c=1; $c<=$cols; $c++) {
    for ($i=0; $i<=2; $i++) {
        $ch[$i]=fgetc($in);
    }
    $avg=(ord($ch[0])+ord($ch[1])+ord($ch[2]))/3;
    fwrite($out,chr($avg),1);
    fwrite($out,chr($avg),1);
    fwrite($out,chr($avg),1);
}
// Read pad bytes at end of line.
for ($p=1; $p<=$nPad; $p++) {
    $pad=fgetc($in);
    if (($r>=$startRow) && ($knt<$K)) {
      // Write text into pad bytes.
      fwrite($out,substr($hiddenText,$knt,1),1);
      $knt++;
    }
    else fwrite($out,$pad,1);
  }
}
fclose($in);
fclose($out);
echo "A grayscale file has been created.<br />";
?>
```

Using `turkey_text.bmp` as the input file, the output from Document 8.9, for row 9, looks like this:

```
949494 949494 949494 939393 808080 757575 898989 787878 848484 929292
939393 108108108 929292 104104104 898989 999999 949494 939393 939393
898989 868686 100100100 777777 686868 797979 848484 616161 797979 828282
636363 606060 515151 737373 666666 666666 505050 707070 555555 383838
585858 575757 505050 303030 353535 292929 111111 222 222 444 111 666 222222
232323 161616 161616 141414 888 111111 777 777 555 181818 111 111 111 111 111
111 222 666 151515 161616 343434 828282 100100100 696969 333 444 666 000
171717 343434 838383 133133133 102102102 105105105 145145145 102102102
123123123 110110110 117117117 132132132 120120120 153153153 115115115
137137137 120120120 138138138 129129129 129129129 122122122 878787
969696 989898 989898 115115115 112112112 929292 989898 979797 979797
123123123 114114114 120120120 106106106 124124124 120120120 909090 808080
959595 109109109 979797 888888 888888 797979 858585 979797 747474
119119119 939393 113113113 Ple
```

The first three characters in the text message ("Ple") are found in the three padding bytes at the end of row 9—remember that this text doesn't affect the image in *any* way. This code doesn't retrieve the location of the first row containing the text message from the header record, to tell you where to start looking for the text message, but it could easily do that.

8.4.3
Transforming and Displaying Images

The GD graphics library for PHP will be discussed in Chap. 12. It includes functions for transforming and displaying existing JPEG, GIF, or PNG images. There is no similar function for BMP images because those images are just "text" files that can be used to create images as discussed in the previous section. Document 8.10 shows how to create and display a PNG image starting with an existing GIF image, using `ImageCreateFromGIF()` and `ImagePNG()`. Similar functions exist for JPEG images. The `Header` specifies the output content type.

Document 8.10 (`TransformImage.php`)

```php
<?php
$imagePath="turkey.gif"; // existing image
$im=ImageCreateFromGIF($imagePath);
Header('Content-type: image/png');
ImagePNG($im); // ImagePNG($im,{filename}) saves to file.
ImageDestroy($im);
?>
```

8

8.4.4
Self-Contained HTML/JavaScript/PHP Documents

> Given an amount of money A, an annual interest rate r percent, and a number of years, y, calculate the future value of that amount, F, assuming interest compounded annually:
>
> $$F = A \cdot \left(1 + r/100\right)^{y}$$

Previously, HTML/JavaScript documents have been kept separate from their related PHP documents, with the understanding that an HTML/JavaScript document will provide an input interface for a PHP document. The PHP document can be stored on a local server—often, in the same directory—or on some remote server. For working locally with documents, it may be convenient to combine an HTML/JavaScript document and its associated PHP code into a single PHP document. Document 8.11 shows how to do this.

Document 8.11 (`CompoundInterest.php`)

```html
<html>
<head>
<title>Calculate Compound Interest</title>
</head>
<body>
<h3>Calculate Compound Interest</h3>
<form action="<?php $_SERVER['PHP_SELF']?>" method="post">
Initial amount (no commas), $: <input type="text"
    name="initial" value="10000" /><br />
Annual interest rate, %: <input type="text" name="rate"
    value="4" /><br />
How many years?: <input type="text" name="years"
    value="20" /><br />
<input type="submit"
    value="Generate compound interest table." />
</form>
<?php
    $initial=$_POST["initial"];
    $rate=$_POST["rate"];
    $years=$_POST["years"];
    echo $initial." ".$rate." ".$years."<br />";
    for ($i=1; $i<=$years; $i++) {
      $amount=$initial*pow(1+$rate/100,$i);
      echo $i." $".number_format($amount,2)."<br />";
    }
```

```
?>
</body>
</html>
```

The "action" specified in the <form> tag,

$ **SERVER** ['PHP SELF']

is a call to the PHP section of the same document. This case was run for 10 years, but after the PHP code is completed, the HTML document reverts to the default value of 20 years.

Calculate Compound Interest

Initial amount (no commas), $: `10000`

Annual interest rate, %: `4`

How many years?: `20`

[Generate compound interest table.]

```
10000 4 10
1 $10,400.00
2 $10,816.00
3 $11,248.64
4 $11,698.59
5 $12,166.53
6 $12,653.19
7 $13,159.32
8 $13,685.69
9 $14,233.12
10 $14,802.44
```

PHP Arrays

9

Abstract Chapter 9 provides an introduction to PHP arrays. The PHP array model provides several new ways of accessing and manipulating data, beyond those available in JavaScript.

9.1
Array Definition

The ability to organize related information in arrays is as important for PHP as it is for JavaScript and other languages. PHP supports *dozens* of functions and constructs for manipulating arrays, corresponding to an array implementation model that is much more complicated than available in JavaScript. Hence, it is often not sufficient simply to translate JavaScript array syntax into PHP. This chapter will present just the basics of working with PHP arrays.

In JavaScript's conceptual model for arrays, array elements can contain a mixture of data types. Each element is accessed with an integer index. The index of the first element is always 0.

PHP arrays include, but are not limited to, this model. In PHP, arrays are created with the array() constructor:

```
$ArrayName = array([(mixed data types)...])
```

where $ArrayName is a generic representation of a user-supplied array name. The elements, which are optional for creating the array, can contain a mixture of data types, just like JavaScript arrays. However, in PHP, each element of an array can have its own user-defined index (**key**) value:

```
$a = array($key1 => $value1, $key2 => $value2,
        $key3 => $value3,...);
```

The => operator associates a key with its value. The keys can be numbers, characters, or strings. Numerical keys can start with any value, not just 0 (which would correspond to the simpler JavaScript array model), and they don't even have to be sequential (although they usually are). Document 9.1 shows an example of an array with named keys.

D.R. Brooks, *Guide to HTML, JavaScript and PHP: For Scientists and Engineers*,
DOI 10.1007/978-0-85729-449-4_9, © Springer-Verlag London Limited 2011

9

Document 9.1 (`keyedArray.php`)

```php
<?php
// Create an array with user-specified keys…
echo '<br />A keyed array:<br />';
$stuff = array('mine' => 'BMW', 'yours' => 'Lexus',
  'ours' => 'house');
foreach ($stuff as $key => $val) {
echo '$stuff[' . $key . '] = '. $val . '<br />';
}
?>
```

```
A keyed array:$stuff[mine]  =  BMW
$stuff[yours]  =  Lexus
$stuff[ours]  =  house
```

The names associated with the keys and array elements can be anything you like—they don't have to be $key and $val, as they are in Document 9.1. A for… loop will not work for an array with string names or non-sequential numerical keys. Instead, a foreach… loop is used, with syntax as shown in the shaded statement. It is the syntax following the as keyword that makes the association between a key name and its array element.

The number of elements in an array is given by the sizeof() or count()) function. Note that a foreach… loop does not require or even allow that you specify the length of the array. The syntax that should be familiar to JavaScript programmers, using sizeof() and an integer index inside a for… loop, won't work with this array because the indices have arbitrary names rather than sequential values:

```php
/* This won't work!
for ($i=0; $i<sizeof($stuff); $i++)
  echo $stuff[$i] . '<br />';
*/
```

This for… loop code won't generate an error message—it just won't generate any output.

If the keys specified are the default integer keys starting at 0, then it is straightforward to use a JavaScript-like for… loop, as shown in Document 9.2, below. It is also possible to use a for… loop if the array is created with a starting index other than 0, or if it has consecutive character keys; these possibilities are also illustrated in Document 9.2.

Document 9.2 (`ConsecutiveKeyArray.php`)

```php
<?php
$a = array('david','apple','Xena','Sue');
echo "Using for… loop<br />";
for ($i=0; $i<sizeof($a); $i++)
```

```
    echo $a[$i] . '<br />';
echo "Using implied keys with foreach... loop<br />";
foreach ($a as $i => $x)
    echo 'a[' . $i . '] = ' . $x . '<br />';
echo "An array with keys starting at an integer other than
0<br />";
$negKey = array(-1 => 'BMW', 'Lexus', 'house');
for ($i=-1; $i<2; $i++)
    echo $negKey[$i] . '<br />';
echo 'A keyed array with consecutive character keys...<br
/>';
$stuff = array('a' => 'BMW', 'b' => 'Lexus', 'c' =>
'house');
for ($i='a'; $i<='c'; $i++)
    echo $stuff[$i] . '<br />';
?>
```

```
Using for... loop
david
apple
Xena
Sue
Using implied keys with foreach... loop
a[0] = david
a[1] = apple
a[2] = Xena
a[3] = Sue
An array with keys starting at an integer other than 0
[−1] = BMW
[0] = Lexus
[1] = house
A keyed array with consecutive character keys...
[a] = BMW
[b] = Lexus
[c] = house
```

Document 9.2 demonstrates that even if specific key definitions are omitted, they still exist and are given default integer values starting at 0. It also shows that it is possible to define just the first key, and the other keys will be assigned consecutively.

The ability to specify just the starting key provides an easy way to start array indices at 1 rather than 0, as might be convenient for labeling columns and rows in a table or the 12 months in a year:

```
$a = array(1 => 63.7, 77.5, 17, -3);
$m = array(1 => January,February,March,April,May,June,
    July,August,September,October,November,December);
```

The first index has a value of 1 and the remaining unspecified indices are incremented by 1. Either a foreach... or a for... loop can be used to access the values, as shown in Document 9.3.

Document 9.3 (base_1Array.php)

```php
<?php
echo '<br />A keyed array with indices starting at 1…
<br />';
$a = array(1 => 63.7, 77.5, 17, -3);
foreach ($a as $key => $val) {
  echo 'a[' . $key . '] = '. $val . '<br />';
}
for ($i=1; $i<=sizeof($a); $i++)
  echo $a[$i] . '<br />';
?>
```

```
A keyed array with indices starting at 1...
a[1] = 63.7
a[2] = 77.5
a[3] = 17
a[4] = -3
63.7
77.5
17
-3
```

Two-dimensional arrays—think of them as row-and-column tables—can be formed from an array of arrays, as shown in Document 9.4.

Document 9.4 (two-D.php)

```php
<?php
echo '<br />A 2-D array<br />';
$a = array(
  0 => array(1,2,3,4),
  1 => array(5,6,7,8),
  2 => array(9,10,11,12),
  3 => array(13,14,15,16),
  4 => array(17,18,19,20)
);
```

```
$n_r=count($a); echo '# rows = ' . $n_r . '<br />';
$n_c=count($a[0]); echo '# columns = ' . $n_c . '<br />';
for ($r=0; $r<$n_r; $r++) {
  for ($c=0; $c<$n_c; $c++)
    echo $a[$r][$c] . ' ';
  echo '<br />';
}
?>
```

```
A 2-D array
# rows = 5
# columns = 4
1 2 3 4
5 6 7 8
9 10 11 12
13 14 15 16
17 18 19 20
```

Document 9.4 uses the count() function to determine the number of rows and columns in the array; this function is completely equivalent to and interchangeable with sizeof(). The number of elements in $a, the "rows," is returned by count($a). Each element in $a is another array containing the "columns," and count($a[0]) (or any other index) returns the number of elements in this array. The count() function counts only defined array elements, so in order for it to work as expected, every element in an array must be given a value. In Document 9.4, defining the first row as

```
0 => array(1,2,3)
```

will result in the number of columns being identified as 3 rather than 4 if you use count($a[0]).

Higher-dimension arrays can be defined by extending the above procedure.

9.2
Array Sorting

PHP supports several functions for sorting arrays, including a sort() function similar to JavaScript's sort() method. Consider Document 9.5.

Document 9.5 (sort1.php)

```php
<?php
// Create and sort an array…
$a = array('david','apple','sue','xena');
echo 'Original array:<br />';
for ($i=0; $i<sizeof($a); $i++)
```

```
  echo $a[$i] . '<br />';
sort($a);
echo 'Sorted array:<br />';
for ($i=0; $i<sizeof($a); $i++)
  echo $a[$i] . '<br />';
?>
```

This code produces the expected results with the array as defined:

```
Original array:
david
apple
sue
xena
Sorted array:
apple
david
sue
xena
```

But it won't do what you probably want for this change to the array, in which two names are capitalized:

```
$a = array('david','apple','Xena','Sue');
```

Recall that JavaScript's sort() method also produced unexpected results because of its default actions in deciding which values were "less than" others. For example, "Sue" is considered to be less than "sue" because the uppercase alphabet comes earlier in the ASCII character sequence than the lowercase alphabet. The same problems exist with PHP's basic sort() function:

```
Original array:
david
apple
Xena
Sue
Sorted array:
Sue
Xena
apple
david
```

JavaScript programmers will also be concerned about potential problems with arrays of numbers because of how JavaScript treats values passed from form fields. For example, because "1" comes before "3" in the ASCII character sequence, JavaScript's sort() will consider "13" to be less than "3" unless the parseFloat() or parseInt()

methods are first applied to the values to convert them explicitly to numbers. Document 9.6 demonstrates that PHPs `sort ()` function does not have this problem with numbers.

Document 9.6 (sort2.php)

```php
<?php
    $a=array(3.3,-13,-0.7,14.4);
    sort($a);
    for ($i=0; $i<sizeof($a); $i++)
      echo $a[$i] . '<br />';
?>
```

```
-13
-0.7
3.3
14.4
```

PHP offers several ways to sort arrays of strings and other combinations of elements, but a simple and reliable approach is to use the `usort ()` function and provide a user-defined function that compares one array element against another using user-supplied criteria. This is comparable to using the JavaScript `sort ()` function with its optional argument giving the name of a user-defined function to compare array elements. The user-supplied comparison function must return an integer value less than 0 if the first argument is to be considered as less than the second, 0 if they are equal, and greater than 0 if the first argument is greater than the second. For an array with strings containing upper- and lowercase letters, the very simple function shown in Document 9.7 makes use of `strcasecmp ()` to perform a case-insensitive comparison of two strings.

Document 9.7 (sort3.php)

```php
<?php
function compare($x,$y) {

   return strcasecmp($x,$y);
}
// Create and sort an array...
$a = array('Xena', 'Sue', 'david', 'apple');
echo 'Original array:<br />';
for ($i=0; $i<sizeof($a); $i++)
   echo $a[$i] . '<br />';
echo 'Sorted array with user-defined comparisons of
elements:<br />';
usort($a, "compare");
for ($i=0; $i<sizeof($a); $i++)
   echo $a[$i] . '<br />';
?>
```

9

```
Original array:
Xena
Sue
david
apple
Sorted array with user-defined comparisons
of elements:
apple
david
Sue
Xena
```

9.3
Stacks, Queues, and Line Crashers

The concepts that apply to and queues are language-independent, so those concepts for storing and retrieving data in arrays are the same for PHP as they are for JavaScript. As is the case for JavaScript, it is very easy to work with queues and stacks in PHP because arrays can be resized dynamically. The sketch in Sect. 5.2, which defined last-in/first-out (LIFO) and first-in/first-out (FIFO) data storage models and operations on stacks and queues, applies equally to PHP.

Because PHP's array model supports user-defined keys for each element, the possibilities for adding elements to and removing them from stacks or queues (or other array operations models) is complicated. This section will deal only with the basics, assuming arrays with integer indices that start at 0. This limited approach is sufficient for many science and engineering problems and for basic data handling.

The basic functions are array_pop(), array_push(), array_shift(), and array_unshift(). Document 9.8 demonstrates the use of each of these functions.

Document 9.8 (StacksAndQueues.php)

```php
<html>
<head>
<title>Stacks and Queues</title>
</head>
<body>
<?php
  $a = array(-17,"David", 33.3,"Laura");
// Treat $a like a stack (last in, first out)…
  echo "The original array (element [0] is the \"oldest\"
element):<br />";
```

```php
  print_r($a);
// Add two elements to $a…
  array_push($a,"Susan",0.5);
  echo "<br />Push two elements on top of stack:<br />";
  print_r($a);
// Remove three elements from $a…
  array_pop($a); array_pop($a); array_pop($a);
  echo "<br />Remove three elements from top of stack:<br
/>";
  print_r($a);
// Treat $a like a queue (first in, first out)…
  $a = array(-17,"David", 33.3,"Laura");
  echo "<br />Back to original array:<br />";
  print_r($a);
  echo "<br />Remove two elements from front of queue:<br
/>";
  array_shift($a);
  array_shift($a);
  print_r($a);
  echo "<br />Add three elements to end of queue:<br />";
  array_push($a,"Susan",0.5,"new_guy");
  print_r($a);
  echo "<br />Add a \"line crasher\" to the beginning of
the queue:<br />";
  array_unshift($a,"queue_crasher_guy");
  print_r($a);
?>
</body>
</html>
```

```
The original array (element [0] is the "oldest"
element):
Array ( [0] => -17 [1] => David [2] => 33.3
[3] => Laura )
Push two elements on top of stack:
Array ( [0] => -17 [1] => David [2] => 33.3
[3] => Laura [4] => Susan [5] => 0.5 )
Remove three elements from top of stack:
Array ( [0] => -17 [1] => David [2] => 33.3 )
Back to original array:
Array ( [0] => -17 [1] => David [2] => 33.3
[3] => Laura )
```

(continued)

(continued)

```
Remove two elements from front of queue:
Array ( [0] => 33.3 [1] => Laura )
Add three elements to end of queue:
Array ( [0] => 33.3 [1] => Laura [2] => Susan
[3] => 0.5 [4] => new_guy )
Add a "line crasher" to the beginning of the queue:
Array ( [0] => queue_crasher_guy [1] => 33.3
[2] => Laura [3] => Susan[4] => 0.5 [5] => new_guy )
```

Document 9.8 deserves close study if you need to do this kind of data manipulation in an array.

9.4
More Examples

9.4.1
The Quadratic Formula Revisited

In Document 7.6b (quadrat.php), three coefficients of a quadratic equation were passed from an HTML document and retrieved by name:

```
$a = $_POST["a"];
$b = $_POST["b"];
$c = $_POST["c"];
```

This code requires the PHP application to "know" what names the form fields were given in the corresponding HTML document ("a", "b", and "c"). In PHP terminology, you can think of the form fields being passed as a keyed array, with the key names corresponding to the form field names. For this and similar kinds of problems, it might be desirable to make the code less dependent on names given in the HTML document. Documents 9.9a, b show one way to do this.

Document 9.9a (quadrat2.htm)

```
<html>
<head>
<title>Solving the Quadratic Equation</title>
</head>
<body>
<form method="post" action="quadrat_2.php">
Enter coefficients for ax<sup>2</sup> + bx + c = 0:
<br />
a = <input type="text" value="1" name="coeff[0]" />
   (must not be 0)<br />
```

```
b = <input type="text" value="2" name="coeff[1]" /><br />
c = <input type="text" value="-8" name="coeff[2]" /><br />
<br /><input type="submit" value="click to get roots..." />
</form>
</body>
</html>
```

Document 9.9b (quadrat2.php)

```php
<?php
var_dump($_POST["coeff"]);
echo "<br />";
$coefficientArray=array_keys($_POST["coeff"]);
$a = $_POST["coeff"][$coefficientArray[0]];
$b = $_POST["coeff"][$coefficientArray[1]];
$c = $_POST["coeff"][$coefficientArray[2]];
$d = $b*$b - 4.*$a*$c;
if ($d == 0) {
   $r1 = $b/(2.*$a);
   $r2 = "undefined";
}
else if ($d < 0) {
   $r1 = "undefined";
   $r2 = "undefined";
}
else {
$r1 = (-$b + sqrt($b*$b - 4.*$a*$c))/2./$a;;
$r2 = (-$b - sqrt($b*$b - 4.*$a*$c))/2./$a;;
}
echo "r1 = " . $r1 . ", r2 = " . $r2;
?>
```

```
array(3) { [0]=> string(1) "1" [1]=> string(1) "2" [2]=> string(2) "-8" }
r1 = 2, r2 = -4
```

Document 9.9a is similar to Document 7.6a, but there is an important difference, marked with shaded code. Instead of each coefficient having a unique name, each one is assigned to an element of an array named coeff.

The calculations of the real roots in Document 9.9b are identical to those in Document 7.6b, but this code assumes that the PHP script does not automatically "know" the names of the quadratic coefficients, and that an array containing those coefficients may use keys other than consecutive integers starting at 0. The array_keys() function is used to extract the key names through the coeff[] array, available in $_POST[]; the contents of $_POST[] are displayed by using the var_dump() function. First, the values are placed in $coefficientArray, which uses default integer keys starting at 0. These values are then used as indices to the coeff array passed to the $_POST[] array.

9

If integer array keys starting at 0 are used, then the code for retrieving the coefficients can be simplified a little, as shown in the shaded lines of Documents 9.10a, b, which are otherwise identical to Documents 9.9a, b.

Document 9.10a (`quadrat3.htm`)

```html
<html>
<head>
<title>Solving the Quadratic Equation</title>
</head>
<body>
<form method="post" action="quadrat3.php">
Enter coefficients for ax<sup>2</sup> + bx + c = 0:
<br />
a = <input type="text" value="1" name="coeff[]" />
   (must not be 0)<br />
b = <input type="text" value="2" name="coeff[]" /><br />
c = <input type="text" value="-8" name="coeff[]" /><br />
<br /><input type="submit" value="click to get roots..." />
</form>
</body>
</html>
```

Document 9.10b (quadrat3.php)

```php
<?php
var_dump($_POST["coeff"]);
echo "<br />";
$coefficientArray=$_POST["coeff"];
$a = $coefficientArray[0];
$b = $coefficientArray[1];
$c = $coefficientArray[2];
$d = $b*$b - 4.*$a*$c;
if ($d == 0) {
   $r1 = $b/(2.*$a);
   $r2 = "undefined";
}
else if ($d < 0) {
   $r1 = "undefined";
   $r2 = "undefined";
}
else {
   $r1 = (-$b + sqrt($b*$b - 4.*$a*$c))/2./$a;;
   $r2 = (-$b - sqrt($b*$b - 4.*$a*$c))/2./$a;;
}
echo "r1 = " . $r1 . ", r2 = " . $r2;
?>
```

Note that because no index values are specified for the `coeff[]` array in Document 9.10a, PHP assumes that they are integers starting at 0. You could also specify the keys, for example, as integers starting at 1, but you must then tell the PHP application what the keys are, either by using `array_keys()` or by "hard coding" the key values:

(in the HTML document)
```
a = <input type="text" value="1" name="coeff[1]" />
    (must not be 0)<br />
b = <input type="text" value="2" name="coeff[2]" /><br />
c = <input type="text" value="-8" name="coeff[3]" /><br />
```

(in the PHP document)
```
$coefficientArray=$_POST["coeff"];
$a = $coefficientArray[1];
$b = $coefficientArray[2];
$c = $coefficientArray[3];
```

This code is easier to write with consecutive integer keys than with arbitrarily named keys, but this approach essentially defeats the purpose of simplifying access to form fields, which the example was originally intended to demonstrate.

You might conclude that the code presented in these examples is not much of a simplification and is not worth the extra effort, because the PHP document still needs to "know" the name of the coefficient array entered into the HTML document's form fields. However, if only one name is needed—the name of that array—this might provide some code-writing economy for a longer list of inputs.

9.4.2
Reading `checkbox` Values

The HTML `<input type="checkbox" ... />` form field is used to associate several possible values with a single form field name. Unlike a `type="radio"` field, which allows only one selection from a list, checkboxes allow multiple values to be selected. Consider this problem:

An HTML document asks a user to report cloud observations by checking boxes for cloud types divided into four categories: high, mid, low, and precipitating. Each category has more than one possible cloud type, and multiple cloud types in one or all categories may be observed:

High: cirrus, cirrocumulus, cirrostratus
Mid: altostratus, altocumulus
Low: stratus, stratocumulus, cumulus
Precipitating: nimbostratus, cumulonimbus

Write an HTML document to enter these data and a PHP document that will echo back all the cloud types reported.

9

Document 9.11a (`CloudObs.htm`)

```html
<html>
<head>
<title>Cloud Observations</title>
</head>
<body bgcolor="#aaddff">
<h1>Cloud Observations</h1>
<strong> Cloud Observations </strong>(Select as many cloud
types as observed.)
<br />
<form method="post" action="CloudObs.php" />
<table>
  <tr>
   <td><strong>High</strong> </td>
    <td>
     <input type="checkbox" name="high[]"
       value="Cirrus" /> Cirrus</td>
    <td>
     <input type="checkbox" name="high[]"
        value="Cirrocumulus" /> Cirrocumulus </td>
   <td>
     <input type="checkbox" name="high[]"
        value="Cirrostratus" /> Cirrostratus </td></tr>
  <tr>
    <td colspan="4"><hr noshade color="black" />
     </td></tr>
  <tr>
   <td> <strong>Middle</strong> </td>
   <td>
      <input type="checkbox" name="mid[]"
        value="Altostratus" /> Altostratus </td>
    <td>
      <input type="checkbox" name="mid[]"
        value="Altocumulus" /> Altocumulus</td></tr>
  <tr>
    <td colspan="4"><hr noshade color="black" />
     </td></tr>
  <tr>
    <td> <strong>Low</strong></td>
    <td>
    <input type="checkbox" name="low[]" value="Stratus" />
      Stratus</td>
```

```
    <td>
      <input type="checkbox" name="low[]"
        value="Stratocumulus" /> Stratocumulus</td>
    <td>
    <input type="checkbox" name="low[]" value="Cumulus" />
      Cumulus </td></tr>
  <tr>
    <td colspan="4"><hr noshade color="black" />
      </td></tr>
  <tr>
    <td> <strong>Rain-Producing </strong> </td>
    <td>
      <input type="checkbox" name="rain[]"
        value="Nimbostratus" /> Nimbostratus</td>
    <td>
      <input type="checkbox" name="rain[]"
        value="Cumulonimbus" /> Cumulonimbus </td></tr>
</table>
<input type="submit" value="Click to process..." />
</form>
</body>
</html>
```

Cloud Observations

Cloud Observations (Select as many cloud types as observed.)

High	☐ Cirrus	☑ Cirrocumulus	☑ Cirrostratus

Middle	☐ Altostratus	☐ Altocumulus	

Low	☐ Stratus	☐ Stratocumulus	☐ Cumulus

Rain-Producing ☐ Nimbostratus ☑ Cumulonimbus

[Click to process...]

9

It is very easy to process these data with PHP if the HTML document is written correctly. Each cloud category—high, mid, low, or precipitating—must be specified as an array high[] rather than just high, for example. (Note that you do not need to specify the index values.) The $_POST[] operation performed in PHP will return an array including just those cloud types that have been checked. PHP automatically does the work that would require you to write more code in JavaScript. The PHP code to do this is given in Document 9.11b, below.

Document 9.11b (CloudObs.php)

```php
<?php
  $high = $_POST["high"];
  $n = count($high);
  echo "For high clouds, you observed<br />";
  for ($i=0; $i<$n; $i++)
     echo $high[$i] . "<br>";
  $mid = $_POST["mid"];
  $n = count($mid);
  echo "For mid clouds, you observed<br />";
  for ($i=0; $i<$n; $i++)
     echo $mid[$i] . "<br />";
  $low = $_POST["low"];
  $n = count($low);
  echo "For low clouds, you observed<br />";
  for ($i=0; $i<$n; $i++)
     echo $low[$i] . "<br />";
  $rain = $_POST["rain"];
  $n = count($rain);
  echo "For precipitating clouds, you observed<br />";
  for ($i=0; $i<$n; $i++)
     echo $rain[$i] . "<br />";
?>
```

```
For high clouds, you observed
Cirrocumulus
Cirrostratus
For mid clouds, you observed
For low clouds, you observed
For precipitating clouds, you observed
Cumulonimbus
```

The number of boxes checked for each category is contained in the value of $n, which is reset after each $_POST[]. For mid and low clouds, no boxes are checked, so their corresponding arrays are empty and their for... loops are not executed. It would be a simple matter to use the value of $n to determine whether the message displayed for an empty category should be different; for example, "There were no low clouds observed."

9.4.3
Building a Histogram Array

> Write a PHP application that reads scores between 0 and 100 (possibly including both 0 and 100) and creates a histogram array whose elements contain the number of scores between 0 and 9, 10 and 19, etc. The last "box" in the histogram should include scores between 90 and 100. Use a function to generate the histogram. You will have to create your own data file for this problem.

The solution shown here is a minimal approach to this problem. It assumes that the range of the values is from 0 to some specified number, and that the histogram "boxes" are uniformly distributed over the range. The data file looks like this:

```
73
77
86
...
17
18
```

Your application should not assume that the number of entries in the file is known ahead of time.

Document 9.12 (histo.php)

```php
<?php
  function buildHisto($a,$lo,$hi,$n_boxes) {
    echo "building histogram...<br />";
    $h=array();
    // echo "Number of boxes = ".$n_boxes."<br />";
    for ($i=0; $i<$n_boxes; $i++) {
      array_push($h,0);
      // echo $h[$i]."<br />";
  }
    echo "size of histogram array = ".sizeof($h)."<br />";
    for ($n=0; $n<sizeof($a); $n++) {
      $i=floor($a[$n]/$n_boxes);
      if ($i==sizeof($h)) $i--; // handles value of 100
      $h[$i]++;
    }
    $sum=0;
    for ($i=0; $i<sizeof($h); $i++) {
      echo "h[".$i."] = ".$h[$i]."<br />";
      $sum+=$h[$i];
    }
    echo "# of entries = ".$sum."<br />";
```

```
}
$in=fopen("histo.dat","r");
$a=array();
$i=0;
while (!feof($in)) {
  fscanf($in, "%f", $s);
    $a[$i]=$s;
    $i++;
    // array_push($a,$s); will also work.
    // echo 'a['.$i.'] = '.$a[$i].'<br />';
}
/* Alternative code...
  $i=0;
  while (!feof($in)) {
    fscanf($in,"%f",$a[$i]);
    $i++;
}
*/
  echo 'Number of scores: '.sizeof($a).'<br />';
  buildHisto($a,0,100,10);
  fclose($in);
?>
```

```
Number of scores: 39
building histogram...
size of histogram array = 10
h[0] = 1
h[1] = 5
h[2] = 2
h[3] = 5
h[4] = 5
h[5] = 1
h[6] = 3
h[7] = 3
h[8] = 8
h[9] = 6
# of entries = 39
```

The first step is to open and read the data file. This code demonstrates how to store values in an array as they are read, one at a time, from a data file. Each value is read into a variable and that variable is then assigned to the appropriate array element. This is a good approach if there is a reason to test or modify the value read before saving it in the array. Alternative code is also shown which reads every value directly into an array element. An echo statement included to display the values as they are read, during code testing, is later commented out of the script.

Next, the histogram function is called. In addition to the number of histogram bins, the lower and upper limits to the range of values are provided in case the code needs to be modified later to accommodate data values that don't have 0 as their lower limit. In this simple solution, the lower and upper limits on the range of the values are not needed.

In function buildHisto(), the contents of each "bin" are initialized to 0. The array index value for the histogram array is calculated as $i=floor($a[$n]/$n_boxes);. In the case of a score of 100, this index would have a value of 10, which is beyond the 10 allowed boxes (indices 0–9), so in this case the index value is reduced by 1 and that value is put in the box holding values from 90 to100. This simple calculation of histogram array indices is possible only because the original data values lie between 0 and 100. In general, a more sophisticated calculation would be required to associate values with the appropriate histogram array element.

The buildHisto() function includes some echo statements for testing which are later commented out. It is very important to include these intermediate outputs whenever you are developing a new application, to ensure that your code is doing what you expect it to do.

9.4.4
Shuffle a Card Deck

> Write a PHP application that will shuffle a deck of 52 "cards." Represent the cards as an array of integers having values from 1 to 52. After the results of shuffling this "deck" are displayed, sort the deck in ascending order and display it again.

This is a very simple statement of a random shuffling problem. The solution presented is to read once through the deck and exchange each element with another randomly chosen element in the array, using the rand() function to select the element. Note that you cannot simply use the rand() function to generate 52 random "cards," because, almost always, some card values will be duplicated and some will not appear at all.

Document 9.13 (cardShuffle.php)

```php
<?php
  $deck = array();
  for ($i= 0; $i<52; $i++) {
    $deck[$i]=$i+1;
      echo $deck[$i]." ";
  }
  echo "<br />";
  for ($i=0; $i<52; $i++) {
    $j=rand(0,51);
      $save=$deck[$i];
      $deck[$i]=$deck[$j];
      $deck[$j]=$save;
  }
```

```
for ($i=0; $i<52; $i++)
  echo $deck[$i]." ";
echo "<br />";
sort($deck);
echo "Resort deck...<br />";
for ($i=0; $i<52; $i++)
  echo $deck[$i]." ";
echo "<br /";
?>
```

---

1 2 3 4 5 6 7 8 9 10 11 12 13 14 15 16 17 18 19 20 21 22 23 24 25 26 27 28 29 30 31 32
33 34 35 36 37 38 39 40 41 42 43 44 45 46 47 48 49 50 51 52
17 6 23 38 22 28 49 40 10 11 33 36 5 25 4 31 30 7 2 15 47 12 46 29 16 26 8 37 44 19
41 45 35 34 52 1 43 13 21 39 27 48 24 14 50 32 20 42 18 3 9 51
Resort deck …
1 2 3 4 5 6 7 8 9 10 11 12 13 14 15 16 17 18 19 20 21 22 23 24 25 26 27 28 29 30 31 32
33 34 35 36 37 38 39 40 41 42 43 44 45 46 47 48 49 50 51 52

The multiple `echo` statements in the code show the results of the code at each step. The purpose of resorting the deck and displaying the results is to make sure that the code actually moves the original elements around and does not, for example, overwrite elements in a way that might produce duplicate or missing values.

9.4.5
Manage a Data File

Write an HTML/PHP application that allows you to manage entries in a text file stored on a server. The application should be able to:

(a) Display all records.
(b) Look for a specified date or value in the file.
(c) Insert a new data report into the file.
(d) Optionally, remove a record.
(e) Optionally, reset the file to a previous version.

There can be duplicate values or dates (but not duplicate complete records), so you must look for all of them. When you insert a new data report into the file, it must be inserted into its chronologically correct position in the file. Make sure that a record with the same date and value as an existing record is not duplicated.

To determine where a new record goes, or to look for a requested date, you need to know whether the date of a record is later than ("greater than"), the same as ("equal to"), or earlier than ("less than") some other record. You can do this with the `strtotime($date)` function, which converts a date given in any reasonable format, including the mm/dd/yyyy format shown in the sample file below, into the integer number of seconds since (probably)

01 January, 1970.[1] Hence, this function allows you to compare dates as needed. For example, to see if you have matched a requested date $date to a date $d in the file,

```
if (strtotime($d) == strtotime($date)) {…
```

The HTML document interface for this program should look something like this:

Date (mm/dd/yyyy format): 01/01/2007

Value (number): 17.7

Find date: ○   Find value: ○

Insert new report (in chronological order): ○   View all reports: ◉

Submit request

Your PHP application must process the radio button selection. This is easy, because $_POST["*{name of your radio button}*"] returns the text value of the value attribute of the selected button.

Here is a sample initial file. It consists of a header line, followed by a series of data entries consisting of a date in mm/dd/yyyy format and a value separated by a space.

```
Date        Value
01/15/2006  17.3
01/20/2006  0.55
05/17/2006  83.9
09/09/2006  9.33
11/13/2006  15
01/01/2007  74.4
02/28/2007  64.4
05/05/2007  100
06/06/2007  64.4
12/12/2007  22.54
```

The "insert new data" option for this program will require you to open a file for reading, close it, and then open it again for writing in order to insert the new record in its appropriate place. Because these are sequential access files—opened only for reading or writing starting at the beginning, but not both at the same time—you cannot simply write the new record into your existing open file. Instead, you need to read the data in the file into an array, insert the new record into its appropriate position in the array, close the original file, and then open the file again in "write" mode so you can copy the expanded array back into the original file. Alternatively, you might write all records, including a new record, directly into a temporary file and then copy this new file back to the original file.

---

[1]This is the usual reference date, but it is certainly possible for some operating systems to choose a different reference. In any event, the starting date does not matter.

```
if (!copy("values.out","values.dat") )
echo "Failed to copy file.";
```

Depending on how you approach this problem it might not require the use of arrays at all. Documents 9.14a, b show one way to implement this basic data file management application. It is incomplete because the section of code that inserts a new record doesn't actually write data into a new file. Instead, it uses echo statements to show what records, including the new record, should be written into the file. (The completion of this application is left as an exercise.)

Document 9.14a (DataReport.htm)

```
<html>
<head>
  <title>Data Management Application</title>
</head>
<body>
<form method="post" action="DataReport.php">
Date (mm/dd/yyyy format): <input type="text" name="date"
value="12/12/2007" /><br />
Value (number): <input type="text" name="x" value="17.7"
/><br />
find date: <input type="radio" name="choose"
value="find_date" />      
find value: <input type="radio" name="choose"
value="find_value" />      
insert new report in chronological order: <input
type="radio" name="choose" value="insert" />
       
view all reports: <input type="radio" name="choose"
value="view_all" checked /> <br />
<input type="submit" value="Click here." />
</form></body></html>
```

Document 9.14b (DataReport.php)

```
<?php
$new_date=$_POST["date"];
$new_value=$_POST["x"];
$choose=$_POST["choose"];
$fileName="FinalExam2009_3.txt";
echo $new_date." ".$new_value." ".$choose."<br />";
$in=fopen($fileName,"r");
$line=fgets($in); // read header
```

```php
echo $line."<br />";
switch($choose) {
  case "view_all":
        while (!feof($in)) {
           fscanf($in,"%s %f",$date,$x);
           echo $date." ".$x."<br />";
        }
        break;
  case "find_date":
    $found=false;
        while (!feof($in) && (!$found)) {
          fscanf($in,"%s %f",$date,$x);
          if (strtotime($date)==strtotime($new_date)) {
            echo $date." ".$x."<br />";
              $found=true;
          }
        }
        if (!$found) echo "This record not found.<br />";
        break;
case "find_value":
  $found=false;
    while (!feof($in)) {
      fscanf($in,"%s %f",$date,$x);
      if ($x==$new_value) {
        echo $date." ".$x."<br />";
          $found=true;
      }
    }
    if (!$found) echo "This record not found.<br />";
    break;
case "insert":
    $temp=array(); $i=0;
    $added=false; $duplicate=false;
    // copy data into array
    while (!feof($in)) {
      fscanf($in,"%s %f",$date,$x);
      if ((strtotime($date)==strtotime($new_date)) &&
        ($x==$new_value)) $duplicate=true;
      if ((strtotime($date)>strtotime($new_date)) &&
        (!$added) && (!$duplicate)) { // insert new record
        $temp[$i][0]=$new_date; $temp[$i][1]=$new_value;
        $added=true; $i++;
      }
      $temp[$i][0]=$date; $temp[$i][1]=$x; $i++;
    }
```

```
    if (strtotime($new_date)>strtotime($temp[$i-1][0])) {
      $temp[$i][0]=$new_date; $temp[$i][1]=$new_value;
    }
    echo "new array...<br />";
    for ($i=0; $i<count($temp); $i++) {
      echo $temp[$i][0]." ".$temp[$i][1]."<br />";
    }
if ($duplicate) echo "Duplicate record, not added.<br />";
  break;
}
fclose($in);
?>
```

Date (mm/dd/yyyy format): 12/12/2007

Value (number): 64.4

find date: ○   find value: ○   insert new report in chronological order: ⦿   view all reports: ○

Click here.

```
02/12/2007 64.4 insert
Date Value
new array...
01/15/2006 17.3
01/20/2006 0.55
05/17/2006 83.9
09/09/2006 9.33
11/13/2006 15
01/01/2007 74.4
02/12/2007 64.4
02/28/2007 64.4
05/05/2007 100
06/06/2007 64.4
12/12/2007 22.54
```

The sample output shows the result of entering a new record in the file. (The value is duplicated, but not the date.) This application could be written with random rather than sequential access file structures (which might make inserting or removing records easier), or by using PHP-accessible databases, but that is beyond the scope of this book. Although the simple approach implemented in Document 9.14 might be unwieldy for very large and complicated data files, it is perfectly satisfactory for small and simple files that you might need to maintain for your own work for nothing more complex than basic recordkeeping and table lookups.

9.4.6
Recursive Insertion Sort

PHP supports recursive functions, using code similar to the JavaScript code discussed in Chap. 6. Document 9.15 gives a recursive implementation of the Insertion Sort algorithm. (In general, it is not as efficient as PHP's `sort()` function, but it works well for arrays that are already almost in order.) Note the "&" preceding the name of the array argument ($a) in both functions. This symbol means that the array $a is passed "by reference" so that PHP can modify its contents in memory. If the array is not passed by reference, it will not be sorted.

Document 9.15 (`InsertionSort.php`)

```php
<?php
function insertionSort(&$a,$first,$last) {
    if ($first<$last) {
        insertionSort($a,$first,$last-1);
        insertInOrder($a[$last],$a,$first,$last-1);
    }
    return $a;
}
function insertInOrder($element,&$a,$first,$last) {
    if($element>=$a[$last]) $a[$last+1]=$element;
    else if ($first<$last) {
        $a[$last+1]=$a[$last];
        insertInOrder($element,$a,$first,$last-1);
    }
    else {
        $a[$last+1]=$a[$last];
        $a[$last]=$element;
    }
}
$x=array(7,3,4,13,544,-17,-1,0);
$x=insertionSort($x,0,7);
var_dump($x);
?>
```

```
array(8) { [0]=> int(-17) [1]=> int(-1) [2]=> int(0) [3]=>
int(3)  [4]=>  int(4)  [5]=>  int(7)  [6]=>  int(13)  [7]=>
int(544) }
```

Summary of Selected PHP Language Elements

10

Abstract Chapter 10 provides a summary of PHP language elements that are necessary or helpful to create the kinds of applications that have been discussed in this book. Most, but not all, of the functions given have been used in previous chapters. As with other parts of this book, the descriptions are not necessarily intended to be comprehensive or complete, and they are not intended to take the place of a reference manual. Nonetheless, the language elements and examples presented in this chapter cover a large range of practical PHP programming situations.

10.1
Data Types and Operators

10.1.1
Data Types

PHP supports four scalar primitive data types:

Boolean *(bool)*
Integer *(int)*
Float *(float)*
String *(string)*

Boolean data can have values of `true` or `false`. The maximum size of an integer that can be represented is system-dependent, but integers are often represented with a 32-bit word, with 1 bit allocated for a sign. This gives a maximum integer value of 2,147,483,647. If presented with an integer larger than the allowed maximum, PHP will convert it to a floating point number, possibly with some loss of precision. The precision of floating point numbers is also system-dependent, but is often approximately 14 digits. In other programming languages you will sometimes find references to a "double" data type. In C, for example, the precision of "float" and "double" real-number values is different, but there is no such distinction in PHP, which supports only a single floating point number

10

representation. Strings are composed of 8-bit characters (giving 256 possible characters), with no limit imposed on string length.

PHP supports arrays and objects as compound data types. This book deals only with the *(array)* type, which can be used to aggregate a mixture of data types under a single name. Array elements can be any of the primitive data types, as well as other arrays.

When a collection of data with various types is specified, such as the elements of a mixed-type array, they can be identified for convenience as *(mixed)*, but this word represents only a **pseudo-data type**, not an actual data type specification. In the definitions of math functions given later (Tables 10.5 and 10.6), inputs and outputs are sometimes identified as having a *(number)* data type. This is also a pseudo-data type that can be either an integer or a floating-point number, depending on context.

Another pseudo-data type is *(resource)*. This refers to any external **resource**, such as a data file, which is accessible from a PHP application.

10.1.2
Operators

PHP supports a large number of operators, some of which are listed in Table 10.1, in order of precedence.

As always, it is good programming practice, especially in relational and logical expressions, to use parentheses to clarify the order in which operations should be performed, rather than depending solely on precedence rules.

Table 10.1   Operators, in decreasing order of precedence

Operator	Description
++, --	Increment/decrement
*, /, %	Multiplication, division, modulus division
+, -, .	Addition, subtraction, string concatenation
<, <=, >, >=	Relational comparisons
==, !=, ===, !==	Relational comparisons
&&[a]	Logical AND
||[a]	Logical OR
=, +=, -=, *=, /=, %=, .=	Arithmetic assignment, string concatenation assignment
and	Logical AND
xor	Logical EXCLUSIVE OR
or	Logical OR

[a]Note the availability of two AND (&& and and) and two OR (|| and or) operators, at different precedence levels (and and or have lower precedence than && and ||).

10.2
Conditional Execution

10.2.1   Conditional Execution

PHP supports if... then... else... conditional execution. The "then" action is implied. Multiple "else" branches can be included. Document 10.1 illustrates typical syntax.

Document 10.1 (conditionalExecution.php)

```php
<?php
  function getRoots($a,$b,$c) {
    echo "This function calculates roots...";
  }
  $i = 2;
  if ($i == 0) {
    echo "i equals 0";
  }
  elseif ($i == 1) {
    echo "i equals 1";
  }
  elseif ($i == 2) {
    echo "i equals 2";
  }
  else {
    echo "i is not 0, 1, or 2";
  }
  echo "<br />";
  $discriminant=0.3;
  if ($discriminant < 0.)
    echo "There are no real roots.<br />";
  elseif ($discriminant == 0.) {
    echo "There is one real root.<br />";
    $r1 = -$b/$a/2;
    echo $r1;
  }
  else {
    echo "There are two real roots.<br />";
    list($r1,$r2) = getRoots($a,$b,$c);
    echo "<br />Print the roots here...";
  }
?>
```

10

```
i equals 2
There are two real roots.
This function calculates roots…
Print the roots here…
```

10.2.2
Case-Controlled Conditional Execution

PHP also has a "switch" construct for conditional execution.

```php
switch ($i) {
  case 0:
    echo "i equals 0.";
    break;
  case 1:
    echo "i equals 1.";
    break;
  case 2:
    echo "i equals 2.";
    break;
  default:
    echo "i does not equal 0, 1, or 2.";
}
```

The order of the case values does not matter. Unlike the if… construct, in which only the first "true" path is executed, the break; statement is needed to exit the construct after the first case match is encountered. Otherwise, all subsequent statements within the construct are executed. There are certainly circumstances under which this might be the desired result, in which case the break; statements wouldn't be needed, although the order of the case values probably *would* matter.

Multiple case values can be associated with the same action, as shown in Document 10.2.

Document 10.2 (daysInMonth.php)

```php
<?php
$month=5;
switch ($month) {
  case 1:
  case 3:
  case 5:
  case 7:
  case 8:
  case 10:
```

```
  case 12:
    echo "There are 31 days in this month.<br />"; break;
  case 4:
  case 6:
  case 9:
  case 11:
    echo "There are 30 days in this month.<br />"; break;
  case 2:
    echo "There are either 28 or 29 days in this month.
<br />"; break;
  default:
    echo "I do not understand your month entry.";
}
?>
```

In PHP, case values can be strings:

```
switch ($fruit) {
case "apple":
    echo "This is an apple.";
    break;
  case "orange":
    echo "This is an orange.";
    break;
  case "banana":
    echo "This is a banana.";
    break;
  default:
    echo "This is not an allowed fruit treat.";
}
```

Comparisons against the value to be tested are case-sensitive. So if $fruit is assigned as $fruit = "Banana", prior to the switch construct (instead of $fruit = "banana";), the default message is printed. If this is a problem, it can be overcome by using the strtolower() or strtoupper() functions.

10.3
Loops

PHP supports both count-controlled and conditional execution loops, including a foreach... loop designed specifically for accessing keyed arrays. In the examples below, generic variable names such as $counter are sometimes used, displayed in *italicized Courier font*. Programmer-supplied text and/or statements are represented by {italicized Times Roman font in curly brackets}.

10

10.3.1

Count-Controlled Loops

The basic count-controlled loop iterates over a specified range of values. The general syntax is:

```
for ((int) $counter = $startValue;
  $counter {relational operator} $endValue;
  $counter = $counter {+ or -} $incrementValue) {
  {statements}
}
```

The statement(s) inside the loop are executed only if (or as long as) the second expression evaluates as true. As a result, it is possible that the statements(s) inside the loop may never be executed. The $startValue can be smaller or larger than the $endValue, as long as the third statement increments or decrements the $counter so that the loop will eventually terminate (that is, the second expression evaluates as false). With appropriately defined conditions, the loop can count "backward." The curly brackets are optional if there is only one statement to be executed inside the loop.

Examples:

Document 10.3 (countdown.php)

```
<?php
  for ($i=10; $i>=0; $i--)
    echo $i . "<br />";
  echo "FIRE!<br />";
?>
```

```
10
9
8
7
6
5
4
3
2
1
FIRE!
```

Document 10.4 (loopExamples.php)

```
<?php
  $a = array(17,-13.3, "stringThing","PHP");
  foreach ($a as $x)
    echo "$x<br />";
  for ($i=0; $i<=sizeof($a); $i++)
    echo $a[$i] . '<br />';
  $a = array(1 => 17,2 => -13.3, 3 => "stringThing",
    4 => "PHP");
  foreach ($a as $k => $x)
    echo "a[" . $k . "] = " . $x . "<br />";
  $b = array(77, 33, 4);
  foreach($b as $x) {
    echo("$x" . "<br />");
  }
?>
```

```
17
−13.3
stringThing
PHP
17
−13.3
stringThing
PHP

a[1] = 17
a[2] = -13.3
a[3] = stringThing
a[4] = PHP
77
33
4
```

See Document 9.2 for an example of how to use a for... loop to access an array with character indices. Document 9.2 also shows that it is possible to define just the first key value in an array, with the remaining keys automatically assigned with consecutive values.

The foreach... loop is used to access keyed elements in an array, including arrays with other than integer indices. The curly brackets are optional if there is only one statement.

```
foreach ( (array) $a as $value) {
   {one or more statements}
}
```

```
foreach ( (array) $a as $key => $value) {
   {one or more statements}
}
```

Example:

Document 10.5 (foreach.php)

```
<?php
  $a = array(17,-13.3,
    "stringThing","PHP");
  foreach ($a as $x)
    echo "$x<br />";

  $a = array(1 => 17,2 => -13.3,
    3 => "stringThing", 4 => "PHP");
```

```php
foreach ($a as $k => $x)
   echo "a[" . $k . "] = " . $x . "<br />";
?>
```

```
17
−13.3
stringThing
PHP
a[1] = 17
a[2] = -13.3
a[3] = stringThing
a[4] = PHP
```

10.3.2
Condition-Controlled Loops

PHP supports both "post-test" and "pre-test" loops. The post-test syntax is:

```
do  (
   {one or more statements}
} while (  (bool)  {logical expression}) ;
```

The conditional do... loop executes statements as long as the *{logical expression}* evaluates as true. Because the expression is evaluated at the end of the loop, the statements inside the loop will always be executed at least once.

The pre-test syntax is:

```
while ( (bool)  {logical expression})  {
   {one or more statements}
}
```

The conditional while... loop executes statements as long as the *{logical expression}* evaluates as true. Because the expression is evaluated at the beginning of the loop, it is possible that the statements inside a while... loop will never be executed.

Examples:

Document 10.6 (squares.php)

```php
<?php
$x=0;
do {
   $x++;
```

```
  echo $x . ', ' . $x*$x . '<br />';
} while ($x*$x < 100.);
?>
```

```
1, 1
2, 4
3, 9
4, 16
5, 25
6, 36
7, 49
8, 64
9, 81
10, 100
```

```php
<?php
  $in = fopen("stuff.dat";, "r") or
    exit("Can't open file stuff.dat.");
  while (!feof($in)) {
    $line=fgets($in);
    echo $line . "<br />";
  }
  fclose($in);
?>
```

10.4
Functions and Language Constructs

There are literally hundreds of PHP functions and language constructs. This section contains a subset of functions and constructs used in or closely related to those used in previous chapters. In these descriptions, the data type of an input parameter or return value is given in italicized parentheses, e.g., *(string)*. Programmer-supplied text is printed in *{italicized Times Roman font}* inside curly brackets. Often, generic variable names are given in *italicized Courier font*, e.g., *$fileHandle*. Optional parameters are enclosed in square brackets.

10.4.1
File Handling and I/O Functions

As noted previously, file access is the primary justification for using a server-side language such as PHP. As a general rule, you can read files from anywhere on a local computer, but you may need to set appropriate access permissions to write or modify files. You may need to need to ask your system administrator about write access on a host computer. Problems with assigning write permissions manifest themselves when PHP refuses to open a file in write ("w") or append ("a") mode.

Format specifiers:

Some of the PHP I/O functions described below for reading read input or displaying output require format specifiers that control how input is interpreted and how output is displayed. Each output format conversion specifier starts with a percent sign (%) followed by, in order, one or more of these *optional* elements:

Sign specifier
   Either a "–" or a "+" forces numbers to be displayed with a leading sign. (By default, negative numbers are preceded by a "–" sign, but positive numbers are not preceded by a "+" sign.)

Padding specifier
   The padding specifier is a character, preceded by a single quote ('), used for padding numerical results to the appropriate string size. The default character is a space. A typical non-default character would be a 0.

Alignment specifier
   By default, output is right-justified. Including a "–" will force left justification.

Width specifier
   A numerical width specifier defines the minimum number of spaces allocated for displaying a number or string. If the width specifier is too small, it will be overridden to allow display of the entire number or string.

Precision specifier
   A numerical precision specifier, preceded by a decimal point, defines how many digits to the right of the decimal point should be displayed for floating-point numbers. It is often used along with the width specifier, for example, 8.3. When applied to a string, this value defines the maximum number of characters displayed. When significant digits are lost, the result is rounded rather than truncated. For example, an *n*.3 specifier applied to 17.4567 will display the number as 17.457. Numbers are right-padded with 0s as needed. For example, an *n*.3 format specifier applied to 17.5 will display 17.500.

Data type specifier (required)
   As opposed to the previous items, a data type specifier is a required part of a format string, to tell PHP how to interpret values being read or displayed. Often, input formats contain *just* the % and a data type specifier. Some type specifiers for strings and base-10 numbers are given in Table 10.2. Format strings can contain characters other than the type specifiers themselves. For example, the statement

Table 10.2 Selected type specifiers for input and formatted output

Specifier	Description
c	Treats argument as an integer, displays an integer as the character having that base-10 ASCII value (assuming the character is printable).
d	Displays numerical value as a signed base-10 integer.
e or E	Displays numerical value in scientific notation, for example, $7.444e-3$.
f	Reads a value as a floating-point number. Displays numerical value as a floating-point number.
s	Reads a value as a string. Displays argument as a string.
u	Reads a value as a base-10 integer. Displays numerical value as a base-10 integer.

Table 10.3 Selected escape characters

Escape character	Description
\n	Insert linefeed, ASCII base-10 value10.
\r	Insert carriage return, ASCII base-10 value 13.
\t	Insert tab, ASCII base-10 value 9.
\$	Display dollar sign.
\'	Display single quote.
\"	Display double quote.
%%	Display percent character.
\\	Display backslash character.

```
fscanf($inFile,"%u,%f",$i,$x);
```

implies that a line in the input file contains an integer and a floating-point number, with a comma directly after the integer. The number of spaces between a comma and the following number does not matter. For example, it does not matter whether two values in a file are stored as

```
17,33.3
```

or

```
17,33.3
```

The same format specifier used for output would display one integer and one floating-point number in default format, separated by a comma. With output, multiple spaces embedded in a format string are collapsed into a single space when they are displayed in a browser, but those spaces are retained if the output is sent to a file.

Table 10.3 gives some escape sequences that are preceded by a backslash, the **escape character**, or a percent sign within format strings.

10

```
(bool) copy((string) $sourceFile,)
              (string) $destinationFile)

(bool) rename((string) $sourceFile,)
                (string) $destinationFile)

(bool) unlink((string) $fileName)
```

copy() copies the entire contents of *$sourceFile* to
$destinationFile. rename() renames a file. unlink() deletes $fileName.
These functions return a Boolean value of true if successful and false if not.

$fileHandle = fopen(*(string) $fileName,(string) {mode}*)

(bool) fclose(*$fileHandle*)

fopen() associates a *$fileName*, the "physical" name of a file, with a specified
access mode and assigns it to the user-supplied resource *$fileHandle*. *$fileHandle* is used in the script as the file's "logical name." *$fileName* can be a variable
name assigned an appropriate value or a string literal. The *{mode}*, which specifies how
the file can be accessed, is usually a string literal. The mode string can be surrounded
by either single or double quotes.

fclose() closes a previously opened file pointed to by a file handle.

There are several possible modes for opening files, including binary files, but this book
assumes that all files are text files and will be opened either for reading or for writing, but
not for both simultaneously. The three modes are summarized in Table 10.4.

Examples:

```
$inFile = "dataFile.dat";
$in = fopen($inFile, 'r');
$out = fopen("outputFile.dat", 'w');
```

Table 10.4   Text file access modes for fopen()

Mode	Description
"r" or 'r'	Open for reading only, starting at beginning of file.
"w" or 'w'	Open for writing only. If the file exists, its contents will be overwritten. If not, it will be created.
"a" or 'a'	Open for writing only, starting at the end of an existing file. If the file does not it exist, it will be created.

For these access modes, all files are sequential access as opposed to random access. When a file is opened in read-only mode, its file handle points to the location of the first byte of the file in memory. Reading from such a file implies that you always must read the contents of the file starting at the beginning, even if you discard some of the information. You cannot jump ahead or backward to a random location within the file.

In write-only mode, data are written to the file sequentially, starting at the beginning of a blank file. If the file handle represents a physical file that already exists, then the old file is replaced by the new data. (Be careful!) In append mode, the pointer to the file in memory is positioned initially at the end of the file, just before the end-of-file character. (In write-only or read-only mode, the file pointer is positioned initially at the beginning of the file.) New data are added to the end of the file without changing whatever was previously in the file.

(bool) feof(*(resource) $fileHandle*)

Tests for the end-of-file marker on *$fileHandle*. Returns a value of true if the end-of-file marker is found and false otherwise.

Example:

```
$f = fopen($fileName,'r');
while (!feof($f)) {
    $line = fgets($f);
    {Statements to process file go here.}
}
fclose($f);
```

(bool) file_exists(*(string) $filename*)

Returns a Boolean value of true if the specified file (or directory) exists, and false otherwise.

(string) fgetc(*(resource) $fileHandle*)

Returns a single character from the file pointed to by *$fileHandle*.

(string) fgets(*(resource) $fileHandle[, (int) $length]*)

Returns a string of up to *$length* − 1 bytes from the file pointed to by *$fileHandle*, or to an end-of line or end-of-file mark. If the optional length parameter is not provided, fgets() will read to the end of the line or the end of the file, whichever comes first.

10

Examples:

```
$line = fgets($in, 128);
$theWholeLine = fgets($in);
```

Text files created on one system may cause problems when using fgets() on a different system. UNIX-based files use only a single character, \n, as a line terminator. Windows systems use two characters, \r\n, as a line terminator. As a result, it is possible that fgets() used in a script running on a Windows computer may not properly detect end-of-line marks in a file created on a UNIX system.

(array) = file(*(string) $filename*)

Reads an entire file into array *$a*. When *$filename* refers to a text file, each line in the file becomes an array element.

Example:

For this data file:

```
Site Lat Lon
brooks 40.01 -75.99
europe 50.5 5.3
south -30 88
farsouth -79 -167
```

this code

```php
<?php
  $a=file("LatLon.dat");
  var_dump($a);
?>
```

produces this output:

```
array(5) { [0]=> string(14) "Site Lat Lon " [1]=> string(21) "brooks 40.01 -75.99
" [2]=> string(17) "europe 50.5 5.3 " [3]=> string(14) "south -30 88 " [4]=> string(17)
"farsouth -79 -167" }
```

(string) file_get_contents(*(string) $fileName*)

Returns the entire contents of *$fileName* as a string. (See fwrite().)

(int) fprintf(*(resource)* *$fileHandle,*
                    (string) {format string}
     [, *{one or more values to be displayed, comma-separated}*])

Writes a text string and optionally (but usually) one or more values according to the
format conversion specifier string, to the file pointed to by *$fileHandle*. The format
type specifiers should match the data type of the values.

   fprintf() returns an integer value equal to the number of characters written to
$fileHandle. Typically, the return value is not needed. The format string is usually
specified as a string literal, but it may be assigned to a variable prior to calling
fprintf(). This capability allows for script-controlled formatting.

Examples:

```
fprintf($out, "Here is some output.\n");
// Writes the text into the file.

$formatString = "%f, %f, %f\n";
fprintf($out,$formatString,$A,$B,$C);
// comma-delimited output
```

   The ability to include commas in the output format string means that it is easy to create
a comma-delimited file that can be opened directly in a spreadsheet. With Microsoft Excel,
for example, these files typically have a .csv extension. On Windows systems, lines written to a text file, but not necessarily to a .csv file that will be opened in a spreadsheet,
should be terminated with \r\n rather than just \n. See printf(), below, for more
examples of how to use format specifiers to control the appearance of output.

(string) fread(*(resource)* *$fileHandle,* *(int)* *$length*)

Reads up to *$length* bytes from *$fileHandle*, up to 8192 bytes, and returns the
result in a string.

(mixed) fscanf(*(resource)* *$fileHandle,*
                   $formatString [, *(mixed)* *$var...*])

Reads a line of text from a file and parses input according to a specified format string.
Without optional *$var* parameters, the output is used to create an array, the elements
of which are determined by the format string. If *$var* parameters are included,
fscanf() returns the number of parameters parsed. fscanf() will not read past the
end-of-line mark if more format specifiers are provided than there are values in the line.
Any white-space character in the format string matches any whitespace in the input
stream. For example, a tab escape character (\t) in the format string can match a space
character in the input stream.

10

(int) fwrite(*(resource) $fileHandle,*
(string) $s[, (int) $length])

Writes the contents of *$s* to the specified file or, optionally, the first *$length*
characters of *$s*. (For the inverse operation, see file_get_contents().)

(int) printf(*(string) $formatString*
[, (mixed) $var…])

Displays a text string according to the format conversion specifier, to the open window.
printf() returns the number of characters written. Typically, the return value is not
needed. *$formatString* is usually given as a string literal, but it may be assigned to
a variable prior to calling printf(), a capability that allows for script-controlled
output formatting.

Examples for fscanf() and printf():

Document 10.7 uses input file dateTime.txt:

```
01/14/2007 17:33:01
02/28/2007 09:15:00
```

Document 10.7 (dateTime.php)

```php
<?php
  $in=fopen("dateTime.txt","r");
  while (!feof($in)) {
    fscanf($in, "%d/%d/%d
%d:%d:%d", $day, $month, $year, $hour, $min, $sec);
      printf("%'02d/%'02d/%4d %'02d:%'02d:%'02d<br
/>", $day, $month, $year, $hour, $min, $sec);
  }
?>
```

```
01/14/2007 17:33:01
02/28/2007 09:15:00
```

Document 10.8 (`formatExample.php`)

```php
<?php
  $a=67;
  $b=.000717;
  $c=-67;
  $d=83.17;
  $e="Display a string.";
  printf("\t%c\n\r%e\n\r%f",$a,$b,$b);
  // no line feeds!
  printf("<br /><br />%s<br />%e<br />%f
          <br />",$a,$b,$b);
  printf("<br />%d %u<br />",$a,$a);
  printf("<br />%d %u<br />",$c,$c);
  // note effect of %u!
  printf("<br />He said, \"Let's go!\"<br />");
  printf("<br />Your discount is \$%'012.2f<br/>",$d);
  printf("<br />%'x26s<br />",$e);
?>
```

```
C 7.17000e-4 0.000717

67
7.17000e-4
0.000717

67 67

-67 4294967229

He said, "Let's go!"

Your discount is
$000000083.17

xxxxxxxxxDisplay a string.
```

Note that `printf()` ignores the `\n`, `\r`, and `\t` characters when it displays results in your browser window because HTML ignores "white space." This explains the presence of the `<br />` tags in the format string. However, `fprintf()` properly interprets these characters when printing to a file. Hence, output to a file should not have `<br />` tags included in the format specifier

---

(mixed) `print_r(`*(mixed)* `$expression` [, *(bool)* `$return`]*)*

Displays information about `$expression`, often an array, in a readable format. Setting `$return` to `true` copies the output into a variable rather than displaying it.

10

Example:

```php
<?php
$cars = array("VW", "GM", "BMW", "Saab");
print_r($cars);
$result = print_r($cars,true);
printf("<br />%s",$result);
?>
```

```
Array ( [0] => VW [1] => GM [2] => BMW [3] => Saab )
Array ( [0] => VW [1] => GM [2] => BMW [3] => Saab )
```

(string) sprintf(*(string)* $formatString
                  [, *(mixed)* $var…])

Returns a string built according to the format specifier string and optional arguments. $formatString is usually given as a string literal, but may be assigned to a variable prior to calling printf(), a capability that allows for script-controlled formatting.

(mixed) sscanf(*(string)* $line,
                  $formatString [, *(mixed)* $var…])

Reads $line and parses its contents according to the format specifier string. Without optional $var parameters, the output is used to create an array, the elements of which are determined by the format string. If $var parameters are included, sscanf() returns the number of parameters parsed. sscanf() will not read past the end of $line if more format specifiers are provided than there are values in the line.

(int) vprintf(*(string)* $formatString, *(array)* $a)

Displays a string built from the arguments of array $a, formatted according to the format string specifier.

Example for sprintf() and vprintf():

Document 10.9 (arrayDisplay.php)

```php
<?php
$a = array("VW", 17.3, "GM", 44, "BMW");
print_r($cars);
$result = print_r($cars,true);
printf("<br />%s",$result);
```

```
vprintf("<br />%s, %f, %s, %u, %s",$a);
$result = sprintf("<br />%s, %f, %s, %um %s",
         $a[0],$a[1],$a[2],$a[3],$a[4]);
echo '<br />' . $result;
?>
```

```
VW, 17.300000, GM, 44, BMW

VW, 17.300000, GM, 44, BMW
```

10.4.2
String Handling Functions

(string) chr((*int*) *$ascii*)

(int) ord((*string*) *$s*)

chr() and ord() are complementary functions. chr() returns the single-character string corresponding to the *$ascii* value. ord() returns the base-10 ASCII value of the first character of *$s*. Apppendix 2 contains a list of the 256 standard ASCII codes (base 10, 0–255) and their character representations for Windows computers. The lowercase alphabet starts at ASCII (base-10) 97 and the uppercase alphabet starts at ASCII 65. Nearly all ASCII characters can be displayed and printed by using their ASCII codes.

(mixed) count_chars((*string*) *$s*[,(*int*) *$mode*])

Counts the number of occurrences of every byte (with ASCII value 0…255) in *$s* and returns it according to *$mode*:

0—the default value, returns an array with the byte value as its keys and the number of occurrences of every byte as its values.
1—same as 0, but only byte values that actually occur in the string are listed.
2—same as 0, but only byte values that do not occur are listed.
3—a string containing all unique characters is returned.
4—a string containing all characters not appearing in *$s* is returned.

(string) ltrim ((*string*) *$s*[,(*string*) *$charlist*])
(string) rtrim ((*string*) *$s*[,(*string*) *$charlist*])
(string) trim ((*string*) *$s*[,(*string*) *$charlist*])

Without the optional list of characters, strips whitespace characters from the left, right, or both left and right ends of a character string. A list of other characters to be trimmed can be specified with the optional *$charlist* parameter. These functions are useful for removing blank characters and return/linefeed characters from strings.

Example:

```php
<?php
$str="x x Mississippi x x";
echo ltrim($str,"x ")."<br />";
echo rtrim($str,"x ")."<br />";
echo trim ($str,"x ")."<br />";
?>
```

> Mississippi x x
> x x Mississippi
> Mississippi

(int) strcasecmp(*(string) $s1, (string) $s2)*

Performs a case-insensitive comparison of $s1 and $s2.

    strcasecmp() returns 0 if $s1 and $s2 are identical, an integer less than 0 if $s1 is less than $s2 (in the lexical sense), and an integer value greater than 0 if $s1 is greater than $s2.

Examples:

```
strcasecmp(("Dave","David"); // returns -4
strcasecmp("DAVID","david"); // returns 0
```

(int) strcmp(*(string) $s1, (string) $s2)*

Performs a case-sensitive comparison of $s1 and $s2.

    strcmp() returns 0 if $s1 and $s2 are identical, an integer value less than 0 if $s1 is less than $s2 (in the lexical sense), and an integer value greater than 0 if $s1 is greater than $s2.

Example:

```
strcmp("david","DAVID"); // returns 1
```

(string) stristr (*(string) $s, (mixed) $lookFor)*

Returns all of $s from the first occurrence of $lookFor to the end of $s. If $look-For is not found, returns false. The search is case-*in*sensitive. If $lookFor is not a string, it is converted to an integer and interpreted as the ordinal value of a character.

Example: stristr("David",'v'); // returns vid

(int) strlen(*(string)* $s);

Returns the length (number of characters) in $s.

(int) strncasecmp(*(string)* $s1, *(string)* $s2,
                    (int) $n_char)

Performs a case-insensitive comparison on the first $n_char characters of $s1 and $s2.

strncasecmp() returns 0 if $s1 and $s2 are identical, an integer value less than 0 if $s1 is less than $s2 (in the lexical sense), and an integer value greater than 0 if $s1 is greater than $s2.

Examples:

```
strncasecmp("Dave","David", 3); // returns 0
strncasecmp(("Dave","David", 4); // returns -4
$len = min(strlen("Dave"),strlen("David"));
strncasecmp("Dave","David",$len);
// compares number of characters contained in shorter
string parameter and returns -4
```

(int) strncmp(*(string)* $s1, *(string)* $s2, *(int)* $n_char)

Performs a case-sensitive comparison on the first $n_char characters of $s1 and $s2.

strncmp() returns 0 if $s1 and $s2 are identical, an integer value less than 0 if $s1 is less than $s2 (in the lexical sense), and an integer value greater than 0 if $s1 is greater than $s2.

Examples:

```
strncmp("Dave","David", 3); // returns 0
$len = min(strlen("Dave"),strlen("David"));
strncmp("Dave","David",$len);
// compares number of characters contained in shorter
string parameter and returns -1
```

(int) strpos(*(string)* $s , *(mixed)* $lookFor
              [, *(int)* $offset])

10

Returns the numeric position of the first occurrence of $lookFor$ in s. If the optional $offset$ parameter is provided (default is 0), the search starts at the specified offset position rather than at the beginning of s.

```
(string) strtolower((string) $s)
(string) strtoupper((string) $s)
```

strtolower() converts the alphabetic characters in s to lowercase.
strtoupper() converts the alphabetic characters in s to uppercase.

```
(string) substr((string) $s ,(int) $start
                    [,(int) $length] )
```

Returns $length$ characters of s, starting at $start$. The first character in a string is at position 0. If the length of s is less than or equal to $start$ characters long, a warning message will be displayed. If $length$ is not specified, all the characters from position $start$ will be returned.

```
(int) substr_compare((string) $s1,
   (string) $s2 ,(int) $offset [,(int) $length
   [,(bool) $case_insensitivity]]
```

Returns 0 if $s1$ is equal to $s2$, <0 if 1 is less than $s2$, and >0 if $s1$ is greater than $s2$. If the optional $length$ parameter is supplied (default is 0), the comparison uses $length$ characters of $s1$. If $length$ is greater than or equal to the length of $s1$, a warning message will be displayed. If the optional $offset$ parameter is specified (default is 0), the comparision starts at the specified offset from the beginning of $s1$. If $offset$ is negative, the comparison starts counting from the end of the string. If the optional $case\_insensitivity$ parameter is given a value of true (default is false), the comparison is case-insensitive.

```
(string) substr_count((string) $s ,(string) $what
   [,(int) $offset[, $length]] )
```

Returns the number of times the string $what$ occurs in s, optionally starting at $offset$ (default is 0) and including the next $length$ characters.

> *(string)* substr(*(string)* $s , *(int)* $start
>   [, *(int)* $length])
>
> Returns $length characters of $s, starting at $start. The first character in a string is at position 0. If the length of $s is less than or equal to $start characters long, a warning message will be displayed. If $length is not specified, all the characters from position $start will be returned.

Document 10.10 shows output from some of the string functions listed in this section.

Document 10.10 (stringFunctions.php)

```php
<?php /* Created on: 6/13/2009 */ ?>
<html>
<body>
<?php
  $str1="Hello, world!";
  $str2="world";
  echo stristr($str1,'w') . "<br />";
  echo substr_compare($str1,$str2,8) . "<br />";
  echo strpos($str1,"wor") . "<br />";
echo stristr($str1,"wor") . "<br />";
?>
</body>
</html>
```

```
world!
-1
7
world!
```

10.4.3
Math Constants and Functions

PHP's math functions return integer or floating-point results, with a system-dependent precision that is often about 14 digits for floating-point numbers. This is sufficient for all but the most specialized calculations. There are also several pre-defined mathematical constants, all of which are floating-point numbers. Constants and functions are built into PHP, with no need for external libraries. Trigonometric functions always assume input parameters in radians or produce angle outputs in radians. Data types are shown in parentheses, for example *(float)*. Optional arguments are enclosed in square brackets.

Constants and built-in math functions are listed in Tables 10.5 and 10.6. In this table, "x" (and other arguments, in some cases) always represents a variable of the appropriate type, even though they are shown without the $ symbol.

10

Table 10.5 Math constants

Named constants	Description
M_1_PI	$1/\pi$
M_2_PI	$2/\pi$
M_2_SQRTPI	$2/(\pi^{1/2})$
M_E	Base of the natural logarithm, $e = 2.71828...$
M_EULER	Euler's constant[a] = $0.577215665...$
M_LN2	Natural logarithm of $2 = 0.693147...$
M_LN10	Natural logarithm of $10 = 2.302585...$
M_LNPI	Natural logarithm of $\pi = 1.1447299...$
M_LOG2E	Log to the base 2 of $e = 1.442695...$
M_LOG10E	Log to the base 10 of $e = 0.434294...$
M_PI	$\pi = 3.1415927...$
M_PI_2	$\pi/2 = 1.5707963...$
M_PI_4	$\pi/4 = 0.7853981...$
M_SQRT1_2	$1/(2^{1/2}) = 0.7071067...$
M_SQRT2	$2^{1/2} = 1.4142136...$
M_SQRT3	$3^{1/2} = 1.7320508...$
M_SQRTPI	$\pi^{1/2} = 1.7724539...$

[a]Euler's constant is the limit as $n \to \infty$ of $(1 + 1/2 + 1/3 + ... + 1/n) - \ln(n)$.

Table 10.6 Math functions

Functions	Returns
(number) abs (*(number)* x)	Absolute value of x, a floating-point or integer number, depending on x
(float) acos (*(float)* x)	Inverse cosine of x, $\pm\pi$, for $-1 \leq x \leq 1$
(float) acosh (*(float)* x)	Inverse hyperbolic cosine of x*
(float) asin (*(float)* x)	Inverse sine of x, $\pm\pi/2$, for $-1 \leq x \leq 1$
(float) asinh (*(float)* x)	Inverse hyperbolic cosine of x*
(float) atan (*(float)* x)	Inverse tangent of x, $\pm\pi/2$, for $-\infty < x < \infty$ (compare with Math.atan2 (y,x))
(float) atan2 (*(float)* y, *(float)* x)	Inverse tangent of angle between x-axis and the point (x,y), $0 - 2\pi$, measured counterclockwise
(float) atanh (*(float)* x)	Inverse hyperbolic tangent of $x^{(2)}$
(float) ceil (*(number)* x)	Smallest whole number (still type *float*) greater than or equal to x
(float) cos (*(float)* x)	Cosine of x, ± 1
(float) cosh (*(float)* x)	Hyperbolic cosine of x
(float) deg2rad (*(float)* x)	Convert x in degrees to radians
(float) exp (*(float)* x)	e to the x power (e^x)
(float) floor (*(float)* x)	Greatest whole number (still type *float*) less than or equal to x

(continued)

Table 10.6 (continued)

Functions	Returns
(float) fmod (*(float)* x, *(float)* y)	Floating-point remainder of *x/y*
(float) log (*(float)* x [, *(float)* b])	Logarithm of *x*, to base *e* unless optional base argument b is included, *x* > 0
(float) getrandmax (*(void)*)	Max value returned by call to rand ()
(float) log10 (*(float)* x)	Base-10 logarithm of *x*
(mixed) max (*(mixed)* x, *(mixed)* y, ...) *(mixed)* max (*(array)* x)	Largest of two or more values, or maximum value in an array
(mixed) min (*(mixed)* x, *(mixed)* y, ...) *(mixed)* min (*(array)* x)	Smallest of two or more values, or minimum value in an array
(float) pi ()	Returns value of π, identical to M_PI
(number) pow (*(number)* x, *(number)* y)	*x* to the *y* power (x^y) Returns a whole number when appropriate
(float) rad2deg (*(float)* x)	Convert radian value *x* to degrees
(int) rand () *(int)* rand ([*(int)* min, *(int)* max])	Random integer in the range 0 − RAND_ MAX, optionally between min and max
(float) round (*(float)* x [, *(float)* p])	*x* rounded to specified precision (*p* digits after decimal point), or to whole number without argument *p*
(float) sin (*(float)* x)	Sine of *x*
(float) sinh (*(float)* x)	Hyperbolic sine of *x*
(float) sqrt (*(float)* x)	Square root of *x*
(float) srand ([*(int)* seed])	Seeds random number generator, optionally with specified integer seed
(float) tan (*(float)* x)	Tangent of *x*, ±∞
(float) tanh (*(float)* x)	Hyperbolic tangent of *x*

*Not implemented in all versions of PHP(?)

10.4.4
Array Functions and Constructs

```
(array) array ( [(mixed) {comma-separated list of arguments}] )
// This is a construct, not a function.
```

Creates an array from specified arguments. It is not necessary to provide arguments when the array is created.

```
(array) array_keys ((array) $a)
```

Returns an array containing the keys of the $a array.

10

> *(mixed)* array_pop ((array) $a)
>
> Treats $a as a stack and removes and returns the last (newest) element of $a, automatically shortening $a by one element. A value of NULL will be returned if the array is already empty. This function resets the array pointer to the beginning of the array after the element is removed.

Example (for array() and array_pop()):

Document 10.11 (arrayPop.php)

```php
<?php
$stack = array("orange", "banana", "apple", "lemon");
$fruit=array_pop($stack);
print_r($stack);
?>
```

```
Array ( [0] => orange [1] => banana [2] => apple)
```

The variable $fruit will be assigned a value of *lemon*.

> *(int)* array_push((array) $a, (mixed) $var [, (mixed)...])
>
> Treats $a as a stack, and pushes the passed variable(s) onto the end of $a. The length of $a increases by the number of variables pushed. Returns the number of elements in the array after the "push."

Example:

Document 10.12 (arrayPush.php)

```php
<?php
$stack = array("red", "grn");
$n = array_push($stack, "blu", "wh");
print_r($stack);
$stack[] = "blk";
printf("<br />%u<br />",$n);
print_r($stack);
printf("<br />%u<br />",sizeof($stack));
?>
```

```
Array ( [0] => red [1] => grn [2] => blu [3] => wh )
4
Array ( [0] => red [1] => grn [2] => blu
        [3] => wh [4] => blk )
5
```

The shaded line in Document 10.11 shows that a new variable can be "pushed" onto the end of an array simply by assigning a new element to the array. Because this avoids whatever overhead might be associated with a function call, and it is shorter to write, it might make sense to use `array_push()` only when you wish to add multiple new values at the same time.

(mixed) `array_shift((array) $a)`

Removes the first element of $a (the "oldest" element) and returns it, then shortens $a by one element and moves everything down one position. Numerical keys will be reset to start at 0. Literal keys are unchanged. `array_shift()` is used to remove the oldest element from an array treated as a queue. It resets the array pointer to element 0 after it is used.

Example:

Document 10.13 (`arrayShift.php`)

```php
<?php
$queue = array("orange", "banana", "raspberry", "mango");
print_r($queue);
$rottenFruit = array_shift($queue);
echo '<br />' . $rottenFruit;
echo '<br />' . count($queue);
?>
```

```
Array ( [0] => orange [1] => banana [2] => raspberry
[3] => mango )
orange
3
```

(int) `array_unshift((array) $a,`
                    `(mixed) $var [, (mixed)...])`

Adds one or more elements to the "front" of the array (the "old" end). The entire list is inserted in order, so the first item in the list to be added is the first element in the modified array. Numerical keys are reset to start at 0. Literal keys are unchanged.

10

Example:

Document 10.14 (`arrayUnshift.php`)

```php
<?php
$a = array("orange", "banana", "raspberry", "mango");
print_r($a);
array_unshift($a, "papaya", "mangosteen");
echo '<br />' . count($a) . '<br />';
print_r($a);
?>
```

```
Array ( [0] => orange [1] => banana [2] => raspberry
     [3] => mango )
6
Array ([0] => papaya [1] => mangosteen [2] => orange
     [3] => banana [4] => raspberry [5] => mango )
```

```
(int) count((mixed) $a [, $mode])

(int) sizeof((mixed) $a [, $mode])
```

count() and sizeof() are equivalent. They return the number of elements in the array $a. If the value of $mode if it is not specified, its default value is 0. Setting $mode to 1 or to COUNT_RECURSIVE will count elements recursively in a multidimensional array.

The "recursive count" might not do what you expect. In a two-dimensional array with five "rows" and four "columns" (refer to Document 9.4, `two-D.php`), the recursive count option counts 5×4 rows, and then five rows again, and returns a value of 25. The number of elements in this two-dimensional array is not 25, but $25 - 5 = 20$.

```
(bool) sort((mixed) $a [,$sort_flag])
(bool) usort((mixed) $a, (string) compare_function_name)
(bool) asort((mixed) $a)
(bool) ksort((mixed) $a)
(bool) arsort((mixed) $a)
(bool) krsort((mixed) $a)
```

sort() sorts an array in ascending order. The $sort_flag is optional:
SORT_REGULAR (default value) compares items without changing types
SORT_NUMERIC compares items as though they are numbers
SORT_STRING compares items as though they are strings

usort() sorts an array by calling a user-supplied function that compares two elements in an array. This can be used to sort an array in descending rather than the default
ascending order.

sort() and usort() will work with keyed arrays, but the key information is lost.
asort() will sort an array by element value but will maintain the relationship between
keys and elements. ksort() will also keep the relationship between keys and elements,
but it will sort the array by key value rather than element value. arsort() and
krsort() do the same thing, but sort in reverse order.

Document 10.15 (SortingFunctions.php)

```php
<?php
function compare($a,$b) {
  return $b-$a;
}
$x=array(7,3,4,13,544,-17,-1,0);
sort($x);
echo "normal sort<br />";
var_dump($x);
sort($x,SORT_STRING);
echo "<br />sort as string<br />";
var_dump($x);
usort($x,"compare");
echo "<br />normal sort, descending order<br />";
var_dump($x);
$a=array('mine' => 'BMW','hers' => 'Lexus',
  'ours' => 'House');
sort($a);
echo "<br />sort keyed array<br />";
var_dump($a);
echo "<br />but the keys haven't been retained:<br />";
foreach($a as $key => $val)
  echo '$a[' . $key . '] = '. $val . '<br />';
$a=array('mine' => 'BMW','hers' => 'Lexus',
'ours' => 'House');
asort($a);
echo "use asort() to retain the keys<br />";
foreach($a as $key => $val)
  echo '$a[' . $key . '] = '. $val . '<br />';
arsort($a);
echo
  "use ursort() to sort keyed array in reverse order<br />";
foreach($a as $key => $val)
  echo '$a[' . $key . '] = '. $val . '<br />';
ksort($a);
```

```php
echo
   "use ksort() to sort by key rather than by value<br />";
foreach($a as $key => $val)
   echo '$a[' . $key . '] = '. $val . '<br />';
krsort($a);
echo
   "use krsort() to sort array in reverse order by key<br />";
foreach($a as $key => $val)
   echo '$a[' . $key . '] = '. $val . '<br />';
?>
```

```
normal sort
array(8) { [0]=> int(-17) [1]=> int(-1) [2]=> int(0)
[3]=> int(3) [4]=> int(4) [5]=> int(7) [6]=> int(13)
[7]=> int(544) }
sort as string
array(8) { [0]=> int(-1) [1]=> int(-17) [2]=> int(0)
[3]=> int(13) [4]=> int(3) [5]=> int(4) [6]=> int(544)
[7]=> int(7) }
normal sort, descending order
array(8) { [0]=> int(544) [1]=> int(13) [2]=> int(7)
[3]=> int(4) [4]=> int(3) [5]=> int(0) [6]=> int(-1)
[7]=> int(-17) }
sort keyed array
array(3) { [0]=> string(3) "BMW" [1]=> string(5)
"House"
[2]=> string(5) "Lexus" }
but the keys haven't been retained:
$a[0] = BMW
$a[1] = House
$a[2] = Lexus
use asort() to retain the keys
$a[mine] = BMW
$a[ours] = House
$a[hers] = Lexus
use ursort to sort keyed array in reverse order
$a[hers] = Lexus
$a[ours] = House
$a[mine] = BMW
use ksort() to sort by key rather than by value
$a[hers] = Lexus
$a[mine] = BMW
$a[ours] = House
use krsort() to sort array in reverse order by key
$a[ours] = House
$a[mine] = BMW
$a[hers] = Lexus
```

10.4.5
Miscellaneous Functions and Language Constructs

```
break [(int) $n]
```

Exits the current conditional or count-controlled loop structure. An optional argument following `break` (not in parentheses) specifies the number of nested structures to be exited.

```
(bool) ctype_alpha( (string) $s)
```

Returns true if all the characters in $s (which could be just one character) are letters, a–z or A–Z, false otherwise. This function will not detect some letters in non-English languages that lie outside the a–z or A–Z range in the ASCII-collating sequence.

```
die( [ (string) $status])

die( [ (int) $status])

exit([ (string) $status])

exit([ (int) $status])
```

Equivalent functions to exit a script. If the argument is a string, it will be printed on exit. An integer argument, in the range 0–254, is available for use as an exit error code in other applications, but it is not printed.

```
(array) explode( (string) $delimiter, (string) $s,
                 [ (int) $n])
(string) implode( (string) $delimiter, (array) $a )
```

`explode()` returns an array of strings consisting of substrings of the string $s, in which the substrings are separated by the $delimiter. When $n is present, `explode()` will build array elements from the first $n values, with the last element containing the remainder of the string. The delimiter must match the file contents exactly. For example, a " " (single space) delimiter implies that the values are separated by one and only one space. In a file with numerical values, the elements of the returned array can be treated as numbers in subsequent code.

`implode()` returns all elements of $a as a concatenated string, with the elements separated by $delimiter.

10

```
(void) list( (mixed) {arguments} ) = $array
//a construct, not a function
```

Assigns contents of an array to several variables.

```
(string) number_format( (float) $n[, (int) $decimals,]
[ (string) $character, (string) $separator) ] )
```

Formats $n, as specified by one, two, or four parameters (not three parameters). With one parameter, a comma is placed between each group of thousands, with no decimal point or fractional digits. With two parameters, $n will include $decimals digits to the right of a decimal point, and with a comma between each group of thousands. With four parameters, $character will be used before the significant digits and $separator designates the character used to separate groups of thousands.

Example:

```
$n=17343789.936;
echo number_format($n)."<br />";
echo number_format($n,2)."<br />";
echo number_format($n,2,',',' ')."<br />";
```

Output:
17,343,790
17,343,789.94
17 343 789,94

```
(int) strtotime( (string) $time )
```

Converts a date and time description, in any common format, into the number of seconds from January 1, 1970, 00:00:00 GMT. For dates specified in xx/xx/xx or xx/xx/xxxx format, strtotime() assumes the U.S. custom of supplying dates as mm/dd/yy or mm/dd/yyyy. (The custom in many other countries is to specify dates as dd/mm/yy or dd/mm/yyyy.) strtotime() can be used to determine whether a date comes before or after another date.

Example:

```
echo strtotime("12/04/2007"); yields the result 1196744400
```

(int) strval(*(mixed) $var*)

Converts any scalar variable (not an array) into a string.

(void) var_dump (*(mixed) $var1* [, *(mixed) $var2*])

Displays structured information about one or more variables. (Displays only defined elements of an array.)

More examples:

Using this data file, LatLon.dat

```
Site Lat Lon
brooks 40.01 -75.99
europe 50.5 5.3
south -30 88
farsouth -79 -167
```

Document 10.16 (ExplodeArray.php)

```php
<?php
  $a=file("LatLon.dat");
  var_dump($a);
  echo "<br />";
  for ($i=1; $i<sizeof($a); $i++) {
    list($s,$la,$lo)=explode(" ",$a[$i]);
      echo $s.", ".$la.", ".$lo."<br />";
}

foreach ($a as $s) {
  list($site,$Lat,$Lon)=explode(" ",$s);
      echo $site.", ".$Lat.", ".$Lon."<br />";
}
?>
```

```
array(5) { [0]=> string(14) "Site Lat Lon " [1]=> string(21) "brooks
40.01 -75.99 " [2]=> string(17) "europe 50.5 5.3 " [3]=> string(14)
"south -30 88 " [4]=> string(17) "farsouth -79 -167" }
brooks, 40.01, -75.99
europe, 50.5, 5.3

south, -30, 88
farsouth, -79, -167
Site, Lat, Lon
brooks, 40.01, -75.99
europe, 50.5, 5.3
south, -30, 88
farsouth, -79, -167
```

Document 10.17 (varDump.php)

```php
<?php
$a = array('david','apple','Xena','Sue');
$b = array();
list($b[0],$b[1],$b[2],$b[3]) = $a;
var_dump($b);
?>
```

```
array(4) {
[3]=> string(3) "Sue" [2]=> string(4) "Xena" [1]=>
string(5) "apple"
[0]=> string(5) "david" }
```

Document 10.18 (arrayList.php)

```php
<?php
$stuff = array('I','love','PHP.');
list($who,$do_what,$to_what) = $stuff;
echo "$who $do_what $to_what" . "<br />";
list($who, , $to_what) = $stuff;
echo "$who $to_what<br />";
$a = array('david','apple','Xena','Sue');
$b = array();
list($b[0],$b[1],$b[2],$b[3]) = $a;
var_dump($b);
echo "<br />Access with for… loop.<br />";
for ($i=0; $i<count($b); $i++) echo $b[$i] . "<br />";
echo "Access with foreach… loop.<br />";
foreach ($b as $key => $x) echo "a[" . $key . "] = " . $x .
"<br />";
?>
```

```
I love PHP.
I PHP.
array(4) { [3]=> string(3) "Sue" [2]=> string(4) "Xena"
[1]=> string(5) "apple" [0]=> string(5) "david" }
Access with for... loop.
david
apple
Xena
Sue
Access with foreach... loop.
a[3] = Sue
a[2] = Xena
a[1] = apple
a[0] = david
```

Note that with scalar, named variables, as in

```php
$stuff = array('I','love','PHP.');
list($who,$do_what,$to_what) = $stuff;
```

the result is what you expect. However, if the target of the list operation is an array, as in

```php
$a = array('david','apple','Xena','Sue');
$b = array();
list($b[0],$b[1],$b[2],$b[3]) = $a;
```

then the output shows that the order of the keys is reversed. That is, the first key for the $b array is 3 and not 0. If you use a for... loop with the numerical indices, you can still get elements printed in the same left-to-right order in which they are defined in $a, but if you use a foreach... loop to display the contents of $b, the order will be reversed.

(Add your own PHP language notes here.)

Using PHP from a Command Line

11

Abstract Chapter 11 gives a brief introduction to using PHP from a command line. This capability does not require that PHP run on a server and it allows user input from the keyboard while a script is executing.

Throughout this book, the typical model for using PHP has been to create an HTML document that serves as an interface to pass form field values as input to a PHP application running on a local or remote server. Those values are automatically sent to the $_POST[] array. Some of the shorter PHP code examples—those that do not require user input—run as stand-alone applications on a server. For example, some of the examples in Chap. 9 use "hard-coded" array elements just to illustrate some syntax for processing arrays.

In the HTML/server PHP implementation, input was provided through form fields and there was no provision for entering input from the keyboard. In some cases, it might be convenient to be able to run stand-alone PHP applications with keyboard input. It is possible to do this from a **command line interface (CLI)**. Doing so removes the possibilities for HTML formatting of PHP output in a browser window, so you may find this to be a practical solution only for calculations with simple output requirements.

The first step toward learning how command line PHP works on a local computer is to find where the php.exe program resides. On a local computer, this is probably not the same folder from which you have previously executed PHP applications on your local server. Assume that this file is located in C:\PHP.

Next, create this simple PHP file with a text editor and store it as hello.php in C:\ PHP:

```
<?php
  echo "Hello, world!";
?>
```

CLI 11.1 (CLI stands for "command line interface") shows a record of a Windows command line session that executes this file. You can type the line as shown or you can type php.exe hello.php—the .exe extension is assumed on Windows computers.

D.R. Brooks, *Guide to HTML, JavaScript and PHP: For Scientists and Engineers*,
DOI 10.1007/978-0-85729-449-4_11, © Springer-Verlag London Limited 2011

11

CLI 11.1

```
C:\PHP>php hello.php
Hello, world!
C:\PHP>
```

This is a trivial PHP "application," but it is important because it differs fundamentally from what has been presented in the previous PHP chapters of this book. This PHP application runs directly from the directory in which the `php.exe` application resides—`C:\PHP` on this computer. In fact, `hello.php` can be executed from any directory that contains a copy of the `php.exe` file. This application did *not* run on a server!

There are several command line options that can be used when a PHP file is executed, but they are not needed for the simple examples shown in this chapter. As always, there are many online sources of more information about using a CLI with PHP.

PHP's command line capabilities make much more sense if you can provide input to a PHP application that actually does something useful. Consider this problem:

> Write a stand-alone application that allows a user to enter an upper and lower limit and then calculates the integral of the normal probability density function,
>
> $$\mathrm{pdf}(x) = \frac{\exp(-x^2/2)}{\sqrt{2\pi}}$$
>
> using those two limits. This function cannot be integrated analytically, so numerical integration is required. There are several ways to integrate functions numerically, but so-called Trapezoidal Rule integration will work well for this problem:
>
> $$\int_{x_a}^{x_b} \mathrm{pdf}(x) \approx \left(\sum_{i=1}^{i=n-1} [f(x_i) + f(x_i + \Delta x)] \right) \frac{\Delta x}{2}$$

Start the code for a CLI application with this short script:

```php
<?php
    $a = $_SERVER['argv'];
    print_r($a);
?>
```

In the same way that $_POST[] contains values passed from an HTML document, the 'argv' element of the $_SERVER[] array contains the values passed from a command line. CLI 11.2 shows the execution of this script:

CLI 11.2

```
C:\PHP>php pdf_1.php -.5 .5
Array
(
      [0] => pdf_1.php
      [1] => -.5
      [2] => .5
)
```

Note that the arguments passed to the PHP application through the `'argv'` array include the file name of the application itself as the first element. Therefore, the lower and upper limits for the numerical integration are the second and third elements of array $a, $a[1] and $a[2]. Document 11.1 shows the complete code for this problem.

Document 11.1 (pdf_1.php)

```php
<?php
  $a = $_SERVER['argv'];
  print_r(+$a);
  $x1=$a[1]; $x2=$a[2];
  $n=200;
  $sum=0; $dx=($x2-$x1)/$n;
  for ($i=1; $i<=$n; $i++) {
    $x=$x1+($i-1)*$dx;
    $y1=exp(-$x*$x/2)/sqrt(2.*M_PI);
    $x=$x1+$i*$dx;
    $y2=exp(-$x*$x/2)/sqrt(2.*M_PI);
    $sum+=$y1+$y2;
  }
  echo "\n" . $sum*$dx/2.;
?>
```

CLI 11.3

```
C:\PHP>php pdf_1.php -.5 .5
Array
(
      [0] => pdf_1.php
      [1] => -.5
      [2] => .5
)
0.38292418907776
C:\PHP>
```

11

CLI 11.3 shows a command line session that executes this code. The application expects you to provide the upper and lower integration limits after the PHP file name. No prompts are provided for this information, and it is the user's responsibility to know what needs to be entered. Note that the HTML formatting tags that have been used in previous chapters—
 to produce a line break, for example—will not work in this environment. Instead, the final echo statement in Document 11.1b contains a line feed escape character, \n.

In general, it would be more helpful to be able to provide prompts to the user about required input from within a PHP application being executed from the CLI. Document 11.2 shows another approach to evaluating the normal probability distribution function which prompts user input from the keyboard, to be entered while the script is executing.

Document 11.2 (pdf_2.php)

```php
<?php
  echo "\nGive lower and upper limits for evaluating pdf,\
nseparated by a space: ";
  fscanf(STDIN,"%f %f",$x1,$x2);
  echo $x1 . ", " . $x2;
  $n=200;
  $sum=0; $dx=($x2-$x1)/$n;
  for ($i=1; $i<=$n; $i++) {
    $x=$x1+($i-1)*$dx;
    $y1=exp(-$x*$x/2)/sqrt(2.*M_PI);
    $x=$x1+$i*$dx;
    $y2=exp(-$x*$x/2)/sqrt(2.*M_PI);
    $sum+=$y1+$y2;
  }
  echo "\n" . $sum*$dx/2.;
?>
```

CLI 11.4

```
C:\PHP>php pdf_2.php

Give lower and upper limits for evaluating pdf,
separated by a space: -3 3
-3, 3
0.99729820978444
```

Document 11.2 uses the fscanf() function. But, instead of using a file handle as the input resource, fscanf() uses the reserved name STDIN (which must be written in uppercase letters), which identifies the keyboard as the input resource. The keyboard can be designated as the input resource for any of the other input functions that require a resource identifier, such as fgets() and fread().

It is even possible to write PHP applications that will execute either from a CLI or on a server through an HTML document. Document 11.3a provides an HTML interface and 11.3b is a PHP application that will work either on a server or as a stand-alone CLI application.

Document 11.3a (pdf_3.htm)

```html
<html>
<head>
<title>Integrate the normal probability density function
</title>
</head>
<body>
<h3>Evaluate the normal probability density function</h3>
<form method="post" action="pdf_3.php">
x1: <input type="text" name="x1" value="-0.5" /><br />
x2: <input type="text" name="x2" value=".5" /><br />
<input type="submit" value="Click to evaluate." />
</form>
</body>
</html>
```

Document 11.3b (pdf_3.php)

```php
<?php
  if ($_SERVER['argc'] > 0) {
    $a = $_SERVER['argv'];
    print_r($a);
    $x1=$a[1]; $x2=$a[2];
  }
  else {
    $x1=$_POST['x1'];
      $x2=$_POST['x2'];
      echo $x1 . ", " . $x2 . "<br />";
  }
  $n=200;
  $sum=0; $dx=($x2-$x1)/$n;
  for ($i=1; $i<=$n; $i++) {
    $x=$x1+($i-1)*$dx;
      $y1=exp(-$x*$x/2)/sqrt(2.*M_PI);
      $x=$x1+$i*$dx;
      $y2=exp(-$x*$x/2)/sqrt(2.*M_PI);
      $sum+=$y1+$y2;
  }
  echo $sum*$dx/2.;
?>
```

When Document 11.3b is run from a server, the output looks like this:

> −0.5, .5
> 0.38292418907776

When Document 11.3b is run from a CLI, the output looks like it did for CLI 11.3.

In Document 11.3b, the `'argc'` element of `$_SERVER[]` contains the number of command line parameters passed to the script when it is executed in a CLI. If this value is 0, then the alternate path is executed to retrieve the values passed from Document 11.3a.

The capabilities introduced in this chapter for passing arguments from a command line and accepting user input typed at a keyboard should be very familiar to C programmers, an observation that most readers of this book may find totally irrelevant. Whether you find using a CLI for some PHP applications useful or a giant leap backwards into the long-gone and best forgotten days of text-based computing may depend on your previous programming experience and quite possibly your age!

There is no doubt that a text-based CLI is primitive by the standards of today's graphical user interfaces (GUIs), but it still has its place for some kinds of applications. Once programmers started using PHP for web applications, they realized that if scripts could be executed from a CLI, it would be useful for many of the offline system-related tasks that are required to maintain a large web site. Unlike server-based PHP, CLI-based PHP scripts do not require close attention to file access privileges, which can be a major time saver for a web site manager. Also, the programming overhead for these kinds of tasks can be much lower with a simple text-based interface than it would be for more modern GUIs. Finally, CLI scripts run very quickly in this text-based environment because they do not depend on much larger and more complex GUI applications. So, CLI-based PHP quickly became very popular with professional programmers.

For the casual programmer, the arguments favoring the use of a CLI are less compelling. However, it is worth remembering that when PHP scripts run from a CLI, they are completely portable because they do not require a server. You can, for example, store such applications on a directory on a USB pen drive along with the php.exe and (on a Windows XP computer,) php5ts.dll files. Here are the contents of a directory on a USB pen drive that allows PHP applications to be run as CLI scripts.

PHPInfo.php
PHP File
1 KB

php5ts.dll
5.2.8.8
PHP Script Interpreter

php.exe
CLI
The PHP Group

pdf_1.php
PHP File
1 KB

The PHPInfo.php script produces a very hard-to-read unformatted text output when it is run from the CLI, but the output from the pdf_1.php script is perfectly usable. When you develop your own PHP applications, it may be worth considering whether they can or should be made CLI-compatible, considering the output limitations.

Using Graphics with PHP

12

Abstract Chapter 12 introduces the GD graphics library that is often used in PHP applications. It provides sample applications for creating pie charts, bar graphs, and line graphs suitable for displaying scientific and engineering data.

12.1
Introduction

The GD is a library of graphics functions written in the C language, usable directly from other languages such as PHP. This library is included as part of current PHP downloads and is typically activated by default when PHP is installed. It is an "open source" library, maintained by an active user community. GD is used in Web applications for dynamically creating images and it is a natural choice for creating simple science and engineering graphing applications to supplement the text-based capabilities of PHP for reading and processing data files.

The GD includes functions for drawing text, lines, and shapes. These functions work at the pixel level. To draw a line, for example, you must supply the starting and ending coordinates, in pixel units. It requires careful planning and, sometimes, a lot of code to use these functions to build graphics applications for displaying data.

The GD will create images in several popular graphics formats, including GIF, JPG, and PNG. (The applications in this chapter will use GIF graphics.) A typical scientific and engineering application for using GD with PHP is to access data on a server and create graphic output "on the fly" that can then be displayed by your browser. It is also easy to save that output as a separate file and, in fact, you can do both from within the same application. Saved files can be accessed with any graphics application.

12.2
Writing GD Graphics Applications for Displaying Data

This section presents examples of applications for creating four types of graphs—pie charts, horizontal and vertical bar graphs, and line graphs. The intent is not to create sophisticated graphics applications, but to develop some basic capabilities for displaying

D.R. Brooks, *Guide to HTML, JavaScript and PHP: For Scientists and Engineers*, 293
DOI 10.1007/978-0-85729-449-4_12, © Springer-Verlag London Limited 2011

12

modest amounts of data, using code that can be modified to meet problem-specific needs.

Each application assumes that it will receive some input from an HTML document, depending on the type of graph. For example, the user-supplied input required for the pie chart application presented in this chapter consists of an array of up to 12 values that will be used to generate the pie slices and another array containing an equal number of legends to be associated with those values. HTML documents for testing each graphing application are also provided.

In each case, some of the values required to define the graphing space and display the output—for example, the diameter of a pie chart and the colors used for the slices—are "hard-coded" into the application; otherwise, these values would have to be provided by the user each time the function is called. Comments in each function provide information about these properties so they can be changed as needed.

Developing code for graphics applications can be a challenge. The favored strategy for creating text-based applications is to write the code one step at a time, using the echo command or a function such as print_r() to display temporary output and check the results for each new section of code. Once the code has been thoroughly tested, then the temporary output can be removed.

The same strategy is not readily available for GD graphics applications. Once an **image space** has been defined, it is no longer possible to mix text commands such as echo with graphics commands. The nearest GD equivalent of echo is ImageString(). But, because the purpose of this function is only to output a user-supplied string, and because this function must include coordinates to position the text at a particular location within the image space, it is not nearly as convenient to implement as an echo command.

Not surprisingly, when graphics code contains an error, the resulting messages may not be very helpful. The line position of actual syntax errors will be given, but often the message consists of nothing more than some version of "Your code contains an error so I can't run it." This will happen whenever you provide inappropriate input to a GD graphics routine even though that input doesn't create a syntax error. So, when you write graphics code, you should start with something very simple, such as defining an image space with a nonwhite background color (so you can see how big the space is on your monitor) and displaying some text. After that, every change should be tested before proceeding. If you try to write an entire graphics application all at once, without lots of intermediate testing, you will be sorry!

One strategy for developing a graphing application that requires calculations to convert values to coordinates in an image space is first to write code to do the calculations in a text-based function. For a pie chart, for example, it is necessary to convert the data values into angles that will define the starting and ending points of the pie slices. It may be helpful to display the results of these calculations before actually trying to draw the chart. When the results have been checked, then the echo commands can be commented out or removed and the graphics functions can be added.

Finally, it is helpful to include a default set of data in each graphing function, so the function will display some representative output without needing any external output. This speeds up the process of developing the application because you can concentrate on writing code for managing the graphics output and you don't have to call the function from an HTML document every time you make a change to the code.

In the sections that follow, the applications are developed in stages that follow these guidelines for a step-by-step approach. The graphic output for each significant stage is also shown. Just as it is a mistake to try to write an entire application all at once, it is also a mistake to force you to read and understand the code for an entire application! Although these examples may seem redundant, it is important to study the changes implemented at each step along the way to developing the final application.

12.2.1
Getting Started

The first step in creating any graphics application is to follow the advice given in the previous section and create an image space. This space serves as the pixel-based "canvas" upon which graphic output will be drawn.

Document 12.1 (ImageSpace.php)

```php
<?php
Header ("Content-type: image/gif");
// define title
$TitleString = "Graphics Display Space";
// dimensions of plotting space
$x_max = 800; $y_max = 200;
// define font size (1-5, smallest to largest)
$font_size=5;
// starting point for title
$x_title = 10; $y_title = 30.;
// create image space
$im = ImageCreate($x_max,$y_max) or
   die ("Cannot Initialize new GD image stream");
// define colors -- first call fills background
$background_color = ImageColorAllocate($im, 234, 234, 234);
// define text color
$black = ImageColorAllocate($im,0,0,0);
// display text
ImageString($im,$font_size,0,0,"(0,0)",$black);
ImageString($im,$font_size,720,180,"(800,500)",$black);
ImageString($im,$font_size,$x_title,$y_title,
        $TitleString,$black);
// display image
ImageGIF($im);
```

12

```
// release resources
ImageDestroy($im);
?>
```

```
(0,0)

Graphics Display Space




                                                                                (800,200)
```

Every GD graphics application includes at least these few lines of code:

```
// Identify this as a document that will create an image.
Header ("Content-type: image/gif");
...
// Create an image space.

$x_max = ...; $y_max = ...;
// Define lower right-hand corner of image space.
$im = ImageCreate($x_max,$y_max);
...

// Send the image to a browser.
ImageGIF($im);
// Release the resources needed to store the image.
ImageDestroy($im);
```

Every application must have a Header line before the image can actually be created and sent to a browser (or saved as a file). In Document 12.1, the header text specifies that the document will create a GIF image. Other possibilities include PNG and JPG images, with the content type given as *image/png* or *image/jpeg* in the Header line.

The image space needs a user-supplied resource handle, assigned to $im in Document 12.1; this variable plays the same identifying role as a user-supplied file handle. The variables $x_max and $y_max, which can be "hard-coded" or supplied as user input, contain the (x,y) pixel coordinates for the lower right-hand corner of the image space—in these applications, the upper left-hand corner of the image space is always assumed to be (0,0).

The image is actually created and sent to a browser with a call to ImageGIF($im), ImagePNG($im, or ImageJPEG($im), consistent with the text in the Header line.

The code in Document 12.1 creates an image space 800 pixels wide by 200 pixels tall, with a light gray background and the text "Graphics Display Space" displayed just below the upper left-hand corner. Remember that x-pixels are counted from left to right and *y*-pixels are counted from top to bottom—the upper left-hand corner is at coordinates (0,0) and the lower right-hand corner of this example is at (800,200). Note that pixel offsets, (720,180) instead of (800,200), are required to display the lower right-hand coordinates inside the image space, but not for the text appearing in the upper left-hand corner. This demonstrates that the coordinates expected by ImageString() correspond to the upper left-hand corner of the text string. If the ImageString() function is asked to draw text outside the graphics text, it won't produce an error message, but nothing will be displayed.

The convention of measuring *y*-coordinates positively downward from the top of the image space means that when values are plotted on an *x*–*y* axis, the *y*-values are "upside down." That is, increasing a value along the *y*-axis corresponds to a smaller pixel value.

12.2.2
Pie Charts

A pie chart application is considered first because it is the simplest to implement, using GD functions that make it easy to draw a colored segment of a circle. Start first by defining the image space, as in the previous section.

Document 12.2a (pie1.php)

```php
<?php
Header ("Content-type: image/gif");
// define title
$TitleString = "Pie Chart";
// dimensions of plotting space
$x_max = 800; $y_max = 500;
// starting point for title
$x_title = 10; $y_title = 30.;
// create image space
$im = ImageCreate($x_max,$y_max) or
        die ("Cannot Initialize new GD image stream");
// define colors -- first call fills background
$background_color = ImageColorAllocate($im, 234, 234, 234);
// define text color
$black = ImageColorAllocate($im,0,0,0);
// display text
ImageString($im,5,$x_title,$y_title,$TitleString,$black);
// display image
ImageGIF($im);
// release resources
ImageDestroy($im);
?>
```

There is no need to show the output from this code, which consists just of a blank space and the "Pie Chart" title. The next step is to add some default data and create the legend block. For this application, the number of pie slices is limited to no more than 12.

Document 12.2b shows the code to do this, but these additions should not be made all at once! Start by adding the new variables needed to accomplish the task. Make sure there are no syntax errors and that the application still continues to run even though it doesn't display anything new. Add the code to display the legend at the very end of this process.

Document 12.2b (`pie2.php`)

```php
<?php
Header ("Content-type: image/gif");
// define title
$TitleString = "Pie Chart";
// default data for testing, up to 12 values
$A = array(60,50,40,100,50,50,75,5,10,15,20,35);
$legends =
array("Item1","Item2","Item3","Item4","Item5","Item6",
   "Item7","Item8","Item9","Item10","Item11","Item12");
// upper left-hand corner of legend space
$x0_legend = 400; $y0_legend = 75;
// size of legend color boxes
$legend_size = 25;
// vertical space between legend color boxes;
$dy_legend=30;
// dimensions of plotting space
$x_max = 800; $y_max = 500;
// create image space
$im = ImageCreate($x_max,$y_max) or die ("Cannot Initialize
new GD image stream");
// define colors -- first call fills background
$background_color = ImageColorAllocate($im, 234, 234, 234);
// define text color
$black = ImageColorAllocate($im,0,0,0);
// define pie slice colors
$ColorCode =
array("255,0,0","51,0,255","51,255,51","255,153,0",
   "0,204,153","204,255,102",
   "255,102,102","102,204,255","204,153,255","255,51,153",
   "204,0,255","255,255,51");
$PieColor=array();
for ($i=0; $i<12; $i++) {
  $ColorCodeSplit = explode(',',$ColorCode[$i]);
  $PieColor[$i] =
ImageColorAllocate($im,$ColorCodeSplit[0],
```

```
  $ColorCodeSplit[1],$ColorCodeSplit[2]);
}
// starting point for title
$x_title = 10; $y_title = 30.;
// display text
ImageString($im,5,$x_title,$y_title,$TitleString,$black);
// Display legend
$n = count($A);
for ($i=0; $i<$n; $i++) {
  ImageFilledRectangle($im,$x0_legend,
    $y0_legend+$dy_legend*$i,$x0_legend+$legend_size,
    $y0_legend+$dy_legend*$i+$legend_size,$PieColor[$i]);
  ImageString($im,5,$x0_legend+$legend_size+5,
    $y0_legend+$dy_legend*$i+5,$legends[$i],$black);
}
// display image
ImageGIF($im);
// release resources
ImageDestroy($im);
?>
```

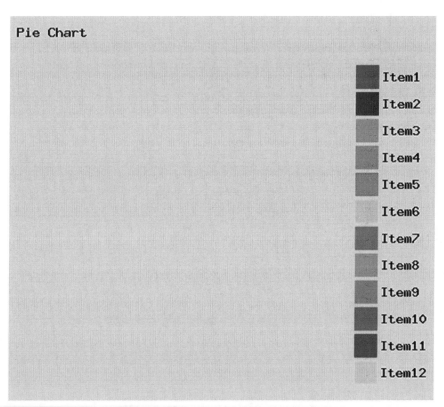

(See Color Example 5 for full-color output.)

12

Note how the pie slice colors are defined as text strings of RGB (red/green/blue) values and converted to an array of color specifiers with the `explode()` function.

The shaded code draws the color squares and their legends. The terminating condition on the for... loop ($i<$n) is set not to a constant value, but to a value determined by the length of the data array; using this kind of calculation to set limits on for... loops is very important in order to make the code as flexible as possible.

All that remains is to convert the data values into pie slice angles and display the chart, as shown in Document 12.2c.

Document 12.2c (`pie3.php`)

```php
<?php
Header ("Content-type: image/gif");
$TitleString = "Pie Chart";
$A=array(60,50,40,100,50,50,75,5,10,15,20,35);
$legends = array("Item1","Item2","Item3","Item4","Item5",
"Item6","Item7","Item8","Item9","Item10","Item11","Item12");
// dimensions of plotting space
$x_max = 800; $y_max=500;
// center point for pie chart
$x0 = 200; $y0 = 250;
// diameter of pie
$dia = 360;
// starting point for title
$x_title = 40; $y_title = 40.;
// upper left-hand corner of legend space
$x0_legend = 400; $y0_legend = 75;
// size of legend color boxes
$legend_size = 25;
// vertical space between legend color boxes;
$dy_legend = 30;
// create image space
$im = ImageCreate($x_max,$y_max) or die ("Cannot Initialize
new GD image stream");
// define colors
$background_color = ImageColorAllocate($im, 234, 234, 234);
// first call fills background
$black=ImageColorAllocate($im,0,0,0);
// pie section colors for up to $n_max sections
$ColorCode =
```

```php
array("255,0,0","51,0,255","51,255,51","255,153,0","0,204,
153","204,255,102","255,102,102","102,204,255","204,153,255",
"255,51,153","204,0,255","255,255,51");
$n_max = count($ColorCode);
$PieColor = array();
for ($i=0; $i<$n_max; $i++) {
  $ColorCodeSplit = explode(',',$ColorCode[$i]);
  $PieColor[$i] = ImageColorAllocate($im,
  $ColorCodeSplit[0],$ColorCodeSplit[1],$ColorCodeSplit[2]);
}
// Convert data array into angles, total of 360 deg.
$sum = array_sum($A);
$n = count($A);
$start = array();
$end = array();
$start[0] = 0;
for ($i=0; $i<$n; $i++) {
  $slice = $A[$i]/$sum*360;
  if ($i>0) $start[$i] = $end[$i-1];
  $end[$i] = $start[$i] + $slice;
}
// Display title
ImageString($im,5,$x_title,$y_title,$TitleString,$black);
// draw filled arcs
for ($i=0; $i<$n; $i++) {
  ImageFilledArc($im,$x0,$y0,$dia,$dia,$start[$i],$end[$i],
    $PieColor[$i],IMG_ARC_PIE);
}
// Display legend
for ($i=0; $i<$n; $i++) {
  ImageFilledRectangle($im,$x0_legend,
    $y0_legend+$dy_legend*$i,$x0_legend+$legend_size,
    $y0_legend+$dy_legend*$i+$legend_size,$PieColor[$i]);
  ImageString($im,5,$x0_legend+$legend_size+5,
    $y0_legend+$dy_legend*$i+5,$legends[$i],$black);
}
// Display and release allocated resources.
ImageGIF($im);
ImageDestroy($im);
?>
```

12

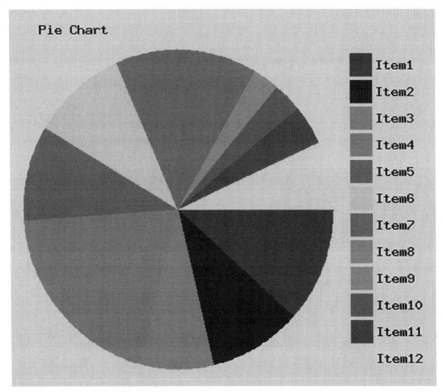

(See Color Example 6 for full-color output.)

The sizing of the pie slices is done in the shaded code. With the starting angle set to 0°, the starting point for the pie slices drawn with `ImageFilledArc()` is the "three o'clock" position (the position of the positive *x*-axis in a conventional *x*–*y* coordinate plane), with angles increasing clockwise from there.

The final steps in creating this application are converting the code from Document 12.2c to a function, writing program code to accept input from an HTML document, and passing that input to the function. It is possible to pass the chart title and all the pie slice values and legends individually from HTML. However, another possibility is to put these values in a text file and pass the name of that file from the HTML document to the PHP application. Document 12.3a gives the very simple HTML code:

Document 12.3a (`pieChartTest.htm`)

```
<html>
<head>
<title></title>
</head>
<body>
```

```
<form method="post" action="pieChart.php" />
  <input type="text" value="pieChart.dat" name="fileName"
  /><br />
  <input type="submit"
  value=
  "Click here to generate pie chart from specified file." />
</form>
</body>
</html>
```

The default data file for generating this chart, `pieChart.dat`, looks like this:

```
Quarterly Sales
17.7      January-March
15        April-June
19.2      July-September
30        October-December
```

Although it may not be obvious, this file is very easy to read because the text for the legends contains no spaces between words. You will have to work harder if there *are* spaces in these legends! (In that case, it might be easiest to put each legend on a separate line.)

The final pie chart application is given in Document 12.3b. The code in Document 12.2c, `pie3.php` is simply copied inside in a function. The only change is that the default title, array values, and legends for the chart have been commented out so they will be replaced with the values passed to the function from the main program.

Document 12.3b (`pieChart.php`)

```php
<?php
function generatePie($TitleString,$A,$legends) {
Header ("Content-type: image/gif");
//$TitleString="Pie Chart";
//$A=array(60,50,40,100,50,50,75,5,10,15,20,35);
//$legends=array("Item1","Item2","Item3","Item4","Item5",
//"Item6","Item7","Item8","Item9","Item10","Item11",
//"Item12");
// dimensions of plotting space
$x_max=800; $y_max=500;
// center point for pie chart
$x0=200; $y0=250;
// diameter of pie
$dia=360;
// starting point for title
$x_title=40; $y_title=40.;
// upper left-hand corner of legend space
```

12

```
$x0_legend=400; $y0_legend=75;
// size of legend color boxes
$legend_size=25;
// vertical space between legend color boxes;
$dy_legend=30;
// create image space
$im = ImageCreate($x_max,$y_max) or
  die ("Cannot Initialize new GD image stream");
// define colors
$background_color = ImageColorAllocate($im, 234, 234, 234);
// first call fills background
$black=ImageColorAllocate($im,0,0,0);
// pie section colors for up to 12 sections
$ColorCode =
array("255,0,0","51,0,255","51,255,51","255,153,0",
  "0,204,153","204,255,102","255,102,102","102,204,255",
  "204,153,255","255,51,153","204,0,255","255,255,51");
$PieColor=array();
for ($i=0; $i<12; $i++) {
  $ColorCodeSplit = explode(',',$ColorCode[$i]);
  $PieColor[$i] = ImageColorAllocate($im,
$ColorCodeSplit[0],$ColorCodeSplit[1],$ColorCodeSplit[2]);
}
// Convert data array into angles, total of 360 deg.
$sum=array_sum($A);
$n=count($A);
$start=array();
$end=array();
$start[0]=0;
for ($i=0; $i<$n; $i++) {
  $slice=$A[$i]/$sum*360;
  if ($i>0) $start[$i]=$end[$i-1];
  $end[$i]=$start[$i]+$slice;
}
// Display title
ImageString($im,5,$x_title,$y_title,$TitleString,$black);
// draw filled arcs
for ($i=0; $i<$n; $i++) {
  ImageFilledArc($im,$x0,$y0,$dia,$dia,$start[$i],$end[$i],
    $PieColor[$i],IMG_ARC_PIE);
}
// Display legend
for ($i=0; $i<$n; $i++) {
  ImageFilledRectangle($im,$x0_legend,
    $y0_legend+$dy_legend*$i,$x0_legend+$legend_size,
    $y0_legend+$dy_legend*$i+$legend_size,$PieColor[$i]);
```

```
    ImageString($im,5,$x0_legend+$legend_size+5,
      $y0_legend+$dy_legend*$i+5,$legends[$i],$black);
}
// Display and release allocated resources.
ImageGIF($im);
ImageDestroy($im);
}
// MAIN PROGRAM -----------------------
$inFile=$_POST["fileName"];
//$inFile="pieChart.dat";
$in=fopen($inFile,"r") or exit("Can't open this file.");
$A=array();
$legends=array();
// rtrim() removes line feeds, etc. from end of string
$Title=rtrim(fgets($in));
$i=-1;
while (!feof($in)) {
  $i++;
  fscanf($in,"%f %s",$A[$i],$legends[$i]);
  $A[$i]=round($A[$i],0);
}
fclose($in);
generatePie($Title,$A,$legends);
?>
```

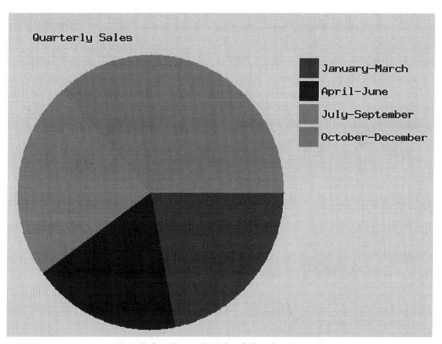

(See Color Example 7 for full-color output.)

12

The main program is responsible for reading data from the piechart.dat file and passing it to function generatePie(). This code is straightforward, but note the use of the rtrim() function to remove return and linefeed characters from the end of the title string. If you don't include this step, "garbage" characters will probably be displayed at the end of the chart title. (Try it and see what happens on your system.)

The data file used to generate this output is, on purpose, different from the default data, just to make sure that the application works with a user-specified number of data values. As noted previously, there is currently a hard-coded limit of 12 for the maximum number of data values, because only 12 pie slice color codes are defined. There is no reason why this limit couldn't be increased if needed, by increasing the number of pie slice color definitions, but pie charts are not the best choice for displaying large numbers of values.

12.2.3
Horizontal Bar Charts

A bar chart application is more difficult to implement than the pie chart application in the previous section, because it requires more data scaling—converting data values to pixel coordinates within a predefined space. As before, the first step is to set up an image space, but there is no reason to show this code separately again. Past this simple first step, some thought is required about what kinds of data the bar chart will display. For now, assume that the data values can have positive or negative values, and that the minimum possible negative value has the same magnitude as the maximum possible positive value.

Document 12.4a shows the code required to display such data. The default arrays of values and labels represent monthly deviations from climatological mean temperatures, so there will be 12 labels with 12 horizontal bars. The values are assumed to fall within the range $\pm 2.5°$.

Document 12.4a (Hbar1.php)

```php
<?php
Header ("Content-type: image/gif");
// define default data
$chartTitle = "Monthly temperature deviations from
climatological average";
// Assumes equal +/- values --> odd number of values
$x_labels = array("-2.5","-2.0","-1.5","-1.0","-0.5",
  "0.0","+0.5","+1.0","+1.5","+2.0","+2.5");
$y_labels =
array("Jan","Feb","Mar","Apr","May","Jun","Jul","Aug","Sep",
      "Oct","Nov","Dec");
$x_values = array(1.3,0.9,-0.2,-0.5,1,0,-2.5,
                  -.5,.6,.2,.7,2.3);
$n_x = count($x_labels); // number of x labels
$n_y = count($y_labels); // number of y labels
```

```php
$xvalue_max = 2.5;
// define image space
$x_max = 800;
$y_max = 500;
// starting coordinates for title
$x0_title = 10; $y0_title = 10;
// space between x-axis labels
$dx = 50;
// space between horizontal bars
$dy = 30;
// y-tic size
$y_tic = 10;
// bar height
$bar_height = 25;
// label offsets
$xlabel_offset = 40; $ylabel_offset = 80;
$xaxis_xoffset = 0; $xaxis_yoffset = 20;
$x0 = 100; $y0 = 60; // starting coordinates for of x-axis
// create and color image space background
$im = imageCreate ($x_max, $y_max) or die ("Cannot
Initialize new GD image stream");
$background_color = ImageColorAllocate($im,234,234,234);
// define colors
$text_color = ImageColorAllocate($im,0,0,0); // text color
$line_color = ImageColorAllocate($im,0,0,0); // line color
$title_font_size = 5; // large font for title
// black text for title
$title_color = ImageColorAllocate($im,0,0,0);
// draw chart title
ImageString($im,$title_font_size,$x0_title,$y0_title,
  $chartTitle,$title_color);
// draw x-axis
ImageLine($im,$x0,$y0,$x0+$dx*($n_x-1),$y0,$line_color);
// draw x labels
for ($i=0; $i<$n_x; $i++) {
  ImageString($im,$title_font_size,$x0+$xaxis_xoffset+$i*$dx,
    $y0-$xaxis_yoffset,$x_labels[$i],$text_color);
  ImageLine($im,$x0+$xaxis_xoffset+$i*$dx,$y0,
    $x0+$xaxis_xoffset+$i*$dx,$y0+$y_tic,$line_color);
}
// draw y labels
for ($i=0; $i<$n_y; $i++) {
  ImageString($im,$title_font_size,$xlabel_offset,
    $ylabel_offset+$i*$dy,$y_labels[$i],$text_color);
}
```

```
// Create GIF image.
ImageGIF($im);
// Release allocated resources.
ImageDestroy($im);
?>
```

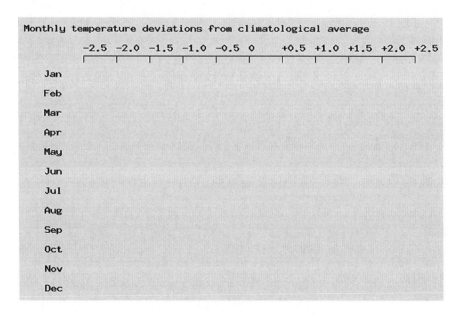

The last step is to scale the data values and generate their bars. Inside a for... loop, this code will do the scaling from values to pixels:

```
$x_scaled = $x_values[$i]/$xvalue_max*$dx*floor($n_x/2);
```

Where $xvalue_max is the magnitude of the largest possible data value. Document 12.4b shows the complete code.

Document 12.4b (Hbar2.php)

```php
<?php
Header ("Content-type: image/gif");
// define default data
$chartTitle = "Monthly temperature deviations from average";
// Assumes equal +/- values --> odd number of values
$x_labels = array("-2.5","-2.0","-1.5","-1.0",
    "-0.5","0","+0.5","+1.0","+1.5","+2.0","+2.5");
```

```
$y_labels =
array("Jan","Feb","Mar","Apr","May","Jun","Jul","Aug","Sep",
     "Oct","Nov","Dec");
$x_values = array(1.3,0.9,-0.2,-2.5,1,0,-1.1,
                 -.5,.6,2.2,.7,.3);
$n_x = count($x_labels); // number of x labels
$n_y = count($y_labels); // number of y labels
$xvalue_max = 2.5;
// define image space
$x_max = 800;
$y_max = 500;
// starting coordinates for title
$x0_title = 10; $y0_title = 10;
// space between x-axis labels
$dx = 50;
// space between horizontal bars
$dy = 30;
// y-tic size
$y_tic = $dy*($n_y+1);
// bar height
$bar_height = 25;
// label offsets
$xlabel_offset = 40; $ylabel_offset = 80;
$xaxis_xoffset = 0; $xaxis_yoffset = 20;
$x0 = 100; $y0 = 60; // starting coordinates for of x-axis
// location of vertical 0-axis
$x0axis_offset = $x0 + $dx*floor($n_x/2);
$x_length = 100;
// create and color image space background
$im = imageCreate ($x_max, $y_max) or die ("Cannot
Initialize new GD image stream");
$background_color = ImageColorAllocate($im,234,234,234);
// define colors
// text color
$text_color = ImageColorAllocate($im,0,0,0);
// line color
$line_color = ImageColorAllocate($im,0,0,0);
// negative bar color
$negative = ImageColorAllocate($im,0,0,255);
// positive bar color
$positive = ImageColorAllocate($im,255,0,0);
// large font for title
$title_font_size = 5;
// black text for title
```

```php
$title_color = ImageColorAllocate($im,0,0,0);
// draw chart title
ImageString($im,$title_font_size,$x0_title,$y0_title,
  $chartTitle,$title_color);
// draw x-axis
ImageLine($im,$x0,$y0,$x0+$dx*($n_x-1),$y0,$line_color);
// draw x labels
for ($i=0; $i<$n_x; $i++) {
  ImageString($im,$title_font_size,$x0+$xaxis_xoffset+$i*$dx,
    $y0-$xaxis_yoffset,$x_labels[$i],$text_color);
  ImageLine($im,$x0+$xaxis_xoffset+$i*$dx,$y0,
    $x0+$xaxis_xoffset+$i*$dx,$y0+$y_tic,$line_color);
}
// draw y labels and bars
for ($i=0; $i<$n_y; $i++) {
  $x_scaled =
ImageString($im,$title_font_size,$xlabel_offset,
  $ylabel_offset+$i*$dy,$y_labels[$i],$text_color);
}
// draw bars
for ($i=0; $i<$n_y; $i++) {
  $x_scaled = $x_values[$i]/$xvalue_max*$dx*floor($n_x/2);
  $color = $negative;
  if ($x_scaled >= 0) $color = $positive;
  ImageFilledRectangle($im,$x0axis_offset,
    $ylabel_offset+$i*$dy,$x0axis_offset+$x_scaled,
    $ylabel_offset+$i*$dy+$bar_height,$color);
}
// draw vertical 0-axis
ImageLine($im,$x0axis_offset,$y0,$x0axis_offset,
  $y0+$dy*$n_y+$dy,$line_color);
// draw line across bottom
ImageLine($im,$x0,$y0+$dy*$n_y+$dy,$x0+$dx*($n_x-1),
  $y0+$dy*$n_y+$dy,$line_color);
// Create GIF image.
ImageGIF($im);
// Release allocated resources.
ImageDestroy($im);
?>
```

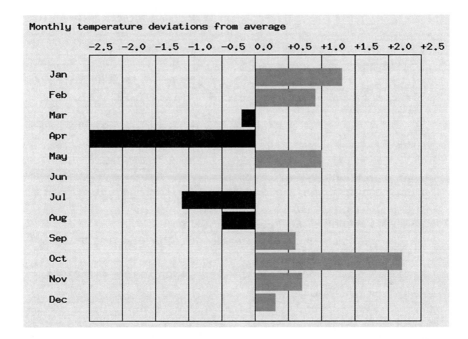

Note that the order in which lines and objects are drawn determines which lines and objects are "on top." The vertical grid lines are drawn before the bars and the vertical line down from $x=0$ is drawn after the bars, so it is visible over them.

There are some questions about the general applicability and flexibility of this code. What happens if the maximum data range is reduced or expanded? What happens if there are no negative data values and the x-axis should start at 0? Or if both the minimum and maximum values for a bar are greater than 0? Or if the magnitudes of the minimum negative and maximum positive value are not the same?

The final version of this application will address these issues, with an HTML interface that will allow testing of various options. Some "housekeeping" inputs will also be allowed, such as the number, width, and spacing of bars.

Document 12.5a (HbarChartTest.htm)

```html
<html>
<head>
<title></title>
</head>
<body>
<h3>Create a horizontal bar chart</h3>
<form method="post" action="Hbarchart.php">Chart title
(text): <input size="50" type="text" name="Title"
value="Monthly ranges" /><br />
   Data arrays (values separated by one space):<br />
   Minimum values: <input size="50" type="text"
```

12

```
name="A_min" value="0.1 6 3 5.3 9.9 8.7 0.5 2 3 4 5 6"
/><br />
Maximum values: <input size="50" type="text"
 name="A_max"
 value="1.5 2 7.8 4.5 6.4 7 9 10 3.3 0.5 4.4 3.3" /><br />
Minimum data value: <input size="4" name="min" value="0"
 /><br />
Maximum data value: <input size="4" name="max" value="10"
 /><br />
X-axis labels (string values separate by one space):
<input size="50" type="text" name="X"
 value="0 1 2 3 4 5 6 7 8 9 10" /><br />
Bar labels (string values separated by one space):
<input size="80" type="text" name="Y"
  value="Jan Feb Mar Apr May Jun Jul Aug Sep Oct Nov Dec"
 /><br />
Bar height (pixels): <input type="text" name="BarHeight"
 value="25" size="3" /><br />
Vertical space between bars (pixels):
<input type="text" name="dy" value="30" size="3" /><br />
<input type="submit"
  value="Click here to generate horizontal bar chart." />
<br />
  <input type="reset"
Value =
"Click here to reset all fields to their original values."
/><br />
</form>
</body>
</html>
```

Create a horizontal bar chart

Chart title (text): `Monthly ranges`

Data arrays (values separated by one space):

Minimum values: `0.1 6 3 5.3 9.9 8.7 0.5 2 3 4 5 6`

Maximum values: `1.5 2 7.8 4.5 6.4 7 9 10 3.3 0.5 4.4 3.3`

Minimum data value: `0`

Maximum data value: `10`

X-axis labels (string values separate by one space): `0 1 2 3 4 5 6 7 8 9 10`

Bar labels (string values separated by one space):

`Jan Feb Mar Apr May Jun Jul Aug Sep Oct Nov Dec`

Bar height (pixels): `25`

Vertical space between bars (pixels): `30`

`Click here to generate horizontal bar chart.`

`Click here to reset all fields to their original values.`

Document 12.5a allows the user to specify two data arrays—one holding the minimum data values for each bar and one holding the maximum values. This provides the flexibility needed to process both negative and positive data values. Note that it makes no difference whether a value in the "minimum" array is actually smaller than its corresponding "maximum" value—these values just mark the bounds of the bar, which can be drawn either from left to right or right to left.

Document 12.5b gives the PHP code to process these data. The code from Document 12.4b is modified to draw bars using pixel values along the x-axis scaled from the minimum and maximum data arrays. This code is incorporated into a function called from a main program that extracts values from the HTML document.

Document 12.5b (HbarChart.php)

```php
<?php
function HorizontalBarChart($Title,$A_min,$A_max,$X,$Y,
                            $bar_height,$dy) {
Header ("Content-type: image/gif");
// define default data
$chartTitle = $Title;
// Allows +/- values
$xmin_values = explode(' ',$A_min);
$xmax_values = explode(' ',$A_max);
$x_labels = explode(' ',$X);
$y_labels = explode(' ',$Y);
$n_x = count($x_labels); // number of x labels
$n_y = count($y_labels); // number of y labels
$xvalue_max=$_POST["max"];
$xvalue_min=$_POST["min"];
// define image space
$x_max = 800;
$y_max = 500;
// starting coordinates for title
$x0_title = 10; $y0_title = 10;
// space between x-axis labels
$dx = 50;
// space between horizontal bars
// y-tic size
$y_tic=$dy*($n_y+1);
// label offsets
$xlabel_offset = 40; $ylabel_offset = 80;
$xaxis_xoffset = 0; $xaxis_yoffset = 20;
$x0 = 100; $y0 = 60; // starting coordinates for x-axis
// location of vertical 0-axis
$x0axis_offset = $x0 + $dx*floor($n_x/2);
$x_length = 100;
```

```php
// create and color image space background
$im = imageCreate ($x_max, $y_max) or die ("Cannot
Initialize new GD image stream");
$background_color = ImageColorAllocate($im,234,234,234);
// define colors
$text_color = ImageColorAllocate($im,0,0,0); // text color
$line_color = ImageColorAllocate($im,0,0,0); // line color
// negative bar color
$negative = ImageColorAllocate($im,0,0,255);
// positive bar color
$positive = ImageColorAllocate($im,255,0,0);
$title_font_size = 5; // large font for title
// black text for title
$title_color = ImageColorAllocate($im,0,0,0);
// draw chart title
ImageString($im,$title_font_size,$x0_title,$y0_title,
  $chartTitle,$title_color);
// draw x-axis
ImageLine($im,$x0,$y0,$x0+$dx*($n_x-1),$y0,$line_color);
// draw x labels
for ($i=0; $i<$n_x; $i++) {
  ImageString($im,$title_font_size,$x0+$xaxis_xoffset+$i*$dx,
    $y0-$xaxis_yoffset,$x_labels[$i],$text_color);
  ImageLine($im,$x0+$xaxis_xoffset+$i*$dx,$y0,
    $x0+$xaxis_xoffset+$i*$dx,$y0+$y_tic,$line_color);
}
// draw y labels and bars
for ($i=0; $i<$n_y; $i++) {
  ImageString($im,$title_font_size,$xlabel_offset,
    $ylabel_offset+$i*$dy,$y_labels[$i],$text_color);
}
// draw bars
for ($i=0; $i<$n_y; $i++) {
  $xmin_scaled = ($xmin_values[$i] - $xvalue_min)/
      ($xvalue_max - $xvalue_min)*($n_x-1)*$dx;
    $xmax_scaled = ($xmax_values[$i] -
    $xvalue_min)/($xvalue_max - $xvalue_min)*($n_x-1)*$dx;
    $color = $negative;
  if ($xmin_values[$i] >= 0) $color = $positive;
  ImageFilledRectangle($im,$x0 + $xmin_scaled,
    $ylabel_offset + $i*$dy,$x0 + $xmax_scaled,
    $ylabel_offset + $i*$dy + $bar_height,$color);
}
// draw vertical 0-axis
//
```

```
ImageLine($im,$x0axis_offset,$y0,$x0axis_offset,$y0+$dy*$n_y
+$dy,$line_color);
// draw line across bottom
ImageLine($im,$x0,$y0+$dy*$n_y+$dy,
  $x0+$dx*($n_x-1),$y0+$dy*$n_y+$dy,$line_color);
// Create GIF image.
//ImageGIF($im,"HbarChart.gif");
ImageGIF($im);
// Release allocated ressources.
ImageDestroy($im);
}
// MAIN PROGRAM --------------------------------------
$Title = $_POST["Title"];
$A_min = $_POST["A_min"];
$A_max = $_POST["A_max"];
$X = $_POST["X"];
$Y = $_POST["Y"];
$BarHeight = $_POST["BarHeight"];
$dy = $_POST["dy"];
HorizontalBarChart($Title,$A_min,$A_max,$X,$Y,$BarHeight,
  $dy);
?>
```

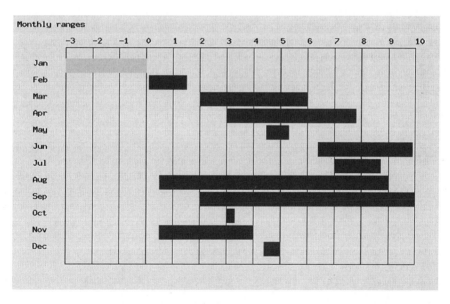

Depending on the choices a user makes in the HTML document interface, it is possible that the requested bar chart may not fit in the defined image space, 500 pixels high by 800 pixels wide. This is because some values are "hard-coded" in the PHP document. For example, the distance between x-axis labels is set at 50 pixels. The chart shown in the

12

sample output is 13 x-axis units wide and that is the maximum that can be accommodated with the existing code. It is certainly possible to add code in the PHP document to scale the x-axis spacing so the data will fit within the available space, but every such increase in flexibility comes at the cost of increasingly complicated code.

12.2.4
Vertical Bar Charts

As usual, the first step is to set up an image space. The next step is to define the graphing space within the image space. One approach is to define the graphing space not in terms of absolute pixels, but based on multiples of the number of x-axis and y-axis labels. To do this, both the number of x-axis and y-axis labels and the space between labels must be specified. Document 12.6a shows how to do this. This document also includes a set of default x- and y-axis labels; these define a bar chart with 31 values (which could represent days of the month) between 0 and 100.

Document 12.6a (Vbar1.php)

```php
<?php
Header ("Content-type: image/gif");
// define default data
$y_labels=array("0","10","20","30","40","50","60","70","80"
,"90","100");
$x_labels=array("0","1","2","3","4","5","6","7","8","9",
"10","11","12","13","14","15","16","17","18","19","20",
"21","22","23","24","25","26","27","28","29","30","31");
$n_x=31; // number of x-axis labels
$n_y=11; // number of y-axis labels
// define image space
$x_max = 800;
$y_max = 300;
// define graphing space in terms of intervals
// lower left-hand corner of graphing space
$x0 = 80; $y0 = 250;
$x_gap = 20; $y_gap = 20; // interval between axis labels
// create and color image space background
$im = imageCreate ($x_max, $y_max) or die ("Cannot
Initialize new GD image stream");
$background_color = ImageColorAllocate($im,234,234,234);
$title_font_size = 5; // large font for title
// black text for title
$title_color = ImageColorAllocate($im,0,0,0);
$chartTitle = "Bar Graph";
// starting coordinates for title
$x0_title = 10; $y0_title = 10;
```

```
ImageString($im,$title_font_size,$x0_title,$y0_title,$chartT
itle,$title_color);
// draw graphing space
// black lines for graphing space borders
$line_color=ImageColorAllocate($im,0,0,0);
// medium line width for graphing space borders
ImageSetThickness($im,2);
// draw x-axis
ImageLine($im,$x0,$y0,$x0+$n_x*$x_gap,$y0,$line_color);
ImageLine($im,$x0,$y0-($n_y-1)*$y_gap,$x0+$n_x*$x_gap,$y0-
($n_y-1)*$y_gap,$line_color); //top border
// y-axis
ImageLine($im,$x0,$y0,$x0,$y0-($n_y-1)*$y_gap,$line_color);
// right border
ImageLine($im,$x0+$n_x*$x_gap,$y0,$x0+$n_x*$x_gap,
  $y0-($n_y-1)*$y_gap,$line_color);
// Create GIF image.
ImageGIF($im);
// Release allocated resources.
ImageDestroy($im);
?>
```

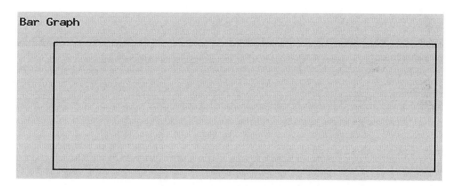

Of course, the entire graphing space does not need to be outlined, but including this outline during the application development process will make it easier to check that everything is working as planned.

Look closely at the parameters in the calls to ImageLine() that outline the graphing space. These parameters are not given as absolute pixel values, but start at the lower left-hand corner of the graphing space (the outlined space resulting from executing Document 12.6a), (x_0,y_0), and draw lines of a length equal to (number of x-labels)×(pixels per x-label) and (number of y-labels−1)×(pixels per y-label)−(number of y-labels−1) because there will be a y-axis label at the bottom of the axis as well as at the top. (This is not true for the x-axis, which will have one label per bar.)

The next step is to draw the *x*- and *y*-axis labels and vertical and horizontal grid lines. A particular application may not need grid lines, but including them will make it easier to check the code. Quite a bit of code is required to add these features to the output, as shown in Document 12.6b.

Note that the output from Document 12.6a does not yet use the label information and some of the other "hard-coded" values for creating the graphing space. However, it is helpful to make sure these values have been defined and that the resulting code is free from syntax errors before proceeding to the next step.

Document 12.6b (Vbar2.php)

```php
<?php
Header ("Content-type: image/gif");
// define default data
$chartTitle = "Bar Graph";
$x_title = "X-axis"; $y_title = "Y-axis";
$y_labels=array("0","10","20","30","40","50","60","70","80"
,"90","100");
$x_labels=array("0","1","2","3","4","5","6","7","8","9",
"10","11","12","13","14","15","16","17","18","19","20","21",
"22","23","24","25","26","27","28","29","30","31");
$n_x=31; // number of x-axis labels
$n_y=11; // number of y-axis labels
$ylabel_mask=" "; // Mask for right-justifying y-labels
$ylabel_length=4; // Maximum length of y-axis label
// define image space
$x_max = 800;
$y_max = 300;
// define graphing space in terms of intervals
// lower left-hand corner of graphing space
$x0 = 80; $y0 = 250;
$x_gap = 20; $y_gap = 20; // interval between axis labels
// label and title offsets from x-y origin _
// trial-and-error
$xlabel_xoffset=-15;
$xlabel_yoffset=10;
$ylabel_xoffset=-28;
$ylabel_yoffset=-8;
$xtitle_xoffset=260;
$xtitle_yoffset=25;
$ytitle_xoffset=-45;
$ytitle_yoffset=-75;
// create and color image space background
$im = imageCreate ($x_max, $y_max) or
  die ("Cannot Initialize new GD image stream");
```

```php
$background_color = ImageColorAllocate($im,234,234,234);
$title_font_size = 5; // large font for title
// black text for title
$title_color = ImageColorAllocate($im,0,0,0);
// starting coordinates for title
$x0_title = 10; $y0_title = 10; // draw graphing space
ImageString($im,$title_font_size,$x0_title,$y0_title,
  $chartTitle,$title_color);
// black lines for graphing space borders
// medium line width for graphing space borders
$line_color=ImageColorAllocate($im,0,0,0);
ImageSetThickness($im,2);
// draw x-axis
ImageLine($im,$x0,$y0,$x0+$n_x*$x_gap,$y0,$line_color);
ImageLine($im,$x0,$y0-($n_y-1)*$y_gap,$x0+$n_x*$x_gap,
//top border
$y0-($n_y-1)*$y_gap,$line_color);
// y-axis
ImageLine($im,$x0,$y0,$x0,$y0-($n_y-1)*$y_gap,$line_color);
// right border
ImageLine($im,$x0+$n_x*$x_gap,$y0,$x0+$n_x*$x_gap,
  $y0-($n_y-1)*$y_gap,$line_color);
// draw x-axis labels and vertical grid
// black lines for grids
$grid_color = ImageColorAllocate($im,0,0,0); $label_color =
// black text for labels
ImageColorAllocate($im,0,0,0); ImageSetThickness($im,1);
for ($i=0; $i<=$n_x; $i++) {
  $x=$x0+$xlabel_xoffset+$i*$x_gap;
  $y=$y0+$xlabel_yoffset;
  if ($i>0)
  ImageString($im,2,$x,$y,$x_labels[$i],$label_color);
  ImageLine($im,$x0+$i*$y_gap,$y0,$x0+$i*$y_gap,
    $y0-($n_y-1)*$y_gap,$grid_color);
}
// draw y-axis labels and horizontal grid
$black=ImageColorAllocate($im,0,0,0);
// define a black and transparent dashed line for grid lines
$style = array(
  $black,$black,$black,$black,$black,
  IMG_COLOR_TRANSPARENT,IMG_COLOR_TRANSPARENT,
  IMG_COLOR_TRANSPARENT,IMG_COLOR_TRANSPARENT,
  IMG_COLOR_TRANSPARENT
);
ImageSetStyle($im,$style);
```

12

```
for ($i=0; $i<$n_y; $i++) {
    // next two lines right-justify the y-axis labels
    $ylabel=$ylabel_mask . $y_labels[$i];
    $ylabel=substr($ylabel,strlen($ylabel)-$ylabel_length);
    $x=$x0+$ylabel_xoffset;
    $y=$y0+$ylabel_yoffset-$i*$y_gap;
    ImageString($im,2,$x,$y,$ylabel,$label_color);
    ImageLine($im,$x0,$y0-$i*$x_gap,$x0+$n_x*$x_gap,
              $y0-$i*$y_gap,IMG_COLOR_STYLED);
}
// Draw axis titles.
ImageString($im,$title_font_size,$x0+$xtitle_xoffset,
    $y0+$xtitle_yoffset,$x_title,$label_color);
ImageStringUp($im,$title_font_size,$x0+$ytitle_xoffset,
    $y0+$ytitle_yoffset,$y_title,$label_color);
// Create GIF image.
ImageGIF($im);
// Release allocated resources.
ImageDestroy($im);
?>
```

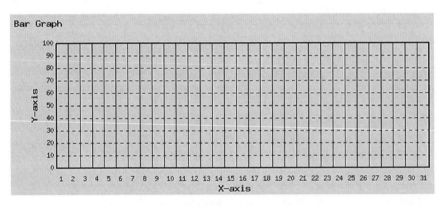

The code required to produce this output includes several pixel offset values, determined by trial and error, as required to position the labels properly to the left of the *y*-axis and below the *x*-axis, and to center the axis titles along their axes. These offsets depend on the length of the titles, of course. In principle, code *could* be written to calculate the pixel offsets, but it seems more trouble than it is worth for this demonstration application.

The *y*-axis labels have been right-justified by concatenating the label string to a mask of blank spaces and extracting a right-hand substring. The *x*-axis labels have been offset to the right so they are placed approximately in the middle of the space where each bar will go. Just for demonstration purposes, code has been included for creating dashed horizontal grid lines consisting of 5 black pixels alternating with 5 transparent pixels.

Document 12.6c adds the code necessary to draw the bars for the hard-coded default data set.

Document 12.6c (Vbar3.php)

```php
<?php
Header ("Content-type: image/gif");
// define default data
$chartTitle = "Bar Graph";
$x_title = "X-axis"; $y_title = "Y-axis";
$y_labels=array("0","10","20","30","40","50","60","70","80",
"90","100");
$x_labels=array("0","1","2","3","4","5","6","7","8","9",
"10","11","12","13","14","15","16","17","18","19","20","21",
"22","23","24","25","26","27","28","29","30","31");
$Y=array(23,10,15,100,0,55,60,16,23,33,44,77,88,91,5,85,80,
66,49,33,22,25,83,90,44,25,11,9,77,20,15);
$n_x=31; // number of x-axis labels
$n_y=11; // number of y-axis labels
$ylabel_mask=" "; // Mask for right-justifying y-labels
$ylabel_length=4; // Maximum length of y-axis label
// define image space
$x_max = 800;
$y_max = 300;
// define graphing space in terms of intervals
// lower left-hand corner of graphing space
$x0 = 80; $y0 = 250;
$x_gap = 20; $y_gap = 20; // interval between axis labels
$bar_width=10;
$bar_offset=5;
// label and title offsets from x-y origin _
// trial-and-error
$xlabel_xoffset=-15;
$xlabel_yoffset=10;
$ylabel_xoffset=-28;
$ylabel_yoffset=-8;
$xtitle_xoffset=260;
$xtitle_yoffset=25;
$ytitle_xoffset=-45;
$ytitle_yoffset=-75;
// create and color image space background
$im = imageCreate ($x_max, $y_max) or
  die ("Cannot Initialize new GD image stream");
$background_color = ImageColorAllocate($im,234,234,234);
$bar_color=ImageColorAllocate($im,255,0,0);
// large font for title
$title_font_size = 5;
// black text for title
```

```php
$title_color = ImageColorAllocate($im,0,0,0);
// starting coordinates for title
$x0_title = 10; $y0_title = 10; // draw graphing space
ImageString($im,$title_font_size,$x0_title,$y0_title,
  $chartTitle,$title_color);
// black lines for graphing space borders
// medium line width for graphing space borders
$line_color=ImageColorAllocate($im,0,0,0);
ImageSetThickness($im,2);
// draw x-axis
ImageLine($im,$x0,$y0,$x0+$n_x*$x_gap,$y0,$line_color);
ImageLine($im,$x0,$y0-($n_y-1)*$y_gap,$x0+$n_x*$x_gap,
//top border
$y0-($n_y-1)*$y_gap,$line_color);
// y-axis
// right border
ImageLine($im,$x0,$y0,$x0,$y0-($n_y-1)*$y_gap,$line_color);
ImageLine($im,$x0+$n_x*$x_gap,$y0,$x0+$n_x*$x_gap,
  $y0-($n_y-1)*$y_gap,$line_color);
// draw x-axis labels and vertical grid
// black lines for grids
$grid_color = ImageColorAllocate($im,0,0,0);
$label_color = // black text for labels
ImageColorAllocate($im,0,0,0); ImageSetThickness($im,1);
for ($i=0; $i<=$n_x; $i++) {
  $x=$x0+$xlabel_xoffset+$i*$x_gap;
  $y=$y0+$xlabel_yoffset;
  if ($i>0)
  ImageString($im,2,$x,$y,$x_labels[$i],$label_color);
  ImageLine($im,$x0+$i*$x_gap,$y0,$x0+$i*$x_gap,
    $y0-($n_y-1)*$y_gap,$grid_color);
}
// draw y-axis labels and horizontal grid
$black=ImageColorAllocate($im,0,0,0);
// define a black and transparent dashed line for grid lines
$style = array(
  $black,$black,$black,$black,$black,
  IMG_COLOR_TRANSPARENT,IMG_COLOR_TRANSPARENT,
  IMG_COLOR_TRANSPARENT,IMG_COLOR_TRANSPARENT,
  IMG_COLOR_TRANSPARENT
);
ImageSetStyle($im,$style);
for ($i=0; $i<$n_y; $i++) {
```

```
    // next two lines right-justify the y-axis labels
    $ylabel=$ylabel_mask . $y_labels[$i];
    $ylabel=substr($ylabel,strlen($ylabel)-$ylabel_length);
    $x=$x0+$ylabel_xoffset;
    $y=$y0+$ylabel_yoffset-$i*$y_gap;
    ImageString($im,2,$x,$y,$ylabel,$label_color);
    ImageLine($im,$x0,$y0-$i*$y_gap,$x0+$n_x*$x_gap,
              $y0-$i*$y_gap,IMG_COLOR_STYLED);
}
// Draw axis titles.
ImageString($im,$title_font_size,$x0+$xtitle_xoffset,
  $y0+$xtitle_yoffset,$x_title,$label_color);
ImageStringUp($im,$title_font_size,$x0+$ytitle_xoffset,
  $y0+$ytitle_yoffset,$y_title,$label_color);
// Draw bars.
$y_range=$y_gap*($n_y-1);
$ymin=0;  $ymax=100;
for ($i=0;  $i<$n_x;  $i++) {
ImageFilledRectangle($im,$x0+$bar_offset+$x_gap*$i,$y0,$x0+$
bar_offset+$bar_width+$x_gap*$i,
    $y0-($Y[$i]-$ymin)/($ymax-$ymin)*$y_range,$bar_color);
}
// Create GIF image.
ImageGIF($im);
// Release allocated resources.
ImageDestroy($im);
?>
```

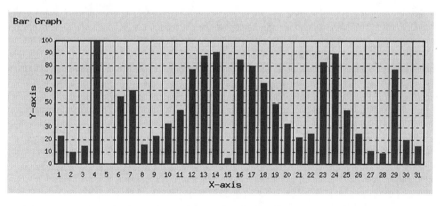

Documents 12.7a, b show the code for creating vertical bar charts using an HTML document interface.

Document 12.7a (VbarChartTest.htm)

```html
<html>
<head>
  <title>Vbar chart interface</title>
</head>
<body>
<h3>Create vertical bar chart</h3>
<form method="post" action="VbarChart.php" >
Data file name: <input type="text" name="FileName"
value="VbarChart.dat" /><br />
Chart title: <input type="text" name="title" size="50"
value="Daily Rainfall (mm)" /><br />
X-axis title: <input type="text" name="xTitle" value="day,
June 2009" /><br />
Y-axis title: <input type="text" name="yTitle"
value="rainfall, mm" /><br />
Number of bars: <input type="text" name="nBars" value="31"
/><br />
Minimum value: <input type="text" name="min" value="0"
/><br />
Maximum value: <input type="text" name="max" value="100"
/><br />
Y-axis labels: <input type="text" name="yLabels" size="50"
value="0,10,20,30,40,50,60,70,80,90,100" /><br />
X-label space (pixels) <input type="text" name="xWidth"
value="20"/><br />
Bar width (% of x-label space): <input type="text"
name="barWidth" value="50" /><br />
Bar color (RRR,GGG,BBB): <input type="text" name="barColor"
value="255,0,0" /><br />
Offset for x-axis title (pixels): <input type="text"
value="250" name="xTitleOffset" /><br />
Offset for y-axis title (pixels): <input type="text"
value="10" name="yTitleOffset" /><br />
<input type="submit" value="Click to draw chart..." /><br />
<input type="reset" value="Click to reset..." ><br />
</form>
</body>
</html>
```

Document 12.7b (VbarChart.php)

```php
<?php
function
drawChart($chartTitle,$barColor,$bar_width,$x_gap,$n_x,
$x_title,$y_title,$xtitle_xoffset,$ytitle_yoffset,$yMin,
$yMax,$x_labels,$y_labels,$Y_lo,$Y_hi){
Header ("Content-type: image/gif");
$n_y=count($y_labels); // number of y-axis labels
$ylabel_mask="    "; // Mask for right-justifying y-labels
$ylabel_length=4; // Maximum length of y-axis label
// define image space
$x_max = 800;
$y_max = 300;
// define graphing space in terms of intervals
$x0=80; $y0=250; // lower left-hand corner of graphing space
$y_range=200; // fixed y-axis graphing space
$y_gap=$y_range/($n_y-1); // interval between y-axis labels
// define bar width as a % of total space for the bar --
$bar_width=$x_gap*$bar_width/100;
$bar_offset=($x_gap-$bar_width)/2;
// label and title offsets from x-y origin
// trial-and-error
$xlabel_xoffset=5;
$xlabel_yoffset=10;
$ylabel_xoffset=-28;
$ylabel_yoffset=-8;
//$xtitle_xoffset=260;
$xtitle_yoffset=25;
$ytitle_xoffset=-45;
$ytitle_yoffset=-$ytitle_yoffset;
// create and color image space background
$im = imageCreate ($x_max, $y_max) or
  die ("Cannot Initialize new GD image stream");
$background_color = ImageColorAllocate($im,234,234,234);
$colorArray=array();
$colorArray=explode(",",$barColor);
//$bar_color=ImageColorAllocate($im,255,0,0);
$bar_color=ImageColorAllocate($im,$colorArray[0],
  $colorArray[1],$colorArray[2]);
// large font for title
$title_font_size = 5;
// black text for title
$title_color = ImageColorAllocate($im,0,0,0);
// starting coordinates for title
```

```php
$x0_title = 10; $y0_title = 10; // draw graphing space
ImageString($im,$title_font_size,$x0_title,$y0_title,
  $chartTitle,$title_color);
// black lines for graphing space borders
// medium line width for graphing space borders
$line_color=ImageColorAllocate($im,0,0,0);
ImageSetThickness($im,2);
// draw x-axis
ImageLine($im,$x0,$y0,$x0+$n_x*$x_gap,$y0,$line_color);
ImageLine($im,$x0,$y0-($n_y-1)*$y_gap,$x0+$n_x*$x_gap,
//top border
$y0-($n_y-1)*$y_gap,$line_color);
// y-axis
// right border
ImageLine($im,$x0,$y0,$x0,$y0-($n_y-1)*$y_gap,$line_color);
ImageLine($im,$x0+$n_x*$x_gap,$y0,$x0+$n_x*$x_gap,
  $y0-($n_y-1)*$y_gap,$line_color);
// draw x-axis labels and vertical grid
// black lines for grids
$grid_color = ImageColorAllocate($im,0,0,0);
$label_color = // black text for labels
ImageColorAllocate($im,0,0,0); ImageSetThickness($im,1);
// draw x-labels
for ($i=0; $i<=$n_x; $i++) {
  $x=$x0+$xlabel_xoffset+$i*$x_gap;
  $y=$y0+$xlabel_yoffset;
  ImageString($im,2,$x,$y,$x_labels[$i],$label_color);
  ImageLine($im,$x0+$i*$x_gap,$y0,$x0+$i*$x_gap,
    $y0-($n_y-1)*$y_gap,$grid_color);
}
// draw y-axis labels and horizontal grid
$black=ImageColorAllocate($im,0,0,0);
// define a black and transparent dashed line for grid lines
$style = array(
  $black,$black,$black,$black,$black,
  IMG_COLOR_TRANSPARENT,IMG_COLOR_TRANSPARENT,
  IMG_COLOR_TRANSPARENT,IMG_COLOR_TRANSPARENT,
  IMG_COLOR_TRANSPARENT
);
ImageSetStyle($im,$style);
for ($i=0; $i<$n_y; $i++) {
  // next two lines right-justify the y-axis labels
  $ylabel=$ylabel_mask . $y_labels[$i];
  $ylabel=substr($ylabel,strlen($ylabel)-$ylabel_length);
  $x=$x0+$ylabel_xoffset;
```

```
    $y=$y0+$ylabel_yoffset-$i*$y_gap;
    ImageString($im,2,$x,$y,$ylabel,$label_color);
    ImageLine($im,$x0,$y0-$i*$y_gap,$x0+$n_x*$x_gap,
              $y0-$i*$y_gap,IMG_COLOR_STYLED);
}
// Draw axis titles.
ImageString($im,$title_font_size,$x0+$xtitle_xoffset,
    $y0+$xtitle_yoffset,$x_title,$label_color);
ImageStringUp($im,$title_font_size,$x0+$ytitle_xoffset,
    $y0+$ytitle_yoffset,$y_title,$label_color);
// Draw bars.
$y_span=$yMax-$yMin;
for ($i=0; $i<$n_x; $i++) {
    ImageFilledRectangle($im,$x0+$bar_offset+$x_gap*$i,
      $y0- ($Y_lo[$i]-$yMin)/$y_span*$y_range,
      $x0+$bar_offset+$bar_width+$x_gap*$i,
      $y0-($Y_hi[$i]-$yMin)/$y_span*$y_range,$bar_color);
}
// Create GIF image.
ImageGIF($im);
// Release allocated resources.
ImageDestroy($im);
}
//--------- MAIN PROGRAM ----------------
$FileName=$_POST["FileName"];
//echo $FileName."<br />";
$title=$_POST["title"];
$xTitle=$_POST["xTitle"];
$yTitle=$_POST["yTitle"];
$nBars=$_POST["nBars"];
$yMin=$_POST["min"];
$yMax=$_POST["max"];
$xWidth=$_POST["xWidth"];
$yLabels=explode(",",$_POST["yLabels"]);
$barWidth=$_POST["barWidth"];
$barColor=$_POST["barColor"];
$xTitleOffset=$_POST["xTitleOffset"];
$yTitleOffset=$_POST["yTitleOffset"];
$in=fopen($FileName,"r");
$xLabels=array(); $Y_lo=array(); $Y_hi=array();
$i=0;
while (!feof($in)) {
    fscanf($in,"%s %f %f",$xLabels[$i],$Y_lo[$i],$Y_hi[$i]);
//echo $xLabels[$i]." ".$Y_lo[$i]." ".$Y_hi[$i]."<br />";
    $i++;
}
```

```
fclose($in);
drawChart($title,$barColor,$barWidth,$xWidth,$nBars,
    $xTitle,$yTitle,$xTitleOffset,$yTitleOffset,$yMin,
    $yMax,$xLabels,$yLabels,$Y_lo,$Y_hi);
?>
```

Documents 12.7a, b include several modifications to the previous code for creating vertical bar charts. The number of pixels allocated along the x-axis to each bar value is specified as input rather than being hard-coded. The width of the bar for each value is given as the percentage of the total space allocated for each value, rather than being speci-fied as a number of pixels, and the bar is centered within the allocated space. It is the user's responsibility to make sure that the total number of pixels required—the number of bar values times the number of pixels for each value—does not exceed the amount of space allocated for the x-axis (about 700 pixels), and also that the x-labels can reasonably be displayed within the space allocated. The bar color is user-selectable in RRR,GGG,BBB format where the color intensities are given as integers between 0 and 255; for example, 255,0,0 produces red bars and 0,0,0 produces black bars.

In Document 12.6c, the number of y-axis values was determined by the number of y-axis labels and the space between labels was hard-coded as 20 pixels. For the sample data, there were 11 y-axis labels, starting at 0, so the y-axis was 200 pixels long. The bars were assumed always to start at 0. In Document 12.7b, the number of pixels allocated for the y-axis is hard-coded as 200 pixels and additional code is added to scale data within this range. Bars do not have to start at 0 and the scaling allows for negative as well as positive values.

The data file specified as an input contains the x-axis labels and the minimum and maximum values for each bar. The y-axis labels are given as a comma-separated string in an <input> field; this string is later converted into an array of labels. It is again up to the user to make sure that the total number of y-labels can reasonably be displayed along a 200-pixel axis. Currently, the code in Document 12.7b right-justifies y-axis labels in a four-character field. For labels containing more than four characters, the code will need to be modified, with the y-labels and y-axis title shifted to the left.

Finally, input values are provided for moving the x-axis label left to right and the y-axis label up and down. (The y-label offset is given as a positive number even though, in the code, this must be converted to a negative number to shift the y-label "up" from the x-axis.) Thus, the HTML interface allows the user to change some, but not all, of the previously hard-coded coordinates for placing labels.

As an example of using this application, consider this data file containing a range of values for components of the air quality index—carbon monoxide, ozone (1- and 8-h values), sulfur dioxide, nitrogen dioxide, and particulates (10 and 2.5 μm):

```
CO  10  15
O3_1  15  30
O3_8  0  0
SO2  50  100
NO2  2  25
PM_10  50  70
PM_2.5  80  95
```

The HTML interface values are:

Create vertical bar chart

Data file name: AQI.dat

Chart title: AQI components

X-axis title: Components

Y-axis title: AQI

Number of bars: 7

Minimum value: 0

Maximum value: 100

Y-axis labels: 0,10,20,30,40,50,60,70,80,90,100

X-label space (pixels) 50

Bar width (% of x-label space): 50

Bar color (RRR,GGG,BBB): 0,0,0

Offset for x-axis title (pixels): 130

Offset for y-axis title (pixels): 90

Click to draw chart...

Click to reset...

For displaying in this book's black-and-white format, the bar color is black (0,0,0). The x- and y-label offset values are selected by trial and error to center the labels on their respective axes and produce this output:

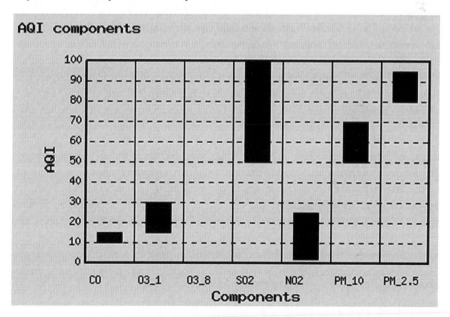

12

12.2.5
Line Graphs

The code required to create a line graph is similar to that required for bar charts, in the sense that the *x*- and *y*-ranges of the data must be scaled to fit within the allocated graphing space. Document 12.8a shows how to set up the image and graphing space. For demonstration purposes, the default *x*- and *y*-axis labels have been chosen for displaying insolation (total solar irradiance reaching Earth's surface) as a function of time for the first 8 days of a summer month.

Document 12.8a (line1.php)

```php
<?php
Header ("Content-type: image/gif");
$title = "Line graph";
// Define axis labels and titles.
$y_labels=array("0","200","400","600","800","1000","1200",
"1400");
$x_labels=array("1","2","3","4","5","6","7","8","9");
// Number of axis labels.
$n_x=count($x_labels);
$n_y=count($y_labels);
$x_title="X-axis title";
$y_title="Y-axis title";
$ylabel_mask=" "; // Mask for right-justifying y-labels
$ylabel_length=4; // Maximum length of y-axis label
$x_gap=100; // The gap between each label on y-axis
$y_gap=50; // The gap between each label on x-axis
$x_max=900; // Maximum width of the graphing space
$y_max=450; // Maximum height of the graphing space
$x0=50; // x-axis origin
$y0=400; // y-axis origin
// Label and title offsets from x-y origin.
$xlabel_xoffset=-5;
$xlabel_yoffset=10;
$ylabel_xoffset=-28;
$ylabel_yoffset=-8;
$xtitle_xoffset=150;
$xtitle_yoffset=25;
$ytitle_xoffset=-45;
$ytitle_yoffset=-50;
// Create and color image space background.
$im = imageCreate ($x_max, $y_max) or die ("Cannot
Initialize new GD image stream");
$background_color = ImageColorAllocate ($im, 234, 234, 234);
```

```php
// Define colors.
$text_color = ImageColorAllocate ($im, 233, 14, 91);
$graph_color = ImageColorAllocate ($im, 25, 25, 25);
$line_color=ImageColorAllocate($im, 0, 0, 0);
$black = ImageColorAllocate ($im, 0, 0, 0);
// Define font size for titles, and style for dashed lines.
$title_font_size=3;
$style = Array(
  $black, $black, $black, $black, $black,
  IMG_COLOR_TRANSPARENT, IMG_COLOR_TRANSPARENT,
  IMG_COLOR_TRANSPARENT, IMG_COLOR_TRANSPARENT,
  IMG_COLOR_TRANSPARENT
);
imagesetstyle($im, $style);
// Set thickness (pixels) for drawing lines.
ImageSetThickness($im, 3);
// Draw x- and y- axes, top and right border.
ImageLine($im, $x0, $y0, $x0+($n_x-1)*$x_gap, $y0, $line_color);
// x-axis
//top border
ImageLine($im, $x0, $y0-($n_y-1)*$y_gap, $x0+($n_x-
1)*$x_gap, $y0-($n_y-1)*$y_gap, $line_color); //top border
ImageLine($im, $x0, $y0, $x0, $y0-($n_y-1)*$y_gap, $line_color);
// y-axis
ImageLine($im, $x0+($n_x-1)*$x_gap, $y0, $x0+($n_x-
1)*$x_gap, $y0-($n_y-1)*$y_gap, $line_color); // right border
// Draw x-axis labels and vertical grid.
ImageSetThickness($im, 1);
for ($i=0; $i<$n_x; $i++) {
  $x=$x0+$xlabel_xoffset+$i*$x_gap;
  $y=$y0+$xlabel_yoffset;
  ImageString($im, 2, $x, $y, $x_labels[$i], $graph_color);
  ImageLine($im, $x0+$i*$x_gap, $y0, $x0+$i*$x_gap,
    $y0-($n_y-1)*$y_gap, $line_color);
}
// Draw y-axis labels and horizontal grid.
for ($i=0; $i<$n_y; $i++) {
      // Next two lines right-justify the y-axis labels.
  $ylabel=$ylabel_mask . $y_labels[$i];
  $ylabel=substr($ylabel, strlen($ylabel)-$ylabel_length);
  $x=$x0+$ylabel_xoffset;
  $y=$y0+$ylabel_yoffset-$i*$y_gap;
  ImageString($im, 2, $x, $y, $ylabel, $graph_color);
  ImageLine($im, $x0, $y0-$i*$y_gap, $x0+($n_x-1)*$x_gap,
```

12

```
         $y0-$i*$y_gap,$line_color);
}
// Draw titles.
ImageString($im,$title_font_size,20,20,$title,$line_color);
ImageString($im,$title_font_size,$x0+$xtitle_xoffset,
  $y0+$xtitle_yoffset,$x_title,$graph_color);
ImageStringUp($im,$title_font_size,$x0+$ytitle_xoffset,
  $y0+$ytitle_yoffset,$y_title,$graph_color);
// Create GIF image.
ImageGIF ($im);
// Release allocated resources.
ImageDestroy($im);
?>
```

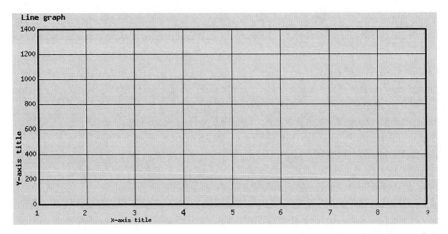

For the next step, assume the insolation values for these 8 days, recorded at one-minute intervals and is saved in file SummerInsolation.txt. The first few lines of this file look like this:

```
DRB Worcester, PA
40.178 -75.3325
4030
mon     day    yr     hr    min    sec     EST             V
6       1      2008   0     0      0       1               0.00031
6       1      2008   0     1      0       1.000694444     0.00031
6       1      2008   0     2      0       1.001388889     0.00031
6       1      2008   0     3      0       1.002083333     0.00031
6       1      2008   0     4      0       1.002777778     0.00031
6       1      2008   0     5      0       1.003472222     0.00031
6       1      2008   0     6      0       1.004166667     0.00031
```

The first line is an identifying header. The second line gives the latitude and longitude of the observing site in decimal degrees, and the third line gives the calibration constant required to convert voltage output from a pyranometer (an instrument for measuring solar irradiance) from volts to physical units of watts per square meter (the units of this constant are (W/m²)/V. The fourth line identifies the columns. The clock times are Eastern Standard Time. The EST column is the day expressed as a decimal value (day+hour/24+ minute/1,440+second/86,400). The last column gives the raw voltage output from the pyranometer.

Document 12.8b gives the code required to read and display these data.

Document 12.8b line2.php

```php
<?php
Header ("Content-type: image/gif");
$fileName = "pyranometerData/SummerInsolation.txt";
$title = "Insolation, W/m^2";
// Define axis labels and titles.
$y_labels = array("0","200","400","600","800","1000","1200",
"1400","1600");
$x_labels = array("1","2","3","4","5","6","7","8","9");
// Number of axis labels.
$n_x = count($x_labels);
$n_y = count($y_labels);
$x_title = "Days, EST";
$y_title = "Insolation, W/m^2";
$ylabel_mask = " "; // Mask for right-justifying y-labels
$ylabel_length = 4; // Maximum length of y-axis label
$x_gap = 100; // The gap between each label on y-axis
$y_gap = 50; // The gap between each label on x-axis
$x_max=900; // Maximum width of the graph or horizontal axis
$y_max=500; // Maximum hight of the graph or vertical axis
$x0 = 50; // x-axis origin
$y0 = 450; // y-axis origin
// Label and title offsets from x-y origin.
$xlabel_xoffset = -5;
$xlabel_yoffset = 10;
$ylabel_xoffset = -28;
$ylabel_yoffset = -8;
$xtitle_xoffset = 375;
$xtitle_yoffset = 25;
$ytitle_xoffset = -45;
$ytitle_yoffset = -120;
// Create and color image space background.
$im = imageCreate ($x_max, $y_max) or die ("Cannot
Initialize new GD image stream");
$background_color = ImageColorAllocate ($im, 234, 234, 234);
```

12

```php
// Define colors.
$text_color = ImageColorAllocate ($im, 233, 14, 91);
$graph_color = ImageColorAllocate ($im, 25, 25, 25);
$line_color=ImageColorAllocate($im, 0, 0, 0);
$black = ImageColorAllocate($im, 0, 0, 0);
// Define font size for titles, and style for dashed lines.
$title_font_size=3;
$style = Array(
  $black, $black, $black, $black, $black,
  IMG_COLOR_TRANSPARENT, IMG_COLOR_TRANSPARENT,
  IMG_COLOR_TRANSPARENT,
  IMG_COLOR_TRANSPARENT, IMG_COLOR_TRANSPARENT
);
imagesetstyle($im, $style);
// Set thickness (pixels) for drawing lines.
ImageSetThickness($im, 3);
// Draw x- and y- axes, top and right border.
// x-axis
ImageLine($im, $x0, $y0, $x0+($n_x-1)*$x_gap, $y0, $line_color);
//top border
ImageLine($im, $x0, $y0-($n_y-1)*$y_gap,
  $x0+($n_x-1)*$x_gap, $y0-($n_y-1)*$y_gap, $line_color);
// y-axis
ImageLine($im, $x0, $y0, $x0, $y0-($n_y-1)*$y_gap, $line_color);
// right border
ImageLine($im, $x0+($n_x-1)*$x_gap, $y0, $x0+($n_x-1)*$x_gap,
  $y0-($n_y-1)*$y_gap, $line_color);
// Draw x-axis labels and vertical grid.
ImageSetThickness($im, 1);
for ($i=0; $i<$n_x; $i++) {
  $x=$x0+$xlabel_xoffset+$i*$x_gap;
  $y=$y0+$xlabel_yoffset;
  ImageString($im, 2, $x, $y, $x_labels[$i], $graph_color);
  ImageLine($im, $x0+$i*$x_gap, $y0, $x0+$i*$x_gap,
    $y0-($n_y-1)*$y_gap, $line_color);
}
// Draw y-axis labels and horizontal grid.
for ($i=0; $i<$n_y; $i++) {
  // Next two lines right-justify the y-axis labels.
  $ylabel=$ylabel_mask . $y_labels[$i];
  $ylabel=substr($ylabel, strlen($ylabel)-$ylabel_length);
  $x=$x0+$ylabel_xoffset;
```

```
    $y=$y0+$ylabel_yoffset-$i*$y_gap;
    ImageString($im,2,$x,$y,$ylabel,$graph_color);
    ImageLine($im,$x0,$y0-$i*$y_gap,$x0+($n_x-1)*$x_gap,
      $y0-$i*$y_gap,$line_color);
}
// Draw titles.
ImageString($im,$title_font_size,20,20,$title,$line_color);
ImageString($im,$title_font_size,$x0+$xtitle_xoffset,
  $y0+$xtitle_yoffset,$x_title,$graph_color);
ImageStringUp($im,$title_font_size,$x0+$ytitle_xoffset,
  $y0+$ytitle_yoffset,$y_title,$graph_color);
// Get data from file.
$in = fopen($fileName,"r");
$title = fgets($in);
fscanf($in,"%f %f",$Lat,$Lon);
fscanf($in,"%f",$Cal1);
$labels = fgets($in);
$i = -1;
while (!feof($in)) {
  $i++;
  fscanf($in,"%f %f %f %f %f %f %f %f",
  $m,$d,$y,$hr,$min,$sec,$EST[$i],$P1[$i]);
}
fclose($in);
// Plot data.
$red = ImageColorAllocate($im,255,0,0);
$yvalue_max = 1600;// W/m^2, y min = 0
$nDays = 8;
$day = 1;
$n_x=count($EST);
$x1 = $x0; $y1 = $y0;
for ($i=0; $i<$n_x; $i++) {
  $x = $x0 + ($EST[$i] - $day)/$nDays*($nDays*$x_gap);
  $y = $y0 - ($P1[$i]*$Cal1)/$yvalue_max*($n_y*$y_gap);
  ImageLine($im,$x1,$y1,$x,$y,$red);
  $x1 = $x; $y1 = $y;
}
// Create GIF image.
ImageGIF ($im);
// Release allocated resources.
ImageDestroy($im);
?>
```

12

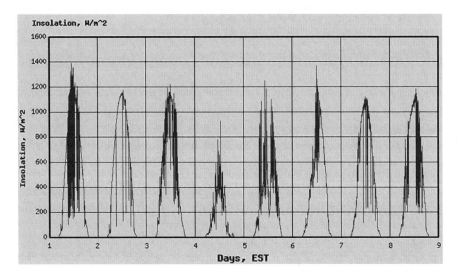

The final step, as in previous applications, is to place the line graph code inside a function and use an HTML interface to provide input values to PHP code that calls the function. Documents 12.9a, b give the HTML and PHP code for this application. This code should be considered just as an example of how to graph values extracted from a data file, rather than as a general-purpose interface, because the drawing of any line graph will depend considerably on the nature of the data being plotted and the format in which it is stored. It is certainly not possible to specify or plan for in advance all the possible formats that will determine the code needed to read and process the data.

Document 12.8b was used to display the first 8 days of solar data, sampled at one-minute intervals, and stored in a file whose name is hard-coded into the document. It was necessary to know the structure of this file in order to process the data. The HTML interface shown in Document 12.9a simply specifies the name of a file that contains *only* pairs of *X–Y* values to be graphed; this represents the simplest possible case of processing data from an external file.

Document 12.9a (lineGraphTest.htm)

```
<html>
<head>
  <title>Line Graph</title>
</head>
<body>
<h3>Draw a line graph</h3>
<form method="post" action="lineGraph.php">
Chart title: <input type="text" name="title"
value="Insolation" /><br />
X-axis title: <input type="text" name="Xaxis_title"
  value="Days, EST" /><br />
Y-axis title: <input type="text" name="Yaxis_title"
```

```
      value="Insolation, W/m2" /><br />
X<sub>min</sub>: <input type="text" name="x_min" value="1"
   /><br />
X<sub>max</sub>: <input type="text" name="x_max" value="32"
   /><br />
Y<sub>min</sub>: <input type="text" name="y_min" value="0"
   /><br />
Y<sub>max</sub>: <input type="text" name="y_max"
   value= "1400" /><br />
X-axis labels: <input type="text" name="X_labels" size="80"
   value="1 2 3 4 5 6 7 8 9 10 11 12 13 14 15 16 17 18 19 20
21 22 23 24 25 26 27 28 29 30 31 32"/><br />
Y-axis labels: <input type="text" name="Y_labels" size="40"
   value="0 200 400 600 800 1000 1200 1400"/><br />
X-title offset (pixels): <input type="text"
   name="xTitleOffset" value="300" /><br />
Y-title offset (pixels): <input type="text"
   name="yTitleOffset" value="150" /><br />
Name of file containing X-Y values:
<input type="text" name="fileName", size="50"
   value="c:/wamp/www/PyranometerData/June2008data.txt" />
<br />
<input type="submit" value="Click here to graph data." />
</form>
</body>
</html>
```

Draw a line graph

Chart title: Insolation

X-axis title: Days, EST

Y-axis title: Insolation, W/m2

X_{min}: 1

X_{max}: 32

Y_{min}: 0

Y_{max}: 1400

X-axis labels: 1 2 3 4 5 6 7 8 9 10 11 12 13 14 15 16 17 18 19 20 21 22 23 24 25 26 27 28 29 30 31 32

Y-axis labels: 0 200 400 600 800 1000 1200 1400

X-title offset (pixels): 300

Y-title offset (pixels): 125

Name of file containing X-Y values: c:/wamp/www/PyranometerData/June2008data.txt

[Click here to graph data.]

12

Document 12.9b (lineGraph.php)

```php
<?php
function lineGraph($title,$x_labels,$y_labels,$x_title,
  $y_title,$xtitle_xoffset,$ytitle_yoffset,$xmin,$xmax,
  $ymin,$ymax,$X,$Y) {
Header ("Content-type: image/gif");
// Define axis labels and titles.
// Number of axis labels.
  $n_x=count($x_labels);
  $n_y=count($y_labels);
//$x_title="X-axis title";
//$y_title="Y-axis title";
  $ylabel_mask=" "; // Mask for right-justifying y-labels
  $ylabel_length=4; // Maximum length of y-axis label
  $xaxis_length=700;
  $yaxis_length=350;
//$x_gap=100; // The gap between each label on y-axis
//$y_gap=50; // The gap between each label on x-axis
  $x_gap=$xaxis_length/($n_x-1);
  $y_gap=$yaxis_length/($n_y-1);
  $x_max=800; // Maximum width of the graphing space
  $y_max=450; // Maximum hight of the graphing space
  $x0=50; // x-axis origin
  $y0=400; // y-axis origin
// Label and title offsets from x-y origin.
  $xlabel_xoffset=-5;
  $xlabel_yoffset=10;
  $ylabel_xoffset=-28;
  $ylabel_yoffset=-8;
  $xtitle_yoffset=25;
  $ytitle_xoffset=-45;
  $ytitle_yoffset=-$ytitle_yoffset;
  $title_yoffset=380;
// Create and color image space background.
  $im=imageCreate ($x_max, $y_max) or
        die ("Cannot Initialize new GD image stream");
  $background_color=ImageColorAllocate ($im, 234, 234, 234);
// Define colors.
  $text_color=ImageColorAllocate($im, 233, 14, 91);
  $graph_color=ImageColorAllocate($im,25,25,25);
  $data_color=ImageColorAllocate($im,255,0,0);
  $line_color=ImageColorAllocate($im,0,0,0);
  $black=ImageColorAllocate($im,0,0,0);
```

```
// Define font size for titles, and style for dashed lines.
  $title_font_size=3;
  $style=Array(
    $black,$black,$black,$black,$black,
    IMG_COLOR_TRANSPARENT,IMG_COLOR_TRANSPARENT,
    IMG_COLOR_TRANSPARENT,IMG_COLOR_TRANSPARENT,
    IMG_COLOR_TRANSPARENT
  );
  Imagesetstyle($im, $style);
// Set thickness (pixels) for drawing lines.
  ImageSetThickness($im,3);
// Draw x- and y- axes, top and right border.
  ImageLine($im,$x0,$y0,$x0+
    ($n_x-1)*$x_gap,$y0,$line_color); // x-axis
  ImageLine($im,$x0,$y0-($n_y-1)*$y_gap,
    $x0+($n_x-1)*$x_gap,$y0-($n_y-1)*$y_gap,$line_color);
//top border
  ImageLine($im,$x0,$y0,$x0,
    $y0-($n_y-1)*$y_gap,$line_color); // y-axis
  ImageLine($im,$x0+($n_x-1)*$x_gap,$y0,
    $x0+($n_x-1)*$x_gap,$y0-($n_y-1)*$y_gap,$line_color);
// right border
// Draw x-axis labels and vertical grid.
  ImageSetThickness($im,1);
  for ($i=0; $i<$n_x; $i++) {
    $x=$x0+$xlabel_xoffset+$i*$x_gap;
    $y=$y0+$xlabel_yoffset;
    ImageString($im,2,$x,$y,$x_labels[$i],$graph_color);
    ImageLine($im,$x0+$i*$x_gap,$y0,$x0+$i*$x_gap,
      $y0-($n_y-1)*$y_gap,$line_color);
}
// Draw y-axis labels and horizontal grid.
  for ($i=0; $i<$n_y; $i++) {
    // Next two lines right-justify the y-axis labels.
    $ylabel=$ylabel_mask . $y_labels[$i];
    $ylabel=substr($ylabel,strlen($ylabel)-$ylabel_length);
    $x=$x0+$ylabel_xoffset;
    $y=$y0+$ylabel_yoffset-$i*$y_gap;
    ImageString($im,2,$x,$y,$ylabel,$graph_color);
    ImageLine($im,$x0,$y0-$i*$y_gap,$x0+($n_x-1)*$x_gap,
      $y0-$i*$y_gap,$line_color);
}
```

12

```php
// Draw titles.
  ImageString($im,$title_font_size,20,$y0-
$title_yoffset,$title,$line_color);
ImageString($im,$title_font_size,$x0+$xtitle_xoffset,
    $y0+$xtitle_yoffset,$x_title,$graph_color);
ImageStringUp($im,$title_font_size,$x0+$ytitle_xoffset,
    $y0+$ytitle_yoffset,$y_title,$graph_color);
// Scale and plot data.
  $n=count($X);
  $x1=($X[0]-$xmin)/($xmax-$xmin)*$xaxis_length;
  $y1=($Y[0]-$ymin)/($ymax-$ymin)*$yaxis_length;
  for ($i=1; $i<$n; $i++) {
    $x_plot=($X[$i]-$xmin)/($xmax-$xmin)*$xaxis_length;
    $y_plot=($Y[$i]-$ymin)/($ymax-$ymin)*$yaxis_length;
    ImageLine($im,$x0+$x1,$y0-$y1,$x0+$x_plot,
      $y0-$y_plot,$data_color);
    $x1=$x_plot; $y1=$y_plot;
}
// Create GIF image.
  ImageGIF ($im);
// Release allocated resources.
ImageDestroy($im);
}
// MAIN PROGRAM -------------------------------------------
$S=$_POST["X_labels"];
$X_labels=explode(' ',$S);
$S=$_POST["Y_labels"];
$Y_labels=explode(' ',$S);
$title=$_POST["title"];
$Xaxis_title=$_POST["Xaxis_title"];
$Yaxis_title=$_POST["Yaxis_title"];
$xmin=$_POST["x_min"]; $xmax=$_POST["x_max"];
$ymin=$_POST["y_min"]; $ymax=$_POST["y_max"];
$xTitleOffset=$_POST["xTitleOffset"];
$yTitleOffset=$_POST["yTitleOffset"];
// Read X-Y values from file.
$fileName=$_POST["fileName"];
$in=fopen($fileName,"r");
$X=array(); $Y=array(); $i=-1;
while (!feof($in)) {
  $i++;
  fscanf($in,"%f %f",$X[$i],$Y[$i]);
}
```

```
fclose($in);
lineGraph($title,$X_labels,$Y_labels,$Xaxis_title,
  $Yaxis_title,$xTitleOffset,$yTitleOffset,$xmin,$xmax,
  $ymin,$ymax,$X,$Y);
?>
```

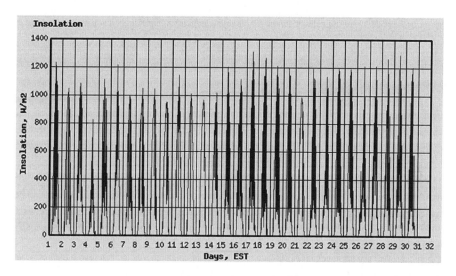

The input file used to test this application, June2008data.txt, contains one-minute data sampled insolation for the entire month of June—43,200 X–Y pairs. These values are read into two arrays in the main program section of Document 12.9b and passed to the lineGraph() function, rather than passing the file name to the function and reading and graphing the values one X–Y pair at a time within the function. The latter choice is perfectly acceptable, but the choice implemented in Document 12.9b shows that PHP is capable of handling very large arrays.

Here is a much smaller data file that can easily be copied and tried with this application:

```
0.582    0.003    8.2398
0.681    0.003    7.0438
0.746    0.003    6.2972
0.799    0.003    5.6974
0.849    0.003    5.1569
0.896    0.003    4.7228
0.931    0.003    4.4054
0.962    0.003    4.1332
1.006    0.003    3.7906
1.037    0.003    3.5338
1.068    0.003    3.2936
```

1.091	0.003	3.0758
1.121	0.003	2.8257
1.158	0.003	2.6090
1.176	0.003	2.4870
1.203	0.003	2.3003
1.223	0.003	2.1956
1.24	0.003	2.1043
1.25	0.003	1.9784
1.272	0.003	1.8467

The first and second columns are voltage outputs V and V_0 from a sun-viewing instrument called a sun photometer. The third column is the "relative air mass" m—a measure of the amount of atmosphere between the instrument, starting early in the morning. For this set of measurements, the quantity $\ln(V - V_0)$ plotted against m should be a straight line.

As is often the case with these applications, some modifications need to be made in the main program to prepare the arrays for graphing. These are shown in the shaded code below. In the main program, the logarithm of the first column minus the second is calculated and placed in the Y array. In the graphing function, code is added to mark each data point with a filled circle.

```php
$x1=($X[0]-$xmin)/($xmax-$xmin)*$xaxis_length;
$y1=($Y[0]-$ymin)/($ymax-$ymin)*$yaxis_length;
ImageFilledEllipse($im,$x0+$x1,$y0-$y1,10,10,$data_color);
for ($i=1; $i<$n; $i++) {
   $x_plot=($X[$i]-$xmin)/($xmax-$xmin)*$xaxis_length;
   $y_plot=($Y[$i]-$ymin)/($ymax-$ymin)*$yaxis_length;
   ImageLine($im,$x0+$x1,$y0-$y1,$x0+$x_plot,
      $y0-$y_plot,$data_color);
   $x1=$x_plot; $y1=$y_plot;
   ImageFilledEllipse($im,$x0+$x1,$y0-$y1,10,10,$data_color);
}
...
// MAIN PROGRAM -------------------------------------------
...
$X=array(); $Y=array(); $i=-1;
while (!feof($in)) {
$i++;
   fscanf($in, "%f %f %f",$V,$Vo,$X[$i]);
   $Y[$i]=log($V-$Vo);
}
```

Draw a line graph

Chart title: `Langley Plot for sun photometer calibration`

X-axis title: `Relative air mass`

Y-axis title: `ln(V)`

X_{min}: `0`

X_{max}: `9`

Y_{min}: `-.6`

Y_{max}: `.6`

X-axis labels: `0 1 2 3 4 5 6 7 8 9`

Y-axis labels: `-.6 -.5 -.4 -.3 -.2 -.1 0 .1 .2 .3 .4 .5 .6`

X-title offset (pixels): `200`

Y-title title offset (pixels): `50`

Name of file containing X-Y values: `LangleyPlot.dat`

Click here to graph data.

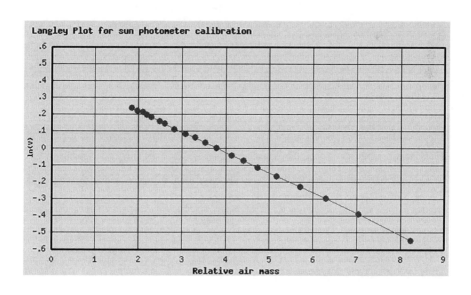

12.3
Summary of Some GD Graphics Functions

The "official" names of GD functions use all lowercase letters. However, taking advantage of the fact that function names are case-insensitive, uppercase letters are used here to separate "words" in function names. Hence, `imagecreate()` is written as `ImageCreate()`. This is simply a style choice, followed throughout this chapter, which may make code a little easier to read. In this section, words in **bold font** do not refer to entries in the glossary, but are intended to provide a visual cue to the purpose of a function. The variable names are just descriptive generic "place holder" names that can be changed as desired.

12.3.1
Create and Destroy Images

```
(resource) ImageCreate((int) $width, (int) $height)
(resource) ImageCreateTrueColor((int) $width,
                                 (int) $height)
```

Returns an **image handle** representing an image space of size width × height pixels.

```
(resource) ImageCreateFromGIF(string) $filename)
(resource) ImageCreateFromJPEG(string) $filename)
(resource) ImageCreateFromPNG(string) $filename)
```

Creates a GD image from an existing GIF, JPEG, or PNG file and returns an image handle.

```
ImageGIF((resource) $image[,(string) $filename])
ImageJPEG((resource) $image[,(string) $filename])
ImagePNG((resource) $image[,(string) $filename])
```

Creates a GIF, JPEG, or PNG file from the specified `$image` and displays it in a browser, optionally, saves the image to `$filename` rather than displaying it in a browser. With two calls, both options can be exercised in the same document. The file type of the original source for the image handle (GIF, JPEG, or PNG) does not matter. (See Document 8.11.)

```
ImageDestroy((resource) $image)
```

Frees memory associated with the image handle `$image`, after the image has been displayed on a browser page and/or saved as a file.

12.3.2
Draw Lines and Shapes

```
(bool) ImageSetThickness((resource) $image,
  (int) $thickness)
```

Sets **thickness** of the line used to draw straight lines and shapes.

```
(bool) ImageArc((resource) $image,(int) $cx,(int) $cy,
  (int) $width,(int) $height,(int) $start,(int) $end,
  (int) $color)
```

Draws an **arc** of an ellipse of size width × height pixels (or a circle if width equals height) centered at the specified (c_x,c_y) coordinates. The arc is drawn clockwise for $end degrees with the specified color. If $start=0, the drawing starts at the "three-o'clock" position.

```
(bool) ImageFilledArc((resource) $image,(int) $cx,
  (int) $cy,(int) $width,(int) $height,(int) $start,
  (int) $end,(int) $color,(int) $style)
```

Draws an **arc** of an ellipse of size width × height pixels (or a circle if width equals height) at the specified (c_x,c_y) coordinates and fills the arc with the specified color, with the following possibilities for $style:

IMG_ARC_PIE draws a circular or elliptical segment
IMG_ARC_CHORD draws a triangular segment
IMG_ARC_NOFILL draws a line only around the outer edge of the segment
IMG_ARC_EDGED produces the same result as IMG_ARC_PIE.

```
(bool) ImageEllipse((resource) $image,(int) $cx,
(int) $cy,(int) $width,(int) $height,(int) $color)
```
Draws an **ellipse** (or **circle**) of size width × height pixels centered at the specified (c_x,c_y) coordinates, with a line of the specified color.

```
(bool) ImageFilledEllipse((resource) $image,
  (int) $cx,(int) $cy,(int) $width,(int) $height,
  (int) $color)
```

Draws an **ellipse** (or **circle**) of size width × height pixels centered at the specified (c_x,c_y) coordinates, filled with the specified color.

```
(int) ImageColorAllocate((resource) $image,(int) $red,
  (int) $green,(int) $blue)
```

Returns a **color identifier** for the color defined by the specified RGB components. The first call fills background color for images created with ImageCreate(). The RGB color specifiers are base-10 integers, in the range 0–255. Often, HTML colors are expressed as hexadecimal values. For example, the hex code for a gold color is #D4A017.These RGB values can be provided as input to ImageColorAllocate() by using the hexdec() function:

```
ImageColorAllocate($im,hexdec('D4'),hexdec('A0'),
                    hexdec('17')
```

(bool) ImageFill(*(resource)* $image,*(int)* $x,*(int)* $y,
  (int) $color)

Floods a bounded area surrounding specified (*x,y*) coordinates with the specified **color**.

(bool) ImageLine(*(resource)* $image,*(int)* $x1,
  (int) $y1,*(int)* $x2,*(int)* $y2,*(int)* $color)

Draws a **line** between two specified pixel coordinates (x_1,y_1) and (x_2,y_2). A black dashed line can be created like this:

```
$black = ImageColorAllocate($image,0,0,0);
$style = Array($black,$black,$black,$black,$black,
  IMG_COLOR_TRANSPARENT, IMG_COLOR_TRANSPARENT,
  IMG_COLOR_TRANSPARENT, IMG_COLOR_TRANSPARENT,
  IMG_COLOR_TRANSPARENT);
ImageSetStyle($im, $style);
...
ImageLine((resource) $image, (int) $x1, (int) $y1,
  (int) $x2, (int) $x2, IMG_COLOR_STYLED);
```

This code draws a **line** with black dashes 5 pixels long and a 5-pixel "open space" between the dashes transparent to the background color. (You could assign this "open space" a different color, rather than have it be transparent.)

(bool) ImagePolygon(*(resource)* $image,(array) $points,
  (int) $n_points, *(int)* $color)

(bool) ImageFilledPolygon(*(resource)* $image,
  (array) $points,*(int)* $n_points,*(int)* $color)

Draws a closed **polygon** using the specified array of points, with a line of the specified color or (with ImageFilledPolygon()) filled with the specified color.

```
(bool) ImageRectangle((resource) $image,(int) $x1,
   (int) $y1,(int) $x2,(int) $y2,(int) $color)
```

```
(bool) ImageFilledRectangle((resource) $image,
   (int) $x1,(int) $y1,(int) $x2,(int) $y2,(int) $color)
```

Draws a **rectangle** using the two specified sets of (*x,y*) coordinates as opposite corners, with a line of the specified color or (with `ImageFilledRectangle()`) filled with the specified color.

12.3.3
Display Text

```
(bool) ImageString((resource) $image, (int) $font,
   (int) $x,(int) $y,(string) $string,(int) $color)
```

Draws a **text string** horizontally starting at specified (*x,y*) coordinates, with a font specified from 1 (smallest) to 5 (largest). The starting coordinates are the upper left-hand corner of the first character.

```
(bool) ImageStringUp((resource) $image, (int) $font,
   (int) $x,(int) $y,(string) $string,(int) $color)
```

Similar to `ImageString()`, but rotates the **text string** by –90° for drawing labels and titles on the *y*-axis of a graph, for example.

```
(bool) ImageTTFText((resource) $image, (int) $size,
   (int) $angle, (int) $x, (int) $y, (resource)
   $font_file, ($string) $text)
```

Draws a **text string** using a TrueType font (`.ttf`) file, `$font_file`. The font size `$size` is specified in pixels or point size, depending on the GD library version. The `$angle` at which the text is displayed is horizontally left to right for 0° and rotating counterclockwise as the angle increases. The `$x` and `$y` coordinates specify the lower left-hand corner of the character, but the `$y` coordinate is the font baseline, not the bottom of a character such as g or p that extends below the baseline. (Compare with the interpretation of coordinates for `ImageString()` and `ImageStringUp()`.)

Appendices

Appendix 1:
List of Document Examples

Starting in Chap. 7, some of the PHP documents require access to external user-generated data files.

D.R. Brooks, *Guide to HTML, JavaScript and PHP: For Scientists and Engineers*,
DOI 10.1007/978-0-85729-449-4, © Springer-Verlag London Limited 2011

349

Appendix 2:
Displaying Special Characters in an HTML Document

There are many symbols that cannot be entered directly into an HTML document from the keyboard. HTML defines so-called escape sequences as a way to embed special characters in a document. Each character can be entered either as a numerical code or by using a mnemonic name. Only the names will be used here. The following list provides some commonly used characters that may be useful for science and engineering applications. The list is a *very* small subset of characters supported by various browsers. In cases where special character names follow a predictable pattern (for the Greek alphabet, for example), just one example is given. (See notes at the end of the list.) There is no guarantee that the escape sequence names will be recognized or that characters will be displayed properly in all browsers or, when printed, by all printers.

`&alpha;`	α	Lowercase Greek alpha[a]
`&asymp;`	≈	Mathematical "almost equal to" symbol
`&aacute;`	á	Lowercase "a" with acute accent[b]
`&acirc;`	â	Lowercase "a" with circumflex[b]
`&aelig;`	æ	Lowercase "ae" ligature (`&AElig;` for uppercase)
`&agrave;`	à	Lowercase "a" with grave accent[b]
`&aring;`	å	Lowercase "a" with ring[b]
`&auml;`	ä	Lowercase "a" with umlaut[b]

`&bull;`	·	Small "bullet" symbol (to indicate multiplication, for example)
`&ccedil;`	ç	Lowercase "c" with cedilla[b]
`&cent;`	¢	Cent symbol
`&cong;`	≅	Mathematical "approximately equal to" symbol
`&copy;`	©	Copyright symbol
`&deg;`	°	Degree (as with temperature)
`&dagger;`	†	Dagger symbol
`&Dagger;`	‡	Double dagger symbol
`&divide;`	÷	Mathematical "divide by" symbol
`&euro;`	€	Euro currency
`&frac12;`	½	Fraction notation for 1/2
`&frac14;`	¼	Fraction notation for 1/4
`&frac34;`	¾	Fraction notation for 3/4
`&ge;`	≥	Mathematical "greater than or equal to" symbol
`&gt;`	>	Mathematical "greater than" symbol (to avoid conflict with angle bracket used in HTML tags)
`&hellip;`	…	Horizontal ellipsis
`&infin;`	∞	Mathematical "infinity" symbol
`&int;`	∫	Mathematical "integral" symbol
`&iques;`	¿	Inverted question mark
`&ldquo;`	"	Left double quote ("smart quote")
`&lsquo;`	'	Left single quote ("smart quote")
`&le;`	≤	Mathematical "less than or equal to" symbol
`&lt;`	<	Mathematical "less than" symbol (to avoid conflict with angle bracket used in HTML tags)
`&micro;`	µ	Micron
`&ne;`	≠	Mathematical "not equal to" symbol
` `		Forced space
`&ntilde;`	ñ	Lowercase n with tilde[b]
`&oelig;`	œ	Lowercase "oe" ligature (`&OElig;` for uppercase)
`&para;`	¶	Paragraph symbol
`&plusmn;`	±	Mathematical "plus-minus" symbol
`&pound;`	£	British pound sterling
`&prop;`	∝	Mathematical "proportional to" symbol
`&quot;`	"	Quote symbol (e.g., for inserting quote marks in quote-delimited text string)
`&radic;`	√	Mathematical "square root" symbol
`&rdquo;`	"	Right double quote ("smart quote")
`&rsquo;`	'	Right single quote ("smart quote")
`&reg;`	®	Product registration symbol
`&sect;`	§	Section symbol
`&szlig;`	ß	"sz" ligature (lowercase only)
`&times;`	×	Mathematical "times " ("multiply by") symbol
`&trade;`	™	Trademark symbol

[a]Other Greek letters can be displayed by spelling the name of the letter. If the name starts with an uppercase character (e.g., Γ), then the uppercase letter is displayed. Otherwise the lowercase character (e.g., γ) is displayed.

[b]Other modified letters follow the same pattern. Start the name with an uppercase or lowercase letter to display a modified uppercase or lowercase character.

Appendix 3:
ASCII Character Codes

The first 127 ASCII character codes are standardized and the remaining characters are system-dependent; the values shown are for Windows-based PCs. These characters can be displayed from a Windows computer keyboard by pressing and holding the Alt key and pressing the corresponding base-10 (Dec) code on the numerical keypad ("locked" with the NumLock key).

Dec	Hex		Dec	Hex		Dec	Hex	
0	0	(a)	27	1B	←	54	36	6
1	1	☺	28	1C	∟	55	37	7
2	2	☻	29	1D	↔	56	38	8
3	3	♥	30	1E	▲	57	39	9
4	4	♦	31	1F	▼	58	3A	:
5	5	♣	32	20	(b)	59	3B	;
6	6	♠	33	21	!	60	3C	<
7	7	•	34	22	"	61	3D	=
8	8	◘	35	23	#	62	3E	>
9	9	○	36	24	$	63	3F	?
10	A	◙	37	25	%	64	40	@
11	B	♂	38	26	&	65	41	A
12	C	♀	39	27	'	66	42	B
13	D	♪	40	28	(	67	43	C
14	E	♫	41	29	)	68	44	D
15	F	☼	42	2A	*	69	45	E
16	10	►	43	2B	+	70	46	F
17	11	◄	44	2C	,	71	47	G
18	12	↕	45	2D	–	72	48	H
19	13	‼	46	2E	.	73	49	I
20	14	¶	47	2F	/	74	4A	J
21	15	§	48	30	0	75	4B	K
22	16	▬	49	31	1	76	4C	L
23	17	↨	50	32	2	77	4D	M
24	18	↑	51	33	3	78	4E	N
25	19	↓	52	34	4	79	4F	O
26	1A	→	53	35	5	80	50	P

Dec	Hex		Dec	Hex		Dec	Hex	
81	51	Q	126	7E	}	171	AB	½
82	52	P	127	7F	△	172	AC	¼
83	53	S	128	80[c]	Ç	173	AD	¡
84	54	T	129	81	ü	174	AE	«
85	55	U	130	82	é	175	AF	»
86	56	V	131	83	â	176	B0	░
87	57	W	132	84	ä	177	B1	▒
88	58	X	133	85	à	178	B2	▓
89	59	Y	134	86	å	179	B3	│
90	5A	Z	135	87	ç	180	B4	┤
91	5B	[	136	88	ê	181	B5	╡
92	5C	\	137	89	ë	182	B6	╢
93	5D	]	138	8A	è	183	B7	╖
94	5E	^	139	8B	ï	184	B8	╕
95	5F	_	140	8C	î	185	B9	╣
96	60	`	141	8D	ì	186	BA	║
97	61	a	142	8E	Ä	187	BB	╗
98	62	b	143	8F	Å	188	BC	╝
99	63	c	144	90	É	189	BD	╜
100	64	d	145	91	æ	190	BE	╛
101	65	e	146	92	Æ	191	BF	┐
102	66	f	147	93	ô	192	CO	└
103	67	g	148	94	ö	193	C1	┴
104	68	h	149	95	ò	194	C2	┬
105	69	i	150	96	û	195	C3	├
106	6A	j	151	97	ù	196	C4	─
107	6B	k	152	98	ÿ	197	C5	┼
108	6C	l	153	99	Ö	198	C6	╞
109	6D	m	154	9A	Ü	199	C7	╟
110	6E	n	155	9B	¢	200	C8	╚
111	6F	o	156	9C	£	201	C9	╔
112	70	p	157	9D	¥	202	CA	╩
113	71	q	158	9E	Pts	203	CB	╦
114	72	r	159	9F	ƒ	204	CC	╠
115	73	s	160	A0	á	205	CD	═
116	74	t	161	A1	í	206	CE	╬
117	75	u	162	A2	ó	207	CF	╧
118	76	v	163	A3	ú	208	D0	╨
119	77	w	164	A4	ñ	209	D1	╤
120	78	x	165	A5	Ñ	210	D2	╥
121	79	y	166	A6	ª	211	D3	╙
122	7A	z	167	A7	º	212	D4	╘
123	7B	{	168	A8	¿	213	D5	╒
124	7C	|	169	A9	⌐	214	D6	╓
125	7D	|	170	AA	¬	215	D7	╫

Dec	Hex		Dec	Hex		Dec	Hex	
216	D8	≠	230	E6	μ	244	F4	⌠
217	D9	⌐	231	E7	τ	245	F5	⌡
218	DA	⌐	232	E8	Φ	246	F6	÷
219	DB	█	233	E9	Θ	247	F7	≈
220	DC	▄	234	EA	Ω	248	F8	°
221	DD	▌	235	EB	δ	249	F9	·
222	DE	▐	236	EC	∞	250	FA	·
223	DF	▀	237	ED	φ	251	FB	√
224	E0	α	238	EE	ε	252	FC	^{n}
225	E1	ß	239	EF	∩	253	FD	^{2}
226	E2	Γ	240	F0	≡	254	FE	■
227	E3	π	241	F1	±	255	FF	(d)
228	E4	Σ	242	F2	≥			
229	E5	σ	243	F3	≤			

[a]ASCII 0 is a null character.

[b]ASCII 32 is a space (as produced by pressing the space bar on your keyboard).

[c]Because the Euro did not exist when the ASCII character sequence was standardized, its symbol, €, does not have a representation in the standard sequence (although it is available as a special character for many fonts in Microsoft Word, for example). On some European computer systems, it may take the place of Ç, the character for ASCII code 128.

[d]ASCII 255 is a blank character.

Appendix 4:
Strategies for Solving Computational Problems

There are two basic skills you must develop while learning to write programs in any language, including JavaScript and PHP. Obviously, you must learn the details of the programming language you are using. But, it is equally important to develop a consistent strategy for solving computational problems that is *independent* of the language you are using.

This strategy requires five steps:

1. Define the problem
2. Outline a solution
3. Design an algorithm
4. Convert the algorithm into program code
5. Verify the operation of the program

Step 1. Define the problem

Real-world computing problems need to be defined carefully. It is often the case that properly defining a problem in terms of the tools that are available is a giant step toward solving that problem. This step involves making sure you understand the problem and can state it clearly in your own words. It is not possible to solve a problem that you can't explain to yourself! And, until you can do this, there is no point in proceeding to Steps 2–5.

Step 2. Outline a solution

This is an informal but very important step. You should focus first on understanding the information needed to solve the problem and then on the nature of the output produced as a result of solving the problem. You need to be sure you understand whatever processing steps or mathematical calculations are required.

It is often difficult to think about solving problems in the straightforward and linear way that is required in order to write a successful computer program:

$$\text{input} \rightarrow \text{calculations or other processing} \rightarrow \text{output}$$

However, you should have these steps clearly in mind before proceeding to Step 3.

Step 3. Design an algorithm

This step is critical to writing successful programs. It may sometimes be combined with Step 2 whenever the conceptual knowledge required to solve a problem is already at hand. In a programming context, an **algorithm** consists of specific steps that must be followed in sequence to attain a clearly defined goal. This may seem obvious, but a common problem for beginning programmers is that the code they write imposes an "algorithm" that does not make sense because it does not proceed in a logical step-by-step fashion. When this happens, conceptual and organizational difficulties are inextricably intertwined with language-specific code problems. The program may "work" without obvious errors, but it will not produce the desired result. It can then become very difficult to isolate and solve problems with a program.

For this step, it is helpful to design algorithms with a generic set of commands that do not depend on the syntax of a particular programming language, as described below.

Step 4. Convert the algorithm into program code

In the early stages of learning a new programming language, this is the most difficult step. But, if you have completed Step 3, then you can focus *just* on programming language details and not on the problem itself.

Step 5. Verify the operation of the program

This step is often overlooked. Beginning programmers are often so overjoyed when a program "works" and produces outputs without any obvious errors that they assume the answers must be right. This is a dangerous assumption! JavaScript and PHP are both relatively forgiving languages in the sense that calculations will appear to "work" even when they are wrong. For example, misnaming a PHP variable does not produce an error message, because variables don't need to be "declared" ahead of time.

Sometimes it is easy to verify the operation of a program by checking calculations by hand or with a calculator. But, for many scientific and engineering calculations, wrong answers will look as reasonable as right answers. Even the most elegantly and cleverly written program has no value if it does not produce correct answers under *all* applicable conditions. It is up to you to define those conditions and test your results.

The algorithm development step, Step 3 in the problem-solving process described above, is critical to writing successful programs. It can best be undertaken using what is called a **pseudocode language**. Pseudocode instructions encompass the range of actions a program can take, but those instructions don't have to follow the syntax rules of a specific language. An algorithm written in pseudocode consists of a series of syntax-free "action commands" which, when translated into the syntax of a specific language, will produce the desired result.

Here is a list of pseudocode commands, given in alphabetical order. If you are reading this section before having actually written any programs, some of the terminology will be unfamiliar. But, the good news is that this relatively short list of commands includes at least conceptually all the actions JavaScript or PHP can take.

ASSIGN

Set a variable equal to a value, another variable, or an expression. See also the *INCREMENT* and *INITIALIZE* commands.

CALL

Invoke a subprogram. (See *SUBPROGRAM*.) This command describes information flow between a subprogram and the point in your pseudocode from which the *CALL* is invoked. It is especially important to differentiate between input to and output from the subprogram. The ability to modularize a program by creating subprograms is an essential element of modern programming languages.

CHOOSE

This command defines actions that can be taken based on selecting one value from a restricted list of possibilities—a selection from a pull-down HTML menu of choices, for example. The choice-dependent action might be some simple calculations or a *CALL* to a *SUBPROGRAM*.

CLOSE

Close an open file.

DEFINE

This pseudocode command provides a mechanism for defining the variables and user-defined data objects such as arrays that your program will need. In scientific and engineering calculations, it is important to identify physical definitions and units when you define variables.

IF... THEN... ELSE...

If something is true, then take a specified action. If it is false, then do something else. The **ELSE...** branch is optional, as there may not be an "else" action when the "if" isn't true. This sequence of actions can be extended:

IF... THEN..., ELSE IF... THEN..., ..., ELSE...

INCREMENT

This is a special kind of assignment command used to indicate operations such as $x = x + 1$. This operation makes no algebraic sense, but has a very specific interpretation in programming languages. It is often used inside loop structures to count the number of times actions inside the loop have been performed.

INITIALIZE

This is a special kind of assignment command used to take into account the fact that variables should be given values before they are **INCREMENT**ed or appear on the right side of an **ASSIGN**ment operator.

LOOP {conditions}... END LOOP

Execute instructions repeatedly until (or as long as) certain conditions are met. In some situations, count-controlled loops are appropriate. In other situations, pre-test or post-test conditional loops are appropriate. With pre-test loops, instructions inside the loop may never be executed, depending on the values of variables prior to the start of the loop. With post-test loops, instructions inside the loop will always be executed at least once, with terminating conditions tested at the end of the loop rather than at the beginning.

OPEN

Open an external file for reading or writing.

READ

Pass information to a program. In an HTML/JavaScript/PHP environment, the source of information is typically values entered in a form field or (with PHP) read from a data file.

SUBPROGRAM

This command marks the start of a separate code module, with the flow of information to and from the module specified through the **CALL** command.

WRITE or DISPLAY

Generate output. The destination of displayed data may be values sent to an `<input>` field in an HTML document, values written to a file, text output generated by JavaScript or PHP, or graphical output generated by PHP.

This set of commands can be modified and extended as convenient for a particular programming environment, in order to take into account language-specific capabilities while deferring concerns about implementation details. For example, when working with HTML/JavaScript, it might be appropriate to extend the **CHOOSE** command to include additional commands such as **CHOOSE CHECKBOX** and **CHOOSE RADIO**, to provide more specific references to these two HTML structures.

Large or complex programming problems may require several iterations through pseudocode. The first step might be just to define input, processing, and output. The next step might include defining local variables, decision points, and repetitive calculations. Finally, the details of each calculation can be given. At this point, translation of pseudocode to actual code should be straightforward if you understand the syntax of the language you are using. If you have problems with language syntax, at least it will be possible to focus just on those details, separate from implementing the algorithm you have designed.

Here is a trivially simple calculation that illustrates how to use pseudocode: Given a radius, calculate the area and circumference of a circle.

DEFINE radius (cm), area (cm^2), circumference (cm)
READ radius
ASSIGN area= π•radius^2, circumference = 2π•radius
DISPLAY area, circumference

Here is a more complicated example, based on Document 8.2.

(HTML user interface)

DEFINE/ASSIGN

longitude and latitude (decimal degrees)
instrument serial number (e.g., WV2-117
date (mm/dd/yyyy)
time (hh:mm:ss UT)
station pressure (mbar)
IR channel 1 voltages (sunlight and dark, V)
IR channel 2 voltages (sunlight and dark, V)

(PHP application)
ASSIGN (using values passed from HTML document)
   longitude, latitude, serial number, date, time,
   IR1 = channel 1 sunlight voltage – minus dark voltage
   IR2 = channel 2 sunlight voltage – minus dark voltage
   (value for pressure not currently used)
OPEN data file containing instrument calibrations
READ past header line
(search for specified instrument serial number)
LOOP (while serial number isn't found)
   READ serial number and calibration data: SN, A, B, C, β, τ
   Look for serial number match. When found, save calibration data.
END LOOP (when serial number match is found)
DISPLAY message if instrument not found?
CLOSE data file
CALL SUBPROGRAM (to calculate relative air mass)
   input: month, day, year, hour, minute, second, latitude,
       longitude
   output: relative air mass (m)

ASSIGN

(using calibration constants and relative air mass)

$$x = Cm\tau - \frac{\left[\ln\left(IR2 / IR1\right) - A\right]}{B}$$

overhead precipitable water = $x^{-\beta}/m$

DISPLAY

summary of instrument calibration constants, IR1 and IR2,
relative air mass (dimensionless)
overhead precipitable water (cm H_2O)

SUBPROGRAM (to calculate relative air mass)
     input: month, day, year, hour, minute, second, latitude, longitude
     CALL SUBPROGRAM (to convert date to Julian Date)
         input: month, day, year, hour, minute, second,
            latitude, longitude
         output: Julian Date
     ASSIGN solar zenith angle z (radians)
       (see astronomical equations, based on location and Julian Date)

ASSIGN cosz = cos(z)

ASSIGN relative air mass = m =

$(1.002432\text{cosz}^2 + 0.148386\text{cosz} + 0.0096467)/(\text{cosz}^3 + 0.149864\text{cosz}^2 + 0.0102963\text{cosz} + 0.000303978)$; (Andrew T. Young, Appl. Opt. 33, 6, 1108-1100, 1994)

output: m

SUBPROGRAM (to convert date to Julian Date)

input: month, day, year, hour, minute, second

output: Julian Date

Whereas the trivial example of calculating the area and circumference of a circle does not really need to be planned in pseudocode, the calculations required in Document 8.2 certainly justify a pseudocode outline. The pseudocode defines the code structure, including needed subprograms, but the details of the calculations of Julian Date and solar position are not yet specified. Once the information flow for the program has been defined in pseudocode, the actual code can be written. In some cases, if you have a good idea about reasonable values for inputs to and outputs from subprograms, it is possible to write subprograms that temporarily return "dummy" values just to check that the rest of the code executes without syntax errors and that the program structure is correct.

The calculations of solar zenith angle based on date, time, and location are lengthy but organizationally straightforward; so the pseudocode does not need to be written at this time. In fact, for Document 8.2, the PHP code to calculate relative air mass was based on code previously written by the author to calculate solar position.

Exercises

1.
Introductory Topics

1.1. Create a new folder on whatever computer you will use with this book. Then create a simple Web page for yourself and store it in that folder. Save your home page file as `index.htm` (or `index.html`). Include the `lastModified` property to show the most recent date on which the page was modified, as in Document 1.4.

1.2. If appropriate, copy your Web page to a location where it will be available through the Internet or an intranet. If you are using this book as a course text, your instructor may provide the information you need to make your work Web-accessible.

2.
HTML Document Basics

2.1. Add some content to your Web page. This could be a short biographical sketch or something less personal. Use some of the HTML elements described in this chapter. Experiment with setting different colors and font sizes. Include at least one image— preferably one you create yourself. Be sure to display the source of the image if it is not your own. Do not use commercial images unless you can demonstrate that you have permission to use them.

2.2. Create a style sheet file for your Web page. Save this as a separate file. Modify your Web page so that it uses this style sheet. Create at least one other Web page that shares this style. The contents of this second page don't matter, but there must be enough content to demonstrate that the style is being implemented. (You may want to combine this with Exercise 2.1.)

2.3. Here's how to create an internal link, essentially a "bookmark" to a specified point in a document:

```
<a href="#section1">Link to Section 1.</a>
...
<a name="section1">Start of Section 1.</a>
```
... {text of Section 1.}

The # sign appearing in the value of the href attribute indicates that this is an internal document link. The `<a name="...">` ... `</a>` tags typically surround a section heading, or perhaps the first few words in a section (see Sect. 2.4).

Create a document with a "table of contents" which is linked to several sections. At the start of each section, include a link back to the table of contents. The sections don't have to be long, as the purpose of this exercise is just to learn how to create internal document links.

2.4. Create an HTML document that contains at least two clickable images that are linked to other HTML documents. In Microsoft Word, for example, you can use the "WordArt" feature to create graphics images that explain the link, as with these examples (see Sect. 2.4).

2.5. Create an HTML document which displays this heading and HTML code:

Here is some HTML code...

```
<html>
<head>
<title>Displaying HTML code in a document</title>
</head>
<body>
Here is an HTML document.
</body>
</html>
```

All the HTML tags, including their left and right angle brackets, should be displayed in red font. Note that this is *not* an HTML code listing. It is the displayed content of an HTML document. Hint: Review Document 2.1 and its explanation.

3.
HTML Tables, Forms, and Lists

3.1. Create a table containing a personnel evaluation form. The first column should contain a statement, such as "Gets along well with others." The second column should contain four radio buttons containing the choices "Never," "Sometimes," "Often," and "Always." The table should have at least four statements. Provide appropriate instructions for filling in the form and submitting it to the creator of the form.

What happens if you submit the contents of a form that does not include the enctype attribute in its <form> tag? What happens if you use method="get" instead of method="post"? Show examples.

3.2. Using Table 2.1 as a guide, create an HTML document and table that displays the 16 standard HTML colors and their hex codes. The color names should be displayed in their color against an appropriate background color.

3.3. Using Table 2.2 as a guide, create a table that displays results of assigning specific and generic font families to text. For example, display an example in serif and Times fonts.

3.4. Modify Document 3.11 so that it e-mails the contents of the form to your address. What happens with the choices you have checked? What about the choices you haven't checked?

3.5. Create a table containing a list of professors. The first column should contain their name, and the second column should allow you to send an email. If you click in the first column, a new window should open that displays information about the professor in that column.

Opening a new window has not been covered in the text. This is done with the window. open() method of the HTML window object; you can find more about the syntax online. Here is some code to get you started.

Creating the table:

```html
<html>
<head>
<title>List of Professors</title>
</head>
<body>
<table border>
<tr><th>Biographical sketch<br />
(click in name box)</th><th>Contact</th></tr>
<tr>
   <td onclick ="window.open('ProfWonderful.htm',
     'ProfWonderful','alwaysRaised=yes,toolbar=no,
     width=600,scrollbars=yes');">
   Professor Wonderful, Super University</td>
   <td><a href="mailto:I.M.Wonderful@superu.edu">
     I.M.Wonderful@superu.edu</a></td>
</tr>
</table>
</body>
</html>
```

The HTML document for Professor Wonderful:

```
<head>
<title>Professor Wonderful</title>
<link href="WindowStyle.css" rel="stylesheet" type="text/
css" />
</head>
<body>
<b><i>Professor I. M. Wonderful, PhD</i></b><br />
  Enter biographical stuff about Professor Wonderful.
</body>
</html>
```

Create a `BiographyStyle.css` file which should be applied to every biography file. You can find much more information online about using the `window.open()` method.

4.
Fundamentals of the JavaScript Language

In these exercises, `prompt()` for input and `alert()` for output can always be replaced by a `form` and `input` fields.

4.1. Prompt the user to enter a temperature in degree Fahrenheit. Calculate and display this temperature converted to degree Celsius and Kelvins (0 K is absolute zero). The conversion from Fahrenheit to Celsius is $T_C = 5(T_F - 32)/9$. The conversion from T_C to Kelvins is $K = T_C + 273.15$.

4.2. Prompt the user to enter two numbers. Print a message that tells which number is smaller or if they are equal. (Do not use the `Math.max()` or `Math.min()` functions.)

4.3. Prompt the user to enter the temperature in degree Fahrenheit and the wind speed V in miles per hour. Calculate and display the windchill temperature according to:

$$T_{WC} = \left(0.279V^{1/2} + 0.550 - 0.0203V\right)\left(T - 91.4\right) + 91.4$$

where T must be less than 91.4°F and $V \geq 4$ mph. Include code to test the input values for T and V and print an appropriate message if they are out of range.

4.4. Prompt the user to enter the month n, date d, and year. Calculate and display the day of the year n, from 1 to 365 or 366, depending on whether the year is a leap year. The formula is

$$n = \text{INT}\left(275m/9\right) - k \cdot \text{INT}\left[(m+9)/12\right] + d - 30$$

where INT() means "the truncated (not rounded) integer value of" and $k = 1$ for a leap year and $k = 2$ otherwise. Note that INT is just mathematical "shorthand" for the desired result, not a JavaScript `Math` method.

To check your code, perform the reverse calculation that converts the day of the year n to its corresponding month and day.

$$
\begin{aligned}
n < 32: & \quad m = 1 \text{ and } d = n \\
\text{otherwise:} & \quad m = \mathrm{INT}[9(k + n)/275 + 0.98] \\
& \quad d = n - \mathrm{INT}(275m/9) + k \cdot \mathrm{INT}[(m + 9)/12] + 30
\end{aligned}
$$

A year is a leap year if it is evenly divisible by 4 and, if it is a centurial year, it is evenly divisible by 400. That is, 2000 was a leap year, but 1900 was not. Provide results for several inputs, including the first and last days of leap and non-leap years, and February 28 or 29 and March 1.

4.5. Rewrite Document 4.7 so that it uses either a pre- or post-test loop. Why did you choose one conditional loop strategy over the other?

4.6. Rewrite Document 4.8 so that it uses a post-test loop.

4.7. Modify Document 4.11 so that if a user enters atmospheric pressure entered in inches of mercury instead of millibars, the code will convert that value into millibars. It is easy to distinguish such an entry because of the large difference in magnitude between the two units. Standard sea level atmospheric pressure is 1013.25 mbar or 29.921 in. of mercury. Therefore, if the user enters a numerical value less than 40, for example, it is safe to assume that it represents inches of mercury. Then,

$$
\frac{P_{\mathrm{mbar}}}{1013.25} = \frac{P_{\mathrm{inches\ of\ mercury}}}{29.921}.
$$

4.8. Using Document 3.1 as a starting point, let a user enter radon values into a table and form. The code should then display an appropriate message in the third column of the table, depending on the radon level.

4.9. Create a table with a form into which a user enters total credit hours and grade points for eight semesters. The code should calculate the GPA for each semester:

$$
\mathrm{GPA} = \frac{\text{grade points}}{\text{credit hours}}
$$

where an A gives four credit points, a B gives three credit points, etc. The last line in the form should be the cumulative GPA:

$$
\mathrm{Cumulative\ GPA} = \frac{\text{cumulative grade points}}{\text{cumulative credit hours}}
$$

4.10. Create a table containing a price list and order form. The first column contains a brief description. The second contains the price for one item. The third column contains a form field in which the user enters the number of items to order. The fourth column contains a form field in which the extended price (price per item times number of items) is calculated. There should be data entry rows for at least three items. Following the items, the table should calculate the total amount for all items ordered, sales tax, shipping, and order total. Provide appropriate instructions for filling in the form and submitting it to the creator of the form.

4.11. The Body Mass Index (BMI) provides a way to characterize normal weights for human adult bodies as a function of height. It is defined as:

$$BMI = \frac{w}{h^2}$$

where w is mass in kilograms (2.2 kg mass per pound weight) and h is height in meters (1 in. = 0.0254 m).

Create a document and form that asks for the user's weight in *pounds* and height in *feet and inches*, and then calculates and displays the BMI.

4.12. A cylindrical liquid storage tank of radius R and length L lies on its side; that is, with its straight sides parallel to the ground. In order to determine how much liquid remains in the tank, a dipstick over the centerline of the tank is used to measure the height of the liquid in the tank. The volume is $L \cdot A$, where A is the area of a partial circle of radius R with a cap cut off horizontally at height H from the bottom of the circle:

$$A = R^2 \cos^{-1}\left[(R-H)/R\right] - (R-H)\left(2RH - H^2\right)^{1/2}$$

where $\cos^{-1}(x)$ is the inverse cosine (arccosine) of x.

Create a document that accepts input values for R, L, and H and then calculates and displays the volume of liquid in the tank.

4.13. Paleontologists have discovered several sets of dinosaur footprints preserved in ancient riverbeds. Is it possible to deduce from these footprints the speed at which dinosaurs walked or ran? The two pieces of information that can be determined directly from the footprints are the length of the dinosaur's foot and the length of its stride, which is defined as the distance between the beginning of a footprint made by one foot and the beginning of the next footprint made by that same foot.

One way to approach this problem is to examine the relationship between size, stride, and speed in modern animals. Because of the dynamic similarities in animal motion, an approximate linear relationship between relative stride and dimensionless speed applies to modern bipedal and quadrupedal animals as diverse and differently shaped as humans, ostriches, camels, and dogs:[1]

$$s = 0.8 + 1.33v$$

---

[1] See R. McNeill Alexander, *Dynamics of Dinosaurs and Other Extinct Giants*. Columbia University Press, New York, 1989.

Relative stride s is defined as the ratio of stride length to leg length, $s = S/L$. Dimensionless speed is defined as the speed divided by the square root of leg length times the gravitational acceleration g, $v = V/(Lg)^{1/2}$. Although it might seem that gravitational acceleration shouldn't influence an animal's speed on level ground, this isn't true, as gravity influences the up and down motions of the body required even for walking.

Leg length from ground to hip joint for dinosaurs of a known species can be determined from fossils. However, even when the dinosaur species responsible for a set of tracks is unknown, its leg length can be estimated by multiplying the footprint length by 4. (Try this for humans.)

Create a document that uses the equation described here to calculate the speed of a dinosaur based on measurements of its footprint and stride length. Use metric units. Test your calculations for a footprint 0.6 m long and a stride length of 3.3 m.

Extra credit note: Is it possible to determine whether the dinosaur was walking or running? Using data for human strides—walking or running—you should be able to speculate about the answer to this question.

4.14. The wavelengths of the Balmer series of lines in the hydrogen spectrum are given by

$$\lambda = \frac{364.6n^2}{\left(n^2 - 4\right)} \text{ nm}$$

Write a script that generates and displays the first ten wavelengths in the Balmer series. Use document.write() to display the results.

4.15. The original population of a certain animal is 1,000,000. Assume that at the beginning of each year (including the first year), the population is increased by 3%. By the end of that year, 6% of the total population (including the births at the beginning of the year) dies. Write a script that calculates and displays the population at the end of each year until the population at the end of the year falls to 75% or less of its original value. Although, in principle, you can figure out how many years this will take, don't do that. Use a conditional loop.

4.16. Section 4.6 briefly discussed some problems with using the Math.random() function to create a series of randomly distributed integers. Write a script that will examine the distribution of 10,000 integers in the range [0,2], using these two expressions:

```
Math.round(Math.random()*2)
```

and

```
Math.floor(3*(Math.random()%1))
```

Show results from several trials. Explain your results.

4.17. Cardiac output is defined as the volume of blood pumped by the heart per minute:

$$\text{Cardiac output} = \text{stroke volume}\,(\text{milliliters}) \times \text{heart rate}\,(\text{beats per minute})$$

A typical resting rate is 60 ml and 70 bpm. During exercise, the stroke volume can double and the heart rate might rise to 200 bpm. During deep sleep, these values might fall to 45 ml and 45 bpm.

Write a JavaScript application that calculates and displays cardiac output for user-supplied values of stroke volume and heart rate.

4.18. Blood pressure is a fundamental indicator of overall general health. It is measured in units of millimeters of mercury and reported as the systolic pressure—the pressure created when your heart is pumping—over the diastolic pressure—the pressure when your heart is at rest between beats. The mean arterial pressure is defined as one third the systolic blood pressure plus two third the diastolic blood pressure.

A good blood pressure reading for adults is 120/80. A consistently measured resting value of 140/90 is considered high, and a condition that should be treated.

Write a JavaScript application that accepts as input the systolic and diastolic blood pressure and:

(a) Displays the mean arterial pressure
(b) Displays a message based on the systolic and diastolic values.

For example, if the blood pressure readings are 140/90, then the message should urge the user to seek treatment. (There may be other appropriate messages for intermediate values. Consult a health care professional!)

5.
Using Arrays in HTML/JavaScript

Each exercise in this chapter should use arrays as appropriate.

5.1. Rewrite the code from Exercise 16 in Chap. 4 so that it looks at the distribution of integers in the range [1,6]. Which of the expressions given in that exercise should be used to simulate the performance of a fair six-sided die? What would be the result of using the wrong expression?

5.2. Rewrite Document 5.12 so that it uses a conditional loop that stops searching when it finds a password match.

5.3. Rewrite Exercise 4.9 to use the `elements` array that is automatically created for the fields in a form.

5.4. The point is made in Sect. 5.1 that assigning one array name to another:

```
var A = ["thing1","thing2","thing3"];
var B = A;
```

doesn't actually create a separate copy of the array A. Instead, both A and B "point" to the same data in memory.

Write code that accepts the names of source and destination arrays and copies the contents of the source array into the destination array, thereby creating an actual copy of the original array. The result should allow you to manipulate the two arrays independently, without changes to one array affecting the contents of the other array. Your code should display the contents of both arrays, before and after the destination array has been created and changes have been made to the contents of the source array.

5.5. Write a script that finds the maximum, minimum, mean, standard deviation, and median of an array.

$$\text{Mean} = \frac{\Sigma x_i}{n}$$

$$\text{Standard deviation}^2 = \frac{\left[\Sigma x_i^2 - (\Sigma x_i)^2 / n\right]}{(n-1)}$$

where the x_i's are the elements of the array, n is the number of elements, and "Σ" means "sum from 1 through n." (Remember that in a JavaScript array, the elements are indexed by value from 0 through $n - 1$, not 1 through n.)

The array must be sorted in ascending or descending order to find the median. For an array with an odd number of elements, the median is the middle value. For an array with an even number of elements, the median is the average of the two middle elements.

5.6. Write a function that will reverse the elements in an array, having the effect of turning a "stack" upside down, for example. Do not do this by creating a "backwards" copy of the original array; make the changes to the original array.

Hint: Start from one end of the array and work toward the middle. Create a temporary variable to hold an element at one end of the array, replace it with its corresponding value from the other end of the array, and then replace the value at the other end of the array with the temporary value.

5.7. Write a function that will create and display a "count histogram" for an array. To do this, specify the minimum and maximum values that will be included in the histogram and the number of "bins" into which that range of values will be divided. For example, you could divide an array of values into quartiles and count the number in the lowest 25%, next 25%, etc. The count histogram should be stored in its own array. Use this array as an example, but be sure to write your code so that it will apply to *any* array.

```
var A=[53,100,66,79,80,81,83,75,91,65,61];
```

You can assume that the values in the array lie within the minimum and maximum values to be included in the histogram. Suppose the array contains test grades. A reasonable choice would be to divide these values into five ranges: 50–59, 60–69, 70–79, 80–89, and 90–100. The contents of the count histogram array should be 1, 3, 2, 3, 2, and the count histogram could be interpreted as showing the distribution of F's, D's, C's, B's, and A's. (Be careful about how you calculate the index for a grade of 100!)

Demonstrate the operation of your script for several choices of ranges and numbers of histogram "boxes."

5.8 Automata can be thought of as artificial life forms that, with the aid of a set of rules for reproducing themselves, appear to be self-organizing. These rules can lead to surprising patterns, related to fractal theory. One well-known pattern is the Sierpinski triangle, shown here.

```
Generation:  0-----------------------*------------------
Generation:  1----------------------*-*-----------------
Generation:  2---------------------*---*----------------
Generation:  3--------------------*-*-*-*---------------
Generation:  4-------------------*-------*--------------
Generation:  5------------------*-*-----*-*-------------
Generation:  6-----------------*---*---*---*------------
Generation:  7----------------*-*-*-*-*-*-*-*-----------
Generation:  8---------------*---------------*----------
Generation:  9--------------*-*-------------*-*---------
Generation: 10-------------*---*-----------*---*--------
Generation: 11------------*-*-*-*---------*-*-*-*-------
Generation: 12-----------*-------*-------*-------*------
Generation: 13----------*-*-----*-*-----*-*-----*-*-----
Generation: 14---------*---*---*---*---*---*---*---*----
Generation: 15--------*-*-*-*-*-*-*-*-*-*-*-*-*-*-*-*---
Generation: 16-------*-------------------------------*--
Generation: 17------*-*-----------------------------*-*-
Generation: 18-----*---*---------------------------*---*-
Generation: 19----*-*-*-*-------------------------*-*-*-*-
Generation: 20---------*-------------------------*-----*-
```

This output is generated by repeatedly printing an array with `document.write()`. In order for the elements to line up, you can specify a monospaced font style inside a `document.write()` before starting to print the output:

```
document.write("<font style='font-family:Courier'>");
```

The pattern starts out with a single "life form" (an asterisk) in the middle of the array. This array has 40 elements. The propagation rules are:

For cell i, if cell $i - 1$ is occupied and cells i and $i + 1$ are not, or if cell $i - 1$ is empty and cell $i + 1$ is occupied, then an organism will appear in cell i in the next generation. Otherwise, the cell will be empty.

Write JavaScript code that reproduces the output shown. HINT: you can't apply the rules to the array itself to determine the distribution of organisms in the next generation. You need to copy the organism distribution array at the start of each generation and test the propagation rules as applied to that copy, in order to update the organism distribution array.

6.
JavaScript Functions

These exercises should always include appropriately designed functions. Note that some
of the exercises for Chap. 4 can be rewritten using functions.

6.1. Recall Document 6.5, which demonstrated how the operation of the `parseInt()`
method without the second optional parameter can cause problems when interpreting an
integer represented as a string that begins with a 0. Write a function that accepts as input
an "integer" value that begins with a 0. The function should create a substring of the original value that doesn't have this leading 0 and should then apply `parseInt()` to this
substring. (See the list of string-related methods given in Table 4.2.)

6.2. Create a document that asks a user to enter a month, day, and year. Then, check the day
to make sure it is an appropriate day for that month. Don't forget about leap years, as
previously defined in Exercise 4.4. Use an "alert" box to display a message if the user
enters an inappropriate day.

6.3 A basic problem in numerical analysis is the solution of systems of linear equations.
Consider a system of equations with three unknowns:

$$a_1x + b_1y + c_1z = d_1$$
$$a_2x + b_2y + c_2z = d_2$$
$$a_3x + b_3y + c_3z = d_3$$

Cramer's Rule can be used to solve equations in two or three unknowns, but becomes
unwieldy for larger systems. For the above system:

$$x = \frac{D_1}{D} \quad y = \frac{D_2}{D} \quad z = \frac{D_3}{D}$$

where D is the determinant for the system:

$$D = a_1b_2c_3 + b_1c_2a_3 + c_1b_3a_2 - a_3b_2c_1 - b_3c_2a_1 - c_3b_1a_2$$

D_1, D_2, and D_3 are found by substituting the constants d_1, d_2, and d_3 for the coefficients in
column 1, 2, and 3, respectively:

$$D_1 = d_1b_2c_3 + b_1c_2d_3 + c_1b_3d_2 - d_3b_2c_1 - b_3c_2d_1 - c_3b_1d_2$$
$$D_2 = a_1d_2c_3 + d_1c_2a_3 + c_1d_3a_2 - a_3d_2c_1 - d_3c_2a_1 - c_3d_1a_2$$
$$D_3 = a_1b_2d_3 + b_1d_2a_3 + d_1b_3a_2 - a_3b_2d_1 - b_3d_2a_1 - d_3b_1a_2$$

It is possible for the value of D to be 0. Then the system of equations has no solution.
Your code should test for this possibility and provide an appropriate message. Include your
solution for this system of equations:

$$3x + 4y + 2z = -1$$
$$5x + 7y + z = 2$$
$$5x + 9y + 3z = 3$$

6.4. Write a modified version of Document 6.9 that demonstrates the relationship between Fibonacci numbers and the Golden Ratio. (Look at the ratio F_n/F_{n-1} as n becomes large. It is easy to find a lot of information about this unexpected (?) relationship online.)

6.5. The `Math.floor()` method, which returns the next-lowest integer below the real number given as its calling argument, truncates non-negative numbers in the way you would expect. For example, `Math.floor(17.9)` equals 17. However, it does not truncate negative numbers. For example, `Math.floor(-17.9)` equals −18, not −17. It might be useful to have a function that simply strips away digits to the right of the decimal point—that is, which actually truncates a number—regardless of its sign.

Fortunately, it is easy to create your own library of methods and properties that act as extensions to the `Math` object. Here's how to set it up:

```
function Math.myMethod(x) {
    {Put code here.}
}
```

Simply give your new method a name and write the appropriate code, with a `return` statement for the desired value. You can also create new properties just be defining them. For example, if you write the statement

```
Math.myPI=5.;
```

You now can use this new property (not that it would be a good idea!) just as you would `Math.PI`.

Write a script that creates and tests a truncation method—call it `Math.trunc()`—that works regardless of whether the calling argument is positive or negative. Also, create at least one other new `Math` method, including a method, `Math.sind()`, that returns the sin of its argument expressed in degrees rather than radians. That is, `Math.sind(30.)` should give a value of 0.5.

Of course, these methods and properties exist only within the script in which they are defined, rather than in a predefined library of `Math` methods and properties available to any browser that supports JavaScript. However, they are treated as "real" extensions of the `Math` object in the sense that you can use them just like other `Math` methods or properties, including referring to just the method or property names inside a `with (Math) { ... }` statement block. Once you create a library of `Math` extensions, you can simply paste them into any script—either literally or by saving them in a `.js` file and referencing that file in a script.

6.6. As noted briefly in Sect. 6.4, the `eval() Global` method is very powerful. Shown below is an HTML document template for an application which will numerically integrate a specified function. The default function is the normal probability density function, which does not have an analytic integral. You can replace this function with any function expressed in proper JavaScript syntax. The function uses Trapezoidal Rule numerical integration. (Refer to the example in Document 4.13 for an example that uses Rectangular Rule integration for a "hard-coded" function.) A "pseudocode" outline of the algorithm is given here:

Specify a function $f(x)$, lower and upper integration boundaries (a and b), and the number of equal intervals (n) into which the range ($b - a$) will be divided. The code outline for the numerical integration is:

Set sum $= 0$, $dx = (b - a)/n$

for $i = 1$ to n,
  $x_1 = a + (i - 1) \cdot dx$, $x_2 = a + i \cdot dx$
  sum $=$ sum $+ f(x_1) + f(x_2)$

return sum $\cdot (dx/2)$

Create an HTML document that uses a JavaScript function and the `eval()` method to implement this algorithm. Consult a probability and statistics text or online source to verify the values produced for the normal probability distribution function. Also, test the application by entering a function that has an analytic integral.

Numerical Integrator

NOTES:
(1) Enter function using JavaScript syntax.
(2) Math methods and properties don't require "Math." in front of their names.
(3) The default function given here is the normal probability density function.
(4) This application uses Trapezoidal Rule numerical integration.

function: `exp(-x*x/2)/sqrt(2*PI)`

lower boundary: `0`   upper boundary: `0.5`

number of intervals: `100`

`Click here to integrate...`

6.7. Assume that the probability of a randomly selected individual in a target population having a disease is PD. Suppose there is a test for this disease, but the test is not perfect. There are two possible outcomes from the test:

1. Test is positive (disease is present).
2. Test is negative (no disease is present).

Because the test is imperfect, if the individual has the disease, result 1 is returned for only PWD (test positive, with disease) percent of the tests. That is, only PWD percent of all individuals who actually have the disease will test positive for the disease. If the individual does not have the disease, result 2 is returned only NND (test negative, no disease) percent of the time. That is, only NND percent of all individuals who do not have the disease will test negative for the disease.

Bayesian inference can be used to answer two important questions:

1. Given a positive test result, what is the chance that I have the disease?
2. Given a negative test result, what is the chance that I have the disease anyhow?

Define the following variables (assuming PWD and NND are expressed as values between 0 and 1 rather than as percentages):

PND = positive test result, but with no disease = $(1 - \text{NND})$
NWD = negative test result, but with disease = $(1 - \text{PWD})$

$$P\_has\_disease = \text{person has disease, given a positive test result}$$
$$= (\text{\# of true positives})/(\text{\# true positives} + \text{\# false positives})$$
$$= (\text{PWD·PD})/[\text{PWD·PD} + \text{PND·}(1 - \text{PD})]$$

Probability that a person does not have the disease, given a positive test result = $1 - \text{P\_has\_disease}$

$$N\_has\_disease = \text{person has disease, given a negative test result}$$
$$= (\text{\# false negatives})/(\text{\# false negatives} + \text{\# true negatives})$$
$$= (\text{NWD·PD})/[\text{NWD·PD} + \text{NND·}(1 - \text{PD})]$$

The probability that a person has the disease even though the test result is negative is called a Type II error. The probability that a person does not have the disease even though the test result is positive is called a Type I error. From a treatment point of view, Type II errors are perhaps more serious because treatment will not be offered. However, it is also possible that treating for a disease that does not actually exist, as a result of a Type I error, may also have serious consequences.

As an example, consider a rare disease for which PD = 0.001, PWD = 0.99, and NND = 0.95. Then the probability that a person has the disease, given a positive test result, is:

$$P\_has\_disease = \frac{0.99 \cdot 0.001}{0.99 \cdot 0.001 + 0.05 \cdot 0.999} = 0.019$$

and for a negative test result:

$$N\_has\_disease = \frac{0.01 \cdot 0.001}{0.01 \cdot 0.001 + 0.95 \cdot 0.999} = 0.0000105$$

The somewhat surprising result that the probability of having this disease is very small despite a positive result from a test that *appears* to be highly accurate is explained qualitatively by the fact that there are many more people without the disease (999 out of 1,000) than there are with the disease. In such a population, approximately 50 people will test positive for the disease even though they don't have it. Approximately one person will test positive for the disease when they have it, so (actual positives)/(all positive test results) ~1/51 ~ 0.02.

The very small probability of having the disease even with a negative test result is explained by the fact that 999 out of 1,000 people don't have the disease and almost all of these people get negative test results.

Write a document that displays results from the indicated calculations. What happens when the tested disease is found in 50% of the population? What happens for both disease situations when the positive and/or negative tests are much less reliable, say 50%?

6.8. Using Document 6.16 as a starting point, write an application that contains contact information for your friends and colleagues. When you select a person's name from the pull-down menu, the remaining fields in a form should be populated automatically with the contact information for that person. Store the contact information in a separate "hidden" file, to be pasted into your document when it is loaded, as shown in Sect. 5.6. Here is a sample of what this contact information file might look like:

```
var contactList = new Array();
function contactArray(name,phone,email) {
  this.name=name;
  this.phone=phone;
  this.email=email;
}
contactList[0]=new contactArray("Mom",
  "222-555-5478","mom@supermail.net");
contactList[1]=new contactArray("My Boss",
  "888-555-0985","MrBig@xyyz.com");
contactList[2]=new contactArray("Sally",
  "111-555-2311","SallyJo@ail.com");
```

Considering previous discussions about sorting arrays in JavaScript, how should you handle the matter of keeping this list sorted in alphabetical order by name? Do you have to sort the contact list array "offline" or is it reasonable to do it in "real time" every time the pull-down menu is created?

6.9. Newton's algorithm for finding the square root of a number—see Document 4.10—can also be implemented (actually, more easily) as a recursive function. Rewrite Document 4.10 so that the iterative calculation is done in a function and then add another function which does the same calculation recursively. Then, add two functions which use a similar approach to finding the cube root of a positive real number:

1. Select an initial guess $g = n/2$.
2. Replace g with $(2g + x/g^2)/3$.
3. Repeat step 2 until the absolute difference between x and $g \cdot g \cdot g$ is sufficiently small.

Of course, you are not allowed to use the Math.pow() method for any part of this calculation, but you could use it to check the results of your work. Implement this algorithm first as an iterative calculation and then, in a separate function, as a recursive calculation.

6.10. Document 5.5 showed how to create two-dimensional arrays which can be accessed with row and column indices, rather than assigning "field names" to one of the dimensions. The code in that example showed how to populate such an array and then display it row-by-row. Add functions to this code which test the sums of each row, column, and main diagonals to verify that the specified assignment of integers 1–9 forms a "magic square." Then expand the code to create a 4 × 4 matrix. Arrange the integers 1–16 in this matrix so that they form a magic square. Use the same functions to check your results. (This means that the size of the matrix must not be "hard coded" into the functions.)

6.11. A recursive algorithm for generating Fibonacci numbers is given in Sect. 6.5. Here is a variation that defines the totally obscure and completely useless "Brooks function" for positive values of n:

$$B_n = 1, n = 1 \ or \ 2$$
$$B_n = 3, n = 3$$
$$B_n = \left(0.5B_{n-1} + 0.75B_{n-2}\right)/ B_{n-3}$$

Give results for at least n = 1, 2, 3, 4, 5, and 20. You *must* use a recursive function to calculate values of the Brooks function.

NOTE: Running this script for large values of n (~100?) may cause your browser to lock up.

EXTRA CREDIT: Invent a new recursively defined function that is actually good for something.

6.12. Consider this HTML interface which defines the calculations for permutations and combinations of n distinct objects taken m at a time, with and without allowing repetitions. For permutations, the same objects in a different order constitute a distinct permutation. That is, for the example shown, CA is different from AC. For combinations, the same objects in a different order do not constitute a distinct combination. That is, CA is equivalent to AC. Hence, there are six permutations of CAT, but only three combinations.

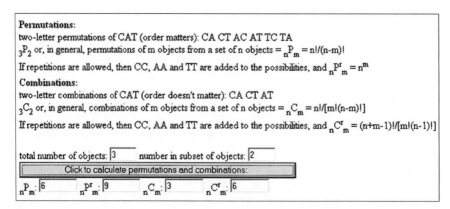

Write a complete HTML/JavaScript application that calculates these permutations and combinations. (You do not have to include all the explanatory text in your HTML document.)

PHP Exercises

These exercises are not keyed to specific chapters, but they are nonetheless presented roughly in order relative to the material presented starting in Chap. 7.

PHP 1. Rewrite Document 8.4 (`windspd.php`) so that it uses the `$array   =  file($filename)` function to copy all the wind speed data into an array. Each line in the file will become an array element, and the `explode()` function can then be used to access the data. This approach can be used to eliminate the long format specifier string required in Document 8.4. To use the `explode()` function, the only requirement is that you know exactly how the values in the file are separated. In the sample file shown in the problem statement for Document 8.4, there is a header line with values separated by a space. Each wind speed value is followed by a comma and a space. Does it matter if the delimiter given in the `explode()` function is `", "` or `",   "`? The documentation for the `explode()` function says that it "returns an array of strings consisting of substrings of the string" specified as a parameter. Does it matter that the contents of the arrays returned by `explode()` should be treated as numbers and not strings?

PHP 2. Create a file of names and densities of various materials. Write an HTML/PHP application that will read this file and display all materials and densities for which the density is greater than or less than some value specified in the HTML document. (Use a radio button to select greater or less than.)

PHP 3. Create a file of unit conversions that lists a "from" unit, a "to" unit, and the number by which the "from" unit must be multiplied to get the value of the "to" unit. For example, to convert from feet to yards, multiply by 0.33333. Write an HTML/PHP application that will allow the user to specify a name and value for a "from" unit and the name of a "to" unit, and will display the equivalent value for the "to" unit.

One problem with such an application is that your HTML document will not "know" which units are included in the data file, and that file can be accessed only through the PHP application. You do not want to "hard code" all possible unit names into your HTML document. There is no simple solution to this problem. The PHP application could search the file entries based on only the first few letters of the unit names passed from the HTML document, which would prevent problems with a user specifying "meters" in the HTML document when the data file contained only "meter."

PHP 4. Write a PHP application that uses one or more functions to find the minimum, maximum, mean, median, and standard deviation of numerical values stored in a file. Note that to find the median, the values need to be sorted. For an odd number of sorted values, the median is the middle value. For an even number of values, the median is the average of the two middle numbers. (See Exercise 5.5).

The mean of a list of n numbers is:

$$m = \sum_{x=1}^{n} x_i$$

and the standard deviation is:

$$s = \sqrt{\frac{\sum_{i=1}^{n} x_i^2 - \left(\sum_{i=1}^{n} x_i\right)^2 / n}{n-1}}$$

PHP 5. Simulation studies in science and engineering often require random numbers drawn from a normal ("bell-shaped") distribution rather than from a uniform distribution. By definition, a set of normally distributed numbers should have a mean of 0 and a standard deviation of 1. PHP has a random number function that generates uniformly distributed values in the range [0,1). That is, the generator could produce a value of 0, but it should never produce a value of 1.

There is a simple way to generate a pair of normally distributed numbers x_1 and x_2 (or at least numbers that *look* like they are normally distributed in some statistical sense) from a pair of uniformly distributed numbers u_1 and u_2 in the range (0,1]:

$$x_1 = \left[-2\ln(u_1)\right]^{1/2} \cdot \cos(2\pi u_2)$$
$$x_2 = \left[-2\ln(u_1)\right]^{1/2} \cdot \sin(2\pi u_2)$$

where ln() is the natural (base e) logarithm.

Write a PHP application to create a file containing 100 normally distributed values. When you do this in a for... loop, remember that each "trip" through the loop calculates two values, x_1 and x_2, not just one. If you like, you can write a simple HTML interface to specify the number of normally distributed values to be generated.

Because ln(0) is undefined, your code will have to check every value of u_1 to make sure it is not 0. If it is, replace u_1 with some arbitrary small value. This should happen only rarely, if ever, so it will not bias the statistics of even a fairly small sample. Note that PHP's random number generator is not supposed to produce a value of exactly 1, for which ln(1) = 0, but if it does, it will cause no problems with these calculations.

Calculate the mean and standard deviation of the numbers you have generated. You can do this by summing the values of x_i and x_i^2 as you generate them. Then use the formulas given in the previous exercise. The mean and standard deviation of these 100 normally distributed values should be close to 0 and 1, but not exactly equal to these values for this finite set. There are other ways to check whether a set of numbers is really normally distributed, but that is beyond the scope of this problem. It is even possible that the numbers generated with this algorithm would pass such tests even though they are not really randomly normal.

PHP 6. Snell's law of refraction relates the angle of incidence θ_i of a beam of light to the angle of refraction θ_r of the beam as it enters a different medium:

$$n_i \sin(\theta_i) = n_r \sin(\theta_r)$$

The table gives the refractive index for four materials. Assuming that the incident material is always air, create a table that shows incident angles from 10° to 90° in steps of 10°. The angle of refraction corresponding to an incident angle of 90° is the angle beyond which light incident from within the refracting material is reflected back into that medium, rather than exiting into air.

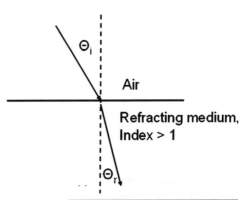

Material	Index of refraction
Air	1.00
Water	1.33
Glass	1.50
Diamond	2.42

PHP 7. A circuit containing an inductance of L henrys and a capacitance of C farads has a resonant frequency f given by:

$$f = \frac{1}{2\pi\sqrt{LC}}\,\text{Hz}$$

Write an HTML/PHP application that allows the user to input a range of inductances and capacitances along with a "step size" for each component, and generates a table containing the resonant frequency for each LC pair of values.

For example, the output could generate a table for inductances in the range from 20 to 100 µH in steps of 20 µH and capacitances from 100 to 1000 µF in steps of 100 µF. It does not make any difference which of these components are the rows in the table and which are the columns.

PHP 8. In a materials testing experiment, samples are given random doses of radiation R every hour. The maximum total radiation exposure R_{max} is specified and the experiment is stopped if the next radiation dose will cause R_{max} to be exceeded. The units for the radiation do not matter for this problem.

Write an HTML document that will provide, as input to a PHP application, the maximum total dose and the maximum individual dose. The PHP application should then generate a table summarizing the random doses delivered to the sample. It could look something like this:

| Maximum cumulative radiation = 1,000 | | |
| Maximum individual dose = 200 | | |
Dose	Amount	Cumulative
1	144	144
2	200	344
3	73	417
4	59	476
5	168	644
6	119	763
7	99	862
8	177	Not delivered

PHP 9. Modify Document 9.12 (`histo.php`) so that the code will accommodate any arbitrary range of input values, with those values distributed in the specified number of equal-size bins. For example, the occurrences of numbers from −30 to +30 could be counted in 12 bins of size 5. It should be up to the user to define the number of bins in a way that makes sense relative to the range of values to be represented by the histogram. The code should save the histogram data in a file.

PHP 10. Create a data file containing an unspecified number of values between 0 and 100. Define an array with letter grades as keys:

```
$a = array("A" => 90, "B" => 80, …);
```

This array defines cutoff points for each letter grade.

Define another array with the same character keys. The elements of this array should be initialized to 0. Then, when you read through your data file, increment the appropriate grade "box" by 1. (This could be done with multiple if… statements, for example.) When you are finished, display the keys and contents of the second array in a table that shows the number of A's, B's, etc.; for example:

```
A   3
B   7
C   5
D   2
F   1
```

This is just another version of the histogram problem, but the boxes are named by the keys of $a, and the limits for letter grades can easily be changed.

PHP 11. Write a PHP application that will read a text file and count the number of occurrences of each letter in the file. (Use the `fgetc()` function to read one character at a time from the file.) Upper- and lowercase letters should be counted as the same character. Store the results in an array with 26 upper- or lowercase character keys and display the contents of the array when all characters have been read from the file. If you like, you can make this an application that runs from a command line, so you can specify the name of the input text file when you execute the application.

PHP 12. Write an HTML/PHP application that will calculate and display a monthly loan repayment schedule. The user specifies the loan amount, the annual interest rate, and the duration of the loan in years. Payments are made monthly.

For n loan payments, where n is the number of years times 12, the monthly payment P for a loan amount A at annual interest rate r (expressed as a decimal fraction, not a percent) is

$$P = \frac{(A \cdot r / 12)}{\left[1 - 1 / (1 + r / 12)^n \right]}$$

At the end of the loan repayment schedule, display the total amount received in loan payments.

Suppose you were thinking about lending this money yourself. The alternative is to deposit the money in an interest-bearing account. What APY (annual percent yield) would that account have to pay in order for you to have the same amount of money at the end of y years as you would have received from the loan repayments?

If you don't reinvest the loan payments as you receive them, calculate the APY from:

$$A_{final} = A_{start} \cdot (1 + r_{APY})^y$$

If you immediately reinvest each loan payment in an account paying an annual rate R (presumably lower than rate r), then at the end of y years (n months), that account will hold

$$A_{final} = \frac{A_{start} \cdot \left[(1 + R / 12)^n - 1 \right]}{(R / 12)}$$

Here is an example. The monthly payments for a 2-year, 8% loan of $200,000 are $9,045.46. The total amount paid is $24 \times \$9,045.46 = \$217,091$. The APY for an account with an initial deposit of $200,000 that would yield this amount is $(A_{final}/A_{start})^{(1/y)} - 1 = 4.19\%$. Suppose you reinvest the monthly payments as you receive them at 4%, compounded monthly. When the loan is repaid, you will have a total of $225,620, which is equivalent to an APY of 6.21% on a 2-year investment of the $200,000.

		Payment	Balance	Reinvestment
			200,000.00	Rate = 4%
Payment #	1	9,045.46	192,287.88	9,045.46
	2	9,045.46	184524.34	18,121.07
	3	9,045.46	176,709.04	27,226.93
	4	9,045.46	168,841.64	36,363.14
	5	9,045.46	160921.79	45,529.81
	6	9,045.46	152,949.15	54,727.04
	7	9,045.46	144,923.35	63,954.92
	8	9,045.46	136844.05	73,213.56
	9	9,045.46	128,710.88	82,503.06
	10	9,045.46	120,523.50	91,823.53
	11	9,045.46	112,281.53	101,175.07
	12	9,045.46	103,984.61	110,557.78
	13	9,045.46	95,632.39	119,971.76
	14	9,045.46	87,224.48	129,417.13
	15	9,045.46	78,760.52	138,893.98
	16	9,045.46	70,240.13	148,402.41
	17	9,045.46	61,662.94	157,942.55
	18	9,045.46	53,028.57	167,514.48
	19	9,045.46	44,336.63	177,118.32
	20	9,045.46	35,586.75	186,754.17
	21	9,045.46	26,778.54	196,422.14
	22	9,045.46	17,911.60	206,122.34
	23	9,045.46	8,985.55	215,854.88
	24	9,045.46	0.00	225,619.85
Total Income		217,091.00		225,619.85
Return		4.19%		6.21%

PHP 13. Modify Document 9.13 (`cardShuffle.php`) so that the code will display four shuffled "hands" of 13 cards each, identified by value and suit:

Three of Clubs
King of Clubs
...
Ten of Spades
Deuce of Spades

PHP 14. Define a "heat wave" as a condition for which the maximum temperature exceeds 90°F on any 3 consecutive days. Write a PHP application that will read and display a file of daily maximum high temperatures, including in your output an appropriate message when a heat wave is in progress.

Note that you can define a heat wave only retroactively, because the heat wave is known to be occurring only on the third day. This means that you must store data from at least the 2 previous days before you can display an appropriate message for the heat wave days.

Here is a sample data file with appropriate output:

```
07/01/2006 89
07/02/2006 90 heat wave day 1
07/03/2006 93 heat wave day 2
07/04/2006 92 heat wave day 3
07/05/2006 94 heat wave day 4
07/06/2006 89
07/08/2006 91 heat wave day 1
07/09/2006 90 heat wave day 2
07/10/2006 92 heat wave day 3
07/11/2006 89
07/12/2006 87
```

PHP 15. The value of equipment used in manufacturing and other businesses declines as the equipment ages. Businesses must recover the cost of "durable" equipment by depreciating its value over an assumed useful lifetime of n years. At the end of n years, the equipment may have either no value or some small salvage value. Depreciation can be computed three ways:

1. *Straight-line depreciation.* The value of an asset minus its salvage value depreciates by the same amount each year over its useful life of n years.
2. *Double-declining depreciation.* Each year, the original value of an asset minus the previously declared depreciation is diminished by $2/n$. (This method does not depend on an assumed salvage value.)
3. *Sum-of-digits depreciation.* Add the integers from 1 through n. For year i, the depreciation allowed is the original value of the asset minus its salvage value, times $(n - i) + 1$, divided by the sum of the digits.

Write an HTML document that allows the user to enter the original value of an asset, the number of years over which the depreciation will be taken, and its salvage value at the end of the depreciation period. Then write a PHP application that will use these values to print out a depreciation table showing the results for each depreciation method. Here is a sample table.

The code that generated this table used echo statements and the round() function to generate the output, because that was a little easier to do while the code was being developed. You can gain more control over the output by, for example, having 100 print as 100.00, using printf() with appropriate format specifiers.

Original value	$1000					
Salvage value	$100					
Lifetime (years)	7					
Year	Straight line	Asset value	Double declining	Asset value	Sum of digits	Asset value
1	128.57	871.43	285.71	714.29	225	775
2	128.57	742.86	204.08	510.2	192.86	582.14
3	128.57	614.29	145.77	364.43	160.71	421.43
4	128.57	485.71	104.12	260.31	128.57	292.86
5	128.57	357.14	74.37	185.93	96.43	196.43
6	128.57	228.57	53.12	132.81	64.29	132.14
7	128.57	100	37.95	94.86	32.14	100

Businesses often like to "front load" the depreciation of an asset in order to realize the maximum tax deduction in the year that the funds were actually spent for the equipment. For this reason, they would likely not choose the straight line method even though it is the simplest of the three.

PHP 16. When analyzing a time sequence of measurements made on a noisy system, it is often useful to smooth the data so that trends are easier to spot. One simple smoothing technique is a so-called unweighted moving average. Suppose a data set consists of n values. These data can be smoothed by taking a moving average of m points, where m is some number significantly less than n. The average is unweighted because old values count just as much as newer values. The formula for calculating the smoothed average value S_i corresponding to the ith value in the data set, is

$$S_i = \frac{\left(\sum_{j=i-m+1}^{i} x_j \right)}{m}, \quad i \geq m$$

Given a set of n points, an algorithm for calculating a moving average of m values is:

1. Calculate the sum s of the first m points. The first average (S_m) equals s/m.
2. For each value of $i = m + 1$ to n, add the ith value to s and subtract the $(i - m)^{th}$ value. Then calculate the average for this new sum.
3. Repeat step 2 until $i = n$.

Write a PHP application that reads a file of numerical values and creates a new file containing the original values and the moving average smoothed values. You may wish to create an HTML interface that specifies the file name and the number of points to be included in the moving average.

PHP 17. The orbit of a body rotating around a gravitational center is characterized by its orbital period τ (the time required to complete one complete revolution starting at perigee—the closest approach to the gravitational center) and its eccentricity e, the departure

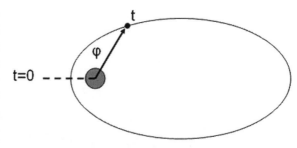

from a circular orbit. Eccentricity is a dimensionless quantity between 0, for a circular orbit, and 1, when the orbit becomes a parabola. For intermediate values of e, the orbit is an ellipse with the gravitational center at one focus of the ellipse. The speed of an orbiting object is maximum at its perigee ($t = 0$), and minimum at its apogee ($t = \tau/2$).

For a circular orbit, the angular position ϕ of an object in its orbit is simply related to time $t \le \tau$:

$$\varphi_{e=0} = 2\pi\left(\frac{t}{\tau}\right) \quad \text{rad}$$

When the orbit is elliptical, the calculation of the angular position of an object in its orbit is much more complicated. The "mean anomaly" M for any orbit is the same as the true angular position for a circular orbit with the same period:

$$M = 2\pi\left(\frac{t}{\tau}\right) \quad \text{rad}$$

But, the actual angular position ϕ, the "true anomaly," for a non-circular orbit cannot be calculated directly. The mean anomaly is related to the so-called eccentric anomaly E_c through a transcendental equation:

$$M = E_c - e \cdot \sin(E_c)$$

After E_c is found, then the true anomaly ϕ can be calculated directly:

$$\varphi_{0<e<1} = \arccos\left\{\frac{[\cos(E_c) - e]}{[1 - e \cdot \cos(E_c)]}\right\}$$

If M is greater than π radians (that is, if $t/\tau > 0.5$), then let $\phi = 2\pi - \phi$. Express your final answer in degrees (degrees = radians $\cdot 180/\pi$).

To solve for E_c using a recursive function with t, τ, e, and the current guess for E_c as the four parameters:

1. As an initial guess, let $E_c = M$ and use this value in the initial call to the function.
2. In the function, calculate $newE_c = M + e \cdot \sin(E_c)$.
3. Recursively call the function with $newE_c$ as the fourth argument.
4. Keep recalculating until the absolute value $|newE_c - E_c|$ is less than some suitably small value—1×10^{-5} is a reasonable choice.

When the terminating condition for recursive calls is satisfied, then calculate ϕ as defined. Use an HTML interface something like this:

period (any unit):	6000
time (same unit):	2500
eccentricity:	0.1
Click to calculate true anomaly.	
true anomaly (deg):	

Values of eccentricity very close to 1 may cause numerical problems, including failure of recursive functions to reach their terminating condition. If eccentricity is equal to 1, then your code should display an appropriate message—that the object's path is a parabola and not an ellipse. Eccentricity values greater than 1 or less than 0 are simply not allowed as input.

PHP 18.   Rewrite the PHP application in Document 9.14b so that it does not store data from the file in an array for any of the operations specified in the problem statement.

PHP 19.   Using Document 4.11 as a guide, write a PHP application that accepts as input the "weather report" barometric pressure and returns the "station" pressure. Except at a few research sites, the reported barometric pressure value is always corrected to sea level—otherwise it would not be possible to understand maps of high and low pressure associated with weather systems. The actual barometric pressure at a site (station pressure) can be obtained from the reported pressure by adjusting it for site elevation h, in units of kilometers:

$$P_{\text{station}} = P_{\text{sea level}} \cdot \exp\left(-0.119h - 0.0013h^2\right)$$

In the United States, barometric pressure is reported in units of inches of mercury. Almost everywhere else in the world, the units are millibars (hectopascals). Values for standard atmospheric conditions at sea level are 1,013.25 mbar or 29.921 in. of mercury. Because these two units have such different values associated with them, your code can determine the units in which the pressure was entered. If the sea level pressure value entered is less than 40, assume the units are inches of mercury and convert that value to millibars:

$$P_{\text{millibars}} = P_{\text{inches of mercury}} \cdot \left(\frac{1,013.25}{29.921}\right)$$

As an example, look at an online weather report for Denver, Colorado, USA. Denver is often called the "mile high city" because its elevation is about 5,300 ft (1.6 km). The barometric pressure will be reported as a value typically just a little above 1,000 mbar, just as it is at sea level. Use your PHP application to calculate the actual barometric pressure in Denver under standard atmospheric conditions.

PHP 20. Recall the basic data management application given in Documents 914a and 9.14b. Document 9.14b contained echo statements to check the performance of each of the options—viewing all records, finding a specified date, finding a specified value, and inserting a new record that is not a duplicate of an existing record. But, it did not actually create a new file containing inserted records.

Complete this application so that the PHP code actually replaces the original file when a new record is inserted. There are two extra credit possibilities:

1. Add an option that removes a specified record and replaces the original file.
2. Add an option that creates a backup copy of the original file whenever a new record is inserted.

PHP 21. Consider a data file that contains the date and time in a 12-h AM/PM tab- or space-delimited format:

```
mon     day     year    hour    min     sec     AM/PM
10      17      2010    9       29      35      AM
...
10      17      2010    12      0       0       PM
```

Write a PHP document that will read such a file and create a new comma-delimited file(with a .csv extension) in which the time is given in a 24-h format, using these substitutions:

```
If (AM/PM is AM) and (hour ≤ 11) the hour is unchanged.
If (AM/PM is PM) and (hour = 12) the hour is 12 (unchanged).
If (AM/PM is PM) and (hour < 12) the hour is hour + 12.
If (AM/PM is AM) and (hour = 12) the hour is 0.
```

PHP 22. The distribution of wind directions recorded over a specified period is typically summarized by using a windrose diagram. Wind directions are often classified according to 16 named 22.5-degree categories:

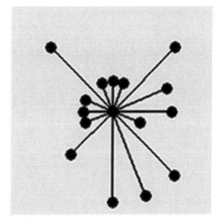

```
N, NNE, NE, ENE, E, ESE, SE, SSE,
S, SSW, SW, WSW, W, WNW, NW, NNW
```

The graphic shows a very simple 16-point windrose. The length of each arm is proportional to the ratio of the number of times that direction was recorded during the sampling interval to the total number of values recorded.

Alternatively, wind directions can be rounded to the nearest 10 degrees, in which case there would be 36 points in the windrose. In any case, directions are measured from due north and represent the direction from which the wind is *coming*. Thus, a NE wind is a wind coming out of the northeast and blowing *toward* the southwest.

Write a PHP application that reads a file of wind direction data, expressed as one of the 16 compass point identifiers, and generates a 16-point windrose.

Extra credit: Write your code so that the 16-point (22-5-degree) windrose can be changed to a 36-point (10-degree) windrose. In that case, the data file should contain wind directions in degrees rather than compass point identifiers. The code required to implement these changes should be accessed as a result of specifying the number of arms as 36 rather than 16.

PHP 23. Modify the line graph application (Documents 12.9a, b) so that two sets of data can be displayed on the same graph.

PHP 24. Modify the vertical bar graph application (Documents 12.7a, b) so that it will display two bars, side-by-side, for each *x*-axis label. The bars should be of different colors and a label identifying the purpose of each bar should be displayed.

PHP 25. Refer to the discussion starting on page 369, which uses the line graph application (Documents 12.9a, b) to plot $\ln(V - V_0)$ against relative air mass, for the data provided. The discussion states that this plot should be a straight line. Modify the line graph application so that the data are plotted just as filled circles, without lines joining the points. Add code to perform a least-squares linear regression analysis and plot the resulting line on the graph. Display the regression equation (in the form $y = a + bx$) and the correlation coefficient (r^2) on the graph.

$$a = \frac{\left[(\Sigma y_i)(\Sigma x_i^2) - (\Sigma x_i)(\Sigma x_i y_i) \right]}{\left[n\Sigma x_i^2 - (\Sigma x_i)^2 \right]}$$

$$b = \frac{\left[n\Sigma x_i y_i - (\Sigma x_i)(\Sigma y_i) \right]}{\left[n\Sigma x_i^2 - (\Sigma x_i)^2 \right]}$$

$$s_{y,x}^2 = \frac{\left(\Sigma y_i^2 - a\Sigma y_i - b\Sigma x_i y_i \right)}{(n-2)}$$

$$s^2 = \frac{\left[\Sigma x_i^2 - (\Sigma x_i)^2 / n \right]}{(n-1)} \qquad r^2 = \frac{1 - s_{y,x}^2}{s_y^2}$$

PHP 26. Exercise PHP 9 asked for code to generate a count histogram from an arbitrary list of numerical values. Using that problem as a starting point, write a PHP application that reads numerical values from a data file, generates a count histogram, and then plots that histogram as a horizontal or vertical bar graph. The numbers can be either positive or negative. An HTML interface should provide the minimum and maximum values to be included in the histogram and the number of "bins" in the histogram. It is OK to assume that the range of values included in each bin—for example, numbers from 0 to 100 divided into 10 bins, 0–9, 10–19,…, 90–100—is constant. However, in this example, note that a value of 100 goes in the 10th bin and not in an 11th bin; that is, this histogram array should have 10 bins and not 11.

It is possible that the maximum and minimum values to be included in the histogram could be different from the maximum and minimum values found in the data file. If the range of histogram values is smaller than the range of values in the data file, some of the data file values could be ignored. If the range of histogram values exceeds the range of values in the data file, some of the bins at the lower and/or upper ends of the histogram range will be empty.

For data samples with possible "tails" of very large or very small values (normal distributions, for example), you might want to include all values less than or equal to some minimum in the "bottom" bin and all values greater than or equal to some maximum in the "top" bin. The choice to include or exclude "outlier" points in the data file should be specified as part of the user input.

Note that for Exercise 5.7, there was no specific requirement to consider data sets that might include negative values. But, for example, both positive and negative values would occur in a sample of values drawn from a standard normal distribution having a mean of 0 and a standard deviation of 1.

PHP 27. Write a PHP application which will reproduce the telephone keypad image shown here. The keypads are filled ellipses of size 75 × 75 pixels. ImageString() was used to draw the letters at the top of the keypads; the "1", "*", and "#" keypads usually don't have text at the top. The text size was specified as 5, the largest allowed value. Text size for ImageString() is just a relative value rather than an actual point size or a size in pixels.

ImageTTFText() was used to draw the larger numbers in the keypads using TrueType fonts, which can be scaled to much larger sizes than is possible for text drawn with ImageString(). The code used to produce this image gets its font information from an arial.ttf font file. To use any .ttf font, find the file on

your computer and copy it into the directory where you store your PHP applications. (On Windows computers, font files should be in the C:\WINDOWS\Fonts\ directory.) The desired font size will need to be specified either in pixels or point size, depending on which version of the GD library you are using—you can quickly figure this out just by trying some size values and observing the results.

Glossary

Glossary entries are highlighted in **bold font** at their first appearance in the text. The reference in parentheses gives the chapter and section where the word or phrase first appears.

algorithm (Appendix 3) A step-by-step process that defines how to solve a computational problem.

ANSI (Preface) American National Standards Institute, an organization which sets voluntary standards and definitions in a number of scientific and engineering areas, including computer programming languages.

append (text file) (7.1) A "write-only" access permission that allows new information to be appended to the end of an existing text file.

array (5.1) A collection of related elements referenced by a common name and accessed by indices.

ASCII character sequence (3.2) A standardized representation of characters.

attribute (1.2) A value used inside an HTML element for the purpose of assigning properties and values to that element.

branching structure (4.1) A structure that determines which section of code will be executed, based on evaluating and comparing values of one or more control variables.

calling argument (1.2) A value passed to a method or function.

cascading style sheet (2.6) A syntax for specifying attributes and values for certain HTML elements in a way that makes it easy to apply the same attributes and values throughout a document, or across many documents.

class name (2.6) As applied to style sheets, a name by which a style definition can be applied to an element.

client side (7.1) Refers to activities taking place on a local computer, outside of a local server environment.

client-side application (1.1) An application that resides on a user's (client's) computer without giving that user access to the host (server side) computer.

client-side language (7.1)   A programming language such as JavaScript that resides on a local browser and can process scripts downloaded to the browser, as opposed to a server-side language such as PHP.

command line interface (CLI) (11.1)   A text-based computer interface that allows a user to type commands, enter data from the keyboard, and display text output from a program.

compiled programming language (1.1)   A programming language in which one or more separate applications translate coded statements into a separate file which then can be used to execute the program.

concatenation operator (4.5)   In JavaScript, the "+" symbol will append (concatenate) one string to another. In PHP, " . " is the concatenation operator.

conditional loop (4.8)   A loop structure whose operation and termination is governed by values generated inside the loop while it is executing.

constructor (5.1)   A method used to create new instances of an object. A means of defining the properties and contents of a built-in or user-defined data object, such as the `new Array()` constructor in JavaScript.

count-controlled loop (4.8)   A loop structure whose operation and termination is governed by an index whose beginning and terminating values are specified ahead of time.

data declaration (4.4)   The process by which a variable is given a name and, optionally, assigned a value.

data type (4.4)   A definition for information stored, accessed, and manipulated in a specific way.

element (1.1, 5.1)   In JavaScript, an element is the contents of one entry in an array.

equality operator (4.7)   An operator such as `==` and `===` in JavaScript and PHP that tests two expressions for equality, with or without automatic type conversion.

escape character (10.4)   A backslash (\), indicating that the following character has a special meaning.

escape sequence (1.2)   A way of displaying characters that are not available on the keyboard or that would be misinterpreted by HTML if entered directly. For example, `&lt;` is the escape sequence for the < symbol, which HTML interprets as the beginning of a tag if it is entered directly from the keyboard.

event handler (4.9)   An HTML attribute that initiates a response to certain user actions on a Web page, such as moving a cursor over a particular form field.

field (3.2)   A component of a form that, through an `input` element, allows user input, displays the results of calculations, or provides controls over form processing.

file handle (7.1)   The "logical" name by which a physical file is identified within a program.

file name extension (7.1) A sequence of characters following a period (.) at the end of a file name which associates that file name with a particular file type.

floating point number (3.1) A real number that includes digits to the right of a decimal point. A method of storing real numbers, as opposed to integer numbers. Whole numbers can be represented either as integers or floating point numbers.

form (3.1) An HTML element that provides an interface between a user and a document. The contents of form fields can (usually) be changed by the user or by a scripting language within the document.

format (7.1) A specification for reading or writing data from or to a file or other resource, such as a keyboard, or a description of how the contents of a file are organized.

format string (7.1) A string of characters that define the data type and format of values being read from or written to a file.

format specification string (7.1) A string containing characters that describe how to interpret data being read or how to display values being written.

format specifier (7.1) A character preceded by a % that is part of a format specification string. For input, the format specifier tells PHP how to interpret data in a file. For output, the specifier, along with other characters such as commas, describes how to display values being written.

frames (3.7) A mechanism for dividing a web page display into separately accessible areas.

free-format language (4.3) A language such as JavaScript or PHP that, within syntax limits, does not restrict where and/or how statements are placed on a document line.

function (6.1) A self-contained code unit that accepts input, performs one or more specific tasks, and returns output.

header line (7.1) One or more lines in a data file which identify and/or describe the contents of that file, as opposed to the data themselves.

hex code (2.5) A number expressed in hexadecimal notation, using values 0 through F (rather than 0 through 9, as in a base-10 number system).

home page (1.3) The top level Web page associated with a Web address. By default, the HTML document containing the home page is called `index.htm` or `index.html`.

HTML (Preface) HyperText Markup Language, a language for displaying and accessing online content, especially on the World Wide Web. HTML is approximately, but not entirely, platform-independent, as different browsers support different subsets and extensions of HTML. An HTML document is any `.htm` or `.html` text file that uses HTML for organizing and displaying text, images, and other content.

HTTP (1.3) HyperText Transfer Protocol, a communications protocol for exchanging information on the World Wide Web.

image space (12.2) A screen area allocated for creating graphics images.

in focus (6.4) The state of a form field or other defined area on a Web page when the cursor is within that field or area.

identifier (4.4) A symbolic name associated with a variable.

indices, (index) (5.1) One or more values that identify a single array element.

input/output (I/O) interface (1.1) A system that manages interactions between a user and a document, program, or script.

Internet (1.3) A globally connected network of computers for exchanging information using an agreed-upon communications format.

intranet (1.3) A system of linked computers that behaves like the Internet, but is accessible only to other computers on an internal network.

interpreted programming language (1.1) A language, such as JavaScript, in which statements are interpreted one line at a time, and the indicated actions are executed "on the fly," without generating a separate executable file. (See **compiled programming language**.)

JavaScript (Preface) An object-oriented programming language designed for manipulating content in an HTML document.

key (9.1) In PHP, a value used to access elements in an array. Integer index values, typically starting at 0, represent a subset of possibilities for PHP array keys.

language construct (7.1) A reserved term or group of terms in a programming language that performs certain operations.

list (3.6) In HTML, one of several ways to impose formatting on lists (in the plain English use of that word) of related items.

literal (4.4) A value entered directly in code, rather than being associated with a variable.

local server (7.1) A server application that runs on a local network or on a user's own computer, as opposed to on another server located physically elsewhere, as opposed to a remote server.

local variable (6.2) A variable defined inside a function that is visible only within that function.

logical operator (4.7) An operator that determines whether two expressions are both true ("AND"), one of two expressions is true ("OR"), or neither of two expressions is true ("NOT").

local server (7.1) In this book, the term "local computer" refers to a user's own computer that is also running a server application, as opposed to a remote server that is physically located elsewhere.

loop structure (4.1) A code structure that enables a section of code to be executed more than once, under the control of one or more index or control variables.

method (1.2) An action that can be applied to an object, or components of an object.

object (1.3) A defined construct that has components, properties, and values, and that allows certain actions to be carried out upon itself or its components.

object-oriented programming language (1.1) Any programming language that makes use of objects.

operator (4.5) A token representing a mathematical, logical, or text action, such as addition.

parameter list (6.2) A list of references to one or more values passed as input to a function.

PHP (Preface) "Personal Home Page" Web programming language that can receive information passed from an HTML document and allows access to data stored on a local or remote server.

PHP document (7.1) Any text document that can be interpreted as a PHP script.

PHP environment (7.1) A local or remote server that includes a PHP script interpreter, a place to store PHP scripts, and a place where files can be created, read, and modified.

PHP interpreter (7.1) A computer application that interprets PHP script files.

PHP script (7.1) A series of statements that follow PHP syntax rules, and that can be executed by a PHP interpreter.

PHP tag (7.1) `<$php... $>`, an HTML tag which contains PHP statements.

platform-independent (Preface) A computer language or application that presents a uniform user interface and behavior regardless of the computer or operating system.

post-test loop (4.8) A conditional loop structure in which tests for termination or continuation are conducted at the end of the loop's statement block.

precedence rules (4.5) The rules governing the order in which operations, including mathematical and logical operations, are performed in a statement.

pre-test loop (4.8) A conditional loop structure in which tests for termination or continuation are conducted at the beginning of the loop's statement block.

primitive (4.4) A basic data type.

property (1.2) An attribute (in the plain English use of that word) of an object or one of its components.

pseudo data type (10.1) A type specifier such as `(mixed)` used to indicate the data type or types associated with a variable name or other identifier.

pseudocode (Appendix 3) A language-independent set of "commands" that can be used to develop algorithms and code for solving computational problems.

queue (5.2) An abstract data structure, often represented by an array, in which the first entry (the "oldest" entry at the "front" of the queue) is always the first to be removed, and new entries are always added at the opposite end ("back") of the queue. Queues are "first in, first out (FIFO)" data structures.

read-only (text file) (7.1) A text file available for access from within a PHP script in a way that only allows its contents to be read but not modified in any way.

recursive algorithm (6.5) An algorithm that depends on being able to refer to itself.

recursive function (6.5) A function that refers to itself by calling itself.

relational operator (4.7) An operator that compares the value of two expressions and returns a value of true or false.

remote server (1.1) A server running somewhere other than on a local computer or local network, as opposed to a local server.

resource (10.1) Any data source, such as a data file or a keyboard, that is external to but accessible to a PHP application. Resources are represented by the pseudo data type `(resource)`.

square bracket notation (5.1) Notation used to specify the index of an array element.

sequential access (7.1) Pertaining to a data file whose contents can be accessed only sequentially, starting at the beginning.

script (1.2) The statements ("code") used to implement a scripting language such as JavaScript.

server (1.1) A software application that provides services such as file access to other computer programs and users on the same computer (a local server) or some other computer (a remote server). A computer on which a server application is running is often referred to as a server even if it is also used for other purposes.

server side (7.1) Refers to activities taking place on a server or data files residing in folders accessible through a server, even if that server is on a user's local computer.

server-side language (7.1) A programming language such as PHP which resides on a computer server, as opposed to being available within a local (client-side) browser.

scripting language (1.1) A language such as JavaScript whose purpose is to access and modify components of an existing information interface.

square bracket notation (5.1) Used to define and access the elements of array.

stack (5.2) An abstract data type, often represented by an array, in which the entries are always added to the "top" of the stack, and the most recent entry is always the first to be removed. Stacks are "last in, first out (LIFO)" data structures.

statement 4.3) A single set of instructions, often followed by a terminating character (a semicolon in JavaScript).

statement block (4.3) Several statements meant to be treated as a group, marked with a special symbol at the beginning and end of the block. JavaScript and other languages use "curly brackets" to define statement blocks: { ... } .

style rule(s) (2.6) One or more attributes and values defined within a style sheet.

style sheet (2.6) (See **cascading style sheet**.)

table (3.1) An HTML element that provides a way to organize and display content in a document.

tag (1.1) A syntax for entering elements in HTML documents (<...>), usually involving both a start tag and an end tag.

terminating character (4.3) A character appearing at the end of a programming statement, to mark the end of the statement. The JavaScript terminating character is a semicolon.

token (4.2) The smallest, indivisible, lexical unit of a programming language. Tokens can be constants, identifiers, operators, reserved words, separators, or terminators.

type conversion (4.4) The process by which a programming language converts data of one type to data of another type. In JavaScript, implicit type conversions from strings of characters to their corresponding numerical equivalents, and vice versa, are common.

URL (1.3) Uniform Resource Locator, the address system used by the World Wide Web.

variable (4.4) A discrete unit of information, associated with a particular data type and stored in a specific part of computer memory.

weakly typed language (4.4) A language that permits variables to be retyped (redefined) "on the fly" based on their contents, and/or allows variables to be used without an initially specified data type.

Web browser (1.1) A computer application designed to access, display, and interpret online content.

Web server (1.3) A computer connected to the Internet that stores documents and other contents for global (but not necessarily public) access by way of a unique address (Uniform Resource Locator, or URL).

World Wide Web, WWW (1.1) A global network of computing resources that uses the hypertext transfer protocol (HTTP) to exchange information on the Internet.

write-only (text file) (7.1) A text file that can be created or overwritten from within a PHP script.

XHTML (1.2) EXtended HyperText Markup Language, a more rigorous version of HTML that vigorously enforces syntax and style rules.

Index

Page numbers greater than 185 reference terms in the PHP chapters of this book. File extensions starting with a period (.), special characters starting with a & symbol, escape characters starting with a backslash (\), file permissions enclosed in single or double quotes (' or "), tags enclosed in angle brackets (<...>) or data type references enclosed in parentheses ((...)) are indexed alphabetically as though those non-letter characters were not present.

Output Examples in Color

In a few cases, color is helpful for understanding the code used to generate output. In those cases, the grayscale output displayed in the text is referenced to these color examples.

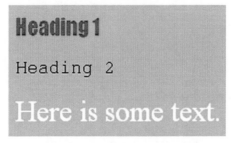

Color Example 1 (Chap. 1, p. 12)

Heading 1

Heading 2

Here is some text.

Color Example 2 (Chap. 2, p. 38)

This text should be blue on a red background

This text should be red on a white background.

This text should be white on a blue background.

Color Example 3 (Chap. 2, p. 39)

Results of radon testing

The table below shows some radon levels measured in residences.
For values greater than or equal to 4 pCi/L, action should be taken
to reduce the concentration of radon gas. For values greater than or
equal to 3 pCi/L, retesting is recommended.

Location	Value, pCi/L	Comments
DB's house, basement	15.6	Action should be taken!
ID's house, 2nd floor bedroom	3.7	Should be retested.
FJ's house, 1st floor living room	0.9	No action required.
MB's house, 2nd floor bedroom	2.9	No action required.

Color Example 4 (Chap. 3, p. 43)

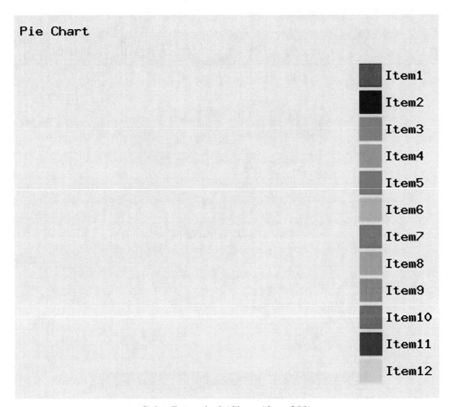

Pie Chart

Item1
Item2
Item3
Item4
Item5
Item6
Item7
Item8
Item9
Item10
Item11
Item12

Color Example 5 (Chap. 12, p. 299)

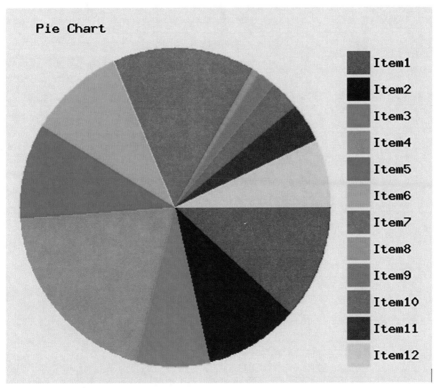

Color Example 6 (Chap. 12, p. 302)

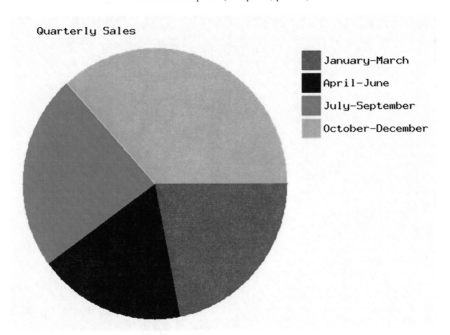

Color Example 7 (Chap. 12, p. 305)